GOING GALT

Surviving Economic Armageddon

Daxton Brown

Los Angeles MMXI

Contact: DaxtonBrown@yahoo.com

ISBN-13: 978-1456413293
ISBN-10: 1456413295

Daxton Brown Is a free lance writer and entrepreneur living in the SouthWest.

Contents

Preface – Going Galt

John Galt is a fictional character in Ayn Rand's novel *Atlas Shrugged* (1957). Although he is absent from much of the text, he is the subject of the novel's often repeated question "Who is John Galt?" and of the quest to discover the answer.

Galt is a creator and inventor who symbolizes the power and glory of the human mind. He serves as an idealistic counterpoint to the social and economic structure depicted in the novel, one of oppressive central control. We now live in a similar society, based on bureaucratic functionaries and a culture that embraces stifling mediocrity and egalitarianism, in short a society of misguided socialistic idealism. In Rand's novel, the industrialists of America were a metaphorical Atlas of Greek mythology, holding up the sky, whom Galt convinces to "shrug," by refusing to lend their productive genius to the regime any longer.

We are close to that same point now, where our creators, inventors and industrialists are "shrugging" and walking away from enterprise because they have been burdened with a stifling bureaucracy which taxes and regulates them from birth to death. That is, at least some of our industrialists are on strike, while others have been co-opted by the system and are now part of the problem (Government Motors, aka General Motors and the entire banking system come to mind). It is clear that those who play by the rules, trying to succeed by merit rather than by government handout, are now being suffocated and are fleeing socialist utopias like California and New York.

Hence the phrase "going John Galt" or simply "going Galt" has been used to refer to productive members of society cutting back on work in response to the projected increases in U.S. tax rates and the use of tax revenues for causes regarded as immoral. Some people who are "going John Galt" were seen at Tea Party protests held in the United States and at banking protests in London, however this movement isn't necessarily part of any specific political agenda. In fact, it may be impossible to distinguish between those who will be dropping out of the system because of philosophical reasons, and those forced to drop out because of world encompassing economic collapse due to out-of-control Central Banks and destructive social spending by governments.

In short, this book *Going Galt* is not concerned with *why* people might want to become self sufficient in the face of an economic collapse, it is only interested in *how* those who wish to prepare for and survive such a collapse can succeed. We are not promoting tax avoidance or protesting any government edicts – any excesses in those realms will take care of themselves. We simply want to prepare the creative and industrious grasshoppers of society for the coming bad times.

The Galt character has been compared to various iconic figures from literature and history. In the novel itself, he is compared with Prometheus from the Greek myths. In contrast to Prometheus, who suffered for bringing a great benefit to mankind, Galt refuses to suffer and withdraws the benefit instead. We aren't suggesting anyone withdraw from anything, we only hope to prepare some for the mathematical certainty that our unfunded liabilities for unachievable social goals cannot be papered over.

Daxton Brown

I   Economic Armageddon

Nearly every nation in the world is now facing serious financial and social stress. If only a few nations were involved, it might be possible to contain the upcoming economic meltdown to a few specific geographical areas as has been successfully done in the past. However, since the entire world is currently on the edge of the cliff, when the meltdown begins it will impact almost everyone on the face of the earth.

The meltdown is no longer avoidable because the world is a giant economic Ponzi scheme with the wheels fast coming off. Our governments and financial institutions are massively in debt and no longer in control of their basic functions. However, to keep the system working just a little longer, our overseers maintain the illusion that they know how to pull all the correct levers.

One fundamental problem is that we (the Human race) can now produce enough to survive without everyone taking part in the workforce. In many ways this is good, but there needs to be a massive restructuring of the economic system to give people money to buy the things being produced. In the West, where people demand high living standards and don't let people starve, we have been making up the slack with "free money" in the public sector. This involves borrowing money, lots of it, but the bill is coming due and a huge realignment of currencies through sovereign defaults is on the horizon.

The prognosis for America is especially discouraging. We have relied too heavily on surplus savings from abroad on top of running massive current account deficits. Until recent times, we ran deficits of this order only when we were engaged in a titanic war; otherwise we sought to achieve budget balances over a complete business cycle. But now we are running annual deficits well over a $trillion dollars, about 10 percent of the total economy. We have compounded the deficits we accumulated over the last decades, so they now are over 60 percent of GDP. Only once before has the ratio of federal debt to GDP come in above 60 percent; that was after World War II. Even worse, our reported federal debt ratio today doesn't even take into account Social Security and Medicare. Total liabilities and unfunded promises for Medicare and Social Security are now over $70 trillion, tripling from the year 2000 to 2010. This unfunded liability is above $200,000 per person and $500,000-plus for the average household. The problem with these trust funds is they're not funded and should be counted as a liability, bringing the debt-to-GDP ratio to 91 percent.

The system is broken, it can't be fixed (not for decades) and everyone knows it. There are two reasons why the system can't be fixed:

- It has grown beyond its own capacity to support itself – you can't tax and spend your way to prosperity.
- It has become so bureaucratically complex that no one can do anything significant to fix it because it is hemorrhaging in too many different places.

Even the poorest poor of the nations on the face of the earth know the meltdown is coming. Wealthy people know it. Poor people know it. Politicians know it. Nobody wants it to happen. But almost everyone is fatalistically waiting for it to begin, just hoping that it doesn't begin too soon before they can squirrel away survival money. Nobody knows when the final meltdown will actually start. It may begin one-month from now. Or a year from now. Or three-years from now. But almost everyone knows that at some near future date the meltdown will occur.

Worst Case Scenario

The widespread knowledge of the impending financial disaster is the reason that when the economic tsunami begins it can quickly and completely spiral out-of-control. Having already having successfully survived years of a "rolling recession", most people do not realize a collapse could overwhelm the world economy in a span of just a few weeks. Most expect a gradual meltdown (if not a recovery!). However, once the avalanche begins it can quickly escalate far beyond anyone's ability to control or manage it on a worldwide basis. Five basic reasons we are at a tipping point are as follows:

1. Banks: The financial institutions around the world cannot withstand a full-scale worldwide bank run - most are already bankrupt holding worthless collateral. Therefore, they already have plans to shut down the instant they are told to do so. Within minutes, all across the globe, all the ATM machines could be offline, all credit card and debit card verification transactions halted, and all banks have their vaults doors locked and their buildings emptied of personnel. High-level bank executives would disappear and telephone calls to financial institutions automatically answered by a pre-recorded computer message.

2. Governments: The majority of government leaders around the world are intelligent enough to understand the ramifications of a "bank holiday" in our computer controlled financial economy. Therefore, it isn't hard to imagine government officials emptying their buildings and locking their doors. Any transactions in progress, including trials, would be halted and postponed until some future date. High-level government officials, including judges and tax officials, could easily disappear to unknown remote locations.

3. Retail Businesses: Since they will be unable to process even simple transactions, retail establishments, large and small, will lock their doors. If possible, they will complete transactions for customers who have enough cash to pay for their purchases, but those wishing to pay by check or credit card or debit card will be told that the verification system is down and their transaction can't be completed. In a manner similar to what happened during the World Trade Center meltdown, store management may demand that employees remain at their stations until further notice or they will lose their jobs , but the more intelligent employees will leave at the same time as the store's last few remaining customers. The security guards might remain to protect the stores, but since most of them are not paid exceptionally well, they would likely return home and protect their own families instead.

4. Criminals: Anyone who has any criminal background would immediately see the collapse as a once-in-a-lifetime opportunity to improve their financial situation. Career criminals already have plans that include exactly which businesses they are going to rob first, second, third, and so on. Any business with a reasonable level of cash-on-hand will be very high on every criminal's list. Every jewelry store and pawn shop that has any type of silver or gold jewelry, or precious stones

(diamonds, rubies, emeralds, etc.), will be very high on everyone's list. Warfare would break out at these establishments between competing criminals.

5. Normal People: Even average people would begin looting (to keep from being left behind). Grocery stores would be broken into and emptied from wall-to-wall. Stores with firearms, ammunition, appliances, clothing, shoes, or anything else needed by the average citizen will be emptied. Everyone will quickly realize there are not ~~are not~~ enough law enforcement personnel to protect everyone and everything. Although the military will probably be ordered to protect specific high priority establishments and resources, there will simply not be enough military personnel to protect individual civilians or businesses. In skirmishes over the few remaining resources, normal average people would go to extremes if they perceived their very survival to be at stake.

Paranoia Or Reality? Is the above scenario exaggerated? Perhaps. Is it out of the realm of possibility? A few years ago, we would all have thought it crazy talk, but now the reported debt and default numbers are so astronomical that the chorus of fear is quite widespread. The crash of 2008 brought us far closer to a systemic failure than anyone realized until the Federal Reserve was forced to divulge the extent of its multi trillion dollar intervention, but now the bullets have been shot. Are you prepared for the stampede when everyone is headed to the exits at the same time?

The Inflation Threat

Sarah Palin made a speech at a trade-association convention in Phoenix in 2010 urging Federal Reserve Chairman Ben Bernanke to "cease and desist" his "pump priming". Palin said the United States, "shouldn't be playing around with inflation." She went on to say, "All this pump priming will come at a serious price. And I mean that literally: everyone who ever goes out shopping for groceries knows that prices have risen significantly over the past year or so. Pump priming would push them even higher."

Critics like the Wall Street Journal's Sudeep Reddy questioned Palin's comments about food inflation, saying that, "Grocery prices haven't risen all that significantly, in fact. The consumer price index's measure of food and beverages for the first nine months of this year showed average annual inflation of less than 0.6%, the slowest pace on record." However, alternative organizations tracking inflation like www.shadowstats.com paint a different picture. Many now believe, with reason, that the government's consumer price index (CPI) numbers are phony. Our own government spokespeople have lost credibility when they tell you the economy is on the mend. Especially as we now know that it required many trillions in bailouts in 2008 to contain that blowout.

The U.S. Bureau of Labor Statistics (BLS)'s CPI is no longer a reliable indicator of U.S. food inflation or any type of price inflation. Estimates are that the real rate of annual food inflation in the U.S. is already 5% and this rate will likely rise above 10%. The BLS has been using both geometric weighting and hedonics to artificially manipulate the CPI downward. The U.S. government has a strong motivation to keep CPI increases as low as possible because since the year 1975, retired Americans receive annual Social Security payment increases that are tied to the CPI. Calculated on the way the BLS's CPI has understated the real rate of price inflation, Americans on Social Security should be receiving payments that are more than double what they receive today. Food and energy inflation can easily become a larger crisis than the mortgage crisis.

When calculating food inflation, the government gives a lower weighting to goods that are rising in price and a higher weighting to goods that are falling in price. If the price of steak is rising while the price of hamburgers is falling, the CPI will give a lower weighting to steak and a higher weighting to hamburgers. The government justifies this by saying that expensive steak prices mean Americans are more likely to eat hamburgers. Therefore, the CPI no longer accounts for the price to maintain the same standard of living. The CPI is now calculated based on the realization that America's standard of living has been in decline and the expectation that it will continue to decline in the future.

Americans subconsciously realize it is becoming harder for them to make ends meet, but they don't realize inflation is the cause. While we've all heard stories about how a gallon of gas used to cost a quarter and we are subliminally aware that the U.S. is currently experiencing heavy price inflation, Americans don't view inflation as a problem because increases have occurred over long time periods. However, the U.S. price inflation that occurred over the past 100 years now seems likely to occur again over just the next 10 years as the Federal Reserve's money printing causes the world to lose confidence in the U.S. dollar.

Another misconception is that American wages have risen at the same rate as inflation. The median household income in the U.S. was $11,800 in 1975 and today is $49,777. Going by the government's CPI, $11,800 in 1975 dollars equals $47,208 in today's dollars. If the government's CPI is to be believed, Americans are earning higher real incomes today than 35 years ago. However, the truth is, once you discount the effects of geometric weighting and hedonics, the median household income in 1975 of $11,800 actually equals $154,000 in today's dollars. This explains how in 1975, a father was able to support a family on just one income and college students were able to afford their own tuition with just a part-time summer job. Today, both parents need to work and families need to get deeply into debt just to survive.

The U.S. government is currently printing money just to survive.

The Federal Reserve has held the Fed Funds Rate at 0-0.25% for nearly two years and there is little doubt that multiple versions of Quantitative Easing (QE1, QE2, QE3 . . .), otherwise known as money printing, will follow.

Increases in commodity prices have been record breaking, with corn rising by 32%, soybeans rising by 32%, orange juice rising by 12%, coffee rising by 19%, and sugar rising by 66%. These agricultural commodity price increases will begin to work their way into grocery stores nationwide in the weeks, months and years ahead, as food manufacturers and retailers are forced to raise their prices. Food manufacturers and retailers who don't raise prices and pass their rising costs on to U.S. consumers will likely go out of business.

Canaries In The Coal Mine China's Dagong Global Credit Rating Co. lowered its credit rating for the U.S. to A+ from AA with an outlook of "negative", saying the Fed's plan to buy government debt will erode the value of the dollar and "entirely encroaches" on the interests of creditors. The Fed, by buying U.S. treasuries, is effectively monetizing the debt. In fact, in 2010 Federal Reserve Bank of Dallas President Richard W. Fisher admitted the Fed's debt laundering, saying in a statement, "For the next eight months, the nation's central bank will be monetizing the federal debt." That monetization process will not stop for eight years much less eight months.

The U.S. has no way of paying off its $13.7 trillion national debt and $80 trillion plus in unfunded liabilities without printing the money and creating massive price inflation!

Fed Chairman Ben Bernanke testified under oath on June 3rd, 2009 in front of Congress that, "The Federal Reserve will not monetize the debt." This must be viewed as perjury, because certainly the man pulling the monetary levers realizes that the United States is bankrupt and the only way to paper over the debt is through inflation

The government's $700 billion 'Emergency Economic Stabilization Act of 2008', clearly did not "jump-start" the economy, but what it did do was jump-start a massive inflationary monetary crisis. The average American family currently spends 13% of their total annual expenditures on food compared to 34% on housing. As the Federal Reserve monetizes our debt and creates massive price inflation, these two numbers will reverse. For every 1% rise in consumer wages, expect to see about a 4% rise in food prices. There are currently 42.4 million Americans on food stamps, up 17% from the pre recession days. The government does not have the resources to make these entitlement payments without printing the money and creating massive food price inflation. Ironically, food stamps are actually making those who receive them, need them even more.

While the U.S. government may be able to avoid going bust due to a worthless U.S. dollar, it is likely that the average middle-class American will become dependent on the government to survive. The Progressive's strategy to get re-elected seems to be to make as many Americans as possible dependent on them and there is faint hope their opposition can hold the fiscal line any better even when they take control. There ~~doesn't~~ is no white knight available to dramatically reduce government spending in an attempt to prevent hyperinflation.

Preparing For Economic Armageddon

Given these dire predictions, surprisingly most Americans haven't taken steps to prepare for an economic disaster, much less natural disasters, terrorist attacks and other emergencies. Only about a third have even made plans with family members about how they would communicate with each other during a crisis. Part of the reason for this is that we have been well off in the United States, and we trust in our bank accounts to sustain us. Unfortunately, money sitting in savings and investments is useless if you become stuck in a perfect storm and the stock market crashes, or the Chinese stop propping up Treasury bond sales.

One disarming reason some people neglect preparedness has to do with an odd defeatism that says, "If current events are prophesied to happen, then there's nothing we can do about it anyway." The notion that calamity is unavoidable if it is divinely predicted is even sanctioned by some who dismiss the pattern for preparedness in the Bible. While it is true that famine was prophesied for Egypt, it is also a fact that God led Joseph to prepare for it, and, as a result, he saved his family and nation.

Yet, perhaps the greatest reason people, never plan for disaster, is that they view the effort to prepare for the unexpected as too complicated and costly. They imagine the back yard being dug up for construction of a massive bomb shelter and the basement crammed with row after row of dry grains and large containers filled with backup water. Fortunately, survival preparation is modestly affordable. Under most circumstances, the ability for individuals to remain mobile for a few days to a week or so by simply grabbing an inexpensive "survival bag" and heading out is more important than silos filled with long term storage foods.

Even when we envision a worst case scenario – such as complete economic collapse, a terrorist nuke or even an ICBM exchange, minimal preparations like water treatment (iodine), low-cost shelters (tents), and some food stores (MREs), would help keep as much as 99 percent of the population alive. While having to endure radioactive fallout is unlikely, other threats from social collapse or Mother Nature are not unbelievable. Every year we read of someone lost in a snowstorm who dies from the exposure to freezing temperatures. If their car had been equipped with a survival kit, they would have had an excellent chance of survival. During Hurricane Katrina, one woman had an emergency supplies kit in her attic that kept her and her two cats alive for days until help arrived.

For reasons such as these, each of us should at least be prepared with a "walk out" kit for the trunks of our cars. These emergency bags contain enough food, water, shelter, first aid, lighting and communication supplies to keep a family alive for a number of days in the case of a vehicle malfunction or other situation where they would need to abandon their car. Many of the items vital for a good survival kit can be found at your local shopping center: an inexpensive poncho, a basic first aid assortment, nylon cord, canvas for temporary shelter, duck tape, a whistle.

Longer term preparation requires items that are a bit trickier to find and may need to be acquired from one of many online emergency preparedness companies. These include five-year-shelf-life food bars, five-year-shelf-life water boxes or pouches, paper-thin thermal blankets designed by NASA to retain body heat, special hand-crank combination flashlights with radios and emergency signals built in, and so on.

Finally, no matter what survival tactics you take, life will still go on and you will have to make a living. So part of the preparation is also knowing how to improve your financial survival. Sitting on the street on a pile of survival stores is not survival, so preparing yourself for a changing economic landscape is also critical and absent from many survival guides.

How far you prepare is up to you, whether it just be to keep an eye on events or go so far as to build a million dollar buried shelter stocked for five years survival. We have written the rest of this book to present you with options that cover a whole range of survival levels. If nothing else, you will find the practical tips useful no matter what your situation.

II   How Life Will Change

Collapse of the Middle Class

In social studies they explain the different kinds of social pyramids. The first pyramid is the basic society - a pyramid with two horizontal lines, dividing those on top (high social class) those in the middle (middle class) and the bottom of the pyramid (the poor, proletarian). The middle of the pyramid, the middle class, acts as a cushion between the rich and the poor, a buffer for social stress.

The second pyramid example has a big middle section, and represents 1st world countries in which the bottom is very thin and arrows show there is a possibility to go from low to middle class, and from middle to the top of the social pyramid. This is the classic, democratic capitalist society. In countries such as European ones, socialists, the pyramid is very similar but a little more fat, meaning that there is a big middle class section and smaller high and low class.

The third pyramid shows a communist society. Where arrows from the low and middle class try to reach the top they bounce off the line. A small high society and one big low society, cushioned by a minimal middle class section of pyramid. Venezuela is the current Petri dish for this pyramid.

Unfortunately there is also a fourth pyramid. This one has arrows from the middle class dropping to the lower, poor class. This is the collapsed country, a country that turns into a 3rd world country where there is almost no middle class, one huge low, poor class , and a very small, very rich, top class. The arrows going from the middle to the bottom of the pyramid represent the middle class turning into poor. The income from the middle class is not enough to function as a middle class any more. Some from the top class fall to middle class, but the vast majority of the middle class turns into poor.

We now have in our own country a middle class that is suddenly becoming poor, headed towards creating a society of basically poor people with no more middle class to cushion tensions. The middle class has suddenly discovered that they are overqualified for the jobs they can find and have to settle for anything they can. Unemployment has sky rocketed, too many workers have too much to offer, but there is too little demand and temporary jobs are displacing permanent jobs.

Just as disturbing is the generation gap: no matter how hard upcoming students study they are preparing for jobs they are not going to get. Eventually the number of students dropping out of college will increase as students either see no point in studying something that will not make much difference in their future salaries, or they have no money to keep themselves in college, or they simply have to drop college to work and support their families. Productive jobs have for two decades been outsourced to China or India, or are now taken by "undocumented workers".

All humans adapt when they have no other choice, but Americans are not now used to adversity. We haven't suffered through civil wars, dictators and dirty social wars since the Civil War. Can we survive the coming collapse? Of course we can, it' just that many won't be prepared. Those are the ones who will be responsible for social unrest once the economic system flatlines; those that were too lazy to take care of themselves, or have gone soft believing that the government will "take care of them because they pay their taxes". In the end, most of them will pull through too. People will adapt, they always do but those who don't adapt to the new reality will die young.

A Different Mentality

In the past, we all got used to living in an affluent society. Some women were able to spend $500 on facial cream, special shampoos and conditioners, as well as having their nails polished. Some men were able to spend even more on Super Bowl tickets or nights out on the town. But $500 is a small generator, or a gun and a few boxes of ammo. It could be a month's worth of food.

A different mentality refers to thinking of a practical use for money, the money we used to throw away. Once the overhanging world debt collapses, money is no longer measured in diversions and entertainment, but in terms of the necessary goods it can buy. Stuff like food, medicine, gas, or private medical care suddenly become very important. Spending 500 dollars on beauty products or a ball game no longer works.

Things may not get economically better for a long time – perhaps twenty years. But even though humans have a capacity to "get used to it", that doesn't mean your own life can't get better even as the ship of state takes on water.

Once you experience the lack of stuff you took for granted, like food or medicines, your set of priorities suddenly change. For example, say you have two wisdom tooth removed and you are prescribed antibiotics along with Hydrocodone for the pain. Now you take the antibiotics, but buy two boxes with the same prescription and keep one box just in case. You don't use the Hydrocodone, adding it to your pile of medicines.

Why? because medicines may not always be available in a new price regulated world that will come from a nationalized health system. Sure, going without painkillers hurts like hell, but making sacrifices to ensure survival is the mentality you should have if you want to be prepared. The stuff that is "nice to have" has to be sacrificed to get the indispensable stuff.

Of course, there are things that are not "basic need stuff" that are important in other ways. Going to the hairdresser once every month or two fits in that category. It's not life or death, but it boosts morale. Buying a game for the Xbox or a movie to watch won't burn a hole in your pocket. It is just that someone who can't survive a week without a credit card, doesn't have the mentality to survive a Great Depression II. Addictions such as alcohol, drugs or even cigarettes should be avoided by the survivalist. They are bad for your health, cost a lot of money that could be much better spent, and create an addiction to something that may not be available in the future. In short, you have to hunker down.

How will your life change?

Everything changes!

The good news is that people adapt, people get "used to". And finally, people accept.

The streets will be more dangerous than ever, thanks to general poverty. Education will suffer, with kids working, or stealing to survive instead of going to school. Tools become expensive, since most come from abroad... remember, your national industry has been sold out or destroyed. But you can thrive in your little bubble.

This self destructive economy created by the stupidity of our previous presidents and politicians, has been a formula for disaster. After years of closing factories and the destruction of our national industry, with extremely low wages, people will get fed up. We are already suffering currency devaluation against the Canadian, Australian, Chinese and Russian currencies. The only reason we are doing well against the Euro is because the European Union is in even worse shape than we are, starting with the PIIGs (Portugal, Italy, Ireland, Greece and Spain) but extending throughout the entire socialized system.

Then comes the devaluation. What happens when one day the Secretary of the Treasury declares that no one can withdraw more than 100 bucks a day from the ATM, nor close out accounts? Imagine what your life will be like if you go to your local market and everything has gone up 200%. How will you survive with your pay check? Eventually, the sheep will get desperate. First, the banks won't return their money to people, then those with the lowest income will find out their salaries aren't high enough to buy the minimum food to survive. You could see the president flee the White House in the Marine 1 chopper.

Banks will be destroyed by people who want their hard earned money back, FDIC or not. Supermarkets and shops will be looted, as well as regular homes. The chaos will spread all over the country, concentrated in the largest cities. Everything you need from food and gas to TVs and refrigerators will rise in price, inaccessible for most people. Things you own and are part of your net worth, like cars and real estate will drop in value.

Food Keep in mind that if society collapses, food will always be in your thoughts. If you don't have it you'll do ANYTHING to get it, and even if you are prepared you'll worry about being able to get more for the future. Once you see food prices go up between 200% and 300%, or simply see it missing, you'll realize what a valuable commodity food really is.

To those that think that food will never be a problem in USA: visit a country like Argentina or Venezuela. Just after WWII Argentina practically fed Europe and was known in Europe as " the world's granary". Cattle and wheat production was enough to feed not only their own country but another continent. After the 2001 Argentinean crisis people in Buenos Aires, the capital city and the richest province, didn't realize how bad things actually were in the other provinces. This was until teachers noted that kids had problems with education - they had problems concentrating, fell asleep, and found it difficult to resolve mathematical equations. They later found out that this was due to malnutrition, kids were not receiving the minimum amount of nutrients for a healthy working body.

Will we see people eating out of trash cans in the United States? In the Third World every night entire families, wife, husband and 2 or 3 kids go through trash cans in search of food. At almost every light stop there's little bare foot kids begging, all dirty and skinny. It's one thing to see those terrible images of a little kid starving in Africa, but now imagine that that kid speaks English, with an American accent, and you see the Hollywood billboard in the background. Both cases are terrible, but the one that looks as if he could be your son and not some kid in Africa or Mexico hits a nerve. Because "those things don't happen here".

However, because the entire world economy is now so fragile, it won't take much to cause sections of our country to go third world. It could be a hurricane, economic collapse, an earthquake or a meteor hitting earth, food and water always come first. Stuff like MRE, Emergency food bars will be impossible to get. Ideally you already have a food plan and have a year's worth of food in your basement. If you don't, your heart will be in your throat all the time, fearing that supermarkets will close permanently and you and your family will be left without food. If you don't have your food needs sorted out already, start buying a little extra every time you go to the supermarket.

Other Changes In a collapse, guns and ammo will be really expensive and sold in small quantities. Forget about buying a "case" of ammo!

Shoes and clothes will be, expensive. Labor will be cheap; maybe you can have a part time maid and a gardener (or be one yourself). There is no "safe" job. With 20% unemployment they pay you whatever they want and if you don't like it there are 100 persons waiting to get your job. Owning a shop/business is hard. You have to consider armed robbery and pay the police for protection (from themselves)

Power might get cut sometimes, though probably not for long. More likely are brownouts or rolling blackouts. A couple of flash lights will help, but a generator will seem like a blessing.

Water might still work but you might not be able to drink because the water is just too dirty.

Entertainment Counter intuitively, when the collapse comes you will want a nice TV and DVD player. Going out for dinner or to the movies will not only be dangerous but also expensive. You will find much better use for that money after the collapse.

There will still be places where you can go out for dinner, movies, or theater shows and have a good time, safely. They will either have their own security or arrange with the police for added security. But these places will either be for tourists or for the extremely wealthy.

As the middle class collapses, even those from the higher socioeconomic levels won't be able to afford to spend the amounts of money they used to every weekend, now it will become every two weekends or once a month. Going out for a walk becomes an alternative, but the view might not be that good, and you may only be able to walk a few blocks in the same direction. If you get out of the area which is guarded by private security, you are on your own.

Once innocent people are getting shot by the police, much less by criminals, it's back to the TV. Good places are too expensive, and just going out for a walk at night with your wife/girlfriend is out of the question. All of a sudden popcorn , pizza and a movie sounds like a good plan.

Of course, don't spend all day in front of the screen like a zombie. Reading is nice, but going out with a date at night won't be that easy, nor will it be that cheap. You will end up paying for that added security that the shop/bar/theater owner hired and for the higher price of gas and food, while a DVD copy can be found everywhere, and costs only a couple of bucks. There will be a lot of "why don't we watch a movie" nights. Like it or not TV is cheap, safe entertainment. A play station or Xbox is also nice to have. Even if the country collapses, there will always be a guy with a DVD writer making copies.

Books If you like reading a lot, buy books now, even if you won't read them for some time. If the economy crashes, you can always burn them to keep warm.

Who To Trust? Obviously, don't trust the media. If you watch the news, reporters say everything is improving, everything will be OK. Journalists are lazy and tend to repeat the government propaganda, but it is clear the statistics have been cooked for a while. When you talk to your neighbor and find no one can afford food or gasoline and it turns out Mr. X got shot yesterday, the nice girl on the next block got kidnapped and raped, all while news reporters are talking about a recovery you will know the media can't be trusted. And if you can't trust the media, then you can't trust most of the sources of information you used to rely on.

You also can't trust the government, because they can't even report the true inflation and unemployment numbers for fear of setting off riots. Try www.shadowstats.com for a better feel for what is happening. You also can't trust bankers because almost everyone one of them is bankrupt, but still has their doors open. In short, you can only trust yourself, that's what happens when the socioeconomic system breaks down.

The New Criminal Class Will crime mostly be simple street crime or will it be highly organized with gangs and cartels/mafia style? The answer is both. Sadly, in dysfunctional societies, the police handle most organized crime as we can see happening in Mexico along the northern border. The cops will be involved in most illegal activities like drugs, prostitution, robbery and kidnappings. Eventually, like in Mexico, 2 or 3 persons will get kidnapped each day when the system collapses. There will be a big chance the "perp" will be wearing a "Police" body armor vest.

The government may even start asking the people for donations to support charity. And the best part is that once they get all the donations (mostly food, milk, blankets and such) the Governors SELL the donated goods to the poor. The problem is that small groups of people both on the left and right want this country as poor as possible to take advantage of it (everyone from Goldman Sachs, to welfare politicians promising bread and circuses).

In other words, in a broken society, the criminals become those you used to trust to create and enforce the laws.

Insecurity Even though crime has always been an issue in the U.S., it has been manageable. There have always been dangerous neighborhoods, but nothing like it will be during an economic crisis. YES, will you need a gun, pepper spray, a machete, a battle axe, a club with a rusty nail sticking out of it, or whatever weapon you can get hold of to defend yourself.

One used to be able to let kids play on the sidewalk, or walk home from a party a few blocks away, and be somewhat safe. This all changes now. There will be no kids playing on the sidewalks anymore, at any time of the day. Maybe a kid rides his bike a few yards on the sidewalk, but always under the supervision of an adult. A kid riding a bike on his own will get that bike stolen in no time, probably getting hurt in the process, therefore no responsible parent leaves a kid alone on the street.

Teenagers present a greater problem. You can't keep a 15 or 16 year old inside a house all day long, and even though they are big enough to go out on their own, when the sun goes down things get much worse. This is when parents will organize themselves; either taking teenagers to someone's house or to a club and picking them up at a certain time. Taxis and limousines can be used sometimes, but after cases of girls getting raped, no parent worth their salt will leave his son or daughter in hands of a stranger. After years of living like this, everyone will learn to be careful; sometimes the hard way.

Practically no one will leave a door or window opened or unlocked. Nor will you hang out in front of the house talking to friends. A bad guy might just see you there, like a sitting duck, pull a gun on you and take you inside your house. In the past, police and social experts have often advised citizens to not resist a robbery, to give thieves what they want so they'll go away. That won't hold true when the criminals are under the influence of drugs, epoxy glue, or just hate your guts because you have a better life than they have. They will hurt and humiliate you as much as they can. Letting a criminal inside your house almost guaranties he will rape/beat/ torture and abuse whoever he finds inside.

By far, the most dangerous moment of the day, is when leaving/entering your house. A solid, secure house cannot be broken into easily, so criminals wait until you are standing on front of the door with the keys on your hand to jump on you. This is why you need to be extra alert when approaching your house, look all around and if you see anything strange, keep walking around the block or keep on driving. No door should ever be opened when there is a strange person around.

Criminals sometimes disguise themselves as electric company employees or repairmen, saying that they have to fix something. If there is something to be fixed they can fix it on the sidewalk. Anything inside your house is your responsibility and the electric company is not going to fix it for you.

Carrying a pistol won't be common for decent working people, but there will be areas where criminals carry their guns openly and no one does anything about it. As drug cartels move up from Mexico. no one will dare mess with them and there are already American neighborhoods where police don't dare to enter. Carrying a handgun, ready for use (loaded and on your person) is illegal, unless you have a Concealed Carry permit, but that may become impossible to get. Carrying a gun, bought on the black market can take you straight to jail. Regarding cops and guns, some of them may understand that you are carrying for self defense if you are in a very dangerous area; if your gun registration shows you bought that gun legally, they MAY be sensitive and let you go. You have to consider all this, and decide if the risk of getting caught is greater than the risk of getting killed for not being able to defend yourself.

Bribery Say you need renew your driver's license after the 20XX crisis. The problem is the DMV is low on personal (they had to let go 25% and 50% are on strike) so you'll have to wait 4 months until you get an appointment. You approach the information desk where you find Tashana. Now, Tashana hasn't had a date since the age of 10, and she weighs as much a healthy manatee, but you kindly ask her to please help you fill the paperwork, and though she's as cold as a Popsicle, you keep calling her by her first name and when you leave she smiles and says good bye.

The next day you drop by and give Tashana a Revlon lipstick for "helping" you fill in the form, which had difficult questions like "Name?"" Age?" It cost you about 4 bucks for lipstick before the crisis but, since it's made in France, it's now $20 dollars and they no longer even import it. Revlon saw that they no longer had a market for their $4 Euro lipstick, and the segment that used to buy it is spending that money in other items like food, so their marketing experts told them that the 4 Euro lipstick is no longer profitable.

Tashana used to love that particular lipstick, she thought it made her look like Cindy Crawford (poor Tashana) but $20 dollars is more than she can spare on her good looks. When she finally decided to drop the 40 pounds of M&M's she ate a month in favor of the lipstick, the girl at the drugstore told her that the item is no longer available. Her face lights up when she sees your present, and tells you that you shouldn't have bothered, and she asks how did it go with your license. You tell her that you actually have a problem, it seems that it takes 4 months to renew, and you ask her if maybe she can do something about it... you get the picture.

In other occasions people will let you know that they want a plain and simple "bribe", and $50 bucks or $100 bucks might get the job done. "Gifts" (like perfume) or bribes when the police stopped you for "inspection" could be life savers. While this does not currently apply to 1st world countries where most officers are honest self sacrificing people, it does apply to 3rd world countries, a point towards which areas of our country are headed. Don't get shot by an angry cop over a few bucks, let them have their bribe.

Trade Items Think of these items not as trade goods, but as "gifts" to buy favors, to build up relationships with police, government officials, doctors, people you might need favors from. Stuff, like liquor/wine, a nice pen, perfume, makeup and other "free shop" kinds of items can go a long way when you need some strings pulled, or a "friend" within certain circles. And it's not only the item, sweet talking also must be applied.

A LIST OF THINGS THAT "If you had it to do over again" YOU WOULD GET.
- Food and Water: You can never have too much canned, or other long shelf life food.
- A generator
- Bullet-proof vest. Get one that can go under the regular clothes.
- Ammunition, you won't be able to get it in bulk.

III   Money In A Collapsing Society

"Banking" in today's Western economies is simply a monopoly-distribution point for the dissemination of fiat currency. Central banks have to distribute money through private banks because the alternative – simply distributing it to people – would reveal the scam for what it is. Filtering money-printed-from-nothing through banks gives the process a mysterious quality and renders it more complex, which is necessary when one is promoting a Ponzi scheme. The situation is incredibly destructive, ruinous and benefits only people who are the most direct beneficiaries of central bank funding stream.

Given that the Federal Reserve's money printing process, coupled with profligate government spending, has lead us to worldwide financial ruin, your survival depends on your ability to make an end run around the monetary system. This can be done in a number of ways, the most obvious being through owning precious metals, but also through barter and investment strategies that focus on commodities. But first, you need to understand just how fragile the current monetary system is.

Who Really Has Money? Most people currently thought of as wealthy have their wealth tied up in credit-related investments of one kind or another—the stock market, bonds, CD's, real estate, etc. Almost nobody keeps a big stash of cash around because there's been no need for large amounts of cash for a long, long time. All these currently wealthy people could suddenly become poor if a financial tsunami were to hit. This doesn't mean metaphorically poor, it means freezing, starving poor, broke, destitute. All their resources will be in the wrong form for the new conditions. Only those who have cash will be wealthy after a national disaster; survival requires cash.

Can't the government simply print enough paper money to replace all the electronic money? The answer is no, it's impossible. The presses at the Bureau of Engraving and Printing are already running at capacity 24 hours a day just to replace the paper money that wears out each year. To replace just the paper currency currently circulating would take years at the current BEP printing capacity. It would take decades to replace the entire $1 trillion in what is called the M0 money supply.

Cash For Survival The answer to the money dilemma is a simple one: Have Cash—coins and green pieces of paper with pictures of dead presidents on them. Convert at least some of your credit investments and electronic forms of money into cash. If you have cash after an economic Armageddon, you will be one of the few wealthy people in your neighborhood. Not only will you be able to survive the disastrous times, you will be able to use your cash to build a prosperous future for you and your family. A word of warning: you must be very careful to keep a low profile both now and in the future. You want to attract as little attention as possible while you convert to cash and later when you use your cash, for two different but equally vital reasons.

First, although you have every right to convert all your investments and savings into cash, doing so may invite the attention of the government DEA agents who may think you're some kind of drug dealer. The drug laws are so powerful regarding the confiscation of suspected drug dealers' wealth that you could find yourself in a protracted legal battle to get back the money that belongs to you. You want to avoid attracting the attention of bank tellers or branch managers who might report to the DEA that you are withdrawing large sums of cash.

Secondly, when everyone around you is impoverished and hungry, it's very prudent to keep your own wealth out of sight. A desperate man will go to extremes to feed his family and keep them sheltered and warm; a hungry man will do what is necessary to procure food. Someone who flashes a lot of cash is courting danger. Get your cash in tens and twenties and a few fifties. If you receive any crisp new bills, stop off at a convenience store and buy a candy bar or something, hand the clerk a new bill and you will receive older, worn bills in change. Afterwards, anyone with brand new money may invite envy as a hoarder or may become a target for robbers. You want to avoid attracting attention to yourself both now and then. You will need ones and fives after a disaster, but it's too noticeable to cash a large check and ask for a lot of very small bills.

Gold And Silver Gold and silver coins are real money, based on their standard precious metal content; they have always been a historical refuge in times of crisis. Because of increased public awareness about possible disasters, gold and silver coins have become more desirable, as evidenced by all the advertisements by people who want to buy your gold jewelry. You are not interested in numismatic collectible coins; you're only interested in gold and silver coins for their precious metal content. The cheapest way to hold silver coins is to buy pre-1965 junk silver dimes and quarters.

No one knows the future value ratio of silver coins to copper-clad coins (our currently circulating ones) after a disaster, but there's no doubt that silver coins will be worth considerably more than clads. You pay a higher premium for silver dollars than you do for silver dimes and quarters, but it would be wise to have some silver dollars on hand as part of your survival plan. They are bigger and more impressive looking than dimes and quarters; even though a silver dollar may have the same metal content as ten silver dimes or four silver quarters, it just looks more valuable. The alternative is to buy brand new American Silver Eagles. These are current manufacture pure Silver coins from the US Mint. Though not commonly seen in circulation, they are legal tender and worth far more than their face value.

Gold coins are the most desirable, most valuable, form of real, hard money. Gold is scarce, it does not rust or corrode, it's very beautiful to look at, it's highly desirable as jewelry, it has industrial uses, and a long, long monetary history in many cultures worldwide. It's the real deal. Right now the price of gold is higher than it's been for 25 years, which should warn us that inflation is on the way (Inflation or the threat of inflation causes an immediate rise in the price of gold). The best gold coins are American coins in one oz., 1/2 oz., 1/4 oz. and 1/10 oz. denominations. People have no experience with real gold money and they will probably more readily accept U.S. gold coins than foreign coins. Although the U.S. 1 oz. Liberty coin is slightly more expensive to buy than the South African Kruger Rand, for example, when you go to spend gold, you'll find it easier to move the American coins. Get smaller denomination gold coins than larger ones. In other words, buy more 1/10 oz. coins than 1/4 oz. coins, and more 1/4 oz. coins than 1/2 oz. coins, etc.

The reason for this is that gold is an immense store of value for its size and weight. You will not be able to go into a local flea market or general store with a one oz. gold coin and be able to buy a few loaves of bread and some local cheese. How will the store owner make change for such a high value coin? You will use the fraying paper money, followed by clad coins and then silver coins before you'll place any gold on the counter. Gold is for large purchases so a small gold coin will be of far greater use on most occasions than a larger one. Save your 1 oz. gold coins to purchase major items.

Everyone wants to buy gold! "I buy gold. Pay cash" signs are everywhere! Most of those buyers deal with junk gold, like jewelry, either stolen or being sold because the owner needs the money, not the gold coins that investors talk about. Be forewarned, no dealer pays the true value of junk gold, unlike people buying gold coins.

Since it is impossible to determine the true mineral percentage of gold, small shops and dealers will pay for it as regular jewelry gold. Besides gold coins, buy a lot of small gold rings and other jewelry. They should be less expensive than gold coins, and you won't be losing money selling premium quality gold coins for the price of junk gold. Buy a small bag worth of gold rings. Small time thieves will snatch gold chains right off of your neck and sell them at these small dealers found everywhere. This will become common at train stations, subways and other crowded areas.

Coins You will also need coins. Gold and silver will be useful during the rebuilding stage after the crisis, but ordinary dimes and quarters, nickels and pennies will be the most easily traded form of money. In a massive deflation, which is what a financial crash would create, real hard money becomes far more valuable. A loaf of bread that costs $1.25 today may cost 5 cents afterwards assuming there's any bread to be had. People are completely used to ordinary pocket change coins, so that's what they will most readily accept for local transactions—and nearly all transactions will be local after a major national disaster. You need to start saving up a coin stash. Once a month or so, take a few $20 bills to a bank in which you do not have an account and trade them for rolls of quarters or dollar coins. Any bank will exchange paper for coins without question.

Storing Cash Now you need to find a safe place to hide your cash. First, tell no one that you have a load of cash, except possibly your spouse, and don't tell your spouse unless absolutely certain of the strength of your marriage. Hard times drive people to do things they would not ordinarily do, and if the hammer hits hard, these may be the hardest times in our country's history. If your spouse is a full trustworthy, consider yourself fortunate and keep no secrets; otherwise, be careful.

If you plan to hide your cash somewhere in your house, you want to make sure to protect it from fire, so go to a Wal-Mart or discount store and buy a fireproof storage box. You should be able to get one for under $40. It will protect your cash from burning for a half hour of direct flame. Put your paper money and your gold and silver in the box. If you fill it up, buy another one and fill that one up too. As you begin changing some of your electronic credit wealth into cash, gold and silver, your money is fully under your control. As long as you keep it safe, it will always be there for you.

Barter Another way to get around the money problem is through barter. Barter is a method of exchange by which goods or services are directly exchanged for other goods or services without using a medium of exchange, such as money. It is usually bilateral, but may be multilateral, and usually exists parallel to monetary systems in most developed countries, though to a very limited extent. Barter usually replaces money as the method of exchange in times of monetary crisis, when the currency is unstable and devalued by hyperinflation.

Swapping is the increasingly prevalent informal bartering system in which participants in Internet communities trade items of comparable value on a trust basis using the Internet. The most notable disadvantage to electronic barter is inherent in Internet commerce, that of trust. How can consumers have confidence that they will receive what they bargained, or paid, for? Although the Internet based consumer market has demonstrated that it works, there is never a guarantee of satisfaction in consumer to consumer transactions and no absolute defense against fraud. However, it can be argued that when a person barters there is less incentive to deliberately mislead. Neither party is paid; each party receives something that would only then have to be converted to cash.

In the United States, the sales a barter exchange makes are considered taxable revenue by the IRS and the gross amount of a barter exchange member's sales are reported to the IRS by the barter exchange via a 1099-B form. Barter exchanges are required to report members sales by the Tax Equity & Fair Responsibility Act of 1982. According to the IRS, "The fair market value of goods and services exchanged must be included in the income of both parties."

Because barter is taxable, it is unlikely to play as large a part in economic survival-plans as one might assume. More likely will be grey and black markets.

MOVING MONEY OUT OF THE COUNTRY

While gold is a great store of value, you can't barter it at a supermarket because you would lose too much money. You can wait until things settle down and change your gold for Dollars/Euros or other stable paper money and save yourself from devaluation. But in the end, you may have to get out of Dodge with your gold and deposit it in a safe country. Foreign accounts should be safe since they are protected by another country's law and aren't affected by national executive orders.

But beware, it is not currently easy to move investment size amounts of money out of the United States, and the situation will only get worse. Nations to consider are:

Canada	Chile	Sweden
Australia	Switzerland	Chile
Singapore	Norway	

Make sure to understand that such transactions don't happen over night because foreign banks are now wary of coming into conflict with US taxation, money laundering and banking laws. So getting out of Dodge will take time and effort because the Federal government doesn't want you to leave, it needs you to stay here so it can help prop up the collapsing Federal government and devalued currency.

IV   Financial Survival

If you have your money invested in 401ks or other standard investment vehicles you already realize that you have been made a sucker. The government not only wants your tax money, it wants ALL your money because it is flat broke. Fortunately, here are some ways to protect your money and income that are still legal:

1   Don't invest all your money in one country. Don't put all your eggs in the same basket, just in case any economy goes to hell. Invest in countries like Canada, Australia, Singapore, Scandinavia; anywhere their debt to GDP ratio is low..

2   Buy Commodities, solid things like gold, or stocks in mining companies. Most banks and financial institutions are currently bankrupt.

3   Keep cash. Both dollars and Euros but also Canadian and Australian dollars. Some don't like European money, but it's the only way you have to cover most bases. It's possible for our national paper money to lose 1/3 of its worth from one day to another.

4   Keep your passport and cash ready. If you can't afford to live in this country, the best thing to do may be getting the hell out of it! Maybe you have family somewhere else, keep in touch just in case.

5   If you have land, have some animals, a garden and fruit trees. Even a few chickens and rabbits can make a huge difference and will complement your staple food.

6   People will be fixing things in the future instead of buying new ones. A handyman will always find a way to survive, no matter what your primary job is.

Until costs and inefficiencies resulting from overly-generous pensions, early retirements, union work rules, long vacations, escalating health care costs, government bureaucracy and inflexible hire-and-fire rules are seriously dealt with the financial problems will continue to come back in one form or another. U.S., voters are not yet ready to accept the major changes needed because so far money can be printed and borrowed to put off the day of reckoning. Eventually that will no longer be possible and then the hard choices will have to be made.

Financial markets are reflecting a diverging expectation. Gold prices have been soaring—a potential indicator of inflation fears—while many other inflation indicators are going the other way. In the United States, the loose monetary policy has not resulted in any significant rise at the consumer level or changes in inflation expectations, as evidenced by the sharply slowing Consumer Price Index and plunging M3 money supply.

Biflation... Not Deflation

Despite the seemingly tame headline inflation numbers, consumers never seem to see price declines in certain categories like education and health. For instance, prescription drug inflation escalated to 5% from less than 3% in 2007 and 2008. So, it is pretty obvious what we have here-- *biflation*--instead of deflation. Biflation is a state of the economy where *inflation and deflation occur simultaneously*.

The price increase of commodities is caused by the increased money flow (via loose monetary policy) chasing them. On the other hand, the growth of economy is tempered with high unemployment and decreasing purchasing power. This has resulted in a greater amount of money directed toward essential items (inflation) and away from non-essential items and things required credit to buy such as house and cars (deflation).

Economic Depression Survival Tips

It hardly matters whether we are in a deflationary, inflationary or biflationary economy, what we know for certain is that we are in a depression. So, what do you need to do to survive?

Keep That Income Keep your job or other income and tough times aren't so tough. In fact, if you are still making the same money when prices are dropping, homes cost less and stocks are on sale, a depression can be an opportunity. So start by finding ways to preserve the income you have.

Find a better job in a more secure industry if possible... Make sure that the boss knows you are a great worker... Transfer to parts of the company that are less likely to face layoffs... Cut costs in your small business as soon as sales start to drop... Find a second job if you have the time... Work overtime or extra shifts and save the money from these... Consider starting a low-investment low-risk business on the side to develop an alternate source of income.

Get Ready Whatever you do, there is always a chance that you will lose your primary income. This is true in good times and bad, but in tough times it may be a long time before you can replace that income. This makes preparation in your personal life very important.

Cut fixed expenses, like payments for rental furniture or appliances. The moment that you hear you are losing your job you can stop trips to the movies or bar, but other expenses are harder to quickly reduce and can drag you down fast. So get rid of the extra car you don't really need to have, or the unused boat that costs you for maintenance and insurance. List all of your household expenses and find ways to reduce each one if possible, but start with those that would be the most difficult to reduce quickly when hard times come.

If you are in particularly insecure industry (auto worker, real estate agent, mortgage broker, etc.), seriously consider downsizing your life in more drastic ways. A $600-per-month apartment in place of a $1,200 one means you can set aside an additional $9,000 in 15 months to be ready for whatever comes your way. It also means you'll have a much easier time finding a way to pay that rent if you lose your job. A nice $3,000 used car (they exist of you look) in place of a payment of $500 per month on a newer one means another $7,500 saved in 15 months, and no repossession risk if your income is lost.

Develop other sources of income to the extent possible. If you have a side business that makes a few hundred dollars per month and some dividend-paying stocks that generate regular checks for you, it's unlikely that you will lose all three sources of income at once.

The last few economic depression survival tips have to do with contingency plans. How much can you live on if you lose your primary income, and how will you do it? You may want to try living on that for a week to see if your plan is realistic. Can you sell some of your things if necessary, and do you know what they'll bring in a fast sale? How quickly can you find another job if you lose your current one? Make a list of possible jobs and who you'll need to contact. Have those numbers ready.

Lower your regular expenses, develop other income, have plans in place and money in the bank. Take those steps and you'll be better prepared than most for recessions, depressions or other tough times.

TAXES

This is book isn't about avoiding your share of taxes, whether fair or not. Others can and have made many arguments on both sides of that debate. However, legally minimizing your taxes is the entire reason for the tax code, for tax lawyers and accountants, and for the IRS itself. If there weren't legal ways to reduce your tax signature, tax law would be trivial and you would just receive a bill and that would be it. That said, there are certain general rules to minimizing your taxes and several categories of expenses that you should consider as possible sources of tax reduction:

Do It Yourself   You aren't taxed on what you do for yourself. Home improvements, gardening, working on your car and other self help crafts are not (as yet) taxed. That isn't to suggest that dropping out of the system completely is wise because being self sustainable requires a huge amount of work – there are cost advantages that markets bring that allow them to produce vast quantities of goods cheaply. Still, anything you can do on your own will not be subject to a tax bite.

Business Expenses   Most of the minimization strategies you will see are for people with small businesses. You open up a world of deductions by starting a business, however this whole area of deductions doesn't apply to most of us. Consider starting a business if you have one in mind. Find side business to generate a schedule C to write off meals and autos.

Tax-Deferred Accounts   Make sure you put any money into your IRA, 401(k), HAS or any other tax advantaged accounts you have. Not having to pay taxes can be a huge savings by itself. When you throw in the capacity of some of the accounts to grow tax-free, they may seem a no brainer. However, be aware that the government may be forced to nationalize pension holdings if things really get bad, as has recently happened to some extent in Ireland during its crash.

Unemployment   This is very relevant to all of us in this economic climate. If you lost your job, many of the expenses that you incur in your job search are tax deductable. Phone calls, agency fees, travel to potential employers as well as costs for printing resumes may all be deductible. Be sure to take advantage of any opportunities to lessen your tax burden in this climate.

Medical   If you had serious medical expenses, you may be able to deduct some of them. Most people will not qualify, but if you spent more than 7.5% of your adjusted gross income on medical expenses, you may be able to deduct the excess. Once again, this can be beneficial to those who are experiencing medical hardship.

Charitable Donations   Be sure to keep these in mind as well. You may have been glad to get rid of that bundle of clothes, but it also had some value and you may be able to deduct that amount. Did you donate some money to Haiti? You may have just wanted to help your fellow man, but why forget to take the tax deduction?

House Expenses Do you still have receipts for any home improvements you did? People often forget that these are deductible. You also of course can deduct mortgage interest as well as property taxes (at least for now).

Investments Sell your losses - look at your portfolio and see which are losers and sell to offset gains. Capital Gains are taxed at a lower rate than income - learn what property qualifies for these reductions in taxes. Find out about Tax Exempt Bonds and Mutual Funds. Do you need a tax professional?

REAL ESTATE

In the past, real estate has been the true store of investment wealth for an individual. Land and buildings on that land are permanent, so the feeling was that real estate investments are a safe store of tangible wealth. Currently, much of the national real estate inventory is "under water", that is the equity in the home or property is not covered by the sale price. Sadly, the investment potential of real property may not recover its luster for a decade or more. That is because with so much inventory being carried below its mortgage value, any increases in market price will be soaked up by properties flooding the market. That said, there are some legitimate reasons to still own a home or land for yourself and some rental properties.

- Mortgage deduction.
- Changing to a better neighborhood.
- You may simply not be able to rent what you need.
- Owning productive land. This means either buying rural property or a home with enough land for gardening.
- Living within your means. If the house you live in is above water, you might as well keep it, or trade up if a good opportunity arrives at rock bottom prices, just don't look for instant appreciation.

For those who own property that is under water, you may be forced to move at a loss. The silver lining to this is that rental homes are now available, often well below what the mortgage would cost to buy that same property.

Property Value

In order to make a rational decision about whether to be in the real estate market, there are three basic strategies to valuing a property.

- Comparable Worth – compare the property price to similar properties.
- Replacement Cost – price based on what the replacement construction, utilities and land cost would be.
- Rent Valuation – Base the price on how large a mortgage the going rent would support.

In the past, during the real estate bubble, one would look first at the comparable worth to set the price, because the feeling was "how could you go wrong" as prices inflated. However, in a Depression era economy the only rational way to estimate the price of a property is through a combination of replacement cost and rent valuation. If the mortgage is above the rent the property could return, that is obviously a red flag for an economic survivalist, especially because rents can also drop further. Pricing by replacement cost is not perfect, but it should at least give you a bottom end target, which must also meet the rent valuation test.

Foreclosure

While no one wants to lose their home, in times of economic stress when your equity is "under water" (your loan is greater than the saleable value of the property), foreclosure may be your only viable option. Strategic Default: That is, walking away from mortgage debt, may be the best alternative for many people.

The process of foreclosure can be rapid or lengthy and varies from state to state, but there are countless people who have spent years rent free as they waited for their eviction. Other options such as refinancing, a short sale, alternate financing, temporary arrangements with the lender, or even bankruptcy may present homeowners with ways to avoid foreclosure and\or being immediately forced out. In some states, particularly those where only judicial foreclosure is available, the constitutional issue of due process has affected the ability of some lenders to foreclose.

We aren't suggesting taking advantage of the system for no purpose, but survival is a damn good purpose. The banks themselves have engaged in "strategic defaults" on properties and have run to the Feds for bailout money (that is, taxpayers bailed them out). The point is, when the whole system is corrupt from the head to the tail, you need to act accordingly. What may have been indefensible in the past may make sense when there is no room left on the lifeboat.

Short Sale

A short sale is a sale of real estate in which the proceeds fall short of the balance owed on the property's loan. It often occurs when a borrower cannot pay the mortgage loan on their property, but the lender decides that selling the property at a moderate loss is better than pressing the borrower. Both parties, the bank and the owner, consent to the short sale process because it allows them to avoid foreclosure, which involves hefty fees for the bank and poorer credit report outcomes for the borrowers. This agreement, however, does not necessarily release the borrower from the obligation to pay the remaining balance of the loan, known as the *deficiency*.

BANKRUPTCY

In the event of an economic collapse, you may very well find yourself bankrupt and forced to seek protection for the sake of survival. The moral issues of bankruptcy – defaulting on debts you legitimately owe – may not even apply because of chains of defaults of your suppliers and your account receivables.   Therefore you need to be aware that there are a number of different bankruptcy strategies.

There are six types of bankruptcy under the Bankruptcy Code, in Title 11 of the United States Code:

- Chapter 7: basic liquidation for individuals and businesses; also known as straight bankruptcy; it is the simplest and quickest form of bankruptcy available

- Chapter 9: municipal bankruptcy; a federal mechanism for the resolution of municipal debts

- Chapter 11: rehabilitation or reorganization, used primarily by business debtors, but sometimes by individuals with substantial debts and assets; known as corporate bankruptcy, it is a form of corporate financial reorganization which typically allows companies to continue to function while they follow debt repayment plans

- Chapter 12: rehabilitation for family farmers and fishermen;

- Chapter 13: rehabilitation with a payment plan for individuals with a regular source of income; enables individuals with regular income to develop a plan to repay all or part of their debts; also known as Wage Earner Bankruptcy

- Chapter 15: ancillary and other international cases; provides a mechanism for dealing with bankruptcy debtors and helps foreign debtors to clear debts.

The most common types of personal bankruptcy for individuals are Chapter 7 and Chapter 13. As much as 65% of all U.S. consumer bankruptcy filings are Chapter 7 cases. Corporations and other business forms file under Chapters 7 or 11.

In Chapter 7, a debtor surrenders his or her non-exempt property to a bankruptcy trustee who then liquidates the property and distributes the proceeds to the debtor's unsecured creditors. In exchange, the debtor is entitled to a discharge of some debt; however, the debtor will not be granted a discharge if they are guilty of certain types of inappropriate behavior (e.g. concealing records relating to financial condition) and certain debts (e.g. spousal and child support, student loans, some taxes) will not be discharged even though the debtor is generally discharged from his or her debt. Many individuals in financial distress own only exempt property (e.g. clothes, household goods, an older car) and will not have to surrender any property to the trustee. The amount of property that a debtor may exempt varies from state to state. Chapter 7 relief is available only once in any eight year period. Generally, the rights of secured creditors to their collateral continues even though their debt is discharged. For example, absent some arrangement by a debtor to surrender a car or "reaffirm" a debt, the creditor with a security interest in the debtor's car may repossess the car even if the debt to the creditor is discharged.

The 2005 amendments to the Bankruptcy Code introduced the "means test" for eligibility for chapter 7. An individual who fails the means test will have his or her chapter 7 case dismissed or may have to convert his or her case to a case under chapter 13.

Generally, a trustee will sell most of the debtor's assets to pay off creditors. However, certain assets of the debtor are protected to some extent. For example, Social Security payments, unemployment compensation, and limited values of your equity in a home, car, or truck, household goods and appliances, trade tools, and books are protected. However, these exemptions vary from state to state. Therefore, it is advisable to consult an experienced bankruptcy attorney.

In Chapter 13, the debtor retains ownership and possession of all of his or her assets, but must devote some portion of his or her future income to repaying creditors, generally over a period of three to five years. The amount of payment and the period of the repayment plan depend upon a variety of factors, including the value of the debtor's property and the amount of a debtor's income and expenses. Secured creditors may be entitled to greater payment than unsecured creditors.

Relief under Chapter 13 is available only to individuals with regular income whose debts do not exceed prescribed limits. If you're an individual or a sole proprietor, you are allowed to file for a Chapter 13 bankruptcy to repay all or part of your debts. Under this chapter, you can propose a repayment plan in which to pay your creditors over three to five years. If your monthly income is less than the state's median income, your plan will be for three years unless the court finds "just cause" to extend the plan for a longer period. If your monthly income is greater than your state's median income, the plan must generally be for five years. A plan cannot exceed the five-year limitation.

In contrast to Chapter 7, the debtor in Chapter 13 may keep all of his or her property, whether or not exempt. If the plan appears feasible and if the debtor complies with all the other requirements, the bankruptcy court will typically confirm the plan and the debtor and creditors will be bound by its terms. Creditors have no say in the formulation of the plan other than to object to the plan, if appropriate, on the grounds that it does not comply with one of the Code's statutory requirements. Generally, the payments are made to a trustee who in turn disburses the funds in accordance with the terms of the confirmed plan.

When the debtor completes payments pursuant to the terms of the plan, the court will formally grant the debtor a discharge of the debts provided for in the plan. However, if the debtor fails to make the agreed upon payments or fails to seek or gain court approval of a modified plan, a bankruptcy court will often dismiss the case on the motion of the trustee. Pursuant to the dismissal, creditors will typically resume pursuit of state law remedies to the extent a debt remains unpaid.

In Chapter 11, the debtor retains ownership and control of its assets and is re-termed a *debtor in possession* ("DIP"). The debtor in possession runs the day to day operations of the business while creditors and the debtor work with the Bankruptcy Court in order to negotiate and complete a plan. Upon meeting certain requirements (*e.g.* fairness among creditors, priority of certain creditors) creditors are permitted to vote on the proposed plan. If a plan is confirmed the debtor will continue to operate and pay its debts under the terms of the confirmed plan. If a specified majority of creditors do not vote to confirm a plan, additional requirements may be imposed by the court in order to confirm the plan.

Chapter 7 and Chapter 13 are the efficient bankruptcy chapters often used by most individuals. The chapters which almost always apply to consumer debtors are chapter 7, known as a "straight bankruptcy", and chapter 13, which involves an affordable plan of repayment. An important feature applicable to all types of bankruptcy filings is the automatic stay. The automatic stay means that the mere request for bankruptcy protection automatically stops and brings to a grinding halt most lawsuits, repossessions, foreclosures, evictions, garnishments, attachments, utility shut-offs, and debt collection harassment.

V   Stocks, Bonds, Real Estate

STOCK MARKET

Which way will the stock market go in a broken biflationary economy ruled by both inflation and deflation? That is of course the million dollar question. When both the Federal government as well as the Federal Reserve are out of control, trust is lost in all sectors of the economy because winners and losers are then chosen by random acts of bureaucrats rather than by market forces. While it is clear that the Fed has gone to extraordinary lengths to prop up the stock market after the 2008 crash, it is also clear that their ability to paper over the losses is not infinite.

Yet there is an argument to be made that the stock market has a use as an inflation hedge. Stocks which derive their profits from overseas ventures, especially those from countries that have their currencies under control, can provide protection from inflation. Also stocks that are based on necessities like food, transportation, and mundane products like cleaning and laundry soaps can also avoid being devalued.

However, be wary, any good news during the initial 1929-33 depressions/recession triggered "euphoric response." Such is human nature and nobody can be blamed for trying to be optimistic; however, in the financial survival game, we have a fiduciary responsibility to be as realistic as possible about the outlook for the economy and the market at all times. The 1929-33 recession saw six quarterly bounces in GDP with an average gain of 8 percent, sending the stock market to a 50 percent rally in early 1930 as investors thought the worst had passed.

Given the possibility of an economic crash in the United States stocks, it seems wise to look towards foreign markets to diversify one's investments.

Emerging markets

One possible investment strategy is for investors to put their money in faster-growing economies like China, India and Brazil which will generate better stock returns. Over the long run, certain emerging markets might be winners simply because their stock-buying population is swelling faster. A key metric to watch is a country's proportion of people in their 40s to those in their 20s.

In our 20s, we spend what little money we have on necessities like rent, tuition loans, social dates, liquor and cars. Only when we grow older, wiser and wealthier— hopefully by the time we hit 40— do we allocate serious money to stocks and plan for retirement. No surprise then that as baby boomers came of age, the old/young ratio in the U.S. shrank from 102% to 56% between 1960 and 1980—drab decades for the stock market. By 2000, however, this ratio rebounded to 109% in a heady ascent that paralleled our stock market boom.

While the U.S. old/young demographic ratio is projected to shrink slightly over the next two decades, the 40s-to-20s horde will surge in many emerging economies— to 84%, from 63%, in India; to 105%, from 73%, in Brazil; to 166%, from 78%, in Poland, and to 125%, from 99%, in China. Of course, things like valuations, financial crises, reforms and busts matter, too, and will create variations from this theme, but there is no escaping the power of demographics. The age ratio will rise the most over the next five to 10 years in Indonesia, India and the Philippines within Asia; and in Brazil, Mexico, Poland and Turkey elsewhere.

If you are going to buy more U.S. and European equities, it should be in stocks that would also interest emerging-market investor, things like the old world's global toothpaste and diaper manufacturers, utilities and health-care outfits. Try stocks like iShares S&P Global 100 Fund (IOO) for exposure to brands like Exxon Mobil (NYSE: XOM), Microsoft (NYSE: MSFT), Procter & Gamble (NYSE: PG) and IBM (NYSE: IBM). In other words, you need to think of the United States as a second tier economy and decide what would be profitable to invest in, the same way as in the past you viewed places like Korea or Colombia for investing.

BONDS

Bonds are a mechanism for loaning someone money, either the federal government, state governments, municipal governments or corporations, at an interest rate. Regarding ederal Treasury Bonds, the problem has been that the federal reserve has lowered the prime lending rate near zero which means returns on Treasuries are in the 2 to 3% range, barely enough to cover inflation risk. Investing in municipal bonds often carries the advantage of their not being taxable, however given the unfunded liabilities of pension funds in the United States, many states and municipalities may be at risk of bankruptcy. While municipalities can go bankrupt, currently states cannot by law file for bankruptcy so their bonds would be at least somewhat protected. However given the size of the deficits in California, New York, and Illinois, it is likely that states will at some point be allowed to go bankrupt as well, defaulting on bondholders.

GRAY/BLACK MARKET

Once an economic collapse begins, black/gray markets will take no time to appear, the question is whether you can capitalize on them. Gray markets will be accepted parts of the economy in the end, as they have been in places like Italy and Argentina. At first it starts as the trading of skills or craft products for food, as already occurs on www.craigslist.com. Localities may also form their own barter markets, and create their own tickets/script, another money really, to trade. However, since script is easy to make on a home computer, eventually barter markets return to paper money.

These markets end up in warehouses or on empty land, and might be managed by some wise guy and a few thugs or hired security. Anyone can rent a kiosk inside and sell their goods and services. Uniformed cops may manage security at these markets as a second job, but you have to be careful. The bad economy hits everyone and once you leave the building, you are on your own. These markets generally run peacefully, free markets at their best, because the managers want to make money and may not wait for the police to solve problems.

VI Employment

If you are unemployed because of the downturn and you're pursuing your dream job, you may need to wake up before Life turns that dream into a nightmare. Your dream job may be one saddled for elimination. But you can save yourself a lot of stress and disappointment by going after jobs with proven longevity. What you need is a career that will stay stable, no matter how much the Dow-Jones rises or falls. Here are a few that will help you survive the dark times:

1. Doctors and Healthcare: These are careers that never goes out of style. People will always get sick; doctors will never want for patients. Despite the failing economy, Health Care in an industry on the rise. We're living longer, but we definitely need people to help us do it. Jobs in the medical and health care professions are not only lucrative, but in demand. And you don't have to be an M.D. Everything from Nurses and Physical Therapists to Medical Coders and Ambulance Drivers are needed.

2. Pharmacist: Immediately after we see the doctor, we head straight for the drug store for our prescription. Whether you're an independent druggist, or working for one of the chains, your position will be in demand, particularly during a recession. Increased unemployment means more people without insurance. And this spells business for pharmacies and manufacturers of pharmaceuticals and medical supplies. The uninsured will forestall an expensive doctor visit with flu shots, over-the-counter drugs, even alternative herb and vitamin therapy.

3. Dentist: Dental hygiene is very important to Americans. This is a safe bet, even when money's tight. While people may not have as much to spend on expensive braces, data from Bureau of Labor Statistics shows that dental offices did increase as much as 2 - 4% during previous economic recessions in 1990, 2001 & 2007. Recession also means people will be eating cheap, rather than healthy. This takes a major toll on the teeth, but creates business for you. No matter how much people hate dentists, they hate toothaches more.

4. Teacher: Sadly, teachers aren't appreciated in this country. But we all remember that one teacher who made difference in our lives. The really good news in this job market is that teachers can always get work. Enrollment is increasing exponentially while veteran teachers are retiring. There's also a growing need for teaching aids with bilingual proficiency and handicap training, to assist children with special needs. Educators with advanced degrees are particularly sought after to meet the rising number of college students.

5. Engineer: There are many different types of engineers, but the great thing is that they are always in demand. And if the government steps in to ignite the economy through infrastructure improvements, it will be engineers that lead the way. We tend to picture them in flannel shirts and hard hats, but engineers can be choosy, and use their skills in either a white or blue collar environment. The Energy industry will bring steady engineer work in any recession, but particularly now, with all the ongoing research for alternative energy sources.

6. Accountant: They say the only two certainties in life are death and taxes. As long as we have taxes, we'll need people to prepare our tax forms. Even in recession, the cost of hiring an expert is offset by the clever loopholes and tax breaks they find. Accountants are spoiled for choice. Every industry and corporation, anyone who makes or handles money, eventually needs one.

7. Mortician: It's macabre and spooky, but career-wise, this is the house that always wins. And you don't need to be a funeral director to get in on the action. There are several lucrative, death-related careers. Here's a list; imagine the details yourself: Coroner, Embalmer, Crematorium Technician, Casket Manufacturer, Obituary Writer, Grave Digger.

8. Politician: Death, Taxes…Politicians, they will always be with us. It's an election year, so it deserves a mention. We like to think them as public servants, but they also get paid. Whether it's the local District Attorney or a Congressman in Washington, our elected officials receive a tidy salary and a budget for the running of their office. Sounds rather cushy, but we all know (wink, wink) they're not in it for the money.

9. Government Employee: It may not be a glamorous politician's life, but somebody has to keep the wheels of bureaucracy well-oiled. The wonderful thing about Government Employment is the longevity. Usually, people leave only when they retire. Not only are they rarely downsized, but during a recession, the government is notable for creating new jobs within its network. Government contracting can also provide stable employment.

10. Utility/Energy Specialist: Another good standby. No matter how bad the economy gets, it isn't likely that people will stop using electricity or heating their homes. These careers offer a variety of specializations from technicians to researchers, particularly as Americans become more environmentally conscious. We want power 'greener' and (hopefully) cheaper.

11. Scientist: The human race is never going to stop wondering about the world around us, which is scientists will feel the cold less than other areas of advanced academia. Now, not everyone can be an Einstein, but thankfully there is a great need for scientists in practical arenas of industry and medicine. Companies like Proctor and Gamble, historically a recession proof corporation, employs many scientists and engineers to develop and test new products.

12. Police Officer: Our finest in blue! Like government employees, police layoffs are rare; nobody wants to jeopardize public safety. This work can be a little more dangerous, depending on where you are keeping the peace, so you may want to opt for security work in the private sector. Or if you don't want to be around criminals (who would?) you can safeguard the public in a fireman's uniform.

13. Soldier: In war or peacetime, a Soldier in the Armed Forces is an honorable profession. And when the nation is in economic trouble, the career choice for many. And it's not hard to see why. The Service provides salary and living expenses, trains soldiers in a variety of marketable skills as well as combat, and helps fund higher education. We all know the downside, of course, so the Army life isn't for everyone. But it's always an option.

14. Social Worker/Career Counselor: Economic turbulence is a time when people need help the most. Ordinary problems seem bigger when money is short. Hence, the need for Social Workers and counselors dramatically increases whenever the economy flops. Social Assistance offers a range of emphasis, from youth and family programs to elderly and handicap services. Career Counselors go hand in glove with economic hardship. They is nothing like being unemployed to make someone feel helpless. Job and industry downsizing will keep Career Counselors busy.

15. Auto Mechanic: We love them, we hate them, but where would we be without our cars? They are a necessity, and so are the mechanics who look nurse them back to health. The career is stable throughout, but during economic recession, mechanics can look forward to an increase in tow truck services.

16. Home Maintenance Specialist: This career is a generic term for a highly skilled worker, such as a Carpenter, Plumber or Roofer. Like the Auto-Mechanic, these jobs provide services that are necessary to daily life. The need for unclogged pipes and a roof without leaks doesn't go away when the economy sours, so these careers, while blue collar, are steady as they come.

17: Bartender: When times get tough, booze sells. And actually, you don't need to be the one mixing drinks and listening to the clients' life story. Anyone involved in the production, manufacture and distribution of alcohol is sure to profit, from the distillery to the bar where you serve it up neat.

18: Cosmetologist: It's the last thing to go. Women may deny themselves new clothes and stylish shoes and every other little luxury. Somehow, they always find enough money for the periodic salon date, complete with haircut, color, manicure and waxing.

19: Veterinarian: Americans adore their pets (sometimes more than people!), and we depend on them when times get tough. Both Veterinary services and sales at pet and pet supply retailers typically take an upward incline during recession.

20: Debt Advisor/Debt Collector: Two sides of the same problem. Collecting and settling debts is probably the single most recession-proof job out there. Debts mount up, and Debt Advisors and Collectors spring up to meet them.

21: Sex Worker: The world's oldest profession is one you can bank on during recession. Illegal it may be, but like bootlegger trade during Prohibition, sex ~~will~~ sells in secret, despite any economic down spirals. And let's not forget, there are similar jobs in this category that, while shady, are totally legal: 'Blue Movie Performers,' 'Massage Therapists,' 'Exotic Dancers.' Hasn't done Diablo Cody any harm.

Employment To Avoid

1: Real Estate While the pay checks can be huge, the amount of work and effort to close deals has also gone up exponentially.

2: Banking and Finance Face it, the banks are in default. While you may be the next Gordon Gekko, the fat is gone

3: Outsourceable Professions Call centers, light manufacturing, some accounting and paralegal work – anything where someone answers the phone with an Indian accent.

4: Journalism The major newspapers are all going belly up and the national broadcasters are losing market share. Blogging is not a living.

VII What To Prepare For?

Before you can prepare for an economic collapse, you must determine what type of events you are preparing to survive and how each disaster threatens you, your safety and the survival of your gamily. What would happen if the stock markets crashed and the banks closed? It isn't hard to guess.

1. The Collapse of Social Order

"Social order" is a delicate thing, and it exists as a psychological barrier that could easily collapse under the right conditions. We saw this years ago during the L.A. Riots following the Rodney King trial verdict as citizens of L.A. set fire to their own town, yanked people from vehicles and beat them literally to death, and even fired guns at firemen attempting to save their buildings! More recently we were all witness to the looting, violence and total breakdown of society following Hurricane Katrina in New Orleans.

What allows this to happen? Simple: the simultaneous melting away of the psychological barrier of "order." Once people realize 911 can't handle the load, or is offline, that the local police are helpless or have abandoned their posts, "Law and Order" ceases to exist in some minds. They then conduct their lives the way they always wanted to, but couldn't because of the police. That is, they run out to the local stores and take whatever they want (looting). Some will take out their racial or other frustrations on innocent victims who happen to be driving through the area, and they let loose on a path of destruction that only stops when men with rifles (the National Guard) are called in to settle things down.

In other words, only the threat of immediate death stops the looting and violence. Rifles work wonders. Imagine store owners lying prone on the roofs of their stores with AK-47's, firing at anyone who approaches. This is exactly what happened in Los Angeles. But worse, imagine the lawless horde firing at the rescue copters trying to bring in supplies to the desperate masses in New Orleans. It took the National Guard to eventually get things under control.

These events were isolated. However, imagine a hundred cities experiencing the same thing. Will the National Guard be able to handle the load? Not likely. What about local police? They aren't fools; if things look bad enough, they'll grab their families and head for the hills, just like they did in New Orleans. No pension is worth getting killed for. A few U.S. cities could be transformed into warzones overnight. It would require all-out martial law and military force to have any chance whatsoever of bringing order to these streets.

This collapse of social order is perhaps the greatest risk of staying in the city during a crisis. What, exactly, would cause this collapse of social order? Lack of three things: food, water, and money. When people run out of food, some will begin ransacking their neighborhood, searching for something to eat. (Remember that in a city, a "neighbor" does not mean the same thing as a "neighbor" in the country. They are not necessarily your friends.)

It won't take long, then, for violence to take over in some cities. While certain regions will certainly manage to keep things under control and people will form lines at the local (depleted) Red Cross shelter, other cities will see an explosion of violence. Imagine the gang-infested regions of L.A., Chicago, New York, St. Louis & New Orleans, those people aren't going to stand in line and wait. They already have guns; now they finally get to use them. Pent-up racial tensions will serve as justification for shooting people of the same or other color in order to get their food.

Even if the food somehow gets into the cities, lack of money (due to the government not sending out checks) could cause the same thing. Eventually, lack of money results in looting and mass theft, accelerating the collapse of social order as the stealing balloons. The breakdown of social order doesn't require any "actual" collapse of the power grid, telecommunications, transportation or banking. Social order is a psychological artifact. It is a frame of mind, and any global panic can quickly remove the mental barrier that now keeps people basically "lawful."

2. The Failure of Water Treatment and Delivery Systems

Will the water treatment facilities fail during a crisis? Many will. Some won't. The problem lies in figuring out whether yours will. Certainly, pumping stations depend on electricity, and if the power goes down, so will the water. The most important question is what happens when the water stops flowing (or if it is flowing, but is not drinkable).

While people can live without food for long periods of time (2-3 weeks), water is needed on a daily basis. You can go 2-3 days without it, at most, but beyond that, you'll quickly turn to dust. That means people will do anything to get water, because to not have it means death. And guess where it's going to be the most difficult to actually get water? You guessed it: in the cities. During the first day of the water crisis, many people still won't figure out what's going on. They'll figure it's a temporary breakage of a water main and the government will get it fixed within hours. As those hours stretch into the next day, these people will get very worried. By the second day, more and more people will realize the water isn't coming.

At that point, you could easily see a breakdown of social order, as described above (these things all tend to cause each other…). People will begin their "search for water," and the first place they're likely to go is where they always go for liquids: the grocery store, the local Wal-Mart, the 7-11. The shelves will be cleaned out rather quickly. Because those liquids won't last long, you'll see a mass-exodus from the cities. They'll take the gas they have left in their tanks and leave the city in search of water.

Some will go to "Grandma's house" out in the country where they might at least find a pond or stream to drink from. Others will simply go on an expanded looting mission, stopping at any house they see and asking the residents (with a gun in their face, likely) if they have any water to "donate." As a result of all this, if water stops flowing, here are the events you can expect to see in some of the worse-off cities:

- Looting of all the grocery stores by the second or third day (remember New Orleans?)
- Minor outbreaks of violence during the looting. Shop owners, for example, may attempt to defend their shops with firearms (ala L.A. Riots)

- Mass exodus of residents from the city in search of water
- Ransacking of any houses or farms within a gas-tank radius of the city, presumably by desperate people with guns
- Mass traffic jams on the outbound highways as people run out of gas and abandon their vehicles (if bad enough, this could actually block the highways and trap people in the cities)
- Mass outbreak of water-borne diseases as people use streams and rivers as both a water fountain and a bathroom. People crapping upstream are going to infect the people drinking downstream. Very few have any kind of water filtration device.

That last point is really critical. Once the water flow stops, disease is going to strike.

3. The Depletion of Food Supplies

Food supplies will dwindle quickly as we approach a crisis due to people stocking up just in case. Once the crisis actually hits, expect to see breakdowns in the transportation sector that will result in major delays in food delivery. This means food may arrive in sporadic fashion in some cities (if at all). Once this happens, food suddenly becomes really valuable to people (even though they take it for granted today). And that means any small shipment of food that arrives will be quickly grabbed and eaten or stored. It only takes one week without food to remind people how much they actually need it, so expect the atmosphere to be that of a "near panic" if food is delayed by as little as three days.

The level of panic will vary from city to city. Some cities or towns may experience very little difficulty receiving food. Others may face near-starvation circumstances. Remember, the cities depend entirely on food shipped in from the farms and food processing companies. Also, note that if there's a water problem and the mass exodus begins, the highways may be jammed up at critical locations, causing gridlock for the trucking industry. If we're lucky, some trucks will continue to roll. If we're not, assume that nothing gets through. A shortage of food ultimately results in the same behavior as a shortage of water. First, people eat what's in the pantry, then they loot the grocery stores. After that, with all local supplies depleted and no hope on the horizon, they leave the city and start ransacking nearby homes. Some will try to hunt or fish nearby forests, but most city-dwellers don't have those skills. In any case, anyone with the means to leave the city will likely do so soon after their food shortage begins.

4. The Failure of the Power Grid

Nothing is as suddenly obvious – nor has such a gigantic psychological impact – as the failure of the power grid. When the electricity stops, almost everybody knows it at the same instant. During the first few hours of power failure, people will assume it's a temporary situation. Maybe a tree fell on some power lines, or perhaps a transformer blew-up somewhere. They'll sit tight and wait for the power to come back on. If it doesn't, the city faces a severe problem. Without power, everything shuts down and within hours, the looting begins in the more crime ridden cities (we saw this in New York a few decades ago…).

The longer the power stays off, the worse the social disorder. The loss of power will bring an entire city to a halt. While vehicles may get around for a few more days (using whatever fuel they have left), businesses obviously won't be operating. Houses that depend on electricity for heat will quickly reach winter temperatures, freezing many occupants to death. Those that depend on electricity for Air Conditioning will just as quickly reach Summer temperatures, resulting in death from heat stroke. Hospitals and police stations may have generators on hand, with a few days' worth of fuel, but in short order, that will be depleted, too. But the water treatment plant will almost certainly be off-line without power, causing all the events mentioned in the water section, above. Let's face it, the power is the worst thing to be without in the city. If you have power, you can survive a food shortage, perhaps even a short water shortage. But without power, all bets are off. If you have a "bug-out" vehicle stocked and ready to go, this might be the time to bail.

5. Quarantine, Marshal Law or city has been sealed off.

A new threat that manifested itself in the aftermath of Hurricane Katrina is the possibility that the government will Quarantine or Seal off the exits of a city to keep all of the residents contained within its boundaries so as not to allow them to flee or leave. This could be done for purely noble reasons like controlling an outbreak of disease/plague from spreading to nearby communities or for more diabolical reasons like exerting control over population centers by stopping the free movement of people. If you lived in New Orleans, the only time you could leave was before and during the Hurricane. Afterwards you were trapped and could only leave when and where you were permitted. Countless people tried to walk out of the city and were sent back at gunpoint by the National Guard into the hell hole until they could be "outprocessed" and evacuated. Regardless of why, the issue is that should you choose to remain in the city, *you may not have the option of leaving once the disaster response begins.*

URBAN OR COUNTRY?

City people and country people have very different views on politics and life in general. Country people tend to be more religious and more conservative. City people tend to be more liberal. So there's more than a little animosity between country people and city people. When a crisis hits, and the country people find they are without electricity and fuel, they will still survive, for the most part, because they're used to surviving. But do you think they will really put "saving city people" high on their list of priorities? Not likely. Any food that's harvested from the fields will be kept and stored by the farmers themselves. They will NOT be shipping this stuff to the cities unless they have excess goods and can find a transportation method that still works (and has fuel).

Unfortunately, if some emergency powers acts are signed into place by the President, the Federal Emergency Management Association will have the legal power to actually confiscate and redistribute food. This makes it all the more likely that farmers will harvest it and HIDE IT in order to keep it. And that means even less food making it to the cities. Bottom line? Cities where food can't be delivered will eventually be gutted, looted, evacuated and even burned to the ground.

Will those who live in the country be better off than city dwellers? There are no simple answers. There are some issues that have to be analyzed, especially security, to decide. Of course, those who live in the country and have some land and animals will be better prepared food-wise. Even without several acres full of crops, a few fruit trees, some animals, such as chickens, cows and rabbits, and a small orchard are enough to be light years ahead of those in the cities. Chickens, eggs and rabbits would provide the proteins, a cow or two for milk and cheese, some vegetables and fruit plants cover the vegetable diet, and some eggs or a rabbit could be traded for flour to make bread and pasta or sugar and salt.

Of course there are exceptions. If you live in a desert climate, and it almost never rains it is almost impossible to live off the land, and animals require food and water you have to buy. Those who live in cities will have to manage as they can if food prices go up 200%-300%. People will cut expenses wherever they can to buy food. Some will eat whatever is available, hunting birds or street dogs and cats; others will starve. When it comes to food, cities are not the place to be in a crisis. The lack of food or the impossibility to acquire is what starts the rioting and looting.

When it comes to security things get even more complicated. Forget about shooting those that mean you harm from 300 yards away with your high powered rifle. Leave that notion to armchair commandos.

Some security facts:

1) Those that want to harm you/steal from you don't come with a pirate flag waving over
2) their heads.
3) Neither do they start shooting at you 200 yards away.
4) A man with a wife and two or three kids can't set up a watch.
5) No 6th sense is going to tell you that there is a guy with a gun pointed at your back when you are trying to fix the water pump that just broke, or a carrying a big heavy bag of dried beans you bought that morning.

The best alarm system anyone can have on a farm are dogs. But dogs can get killed and poisoned. Even though the person that lives out in the country is safer when it comes to small time robberies, that same person is more exposed to extremely violent home robberies. Criminals feeling of invulnerability is boosted knowing that farms are isolated. When they assault a country home or farm, they can stay there for hours or days torturing the owners.

Big cities aren't much safer for the survivalist that decides to stay in the city. He will have to face express kidnappings, robberies, and pretty much risking getting shot for what's in his pockets or even for his clothes.

So, where to go? The concrete jungle is dangerous and so is living away from it, all on your own. The solution is to stay away from the cities but in groups, either by living in a small town community or sub division, or if you have friends or family that think as you do, form your own community small community.

Some may think that having neighbors within "shouting" distance means losing your privacy and freedom, but it's a price that you have to pay if you want to have someone to help you if you ever need it. To those that believe that they will never need help from anyone because they will always have their rifle at hand, checking the horizon with their scope every five minutes and a first aid kit on their back packs at all times.... Grow up

SERVICES

Whatever scenario you are dealing with, basic services are likely to either suffer in quality or disappear all together. Think ahead and analyze possible scenarios and which service would be affected by events in your area. Think about the most likely scenario but also think outside the box. What's more likely? A tornado? A terrorist attack isn't as crazy as you thought it would be a few years ago. Also analyze the consequences of those services going down. If there is no power then you need to do something about all that meat you have in the fridge, you might be able to dry it or can it. Think about the supplies you would need for these tasks before you actually need them. You have a complete guide on how to prepare the meat on your computer... how will you get it out of there if there is no power? Print everything that you consider important.

If you have loved ones around you, black outs won't be as bad. The point is that family helps morale on these situations.

QUESTIONS TO ASK YOURSELF

Determining your options in a crisis isn't tough; it only takes a few minutes of thought. The following exercise will get you started, jot notes or switch into your word processor while you work. Keep in mind that you cannot prepare for everything — only the army tries to do that with far more resources. If you focus on potential disasters that are likely to occur within the next five years, you will realize economic collapse is more likely than the next earthquake or 100 year flood, but remember the survivalist's creed: better safe than sorry.

You'll have to extrapolate, evaluate trends, read the newspaper, conduct your own research. At the very least, take a few minutes and consider your location. Pull out a map and look what's within a two-mile, five-mile 10-mile and 25-mile radius of your home and place of work. Put on your pessimist hat and consider what might go wrong that could directly impact you. Decide if that's something you want to prepare for. For example, if you live a "safe" distance outside of a flood plain, your house might still get flooded in the 100-year flood, should you prepare for it? We would, but it's your call. That nuclear plant 20 miles away has an excellent safety record. Should a nuclear disaster be on your list? Again, you make the call. Are you worried about a meteorite crashing into your house? Well, it has happened, but it's probably not worth preparing for

Here are some questions to ask yourself:

What natural disasters or extreme conditions am I (we) likely to face in the next five years?

Make a list and rank them in order of most to least likely to impact you. Your list might look like this:

Natural Disasters

Weather-related

- Hurricanes Tornadoes Flash flooding slides Heavy thunder storms
- High winds Hail
- Severe winter weather
- Avalanche Extreme
- High Heat Drought
- Wildfire

Non Weather-related

- Earthquake
- Volcano eruption
- Tidal wave/Tsunami

Man-made Disasters

- Severe Economic Depression
- Stock market crash
- War (*conventional, biological, chemical or nuclear*)
- Toxic material emission or spill (*from a train, semi truck or nearby plant*)
- Riot or other civil disorder
- Nuclear plant melt down or other nuclear disaster
- Terrorism
- Fire
- Government action against you

Other

- Plague or disease outbreak
- Comet strike or giant meteor

Personal Emergencies

- Kidnapping Mugging, robbery or other criminal attack
- Unemployment financial disaster
- Death in family Home destroyed by fire
- Random acts of violence

What are the ramifications of each item on your list.??

Now, take your list and create a second column. Put the ramifications of each disaster in the second column. How the disaster or emergency situation could affect you. Everyone's situation is different, a family with children has different concerns than those without or singles.

Potential Disaster Ramifications

- Thunder storm with electrical outage for 2 (average) to 48 hours (severe)

- Food spoilage possible
- Lack of air conditioning/furnace
- Damage to house or car from nearby trees
- Possible local flooding (see below)
- Local transportation impaired by fallen trees, wires
- Lightning damage/fire potential
- Severe winter weather, Electrical power outage for 4hrs (average) to 72 hours (severe)
- Would affect furnace operation
- Exposure problems
- Frozen pipes
- Disruption of travel, transportation
- Self or family members possibly stranded away from home
- Possible food shortages and empty shelves at local markets
- Nearby flash flooding Local transportation disrupted
- Danger while traveling in car or by foot
- Possible loss of some utilities
- Nearby train derailment Possible leak or spill of chemicals
- Short-term exposure problem
- Long-term cancer concerns
- Evacuation may be necessary
- Riot or other civil disorder Disruption of commute (ala Los Angeles)
- Stranded in car or office while family is at home and/or school
- Danger of riot spreading to my neighborhood
- Danger of local kids/low lives taking advantage of situation
- Attack or threat to personal safety
- Looting and rampaging by otherwise lawful citizens
- Fire with potentially no response by authorities
- Police are overwhelmed, cannot protect law-abiding citizens
- Nuclear plant problems
- Reactor vessel damage could result in release of radioactive chemicals to atmosphere
- Evacuation necessary
- Terrorism Threat to safety at work and during business travel
- Disruption of commerce, travel
- Less personal freedom, privacy as a result of government reaction to terrorism

Once you've created a chart like the one above, you know what situations you are most likely to face and can prepare your survival plan.

VIII Survival Priorities

The truth is you could find yourself and your loved ones in a struggle for survival at any time, whether or not this is caused by economic collapse, manmade disasters or by natural disasters. Even if your outdoor skills are better than most, that's not really saying much given our predominantly urban population.

So we won't just be prepping you for for economic survival, because you need to prepare for Survival no matter what sequence of events tips the world against you. An oil spill (like the BP Gulf Oil spill) could be both a natural as well as economic disaster leading to a social collapse, so you need to get your head into a slightly different place than it probably is right now. Hard times are coming, and you need to get back to thinking about survival from the most basic levels on up.

While you need to be proactively conducting your own ongoing risk assessment at multiple levels, from accident avoidance and healthy lifestyle choices to stockpiling food and growing your own , right now just focus on the ramifications of the Rule of Three.

The Rule of Three

The basics of survival can be summed-up in "The Rules of Three" which say (absent sudden death such as an accident or terminal illness) your survival is generally contingent upon you not exceeding:

3 minutes without breathing (drowning, asphyxiation)

3 hours without shelter in an extreme environment (exposure)

3 days without water (dehydration)

3 weeks without food (starvation)

3 Months without hope.

Asphyxiation Asphyxiation kills in three minutes. This is the emergency situation that gives you the least amount of time to react for your survival. This is your Priority One Survival issue. An interior fire is the most common cause of asphyxiation. How many of you have a home escape plan in the event of a fire? Make one. It's free. It takes minutes. And it might save your life.

Unless you've been in a burning building, you cannot imagine how blinding the smoke is nor how quickly a structure can become fully engulfed. If you have children, periodic rehearsal of the escape plan is mandatory. In the unthinkable event of a fire, panic is inevitable. Rehearsal helps to moderate the flight reaction, which might otherwise lead to death. Also, test your smoke detectors. Those in the West can attest to the power, speed and terror of a large scale wildfire. Most of us assume such an occurrence will provide adequate forewarning, thereby allowing avoidance. While normally that's true, you wouldn't be prepping if you only planned for 'typical' events.

While obviously a confluence of enabling conditions is required in order for a firestorm to occur, be assured that this could occur in most parts of the country. While the development of those enabling conditions will be obvious (i.e. extreme drought) to anyone on the lookout, once commenced, the firestorm expands far too quickly to allow for evacuation.

While fire is a common cause, there are other causes of asphyxiation worth your consideration: Carbon monoxide poisoning – usually from a combustion source in the home. This has also occurred in vehicles stranded in snowstorms when the engine is run for heat. Accumulating snow shrouded the tailpipe resulting in vehicle exhaust entering the passenger compartment.

Other poisonous fumes – tanker trucks, rail cars and chemical & other industrial plants often have hazardous materials that, in an emergency situation, could cause you grave bodily harm if exposed. Smothering- confined space entrapment, such as a building collapse (snow or volcanic ash loads on roofs, earthquakes, etc). Consider also avalanches, landslides and mudslides.

Drowning – while using common sense on and around bodies of water is presumed, consider also flash floods, tsunami, the aforementioned breaking ice, catastrophic dam failure, bridge failure while crossing. Flash floods are relatively common and often deadly. While a tsunami is much less common, consider the scale of the 2004 Indian Ocean tsunami before you dismiss its' likelihood. If you live in a coastal region, it would only take one to bring all of your pantry efforts to naught. All of these events are sudden, unexpected and leave you minutes or less to choose a course of action. Taking the proper action may save your life.

Exposure Exposure occurs far more rapidly than dehydration. Hot or cold, you could find yourself unable to function in less than three hours. Immersion in cold water, such as breaking through ice, could reduce your time to act down to mere minutes. So what's your shelter strategy when you're away from base? In the North, with temps possibly below minus 40, if you have an accident on a slick road late at night in such conditions, you will likely not be waking up ever again unless you have prepared for such an eventuality. Similarly, in Nevada in the summer heat above 115 degrees, your lifespan may be less than a day. Exposure can kill in hours, or less. Countering exposure is your number two priority for survival in any emergency situation. Prepare for exposure, especially if you have any chance of being forced onto the road..

Dehydration

Dehydration occurs much more quickly than starvation. As such, water supply is much more critical to address in an emergency. Consider that in a temperate climate and without exertion, the human body requires approximately 2.5 liters of fluids per day. In extreme heat this requirement goes up significantly. Diarrhea can lead to rapid, catastrophic dehydration as well. Given that water is far bulkier to store and/or transport than food, and that dehydration is potentially a far more pressing concern than starvation, your ability to procure water in an emergency should supplant food in your ranking of Survival priorities. Stated simply, water is far more important than food. What is your base plan for water? What is your mobile plan for water?

Starvation

While many of you may be planning on stocking food, starvation is the slowest form of death among the Rule of Three. You would likely have three weeks before you starve. Your level of physical exertion has an impact on the body's caloric requirements and you might survive starvation for five or six weeks if you are sedentary and carrying extra weight. Your survival strategy must consider the likelihood of you being separated from your food supply in an emergency. When that happens, stay calm, focus on any immediate threats or hazards and remember that you have three weeks to implement Food Plan B or Plan C (which you need to prepare as well).

Hope

Three months without hope can defeat the strongest. A sure way to fall into despair during a crisis is to have failed to prepare for it; disasters by nature most times lead to chaos, suffering and distress, but when you add in hunger, thirst and cold to the chaos depression and hopelessness will soon follow. Preparedness, training and a plan can do much to reduce the chaos about you. Though it is true that often chance seems play a great deal in who survives a crisis situation remember the words of Louis Pasteur: *"Chance favors the prepared mind."*

Perils, Perils Everywhere As you continually assess and prioritize your survival risks, take into account those risks specific to the area where you happen to be. Weather patterns for example. Hurricanes in coastal regions, tornados on the plains and thunderstorms or blizzards in the mountains are all hazards to be anticipated and prepped for. Also, consider geologic perils. Earthquakes, volcanoes and rapidly moving lahars are hazards to be aware of and plan for, even if you are merely passing through. Therefore, if you are inclined to take a proactive approach in preparing for what economists might refer to as 'outlier occurrences', then it behooves you to prioritize your risks and review appropriate responses to them in a rational fashion. The scenarios resulting in your death most quickly should command your immediate attention. When you have sufficiently addressed those, by all means move down your list. We all believe in the Boy Scout motto of "Be Prepared". However oftentimes it's the obvious peril that gets overlooked.

Preparedness Test

1. Has your family rehearsed fire escape routes from your home? YES - NO
2. Does your family know what to do before, during, and after an earthquake or other emergency situation? YES-NO
3. Do you have heavy objects hanging over beds that can fall during an earthquake? YES - NO
4. Do you have access to an operational flashlight in every occupied bedroom?
5. (use of candles is not recommended unless you are sure there is no leaking gas) YES-NO
6. Do you keep shoes near your bed to protect your feet against broken glass? YES-NO
7. If a water line was ruptured during an earthquake, do you know how to shut off the main water line to your house? YES - NO

8. Can this water valve be turned off by hand without the use of a tool?
9. Do you have a tool if one is needed? YES-NO
10. Do you know where the main gas shut-off valve to your house is located? YES - NO
11. If you smell gas, do you know how and would you be able to shut off this valve? YES-NO
12. Gas valves usually cannot be turned off by hand. Is there a tool near your valve? YES - NO
13. Would you be able to safely restart your furnace when gas is safely available? YES - NO
14. Do you have working smoke alarms in the proper places to warn you of fire? YES - NO
15. In case of a minor fire, do you have a fire extinguisher that you know how to use? YES - NO
16. Do you have duplicate keys and copies of important insurance and other papers stored outside your home? YES - NO
17. Do you have a functional emergency radio to receive emergency information? YES - NO
18. If your family had to evacuate your home, have you identified a meeting place? YES – NO

IF AN EMERGENCY LASTED FOR THREE DAYS (72 HOURS)
BEFORE HELP WAS AVAILABLE TO YOU AND YOUR
FAMILY

1. Would you have sufficient food? YES - NO
2. Would you have the means to cook food without gas and electricity? YES - NO
3. Would you have sufficient water for drinking, cooking, and sanitary needs? YES - NO
4. Do you have access to a 72 hour evacuation kit? YES - *NO*
5. Would you be able to carry or transport these kits? YES - *NO*
6. Have you established an out-of-state contact? YES - *NO*
7. Do you have a first aid kit in your home and in each car? YES - *NO*
8. Do you have work gloves and some tools for minor rescue and clean up? YES - *NO*
9. Do you have emergency cash on hand? (During emergencies banks and ATMs are closed) YES - *NO*
10. Without electricity and gas do you have a way to heat at least part of your house? YES - *NO*
11. If you need medications, do you have a month's supply on hand? YES - *NO*
12. Do you have a plan for toilet facilities if there is an extended water shortage? YES - *NO*
13. Do you have a supply of food, clothing, and fuel where appropriate?
14. For 6 months? YES - *NO*
15. For a year? YES - *NO*

These are all questions that need answers if you are to be safe in an emergency. If you answered 'No' to any of them, it's now time for some work.

IX   Four Day Survival Kit

In emergency preparedness, a 72 hour kit is widely considered the first step in becoming prepared. Sitting in a closet or some other area close to the front door, it can be grabbed in a moment's notice, should you have to depart your home with little or no warning. If a fire spread and quickly destroyed your family's home, how would you cope? If everything was totally destroyed, or you had to "bug out", how would you survive? That's when you'll wish you had a good 96 hour/four day kit.

Sometimes, whole communities are affected at the same time. One tiny farming village back in 1978 had to be immediately evacuated for several days because of derailed and leaking butane cars. Before that, everyone thought this was a place where disasters 'never happened.' It's not necessary that you live in a tornado or hurricane alley to need a four day survival kit. Every family needs one for the unexpected, filled with all the essential things your family would need to take you through 4 days of being on your own.

There's a reason behind the length of time the kit's contents should last. It generally takes the disaster relief agencies at least 3-4 days to move in and set up before offering assistance. Generally speaking, you're on your own during this time. Depending on how bad the situation is, it could even be longer. In any type of disaster things will be bad. Not having the necessities to sustain your life and the lives of your family members could turn a manageable problem into a personal cataclysm.

Four Day Kit

FIRST AID
Preventative Aid
Personal First Aid Kit
Family First Aid Kit
Foot powder
Body powder, medicated

LIGHT, HEAT, FIRE MAKING
Pack lantern
Spare lantern mantles
Flash light
Spare bulb, batteries
Candle lantern
Spare plumber's candles
Glow sticks
Match safe & matches

Magnesium block
Magnifying glass
Lighter
Spare flints
Book matches, water proof
Pack stove
Windscreen
Fuel bottles

COOKING EQUIPMENT
Frying pan, folding
Cook set, nesting
Can opener, P-38
Eating utensil set

WATER
Poly canteens, 1 quart

Sierra cup
Water purification tablets
Water purifier & extra filters
Water bag, nylon
Water bag liners, plastic
Solar still
Rubber surgical tubing

FOOD
Personal daily rations
MREs, Freeze Dried
Energy bars, tablets
Trail snacks
Condiments
Salt & Pepper
Sugar
Flour

Honey
Milk, dry, instant

NAVIGATION
Map case
Maps
Map measure
Pedometer
Compass
Altimeter
Global positioning system
(GPS)

TOOLS AND REPAIR KITS
Leatherman Gerber tool
Sven saw
Hatchet/Boys axe w/sheath
8 inch mill file
Spare parts: pack, stove,
lantern
Tent/ Pack patch kit: ripstop
tape
Copper wire, spool

HYGIENE & SANITATION
Toilet trowel
Toilet tissue, biodegradable
Feminine hygiene items
Shampoo
Comb and brush
Eye drops
Tooth brush & tooth paste
Shaving gear
Deodorant
Soap & soap dish
Bath towel

FISHING EQUIPMENT
Pack rod case
Pack rod, spin -fly
combination
Ultra lite spinning reel
Ultra lite fly reel

15 lb test Spiderwire
monofilament
7DTF fly line
Fly line leaders, various lb test
Tackle boxes, small double
sided (2)
Hooks, size 8, 10, 12
Fly assortment
Sinkers, split shot
Spinners
Spoons
Small plugs, poppers, bugs

CAMP GEAR
Pack
Frame
Clevis pins
Stuff bags
Fanny Pack.
Compression straps
Camera, lenses, flash and film
Binoculars
Swiss Pocket knife
Sharpening stones and oil

PERSONAL ITEMS
Wallet
Extra house and car keys
Copy of important papers
such as titles etc.
Handkerchief
Watch
Sun & prescription glasses
Pencil and note pad
Scriptures
Chigger powder
Mosquito repellent
Lip balm
Sun block
Body powder, medicated
Corn starch
Hand lotion

EMERGENCY GEAR
Signal flares, night
Signal smoke, day
Signal die, water
Signal mirror
Strobe light
Whistle
Space blanket
Hand warmers
Pack and Pack Frame

CLOTHING REPAIR
Sewing Kit
Spare shoelaces

CLEAN UP
Biodegradable detergent
Woolite
Small scrub brush
Clothes pins
Scouring pads, soap filled
Sanitary tablets & dunking
bag
Dish towel
Plastic garbage bags
Twist ties

SHELTER CASH
$100 in small bills
$10 in Quarters
Credit Cards
Debit Card
A few blank Checks

SHELTER
Tent
Tent fly
Tent poles
Tent pegs
Ground cloth
Ultra light weight tarp
Visk clamps
Nylon line, 50 ft. 2 ea

CLOTHING
Hiking boots
Trail sneakers
Socks
Underclothing
Thermal underwear
Shirts, short sleeve
Shirts, long sleeve
Shorts, hiking
Trousers, long
Belt and buckle
Sweater
Vest
Jacket

Parka
Poncho
Gloves, leather
Mittens, wool
Scarf
Balaclava
Bandanna, large
Hat
Moleskins
Swimsuit

BEDDING
Foam pad, closed cell
Sleeping bag

Air pillow

COMMUNICATION
Pocket radio, battery/solar power
Cell phone ... or
Two way radio: CB, GMRS, FRS
Spare NiCad batteries
Solar battery charger

More Oklahomans reach Calif. via the cotton fields of Ariz.

X   Exposure

Lack of Shelter

The major concern caused by the lack of shelter is that of hypothermia (cold) but we will also discuss hyperthermia which can occur in the southern states.

There are any number of natural and manmade disasters that can render your home unlivable. Without a back-up heat source, losing power/heat to your home in a snow storm can lead to temperatures quickly falling into the range where hypothermia can be a concern. Every year a number of elderly die in their homes of hypothermia due to utility shutoffs and broken heating systems. In desert areas, a lack of cooling can also be devastating. In some cases your home could be flooded or so severely damaged to make it unsafe, especially in the case of a major earthquake (for example Haiti). There may not be enough safe and suitable buildings left in your area to even act as temporary shelters, quickly leaving you and your family at the mercy of the elements.

WHAT IS HYPOTHERMIA?

Hypothermia, also known as 'exposure' is technically when your core body temperature drops below the normal 35 degrees centigrade, your normal body temperature is 37C. It happens when the amount of heat you're losing can't be replaced by your body, so your body temperature falls. The results are serious and can be fatal, one text book lists a drop of 4C as causing disorientation, 7C leaves you in a coma and a drop of 10C can be fatal. So in very simple terms, it's a fall in body temperature when you're losing more heat than you can produce. It's not just feeling 'a bit cold', though that can be the start of it.

Spotting the symptoms Assuming you're not walking around with a thermometer permanently up your butt, you need to be aware of possible signs that you, or your mates are going hypothermic. Bear in mind that it's not always easy to spot, particularly early on, but watch out for:

- clumsiness - might look like drunkenness
- disorientation
- sudden bursts of energy
- exhaustion

Classically a quick test is to ask the suspected victim to do some quick mental arithmetic as a check on their mental function. Exhaustion and hypothermia go hand in hand, if you're very tired, your metabolism slows, you don't kick out enough body heat and you become hypothermic..

Treating Hypothermia Stop and take stock. It's essential that you don't push on regardless unless safety is very, very near. If the symptoms are mild, putting the casualty in some sort of shelter, adding dry, warm clothes and, in particular, a hat, and feeding them warm hot drinks and food may be enough.

- If things don't improve, put the casualty in a sleeping bag and insulate them from the Cold ground with a sleeping mat.
- Recent research suggests that too quick body warming can actually be counterproductive since pooled acidic blood in the muscles is warmed too quickly, reaches the heart and can cause cardiac arrest.
- Heat packs placed at the victim's armpits and groin are a good way of raising the core body temperature without risking shock. Warm drink or soup if the victim is conscious should be given slowly.
- Do not give the victim alcohol or coffee since both can cause heat loss.
- Do not allow the victim to fall asleep.
- Treat the victim gently, in severe cases of hypothermia, rough handling can cause a chilled heart muscle to arrest.
- Even when the victim has apparently recovered, they mustn't be allowed to continue the hike. Instead, call or fetch help and, if possible, get them evacuated from the hill so they can receive professional treatment.

Avoiding Hypothermia The best solution to hypothermia is to avoid it in the first place, which is doubly important when you're on your own, since disorientation makes the condition hard to spot. Wear correct and sufficient clothing. Wind chill and damp are both your enemy since both accelerate heat loss from the body. Wind and water-proof clothing and insulation layers are crucial.

- Cover your head - you lose a lot of heat through your noggin. While the body will restrict blood flow to, say, your feet, your brain needs a blood supply to function, so the stuff is always flowing up there. A warm, windproof hat will make a big difference. Carry a spare too, it's stupid dying because you dropped your hat.
- Eat high energy foods regularly as you go - your body is like an engine and if you don't fuel it, it'll stop running and stop producing heat.
- Don't be over ambitious - tired walkers and climbers are far more likely to get hypothermia, so be realistic about your day - if it's cold and wet or very windy, consider shortening your route or maybe cancelling altogether. If you're a little unfit, don't push yourself too hard.

Kit To Carry Particularly if you're part of a group, carrying the right kit can make the difference between life and death. So, here's what should you bring with you if you are in a situation that could risk hypothermia:

- Your brain. No joke, pressing on regardless is what kills many hypothermia victims. Having the presence of mind to realize that you have a problem and need to deal with it is crucial, but difficult.
- Spare warm clothing and a sleeping bag / down jacket can be crucial in minimizing heat loss in the victim. Bear in mind that other members of the group will also need warm clothing once you stop. Hats are crucial.
- An emergency shelter or bivvy bag - crucial to getting the victim out of the wind. Group survival shelters are excellent and can also be used for sheltered lunch stops and allow you to pool body heat.
- A sleeping or bivvy mat - ideally you want to insulate the casualty from cold ground, if you don't have these, improvise using a pack and / or spare clothing.

- Stove, drinks and food. A lightweight stove and some soup or hot drinks are a good move and you should always carry emergency with high energy food as a backup measure.
- Heat pads - exothermic warming pads are a better way of warming a casualty than body contact. Well worth adding to a group kit list.

You don't have to carry all of these in winter, but they could make the difference between a minor scare and a fatality, so, particularly if you're part of a group, think about sharing the above out between you. Hypothermia's not just for winter, it's perfectly possible to experience it in spring or autumn, or even in summer.

WHAT IS HYPERTHERMIA?   Hypothermia is an elevated body temperature due to failed thermoregulation. Hyperthermia occurs when the body produces or absorbs more heat than it can dissipate. When the elevated body temperatures are sufficiently high, hyperthermia is a medical emergency and requires immediate treatment to prevent disability or death.

The most common causes are heat stroke and adverse reactions to drugs. Heat stroke is an acute condition of hyperthermia that is caused by prolonged exposure to excessive heat or heat and humidity. The heat-regulating mechanisms of the body eventually become overwhelmed and unable to effectively deal with the heat, causing the body temperature to climb uncontrollably.

Treatment for hyperthermia depends on its cause, as the underlying cause must be corrected. Mild hyperthermia from exertion on a hot day might be adequately treated through self-care such as drinking water and resting in a cool place. Hyperthermia that results from drug exposures is frequently treated by cessation of that drug, and occasionally by other drugs to counteract them. Fever-reducing drugs such as paracetamol and aspirin have no value in treating hyperthermia.

When the body temperature is significantly elevated, mechanical methods of cooling are used to remove heat from the body and to restore the body's ability to regulate its own temperatures. Passive cooling techniques, such as resting in a cool, shady area and removing clothing can be applied immediately. Active cooling methods, such as sponging the head, neck, and trunk with cool water, remove heat from the body and thereby speed the body's return to normal temperatures. Drinking water and turning a fan or dehumidifying air conditioning unit on the affected person may improve the effectiveness of the body's evaporative cooling mechanisms (sweating).

Sitting in a bathtub of tepid or cool water (immersion method) can remove a significant amount of heat in a relatively short period of time. However, immersion in very cold water is counterproductive, as it causes vasoconstriction in the skin and thereby prevents heat from escaping the body core. In exertional heat stroke, studies have shown that although there are practical limitations, cool water immersion is the most effective cooling technique and the biggest predictor of outcome is degree and duration of hyperthermia. No superior cooling method has been found for nonexertional heat stroke.

When the body temperature reaches about 40 C, or if the affected person is unconscious or showing signs of confusion, hyperthermia is considered a medical emergency that requires treatment in a proper medical facility. In a hospital, more aggressive cooling measures are available, including intravenous hydration, gastric lavage with iced saline, and even hemodialysis to cool the blood.

XI   Emergency Shelter

Even if you plan to ride out every crisis in the comfort of your home, you should prepare to evacuate anyway. None of us are immune to the possibility of natural or manmade disasters forcing us to flee our homes or our favorite crisis hideaway.

Do you have a tent in your emergency bugout kit?

Some of you may be thinking along these lines in the event of an emergency evacuation, *"I don't need a tent, I'll be in a motel/relative or friend's house/etc."* or *"I can sleep in my car, if I need to."* If this is you talking, then please consider that best laid plans can go wrong. You may have to abandon your vehicle for some reason or another...or face way too many miles of no motel vacancies...houses can burn down...you get the idea.

The paramount rules for survival anytime, anywhere involves shelter, water and food. Naturally, when preparing for emergencies, we always think of food and water...but *how prepared are you for emergency shelter*

Shelter may be defined as anything that protects the human element from nature's elements. In survival as in all aspects of life, it is easier to be organized if we prioritize. The priorities, in order, are shelter, water, heat, food, signal, and utility. You can live 4-6 weeks without food; 3-5 days without water; but hypothermia will kill you in 30 minutes. In desert climates in the summer, water is generally your first priority, but even there desert shelter quickly follows both because desert night temperatures can drop substantially and because shade can help immensely during the day.

We won't discuss clothing yet, other than to say that a good coat can't be beat, and it is easier to survive in the summer with winter clothes than in the winter with summer clothes.

What You Need

A free-standing dome or *A-frame* tent is the only realistic option for a mobile shelter in a short term emergency preparedness kit. There are several things to be aware of in selecting a tent. Construction should be of good quality, breathable materials. The rain fly should extend from the apex of the tent almost to the ground. A small rain fly like those found on many discount shelf specials is unsuitable, because it means the tent walls are made mostly of waterproof material. The human body passes 1-2 quarts of water vapor daily and if you are in a waterproof tent for an extended period of time that water vapor will condense on the walls. It is for this very reason that tube tents should be avoided like the plague.

A heavy-duty space blanket is recommended to put under the tent in order to protect the tent floor. It is much easier and cheaper to replace a $12 space blanket than a $100 tent. Avoid the pocket space blanket—another plague! Their usefulness is limited and they breed a false sense of security.

A sleeping bag is the most critical piece of survival equipment you can possess, especially in winter. Fires are only 50% effective. You cook your front side while your buns freeze, or your toast your buns and your nose freezes—you just can't win! In a sleeping bag, however, you can efficiently maintain body heat.

A good sleeping bag will have the capability to form a hood. It will have a sizable draft tube along the length of the zipper to prevent snags. Another important feature is the ability to zip two bags together to share body heat or to put a child between parents. Select a synthetic insulation rather than down. Qualofill, Polarguard and some of the new materials recently released are excellent. The advantage of synthetic insulation is that when the bag gets wet, it can be wrung out and will still keep you warm. When down gets wet, the insulation value drops to nearly nothing. Emergency survival situations rarely occur on warm sunny days, and you can just about bet it will be on a dark, rainy or snowy night when the world comes apart.

An absolute must in a temperate climate is a sleeping pad. Ground cold can suck the heat right out of your body, through your sleeping bag. A closed-cell foam pad will provide the insulation required, but will give little if any comfort. An air mattress of the type you take to the beach or swimming pool will freeze your whole body during the winter. For true comfort an air mattress such as Thermarest is expensive but worth every cent. For economy, a simple 3/4-length closed cell foam pad is all that you need. Avoid open-cell pads because they soak up water just like a sponge.

Put a 'Shelter Box' in your Emergency Preparedness Plans

If you have not already done so, put a low cost 'shelter box' in your emergency preparedness plans. Make your own custom kit to suit your group. The price and weight of a full shelter kit can be a bear, so the alternative is a combination Shelter Box and 'bugout' bag. The following items can be packed into one or two large sturdy and waterproof boxes (or large bags). Waterproofing is essential, in the event of rain. Use plastic bags inside of the containers, if needed. A well stocked Shelter Box should at least include the following items.

Very Basic Kit. Your personal kit will likely contain more gear than this, but a supply list as long as your leg can be overwhelming to those who are just starting out in their preparedness ventures, or to those who simply can't afford to buy a lot.

1. **Expedient dry shelter** such as a tent (or several heavy duty tarps and rope if you can't afford a tent right now). Instead of including one large/medium tent to shelter your whole group, include two medium (or smaller) tents. Bad things can happen to your one shelter. Better to have a backup, even if it will be a bit cramped.

2. **Bedding and clothing for every person**:
   A. Thermal blankets and thermal sleeping bags, if you can afford it.
   B. Even if it is summertime (or wintertime) when you pack your shelter box, and the next season is far from your mind…don't forget to include a coat and a summer/winter change of clothing and shoes for each person.

3. **One heavy duty plastic tarp for each person,** to serve as a ground cover beneath bedding. Include an inexpensive Mylar blanket for every person to bolster up insulation where needed. In

summer, the same Mylar blanket can be used on top of a tarp shelter to divert the sun's hot rays and to help cool the area beneath the tarp...

4. **Light** - Include an inexpensive solar powered battery charger and rechargeable batteries for several LED flashlights. Get a few of the same kind of flashlight (and other gear), so you can cannibalize one for parts, if needed.

5. **Clean water and several ways and means of purification.** Collapsible water containers.

6. **Heat / cooking** - Two lightweight stoves: one multi-fuel stove and one twig-burning stove. Here are some options/ideas: http://www.modernoutpost.com/gear/camping-stoves.html Include several ways of making fire.

7. **Cooking aids** - 2 cooking pots, cooking spoon, sharp, tough knives, small knife sharpener, folded heavy duty aluminum foil, etc. Include one set of utensils and a bowl for each person. Lightweight mugs if you have room. (A bowl can do multi-duty in a pinch, if needed to save space on plates and mugs).

8. **Food** - Lightweight instant foods that require no refrigeration or extensive cooking. Include dried fruits, nuts, jerky, tasty energy bars, etc.

9. **Tools** - hammer, axe, saw, heavy duty plastic bags of varying sizes, quality duct tape (the 'Gorilla' brand tape is the best!), folding shovel, rope, tent stakes, bungee cords, etc. etc.

10. **Health and special needs**: fever and diarrhea reducing meds, personal medications, basic first aid gear. Your favorite insecticide and mosquito nets if your area calls for it. If you have babies, include the basics for their survival. Pets...decide ahead of time what their emergency plans will involve and plan accordingly.

11. **Communications** - Radio, cell phone, windup battery chargers. Phone numbers.

12. **Sanity savers** - Just to mention a few...

   A. A copy or the originals of your important papers. You know what they are.
   B. A list of details about your employment/educational history. Not many think to include this in their emergency kit, but it is a sanity saver in the event you cannot return home right away, and may need to apply for temporary or permanent work elsewhere.

URBAN CARDBOARD SHELTER

This is the type of shelter you use when everything else has failed and you are out on the street. Just remember, this situation too is survivable and has happened to better people than you.

Materials:
- Refrigerator cardboard box
- Styrofoam found within the same box and dumpster.
- Duct tape
- Box cutter
- Tape measure
- Marker

If the circumstances force you to build the shelter outside, you need to protect it from moisture. You could use multiple layers of trash or any available plastic. (trash bag, tarp, poncho, carpet, sheet metal, wood, rugs) The refrigerator box can be replaced with boxes from big screen TVs or whatever is available. Most families have boxes in their attic. Local furniture stores are usually happy to let people take away their trash. Call and ask for permission. A lot of furniture and hardware stores will give you cardboard.

While rectangular boxes lend themselves to rectangular shelters, you can also build the shelter as a triangular prism, in order to minimize the walls you have to insulate. A smaller shelter is easier to warm up with body heat. If you want to squeeze two people in a shelter, a rectangular configuration would work better.

Use duct tape to stabilize the shelter and close off the ends with a hinged cardboard door using the tape. This is where the cutting device and pen/marker comes into play.

Close up one end of the cardboard a-frame shelter and insulate the box using the Styrofoam and duct tape. Since heat flows from warmer to a cooler spaces, adding insulation lessens conduction from the cold concrete. You minimize convection by trapping air inside the box shelter. You want multiple layers trapping the air and the Styrofoam insulation to get you off the ground.

Once you finish the insulation, build a door so you can shut it behind you. If the shelter is to be used multiple days outside, cover it with multiple layers of cardboard and items such as rugs, carpet, plastic, trash bags anything that would help waterproof the shelter. Insulate the door as much as possible, it will be your number one source of heat loss.

Note: making the shelter completely airtight is pretty difficult. DO NOT MAKE THE SHELTER COMPLETELY AIR TIGHT !

INSIDE THE HOME SHELTERS can be made using your furniture and cushions. A futon mattress can be rolled into a improvised sleeping bag. Several bed mattresses can be structured to build a shelter. Use sheets, blankets, rugs, curtains, and extra clothing to build a shelter within your home. If your home has been destroyed, often debris can be used to build a shelter. Plastic sheets, trash bags, cardboard, wood can be used to build modified a-frame, leanto type shelters.

Cold-weather survival skills should be part of everyone's knowledge base. Knowing how to make a debris hut, snow cave, or igloo, can save your life in a winter emergency, and it is easy to find instructions for constructing these shelters in survival manuals, or on the internet. These types of shelter work well in the outdoors, but for urban winter survival scenarios, you can use man-made materials to construct cold-weather shelters, that is mattress shelters.

XII Water Treatment & Storage

No one can last long without water. When a disaster happens and water is shut off or scarce, a large city where millions live will run out of bottled water within minutes.

A high percentage of the country has no potable water at all. If you can build a well, do so, set it as your top of the list priority as a survivalist. Water comes before firearms, medicines and even food. In a disaster, save as much water as you can. Use plastic bottles, refill soda bottles and place them in a cool place, preferably inside a black garbage bag to protect it from sun light. The water will pick some plastic taste after a few months, but water that tastes a little like plastic is far better than no water at all. Whatever the kind of disaster scenario you are dealing with, water will suffer. In an economic crash, even the water company may reduce maintenance and quality in order to reduce costs

PROPER HYDRATION

Prevent Dehydration with Proper Hydration

Dehydration is a serious concern during outdoor activities. It can happen in summer or winter, on a day hike or several days into a 50-miler, even on a canoe or kayak trip. Vigorous activity, excessive sun exposure, forgotten water breaks, higher altitudes (where humidity levels are lower), and medical conditions are a few factors that can affect your hydration level. Some of the consequences of dehydration are loss of energy and motivation, irritability, headaches, difficulty sleeping, fainting, and, at high altitude, an increased likelihood of altitude sickness, hypothermia, and frostbite. In extreme cases, dehydration can lead to delirium and even death.

Essentially, if you're losing more fluids than you're taking in, dehydration is the result. So it's important to stay sufficiently hydrated while hiking, backpacking, or climbing. However, water sources in the backcountry, or even at the trailhead, are not normally assured of being safe for consumption. So learning how to treat backcountry water is essential to ensure safe water supplies and proper hydration

Dehydration Signs and Symptoms

The rule for judging whether someone is becoming dehydrated is the phrase "Clear and Copious." This means that one's urine should not have a strong color and that urination should be fairly frequent. If your urine is not clear like gin to pale yellow, you are dehydrated. Dark yellow indicates serious dehydration.

It takes time for the body to absorb fluids, so you must drink early and often. Make sure everyone, youths and adults, is drinking plenty of water. "Saving" your water for later can result in dehydration instead. Trip leaders and other adults should make sure to not neglect their own hydration needs.

Thirst is not necessarily an indicator of dehydration. The body's thirst signal starts when you are 2 to 5 percent dehydrated. That person who is acting crankier than usual may be dehydrated, so take frequent water breaks (every 20 to 30 minutes). Consider using a hydration reservoir; its easy access means you never need to stop for a drink.

Rate of Moisture Loss Some of us, especially those brought up in desert regions, were taught to "conserve our water," saving the small amounts available as long as possible; we were told we could quell the thirsty feeling by holding a small round pebble in our mouths and sucking on it. The problem with these misconceptions is that we lose moisture in our breath and by sweating. For example, during eight hours of sleep about one liter of moisture is lost through breathing and another liter is lost through perspiration. The rate is even faster when exercising vigorously.

A good way to find your personal rate of moisture loss during exercise is the same as that used in professional and international competitions—weigh yourself before, during, and after an exercise session. It is, of course, impractical to weigh yourself during a hike, but you can weigh yourself before and after a training hike. Each pound you lose during exercise is a pint (half liter) of water lost. Be sure to account for any water and fluids you take in during the hike. In ultra-marathons and other endurance competitions, competitors are usually pulled from the event if they lose more than 5 percent of their body weight.

How Much Water? The basic rule for avoiding dehydration is to drink plenty of fluids, but this doesn't mean just any fluid. Diuretics (such as caffeine, alcohol, and a number of medicines, including Diamox commonly taken for altitude sickness) promote dehydration. The body does not absorb highly sugared or carbonated beverages as rapidly, which means that soft drinks are less efficient at quenching thirst than plain water. And some adults down a few malt beverages at the end of a hot day believing that they are rehydrating, but research shows quite the opposite. The best way to keep hydrated or to rehydrate is with plain water or water with one of the specially developed rehydration mixes added.

Someone exercising hard may lose more than a liter (quart) of water an hour. So a good guideline for vigorous activities at altitude is a minimum of 4 liters a day, up to as much as 8 liters. For example, this might mean consuming a liter at breakfast (including hot drinks and fluids in cereal and fruit), one liter between breakfast and lunch (take frequent water breaks), a half-liter with lunch, a liter between lunch and supper (more water breaks), and a final liter at supper (including in the form of soups, hot drinks, and the main course). Many people find that staying well-hydrated is key to a good night's sleep. Remember that caffeine is a diuretic, so coffee, tea, and chocolate are not as effective as non-caffeinated drinks.

Keeping Your Water Supply Safe In Camp Whenever and wherever you camp, you must make sure your water supply is not contaminated, as well as take great care not to contaminate the water supply. To prevent contamination, separate your water source from the areas for bodily relief and washing dishes or yourself by at least 100 feet (or as specified by the land manager). Designate a clean water source area and a separate latrine area when you set up camp. If there is a latrine or outhouse available, make this the designated latrine area. Emphasize to everyone in your party (adults and youth) that they must use the designated latrine area, and must not just step outside the tent during the night or first thing in the morning. When designating the latrine area, keep in mind that other people may be using the area in the future. In winter, consider the impact when the snow melts.

In Winter It is tempting to think that snow, especially in winter, is uncontaminated, but this is not necessarily true. Avoid yellow or brown snow, but also keep in mind that animals roam the snowfields and can contaminate the snow, just as humans do. Purify the water, just as in summer. If you are melting snow, continue heating it up to the boiling point. While it's obvious when thinking about it, the shovel or scoop used for gathering snow to melt into water should be different from the shovel used for the latrine or other purposes.

In Wilderness Areas In an increasing number of wilderness areas, camping and backpacking groups are required to carry out all human waste. This can be accomplished by using one of the commercial waste bags (RestStop or WAG Bags, for example) or by using doubled plastic garbage bags. In the latter example, one garbage bag is used as a liner, either for a bucket carried in for that purpose (some groups carry a toilet seat for the can) or for a hole dug for that purpose. The person changing the liner bag should wear disposable gloves (the same type of surgical gloves everyone should have in their first aid kits), tightly close and tie-wrap the liner bag, and place it inside a second bag, which is also tightly closed and tie-wrapped. The now-contaminated gloves are disposed of in the new liner bag. A handful of cat litter can help reduce odor and will make the operation less unpleasant for the designee. In winter, waste matter usually freezes quickly. To reduce volume, reserve the bags for fecal matter and have people urinate a short distance away. The bags can be emptied into a latrine or a dumpster at the trailhead (check with the local land managers for their standardized practices).

During a Natural Disaster It is also important to be aware of the potential contamination of water supplies during natural disasters, such as earthquakes in California, floods in the Midwest, and hurricanes in the Gulf States. While this does not relate directly to camping, knowledge and practice in dealing with water supplies in the backcountry can help with preparedness for natural disasters or other interruptions of normal water supplies.

Clean Hands Cleanliness is more difficult in the backcountry. It is important that the cook always has clean hands, as should everyone when eating (especially finger foods like sandwiches). Certainly, the person on latrine duty should not also be the cook. And when rotating duties, do not have the latrine person's next task involve food preparation. If possible, the latrine person should thoroughly wash his or her hands with soap and water.

Do not wash your hands in *any* stream, lake, or spring. That is your water supply and that of other parties and the local wildlife. You can carry a folding basin for this purpose; do the washing at least 100 feet from water sources. Alternatively, use the sterilizing solutions or gels, such as Pure Touch and Purell, found in many drug, grocery, and camping stores.

Clean Dishes Rinsing soap off dishes, especially aluminum pots, requires enough hot water that the extra fuel to be carried becomes a significant factor. Part of the solution to having clean dishes is to prepare foods that produce minimal mess. Much of the mess can be cleaned off dishes and cooking utensils by scrubbing with snow and following with a hot water rinse (remember to pack out all food waste!). Also, remember to dispose of any soapy wash or rinse water in an ecologically sound manner, at least 100 feet from water sources. You can also clean dishes as much as possible at the end of each meal, then sterilize dishes, cups, spoons, etc. in boiling water just before use in the water to be used for cooking.

What Is In Backcountry Water?

There are two major groups of contaminants found in water that can cause serious illness (potentially ruining a trip), and one aesthetic ingredient that makes water unattractive (and affects methods for removing the other two groups of contaminants). The first two groups are biological contaminants and chemical contaminants. The aesthetic group is material suspended in the water that may not cause illness itself, but looks unattractive and can interfere with removal of the first two. First, it should be noted that extensive testing of water in U.S. and Canadian areas popular for backpacking and canoeing, in all seasons, indicates that whether there is contamination and how dangerous it is varies widely from place to place, even within a given area.

For example, studies in the Sierra have found front-country streams (at the trailhead) that have virtually no contamination, while some streams far from the trailhead and not frequented by humans or pack animals have a high concentration of biological contaminants. Some backcountry users take no precautions and do not get sick, while others diligently use filters and chemical purifiers and get extremely sick. The most common thread for those who come down with digestive problems appears to be, not contaminated water, but carelessness in basic sanitation, particularly diligent washing and sterilizing of hands when handling food. The situation is different in Third World countries. In tropical climates, especially, the abundance of wildlife living in potential water sources and the poor sanitation practices of local populations mean that there are many varieties of bacteria, viruses, and parasites that are unknown in colder climes, and against which those of us who live in North America have developed no resistance.

Biological Contaminants: Parasites, Bacteria, Viruses

The biological contaminants are generally grouped into parasites (or protozoa), bacteria, and viruses. Protozoa are the largest at about 1 micron, bacteria measure approximately 0.5 to 2 microns, and viruses measure around 0.02 - 0.3 microns.

The most infamous villain of backcountry water is the dreaded giardiasis, caused by the parasite giardia lamblia. Giardiasis was known among the pioneers and trappers as "beaver fever," since it was often associated with beaver ponds. This emphasizes the fact that biological contaminants in water come not only from human activity, but also from animals that live in the wilderness, as well as pack animals and domesticated animals that graze in such areas (sheep, goats, and cattle, among others).

Some plant materials (certain algae in particular) can produce physical symptoms. In areas where sanitation practices are poor, sewage seepage and runoff often include the organisms that cause cholera, hepatitis, and other diseases, along with a large variety of viruses. Illness from biota can appear quickly, though most frequently; it takes several days for bacteria, viruses, and parasites to reproduce sufficiently to produce nausea, headaches, vomiting, and diarrhea. This delay in the appearance of symptoms often leads people to believe that they got away with drinking untreated water, and that the symptoms are due to something else not associated with their weekend trip.

Chemical Contaminants

Chemical contaminants can come from man-made or natural sources. Most common are manmade sources such as industrial and agricultural runoff. There are many "backcountry" areas that are affected by such runoff into water sources. For example, mining operations took place throughout much of the Sierra Nevada and Rocky Mountains, resulting in seepage of heavy metal compounds and chemicals used in leeching operations.

There was extensive mercury mining in the Santa Cruz Mountains until the 1960s. In the Almaden Valley, many streams are posted to warn fishermen not to eat any fish, because of the high concentrations of mercury in the fish in those streams. You should be aware of your water sources before going into any area, so you can prepare accordingly. Illness due to chemical contamination may be rapid, but more often is a very long-term problem. Heavy metals, such as mercury or selenium (found in areas of agricultural runoff), sometimes take several years of continual use of the contaminated water to show up. In some cases the available water may be highly saline. This includes ocean sailing trips or trips to offshore islands where your party is dropped off and later picked up. This book does not cover desalination. Critters do not pay attention to where they relieve themselves). Basic sanitation—diligent washing and sterilizing hands when handling food—is as important as treating water.

Methods for Making Water Safe

Short of transporting all your water from civilization and municipal water supplies, there are three general methods for treating your water for drinking and cooking, and two more recent additions:

- Boiling
- Filtering
- Chemical Treatment
- Ultraviolet Radiation
- PUR Clean Drinking Water Kit

Which Treatment Methods Remove What

Boiling Although sterilization by heating is referred to as "boiling," it is not necessary to actually bring water to a full rolling boil or to boil for 5 to 10 minutes, as is often stated. Raising the temperature of water to 155°F (70°C) is sufficient to kill most biota encountered by backpackers.

This is also the temperature required for pasteurizing milk.

The temperature at which water boils decreases with altitude. However, the boiling temperature is higher than 155°F (70°C) at all altitudes that you would camp at (even on Mt. Everest with a boiling point of approximately‑167°F / 75°C). Since few people carry a thermometer capable of measuring water temperature on a backpack, the most practical approach is to heat water until it starts bubbling.

Note: the Environmental Protection Agency (EPA) and the Centers for Disease Control and Prevention (CDC) both recommend boiling water for one minute. If you are above 6,562 feet (2,000 meters), the recommended boiling time increases to three minutes.

Advantages of Boiling:

- Boiling kills most microorganisms.
- Boiling is the most practical and simplest approach to sterilizing water for meals, since you have to raise the water to boiling for most backpacking foods anyway.
- In winter, when you often must melt snow or ice, you usually will raise the water to boiling, as well.

Disadvantages of Boiling:

- Boiling does not remove silt, glacial flour, or volcanic ash, though it will sometimes reduce turbidity from plant material in the water.
- Boiling does not remove chemical contamination, though it can drive off some of the sulfur compounds.
- Boiling requires burning fuel. Since you generally will be carrying your stove fuel with you, this means carrying extra weight.

Filtering Filters depend primarily on forcing water through a medium with tiny holes to physically remove microbes and matter. Anything larger than the hole size is blocked, so a filter's effectiveness depends on its "pore" size. Most filters available for backpackers remove all parasites and bacteria, plus some viruses. They remove most of the particles that cause turbidity. However, few filters for backpackers remove the smallest viruses.

Filters sold as "purifiers" (First Need, for example) use a chemical purifier to kill viruses, usually an iodine resin. Purifiers must prove inactivation of all three biological contaminants (protozoa, bacteria, and viruses) to meet the EPA Guide Standard for Testing Microbiological Purifiers. There are filters, known as "reverse-osmosis filters," available for desalination. However, their size makes them impractical for backpacking, though usable for ocean-going sailboats and other larger vessels.

Backpacking filters may work via a pump (a manual pump forces the water through the filter element), "straw" (your suction pulls the water through the filter), or gravity. Ease of use and the speed of filtering are considerations when selecting a filter.

Advantages of Filtering:

- Most filters are effective against bacteria and parasites.
- Some filters remove larger viruses.
- Filters remove some turbidity.
- Filters are usually convenient and fast.

Disadvantages of Filtering:

- In areas where viral contamination is present (Third World countries, for example), additional purification by boiling or chemical treatment is still required.
- Few filters remove chemical contamination; those that do remove only a limited range of chemical contaminants (usually with an activated carbon element).
- Fine particles like silt, glacial flour, and volcanic ash will clog any filter, requiring field maintenance (back flushing, cleaning with a brush made for the purpose, or replacement of the filter element). Many filters have pre-filters available to reduce the amount of material that will cause clogging – use them. Settling can also help.
- If the filter freezes with even a tiny amount of water in the element, the element can crack, rendering the filter useless.
- The moving parts of pump filters can break, rendering the pump useless.
- Pumping can be tiring.

Proper Use of Filters:

Always store the intake hose separately from the rest of the pump. Use the covers for the inlet and outlet to prevent contaminating the filter element on the outlet side.

Protect the filter from freezing.

Clean the filter regularly according to the manufacturer's specifications.

Use a bucket, pan, fold-up basin, or other container as the source of the water for the pump, rather than pumping directly out of the stream or lake (at least 100 feet from the water source).

This is both for avoiding the watering area for local animals and to reduce the amount of suspended material entering the screen on the pickup and into the pre-filter.

If possible, let water stand overnight to allow suspended material to settle out.

Chemical Treatment: Iodine and Chlorine

The chemical treatment approach uses one of two halogens (chlorine or iodine) to kill biota. This is the method most used by municipal water supplies around the world. The backpacker's approach is to use a small amount of the halogen, rather than the massive treatment plant used by your local water company. The halogen may be applied in one of two forms – a tablet that is dissolved in the water to be treated or in a solution of the halogen in water. Both iodine and chlorine are very effective against the most common pathogens, but they require sufficient time to act. Like all chemical reactions, the time required increases as the temperature decreases.

Iodine   Iodine is most commonly used in the form of tablets, such as Potable Aqua water purification tablets. One or two tablets are added to each liter of water, with the time required being about 30 minutes for "room temperature" water (always follow the manufacturer's instructions). Alternatively, a small amount of a saturated solution made from iodine crystals is added to the water to be treated. The most common form of this treatment is Polar Pure. With Polar Pure, the crystals are in a bottle that has a "trap" in the mouth of the bottle to ensure that only the saturated solution of iodine in water and no crystals gets into your drinking water. One capful of the solution is measured out and poured into your one-liter water bottle. Then the Polar Pure bottle is refilled to allow a saturated solution to be formed for the next treatment.

Advantages of Iodine

- Chemical treatments, like iodine, are very effective against most common pathogens.
- Iodine is faster than chlorine, approximately 30 minutes versus up to 4 hours.

Disadvantages of Iodine

- Does not kill the parasite cryptosporidium.
- Chemical treatments do not remove chemical contaminants or turbidity.
- Requires time to work (approximately 30 minutes); Temperatures below 70°F (20°C) and turbid water require increasingly longer times.
- Some people react badly to iodine, particularly people with thyroid problems.
- The medical community recommends that continuous usage of iodine-treated water last no more than 3 to 4 weeks.
- Many people find the iodine taste objectionable (mixing in some citric acid in the form of lemon juice or tablets will kill the taste, but be sure to wait until sterilization has had plenty of time to take place).

Chlorine   Aquamira water treatment drops use chlorine. Chlorine is most commonly used in the form of chlorine dioxide tablets or drops, such as in Aquamira, Katadyn Micropur, and Potable Aqua Chlorine Dioxide. It can also be used in the form of laundry bleach (be sure it is pure hypochlorous acid and not mixed with perfumes or other chemicals) or a solution generated from rock salt, such as done by MSR's MIOX purifier.

While chlorine will kill most bacteria and parasites in a few minutes, a much longer time is required to kill the cysts of giardia and cryptosporidium, as well as many viruses. Typically 4 hours or more is the recommended time for room temperature water (70°F/20°C), with an increase for colder water, such as from mountain streams (always follow the manufacturer's instructions). Chlorine can be used indefinitely, unlike iodine. It's what you drink in most city water systems. On the other hand, one of the joys of fresh stream water is its clean taste with no chemical smell or taste.

The much longer time required for chlorine treatment is also a problem. The solution is to carry two water bottles, which are alternately refilled and the chlorine added at each water source. That way, you have a full bottle available when you empty the other. Chemical treatments do not remove chemical contamination, and in fact can react with certain agricultural runoff. This is unlikely to be a significant problem for the backcountry traveler, however. Chemical treatment also does not remove turbidity. Turbid water requires longer treatment times or an increased amount of the halogen.

Advantages of Chlorine:

- Chemical treatments are very effective against most common pathogens, and chlorine kills most bacteria and parasites in minutes.
- Chlorine can be used indefinitely.

Disadvantages of Chlorine:

- Chemical treatments do not remove chemical contaminants or turbidity.
- Requires time to work, up to 4 hours, for full treatment; Temperatures below 70°F (20°C) and turbid water require increasingly longer times.

Ultraviolet Radiation

A recent addition to the quiver of techniques for purifying water in the field is ultraviolet (UV) radiation. The most widely available device for doing this is the SteriPen. This is a battery operated device that is stirred in the water (preferably a one-liter water bottle with a wide mouth) for a short period of time (couple of minutes).

To prepare for purification, fill a bottle with water, press a button on the SteriPen according to the directions (single push for one liter), then insert the pen into the water. When the contacts on the side of the pen are immersed, the light will light up. Stir the water until the light extinguishes, and the water is sterilized. The UV radiation is extremely effective against biological contaminants. However, like the other treatments mentioned above, UV radiation does not remove chemical contaminants or turbidity. The water should be fairly clear (it need not be crystal clear), so the water should be allowed to settle or a filter used to remove most of the sediment (a coffee filter is sufficient, according to the last word we had from the SteriPen people). If the water appears slightly milky from glacial flour or volcanic ash, you may want to run a second treatment. We used this approach on Kilimanjaro with the water taken from streams on the mountain.

A disadvantage of the SteriPen is that it requires batteries. However, one of the optional packages includes a carrying case with a solar charger in the lid. This requires 8 to 10 hours to recharge a pair of batteries. Since a charge will suffice for 10 liters or so of water (a couple day's worth), this is adequate. You can carry two or three sets of the batteries as backups, although the batteries (both primary and rechargeable) are lithium-based, hence subject to the TSA restrictions on carrying no more than two spare batteries in your carry-on baggage and none in your checked baggage.

Advantages of UV Radiation:

- Effective against biological contaminants—parasites, bacteria, and viruses.
- Fast and convenient.

Disadvantages of UV Radiation:

- Does not remove chemical contamination nor reduce turbidity.
- Water should be fairly clear, though it does not have to be perfectly clear.
- Requires batteries, but a solar charger is available.

PUR Water Treatment Kit

PUR, a Swiss division of Proctor and Gamble, developed a water treatment kit for use in Third World countries a couple of years ago. They have now made the PUR Clean Drinking Water Kit available in North America. This kit will purify water, removing biological and many chemical contaminants, along with suspended particulates. The complete kit includes two 10-liter containers (one for the untreated water to be treated, the other for the treated water to be decanted into), a stirring tool, a cotton cloth filter to remove the flocculus with the trapped contaminants, packets of the treatment chemical, and a packet opening tool. The first container is filled with the water to be treated. The premeasured chemical packet, containing iron sulphate and calcium hypochlorite, is poured into the water and the stirring tool is used to stir the water to mix the chemical thoroughly. The container is then closed and let stand for 10 minutes. The iron sulphate forms a flocculus (similar in appearance to fluffy cotton), which settles to the bottom, carrying most of the biological contaminants, silt and other suspended particulates, and most chemical contaminants (including heavy metal compounds) to the bottom. After 10 minutes, the water is carefully decanted through the cloth filter into the second container, which is allowed to sit for an additional 10 minutes, during which the remaining pathogens (viruses) are killed by the calcium hypochlorite acting as the purifying agent. At this point the water is pure enough to pass international standards for drinking water.

The two major problems with the PUR kit are that it is currently somewhat difficult to obtain, and that the packets are pre-measured for 10 liters. You cannot use a partial packet for a smaller amount of water (the powder does not necessarily have the components uniformly mixed throughout the packet, so you must empty the complete packet into the water). While this is ok for a group (or, in Third World communities, for a family group), this is inconvenient for the individual backpacker or a small group of backpackers. However, the cost is very small, less than the cost per liter of most of the other methods described. The big advantage is that this is the only method available for water contaminated heavily with suspended particulates, many chemical contaminants, and virtually all biological contaminants. It would work well for larger backcountry groups, as well as in case of a natural or man-made disaster that interrupts municipal water supplies. It will not desalinate water.

Advantages of PUR Clean Drinking Water Kit:
- Removes biological, particulate, and some chemical contamination.
- Particularly good for Third World and highly contaminated water sources, and during natural or man-made disasters.
- Inexpensive.
- Simple procedure.
- Treats 10 liters at a time, so is best for large groups.

Disadvantages of PUR Clean Drinking Water Kit:

- Treats 10 liters at a time—no smaller, no larger—so inconvenient for most backpackers.
- Takes 20 minutes total time for treatment.

The Bottom Line

For backcountry travelers in the United States and Canada, the major source of digestive tract illness is not waterborne pathogens or other contamination, but poor sanitation. The best prevention is paying diligent attention to simple sanitation measures: Wash your hands frequently, particularly after relieving yourself. Use soap and water and/or Purell or another alcohol-based purifier. Wash and sterilize your hands before eating, particularly finger foods (sandwiches, bars, trail mix, etc.)

All individuals preparing or serving food for the group must wash and sterilize their hands, and should consider using gloves of the type now mandated for restaurant workers. All dishes and utensils should be washed before meal preparation and serving. Sterilizing by dunking in boiling water is one of the easiest and quickest ways to assure sterile utensils. It is all too easy to be careless and neglect simple sanitation while hiking, backpacking, and climbing. But, by treating your backcountry water, staying hydrated, and practicing proper hygiene, you'll help ensure that you, and everyone in your group, has a great trip and will be back on the trail again soon.

Water Treatment/Water Storage

Quantity A water ration of as little as a pint per day has allowed life raft survivors to live for weeks, but a more realistic figure is 1 gallon per person per day for survival. 4 gallons per person/day will allow personal hygiene, washing of dishes, counter tops, etc. 5 to 12 gallons per day would be needed for a conventional toilet, or 1/2 to two gallons for a pour flush latrine. For short-term emergencies, it will probably be more practical to store paper plates and utensils, and minimize food preparation, than to attempt to store more water.

In addition to stored water, there is quite a bit of water trapped in the piping of the average home. If the municipal water system was not contaminated before you shut the water off to your house, this water is still fit for consumption without treatment. To collect this water, open the lowest faucet in the system, and allow air into the system from a second faucet. Depending on the diameter of the piping, you may want to open every other faucet, to make sure all of the water is drained. This procedure will usually only drain the cold water side, the hot-water side will have to be drained from the water heater. Again, open all of the faucets to let air into the system, and be prepared to collect any water that comes out when the first faucet is opened. Toilet tanks (not the bowls) represent another source of water if a toilet bowl cleaner is not used in the tank. Some people have plumbed old water heaters or other tanks in line with their cold water supply to add an always rotated source of water. Two cautions are in order:

(1) Make sure the tanks can handle the pressure (50 psi min.), and

(2) if the tanks are in series with the house plumbing, this method is susceptible to contamination of the municipal water system.

The system can be fed off the water lines with a shutoff valve (and a second drain line), preventing the water from being contaminated as long as the valve was closed at the time of contamination. Water can only be realistically stored for short-term emergencies, after that some emergency supply of water needs to be developed

Water Collection Wells

Water can only be moved by suction for an equivalent head of about 20'. After this cavitation occurs, that is the water boils off in tiny bubbles in the vacuum created by the pump rather than being lifted by the pump. At best no water is pumped, at worst the pump is destroyed. Well pumps in wells deeper than this work on one of the following principles:

1) The pump can be submerged in the well; this is usually the case for deep well pumps. Submersible pumps are available for depths up 1000 feet.

2) The pump can be located at the surface of the well, and two pipes go down the well: one carrying water down, and one returning it. A jet fixture called an ejector on the bottom of the two hoses causes well water to be lifted up the well with the returning pumped water. These pumps must have an efficient foot valve as there is no way for them to self-prime. These are commonly used in shallow wells, but can go as deep as 350 feet. Some pumps use the annular space between one pipe and the well casing as the second pipe, but this requires a packer (seal) at the ejector and at the top of the casing.

3) The pump cylinder can be located in the well, and the power source located above the well. This is the method used by windmills and most hand pumps. A few hand pumps pump the water from very shallow wells using an aboveground pump and suction line.

A variety of primitive, but ingenious, pump designs also exist. One uses a chain with buckets to lift the water up. Another design uses a continuous loop rope dropping in the well and returning up a small diameter pipe. Sealing washers are located along the rope, such that water is pulled up the pipe with the rope. An ancient Chinese design used knots, but modern designs designed for village level maintenance in Africa use rubber washers made from tires, and will work to a much greater depth. Obviously a bucket can be lowered down the well if the well is big enough, but this won't work with a modern drilled well. A better idea for a drilled well is to use a 2' length or so of galvanized pipe with end caps of a diameter that will fit in the well casing. The upper cap is drilled for a screw eye, and a small hole for ventilation. The lower end is drilled with a hole about half the diameter of the pipe, and on the inside a piece of rigid plastic or rubber is used as a flapper valve. This will allow water to enter the pipe, but not exit it. The whole assembly is lowered in the well casing, the weight of the pipe will cause it to fill with water, and it can then be lifted to the surface. The top pipe cap is there mostly to prevent the pipe from catching as it is lifted.

Springs Springs or artesian wells are ideal sources of water. Like a conventional well, the water should be tested for pathogens, VOCs (Volatile Organic Compounds such as fuel oil or benzene), pesticides and any other contaminants found in your area. If the source is a spring it is very important to seal it in a spring box to prevent the water from becoming contaminated as it reaches the surface. It is also important to divert surface runoff around the spring box. As with a well, you will want to periodically treat the spring box with chlorine, particularly if the spring is slow moving. The spring may also be used for keeping food cool if a spring-house is built. If this is the case, it is still recommended to build a spring box inside the house to obtain potable water.

Surface water Most US residents served by municipal water systems supplied with surface water, and many residents of underdeveloped countries rely on surface water. While surface water will almost always need to be treated, a lot of the risk can be reduced by properly collecting the water. Ideal sources of water are fast flowing creeks and rivers which don't have large sources of pollution in their watershed. With the small amounts of water needed by a family or small group, the most practical way to collect the water is though an infiltration gallery or well. Either method reduces the turbidity of the collected water making it easy for later treatment.

Organic compounds Water can be contaminated by a number of organic compounds such as chloroform, gasoline, pesticides, and herbicides. These contaminants must be identified in a lab test. It is unlikely ground water will suddenly become contaminated unless a quantity of chemicals is allowed to enter a well or penetrating the aquifer. One exception is when the aquifer is located in limestone. Not only will water flow faster through limestone, but the rock is prone to forming vertical channels or sinkholes that will rapidly allow contamination from surface water. Surface water may show great swings in chemical levels due to differences in rainfall, seasonal crop cultivation, and industrial effluent levels

Water purification heavy metals Heavy metals are only a problem is certain areas of the country. The best way to identify their presence is by a lab test of the water or by speaking with your county health department. Unless you are down stream of mine tailings or a factory, the problem will probably affect the whole county or region. Heavy metals are unlikely to be present in sufficient levels to cause problems with short-term use.

Turbidity Turbidity refers to suspended solids, i.e. muddy water, is very turbid. Turbidity is undesirable for 3 reasons:

1) Aesthetic considerations

2) Solids may contain heavy metals, pathogens or other contaminants,

3) Turbidity decreases the effectiveness of water treatment techniques by shielding pathogens from chemical or thermal damage, or in the case of UV treatment, absorbing the UV light itself.

Organic compounds Water can be contaminated by a number of organic compounds such as chloroform, gasoline, pesticides, and herbicides. These contaminants must be identified in a lab test. It is unlikely ground water will suddenly become contaminated unless a quantity of chemicals is allowed to enter a well or penetrating the aquifer. One exception is when the aquifer is located in limestone. Not only will water flow faster through limestone, but the rock is prone to forming vertical channels or sinkholes that will rapidly allow contamination from surface water. Surface water may show great swings in chemical levels due to differences in rainfall, seasonal crop cultivation, and industrial effluent levels.

Pathogens

Protozoa Protozoa cysts are the largest pathogens in drinking water, and are responsible for many of the waterborne disease cases in the US. Protozoa cysts range in size from 2 to 15 μm (a micron is one millionth of a meter), but can squeeze through smaller openings. In order to insure cyst filtration, filters with an absolute pore size of 1μm or less should be used. The two most common protozoa pathogens are Giardia lamblia (Giardia) and Cryptosporidium (Crypto). Both organisms have caused numerous deaths in recent years in the US, the deaths occurring in the young and elderly, and the sick and immune compromised. Many deaths were a result of more than one of these conditions. Neither disease is likely to be fatal to a healthy adult, even if untreated. For example in Milwaukee in April of 1993, of 400,000 who were diagnosed with Crypto, only 54 deaths were linked to the outbreak, 84% of whom were AIDS patients. Outside of the US and other developed countries, protozoa are responsible for many cases of amoebic dysentery, but so far this has not been a problem in the US, due to better wastewater treatment. This could change during a survival situation. Tests have found Giardia and/or Crypto in up to 5% of vertical wells and 26% of springs in the US.

Bacteria Bacteria are smaller than protozoa and are responsible for many diseases such as typhoid fever, cholera, diarrhea, and dysentery. Pathogenic bacteria range in size from 0.2 to 0.6 μm, and a 0.2 μm filter is necessary to prevent transmission. Contamination of water supplies by bacteria is blamed for the cholera epidemics which devastate undeveloped countries from time to time. Even in the US, E. coli is frequently found to contaminate water supplies. Fortunately E. coli is relatively harmless as pathogens go, and the problem isn't so much with E. coli found, but the fear that other bacteria may have contaminated the water as well. Never the less, dehydration from diarrhea caused by E. coli has resulted in fatalities.

Viruses Viruses are the 2nd most problematic pathogen, behind protozoa. As with protozoa, most waterborne viral diseases don't present a lethal hazard to a healthy adult. Waterborne pathogenic viruses range in size from 0.020-0.030 μm, and are too small to be filtered out by a mechanical filter. All waterborne enteric viruses affecting humans occur solely in humans, thus animal waste doesn't present much of a viral threat. At the present viruses don't present a major hazard to people drinking surface water in the US, but this could change in a survival situation as the level of human sanitation is reduced. Viruses do tend to show up even in remote areas, so case can be made for eliminating them now.

Physical Treatment

Heat Treatment Boiling is one guaranteed way to purify water of all pathogens. Most experts feel that if the water reaches a rolling boil it is safe. A few still hold out for maintaining the boiling for some length of time, commonly 5 or 10 minutes, plus an extra minute for every 1000 feet of elevation. If one wishes to do this, a pressure cooker would allow the water to be kept at boiling without losing the heat to evaporation. One reason for the long period of boiling may be to inactivate bacterial spores (which can survive boiling), but these spore are unlikely to be waterborne pathogens. African aid agencies figure it takes 1 kg of wood to boil 1 liter of water. Hardwoods and efficient stoves would improve on this. Water can also be treated at below boiling temperatures, if contact time is increased. A commercial unit has been developed that treats 500 gals of water per day at an estimated cost of $1/1000 gallons for the energy. The process is similar to milk pasteurization, and holds the water at 161° F for 15 seconds. Heat exchangers recover most of the energy used to warm the water. Solar pasteurizers have also been built that would heat three gallons of water to 65° C and hold the temperature for an hour. A higher temperature could be reached if the device was rotated east to west during the day to follow the sunlight. Regardless of the method, heat treatment does not leave any form of residual to keep the water free of pathogens in storage.

Reverse Osmosis Reverse osmosis forces water, under pressure, through a membrane that is impermeable to most contaminants. The most common use is aboard boats to produce fresh water from salt water. The membrane is somewhat better at rejecting salts than it is at rejecting non-ionized weak acids and bases and smaller organic molecules (molecular weight below 200). In the latter category are undissociated weak organic acids, amines, phenols, chlorinated hydrocarbons, low molecular weight alcohols. Larger organic molecules, and all pathogens are rejected. Of course it is possible to have an imperfection in the membrane that could allow molecules or whole pathogens to pass through. Using reverse osmosis to desalinate seawater requires considerable pressure (1000 psi) to operate, and for a long time only electric models were available.

Competing for a contract to build a hand powered model for the Navy, Recovery Engineering designed a model that could operate by hand, using the waste water (90 percent of the water is waste water, only 10% passes through the filter) to pressurize the back side of the piston. The design was later acquired by PUR. While there is little question that the devices work well, the considerable effort required to operate one has been questioned by some survival experts such as Michael Greenwald, himself a survivor of a shipwreck.

On the other hand the people who have actually used them on a life raft credit the availability of water from their PUR watermaker for their survival. PUR manual watermakers are available in two models: The Survivor 06 ($500) produces 2 pints per hour, and the Survivor 35 ($1350) produces 1.4 gal/hr. The latter model is also available as the Power Survivor 35 ($1700), which produces the same water volume from 4 Amps of 12 VDC, and can be disconnected and used as a hand held unit. A number of manufactures, including PUR, make DC powered models for shipboard use. PUR recommends replacing the O rings every 600 hours on its handheld units, and a kit is available to do this. Estimates for membrane life vary, but units designed for production use may last a year or more. Every precaution should be taken to prevent petroleum products from contacting the membrane as they will damage or destroy the membrane. The prefilter must also be regularly changed, and the membrane may need to be treated with a biocide occasionally Reverse osmosis filter are also available that will use normal municipal or private water pressure to remove contaminates from water, as long as they aren't present in the levels found in sea water. The water produced by reverse osmosis, like distilled water, will be close to pure H_2O. Therefore mineral intake may need to be increased to compensate for the normal mineral content of water in much of the world.

Distillation

Distillation is the evaporation and condensation of water to purify water. Distillation has two disadvantages: 1) A large energy input is required and 2) If simple distillation is used, chemical contaminants with boiling points below water will be condensed along with the water. Distillation is most commonly used to remove dissolved minerals and salts from water. The simplest form of a distillation is a solar still. A solar still uses solar radiation to evaporate water below the boiling point, and the cooler ambient air to condense the vapor. The water can be extracted from the soil, vegetation piled in the still, or contaminated water (such as radiator fluid or salt water) can be added to the still. While per still output is low, they are an important technique if water is in short supply.

Other forms of distillation require a concentrated heat source to boil water which is then condensed. Simple stills use a coiling coil to return this heat to the environment. These can be improvised with a boiler and tight fitting lid and some copper tubing (Avoid using lead soldered tubing if possible). FEMA suggests that, in an emergency, a hand towel can be used to collect steam above a container of boiling water. More efficient distillations plants use a vapor compression cycle where the water is boiled off at atmospheric pressure, the steam is compressed, and the condenser condenses the steam above the boiling point of the water in the boiler, returning the heat of fusion to the boiling water. The hot condensed water is run through a second heat exchanger which heats up the water feeding into the boiler. These plants normally use an internal combustion engine to run the compressor. Waste heat from the engine, including the exhaust, is used to start the process and make up any heat loss. This is the method used in most commercial and military desalinization plants.

Inflatable solar stills are available from marine supply stores, but avoid the WW2 surplus models, as those who have used them have had an extremely high failure rate. Even new inflatable solar stills may only produce from 30-16 oz under actual conditions, compared to a rating of 48 oz/day under optimum conditions.

Microfilters

Microfilters are small-scale filters designed to remove cysts, suspended solids, protozoa, and in some cases bacteria from water. Most filters use a ceramic or fiber element that can be cleaned to restore performance as the units are used. Most units and almost all made for camping use a hand pump to force the water through the filter. Others use gravity, either by placing the water to be filtered above the filter (e.g. the Katadyn drip filter), or by placing the filter in the water, and running a siphon hose to a collection vessel located below the filter (e.g. Katadyn siphon filter). Microfilters are the only method, other than boiling, to remove Cryptosporidium. Microfilters do not remove viruses, which many experts do not consider to be a problem in North America.

Despite this the Katadyn microfilter has seen considerable use around the world by NATO-member militaries, WHO, UNHCR, and other aid organizations. Microfilters share a problem with charcoal filter in having bacteria grow on the filter medium. Some handle this by impregnating the filter element with silver such as the Katadyn, others advise against storage of a filter element after it has been used. The Sweetwater Guardian suggests using a freezer for short-term storage. Many microfilters may include silt prefilters, activated charcoal stages, or an iodine resin. Most filters come with a stainless steel prefilter, but other purchased or improvised filters can be added to reduce the loading on the main filter element. Allowing time for solids to settle, and/ or prefiltering with a coffee filter will also extend filter life.

Iodine matrix filters will kill viruses that will pass through the filter, and if a charcoal stage is used it will remove much of the iodine from the water. Charcoal filters will also remove other dissolved natural or manmade contaminates. Both the iodine and the charcoal stages do not indicate when they reach their useful life, which is much shorter than the filter element. If you are depending on the stage for filtering the water you will have to keep up with how much water passes through it.

New designs seem to be coming out every month. The best selling brands seem to be the PUR, and Sweetwater Guardian. The Katadyn doesn't sell as well to outdoor enthusiasts due to its high cost, but for years it was state of the art for water purification and still has a loyal following, especially among professionals in relief work. Below is the data on a few of the more common units, for an excellent field test of some common units, see the December 96 issue of Backpacker magazine. Note that the first price is for the filter, the second for the replacement filter.

Basic Designs Ceramic Filter Pump ($29/$15, 8 oz.)

Cheap flimsy filter, claimed to filter up to 500 gallons with a 0.9 μm ceramic filter. Not EPA rated, may not have passed independent lab tests, prone to damage, filter element must be submerged in water.

General Ecology- First Need Deluxe ($70/$30, 20oz)

This filter uses a structured matrix micro strainer, though General Ecology won't reveal what the structure is. It has survived independent lab tests, and filters particles to 4 μm, while actually removing viruses (the only filter capable of doing this) through electrostatic attraction. The filter cartridges can't be cleaned (other than by back flushing), but are good for 100 gallons. Pump design isn't the best. Other models are available from the manufacturer.

Katadyn PF ($295/$145, 22.7 oz).

The original microfilter using a 0.2 μm silver impregnated ceramic candle. An extremely thick filter allows it to be cleaned many times for up to 14,000 gallons capacity. While the Katadyn seems well made, one reader of this list reported breaking the candle, and Backpacker Magazine broke the case during a field test. The pump, while probably indestructible, is somewhat slow and hard to use, requiring 20 lbs. of force on a small handle. The PF also lacks an output hose as the Katadyn engineers felt it would be a source of contamination.

Katadyn Combi ($185/$75 (ceramic)/$19 (carbon), 29 oz)

A cheaper version of the PF incorporating both ceramic and carbon stages. Much faster filter than the PF.

Katadyn Minifilter ($139/$59, 8.3 oz)

A smaller and cheaper version of the PF, easier to pump, but generally not well received. Good for 200 gallons.

Katadyn Expedition ($680/$77, 13 lb.)

Similar filter to the PF (exact same cartridge as the Drip Filter Below), but designed for much higher production, stainless steel case with spade type D handle, produces 0.75 gpm. Filter good for 26,000 gallons.

Katadyn Drip Style Filter ($240, $77, 12.5 lb.)

Filter elements similar to those in the PF are mounted vertically in top 3 gallon plastic bucket, water drips through filters into second 3 gallon bucket with faucet. 1 qt, per hour with the 2 filters included, a third filter can be added to increase rate 50%. Each filter good for 13,000 gallons. The mounting hardware for the filters is available for $10 to allow you to make your own filter of whatever size is needed. Each mounting kit requires a ½" hole in the bottom of the raw water container.

Katadyn Siphon Filter ($92, 2 lb.)

Similar design to PF filter element, but a siphon hose replaces the pump, filters 1-2 quarts per hour (allow 1 hour for the filter to "prime" itself via capillary action), but multiple filters can be used in the same container. Collection vessel must be lower than raw water container. Good for13,000 gallons.

MSR Miniworks ($59/$30, 14 oz)

MSR's smaller filter, using a 0.3 μm ceramic element. Pump is well designed, and easy to use. Main drawback is that the clean water discharge is from the bottom of the filter, and no hose is provided. While the bottom is threaded for a Nalgene bottle, it is a pain in the butt to fill a canteen or 2 liter bottle. Claimed to filter 100 gallons, Backpacker Magazine feels this may be one of the few filters without a grossly inflated rating.

MSR Waterworks ($140/$30/$30, 17 oz)

MSR's first filter with a 0.2 μ ceramic and membrane stage and a carbon stage. Other wise similar to the Miniworks.

PUR Pioneer ($30/$4, 8 oz)

Newly introduced low-end microfilter. 0.5 μm, 1 lpm filter rate, 12 gallon capacity

PUR Hiker ($50/$20, 12 oz)

PUR's microfilter only design, filters to .5 μm. Well liked, as are the other PUR filters. Very compact. 200 gallon capacity

PUR Scout ($70/$35/$15, 12 oz)

Combines a iodine resin stage, a 1.0 μm filter, and a activated charcoal filter. 200 gallon capacity

PUR Explorer ($130/$45, 22 oz)

PUR's top of the line model. Bulky, but well made, with a high output (1.4 lpm, faster than any of the hand held models listed and one of the easiest to pump) Has a 1.0 μm filter plus a iodine resin stage, 300 gallon capacity

Sweetwater Walkabout ($35/$13, 8.5 oz.)

Sweetwater's low end filter, 0.2 μm, .7 lpm, 100 gal capacity

Sweetwater Guardian ($60/$20, 11 oz)

Uses a glass fiber and carbon filter, filters to .2 µm, claimed to last for 200 gallons. An iodine resin stage can be added that will kill viruses, and will last for 90 gallons. Pump is well designed, but it takes a few seconds to pull a captive pin to fold for storage. Available in white or OD.

Timberline Eagle ($20/$13, 8 oz)

At 1 µm, this filter only does protozoa, but is much easier to pump, lighter, and cheaper. Filter is attached to pump, and must rest (but doesn't have to be submerged) in water to be purified. Looks flimsy, but seems to hold up. Claimed to last for 100 gallons. It is also possible to build your own microfilter using *diatomaceous earth*, sold for swimming pool filters (DE). Usually pressure is required to achieve a reasonable flow rate. A DE filter will remove turbidity as well as pathogens larger than 1 um.

[This type of diatomaceous earth is NOT the type you want for food storage. Don't get them confused.]

Slow Sand Filter

Slow sand filters pass water slowly through a bed of sand. Pathogens and turbidity are removed by natural die-off, biological action, and filtering. Typically the filter will consist of 24 inches of sand, then a gravel layer in which the drain pipe is embedded. The gravel doesn't touch the walls of the filter so that water can't run quickly down the wall of the filter and into the gravel. Building the walls with a rough surface also helps. A typical loading rate for the filter is 0.2 meters/hour day (the same as .2 m^3/m^2 of surface area). The filter can be cleaned several times before the sand has to be replaced.

Slow sand filters should only be used for continuous water treatment. If a continuous supply of raw water can't be insured (say using a holding tank), then another method should be chosen. It is also important for the water to have as low turbidity (suspended solids) as possible. Turbidity can be reduced by changing the method of collection (for example, building an infiltration gallery, rather than taking water directly from a creek), allowing time for the material to settle out (using a raw water tank), prefiltering or flocculation (adding a chemical such as alum to cause the suspended material to floc together.) The SSF filter itself is a large box, at least 1.5 meters high. The walls should be as rough as possible to reduce the tendency for water to run down the walls of the filter, bypassing the sand. The bottom layer of the filter is a gravel bed in which a slotted pipe is placed to drain off the filtered water. The slots or the gravel should be no closer than 20 cm to the walls, again to prevent the water from bypassing the sand. The sand for a SSF needs to be clean and uniform, and of the correct size. The sand can be cleaned in clean running water, even if it is in a creek.

The ideal specs on sand are effective size (sieve size through which 10% of the sand passes) between 0.15 and 0.35 mm, uniformity coefficient (ratio of sieve sizes through which 60% pass and through which 10% pass) of less than 3, Maximum size of 3 mm, and minimum size of 0.1 mm. The sand is added to a SSF to a minimum depth of 0.6 meters. Additional thickness will allow more cleanings before the sand must be replaced. 0.3 to 0.5 meters of extra sand will allow the filter to work for 3-4 years. An improved design uses a geotextile layer on top of the sand to reduce the frequency of cleaning. The outlet of a SSF must be above the sand level, and below the water level. The water must be maintained at a constant level to insure an even flow rate throughout the filter. The flow rate can be increased by lowering the outlet pipe, or increasing the water level.

One common idea for maintaining the water level is to use an elevated raw water tank or pump, and a ball valve from a toilet. While the SSF will begin to work at once, optimum treatment for pathogens will take a week or more. During this time the water should be chlorinated if at all possible (iodine can be substituted). After the filter has stabilized, the water should be safe to drink, but chlorinating of the output is still a good idea, particularly to prevent recontamination. As the flow rate slows down the filter will have to be cleaned by draining and removing the top few inches of sand. If a geotextile filter is used, only the top ½" may have to be removed. As the filter is refilled, it will take a few days for the biological processes to reestablish themselves.

Activated Charcoal Filter

Activated charcoal filters water through adsorption, chemicals and some heavy metals are attracted to the surface of the charcoal, and are attached to it. Charcoal filters will filter some pathogens though they will quickly use up the filter adsorptive ability, and can even contribute to contamination as the charcoal provides an excellent breeding ground for bacteria and algae. Some charcoal filters are available impregnated with silver to prevent this, though current research concludes that the bacteria growing on the filter are harmless, even if the water wasn't disinfected before contacting the filter.

One of the fewfilters that uses only activated charcoal, and doesn't require pressurized water is the Water Washer ($59). Activated charcoal can be used in conjunction with chemical treatment. The chemical (iodine or chlorine) will kill the pathogens, while the carbon filter will remove the treatment chemicals. In this case, as the filter reaches its capacity, a distinctive chlorine or iodine taste will be noted. Activated charcoal can be made at home, though the product will be of varying quality compared to commercial products. Either purchased or homemade charcoal can be recycled by burning off the molecules adsorbed by the carbon (This won't work with heavy metals of course.)

The more activated charcoal in a filter, the longer it will last. The bed of carbon must be deep enough for adequate contact with the water. Production designs use granulated activated charcoal (effective size or 0.6 to 0.9 mm for maximum flow rate. Home or field models can also use a compressed carbon block or powered activated charcoal (effective size 0.01) to increase contact area. Powered charcoal can also be mixed with water and filtered out later. As far as life of the filter is concerned, carbon block filters will last the longest for a given size, simply due to their greater mass of carbon. A source of pressure is usually needed with carbon block filters to achieve a reasonable flow rate.

Sol-Air Water Treatment

If sufficient dissolved oxygen is available, sunlight will cause the temporary formation of reactive forms of oxygen such as hydrogen peroxide and oxygen free radicals. This form of water treatment is called solar photo oxidative disinfection or sol-air water treatment. Sol-Air water treatment has been shown to dramatically reduce the level of fecal coliform bacteria. There is some evidence that other bacteria and viruses may be affected also. While not as reliable as other methods, it does offer a low-tech solution in emergencies.

Sol-Air treatment requires bright sunlight, and has been shown to be effective whenever the sun causes a distinct shadow to be cast. Exposure to 4.5 hours of bright sunlight has been shown to cause a thousand fold reduction in fecal coliforms in lab tests. In order for Sol-Air to be effective, oxygen must be present. Experiments have shown that shaking a bottle filled 3/4 with air will restore oxygen levels to near saturation. As the treatment continues, some of the oxygen will come out of solution, while other oxygen will be consumed by the killed pathogens, so the shaking should be repeated every few hours.

Data shows that maximum activity occurs when the water temperature is above 50° C (122° F), so this method may be unsuitable in colder climates unless special solar collectors are used. Either glass or plastic bottles may be used. Plastic bottles will allow short wave ultraviolet radiation to pass, increasing the rate of microbial inactivation, but may yellow with age, reducing light transmission, and may leach plasticizers into the water at the elevated temperatures that will occur. The leaching of plasticizers can be reduced by using bottles of PET (polyethylene terephtalate) rather than PVC. Glass bottles on the other hand are more durable.

Research has used bottles with 2 liters of capacity, but if the water is free of turbidity, larger containers can be used. Plastic bags, or some sort of flat glass container represent the ideal container as this maximizes the solar energy received per ounce of water. Bottles should be filed 3/4 full in the early morning with water as free of turbidity as possible. After capping the bottles should be shaken vigorously for a few minutes then placed upright in the sun, where they will be not be shaded later in the day. The shaking should be repeated at least three times during the day. At the end of the day the water should be reasonably freed of bacteria, though it is most practical to let the water cool for consumption the following day. Each day a new batch should be treated due to the lack of a residual disinfected. After consumption of the water the bottle should be air dried to prevent algae growth with continual use.

Improvised Mechanical Filter

If the materials aren't available to build a slow sand filter, or some other means of water treatment is preferred, it may still be advantageous to mechanically filter the water before treating it with chemicals or passing through a microfilter. Generally the idea is to allow the water to flow as slowly as possible through a bed of sand. In a municipal water treatment plant this is called a rapid sand filter. The particular design below is included, because the designer, a research engineer at Oak Ridge National Laboratories, found it particularly effective at removing fallout from water. The filter will do little or nothing to remove pathogens, though removing suspended solids allow others water treatment methods to work more effectively.

Expedient water filter

Survival Skills,

1) Perforate the bottom of a 5 gallon bucket, or similar container with a dozen nail holes even spread over a 4" diameter circle in the center of the container.

2) Place a 1.5" layer of small stones or pebbles in the bottom of the can. If pebbles aren't available, marbles, clean bottle caps, twisted coat hangers or clean twigs can be used.

3) Cover the pebbles with one thickness of terrycloth towel, burlap sackcloth, or other porous cloth. Curl the cloth in a roughly circular shape about three inches larger than the diameter of the can.

4) Take soil containing some clay (pure clay isn't porous enough, pure sand is too porous) from at least 4" below the surface of the ground (nearly all fallout particles remain near the surface except after disposition on sand or gravel.)

5) Pulverize the soil, then gently press it in layers over the cloth that covers the pebbles, so that the cloth is held snugly against the walls of the can. The soil should be 6-7" thick.

6) Completely cover the surface of the soil layer with one thickness of fabric as porous as a bath towel. This is to keep the soil from being eroded as water is being poured into the filter. A dozen small stones placed on the cloth near its edges will secure it adequately.

7) Support the filter on rocks or sticks placed across the top of a container that is larger than the filter can (such as a dishpan) The contaminated water should be poured into the filter can, preferably after allowing it to settle as described below. The filtered water should be disinfected by some method.

If the 6 or 7 inches of filtering soil is a sandy clay loam, the filter will initially deliver about 6 quarts/hour. If the filter is any faster than this then the fabric layer needs to be removed and the soil compressed more. The filtering rate will drop over time as the filter begins to clog up. When this happens the top 1/2" of soil can be removed to increase the filtering rate. After 50 or so quarts, the filter will need to be rebuilt with fresh soil. As with any filter, optimum performance will be achieved if sediment in the water will be allowed to settle out before passing the water through the filter. If the water is contaminated with fallout, clay can be added to help the fallout particles to settle out. The procedure is as follows:

- Fill a bucket or other deep container 3/4 full with contaminated water.
- Dig pulverized clay or clayey soil from a depth of four or more inches below ground surface and stir it into the water.
- Use about 1 inch of dry clay or clayey soil for every 4" depth of water. Stir until practically all of the clay particles are suspended in the water.
- Let the clay settle for at least 6 hours. This will carry the fallout particles to the bottom and cover them.
- Carefully dip out or siphon the clear water and disinfect it.

Chemical Treatment

Chlorine: Chlorine is familiar to most Americans as it is used to treat virtually all municipal water systems in the United States. For a long time chlorine, in the form of Halazone tablets, was used to purify small batches of water for campers and military troops. Later questions emerged about the effectiveness of Halazone, and in 1989, Abbot Labs pulled it off the market. If Halazone tablets are are encountered outside the US, the nominal shelf life is 6 months and the dosage is 2 tabs per liter.

Until recently, there was no chlorine product designed for wilderness/ survival use available in the US. Chlorine has a number of problems when used for field treatment of water. When chlorine reacts with organic material, it attaches itself to nitrogen containing compounds (ammonium ions and amino acids), leaving less free chlorine to continue disinfection. Carcinogenic trihalomethanes are also produced, though this is only a problem with long-term exposure. Trihalomethanes can also be filtered out with a charcoal filter, though it is more efficient to use the same filter to remove organics before the water is chlorinated. Unless free chlorine is measured, disinfection cannot be guaranteed with moderate doses of chlorine. One solution is superchlorination, the addition of far more chlorine than is needed. This must again be filtered through activated charcoal to remove the large amounts of chlorine, or hydrogen peroxide can be added to drive the chlorine off. Either way there is no residual chlorine left to prevent recontamination. This isn't a problem if the water is to be used at once.

Chlorine is sensitive to both the pH and temperature of the treated water. Temperature slows the reaction for any chemical treatment, but chlorine treatment is particularly susceptible to variations in the pH as at lower pHs, hypochlorous acid is formed, while at higher pHs, it will tend to dissociate into hydrogen and chlorite ions, which are less effective as a disinfectant.- As a result, chlorine effectiveness drops off when the pH is greater than 8.

Chlorine, like iodine, will not kill Cryptosporidium.

Methods of chlorine treatment:

Bleach: Ordinary household bleach (such as Clorox) in the US contains 5.25% sodium hypochlorite (NaOCL) and can be used to purify water if it contains no other active ingredients, scents, or colorings. Bleach is far from an ideal source due to its bulkiness (only 5% active ingredient), and the instability over time of the chlorine content in bleach. Chlorine loss is farther increased by agitation or exposure to air. One source claims chlorine loss from a 5% solution at 10% over 6 months if stored at 70° F. Nevertheless, this may be the only chemical means available to purify water, and it is far better than nothing. Normal dosage is 8 drops (0.4 ml) per gallon. Allow the treated water to sit for 30 min., and if there isn't a slight chlorine smell, retreat.

Note: USP standard medicine droppers are designed to dispense 0.045-0.055 ml per drop. Use of other solvents or some chemicals can change this. The dropper can be calibrated against a graduated cylinder for greater accuracy.

Some small treatment plants in Africa produce their own sodium hypochlorite on site from the electrolysis of brine. Power demands range from 1.7 to 4 kWh per lb. of NaOCL. 2 to 3.5 lbs. of salt are needed for each pound of NaOCL. These units are fairly simple and are made in both the US and the UK. Another system, designed for China, where the suitable raw materials were mined or manufactured locally, used a reaction between salt, manganese dioxide, and sulfuric acid to produce chlorine gas. The gas was then allowed to react with slaked lime to produce a bleaching powder that could then be used to treat water. A heat source is required to speed the reaction up.

AquaCure: Designed for the South African military, these tablets contain chlorine and alum. The alum causes the suspended solids to flocculate and the chlorine adds 8 PPM chlorine. This is a great way to treat turbid water, though it will leave a lot of chlorine in clear water (The one tablet/liter could be halved for clear water.)

The US distributor for Aqua Cure is: Safesport Manufacturing, Box 11811, Denver, CO 80211 1 800 433 6506

Bleaching Powder (Chlorinated Lime): Can also be purchased and used as a purification means if nothing else is available. Bleaching powder is 33-37% chlorine when produced, but losses its chlorine rapidly, particularly when exposed to air, light or moisture.

Calcium Hypochlorite: Also known as High Test Hypochlorite (HTH). Supplied in crystal form, it is nearly 70% available chlorine. One product, the Sanitizer (formally the Sierra Water Purifier) uses these crystals to superchlorinate the water to insure pathogens were killed off, then hydrogen peroxide is added to drive off the residual chlorine. This is the most effective method of field chlorine treatment. The US military and most aid agencies also use HTH to treat their water, though a test kit, rather than superchlorination, is used to insure enough chlorine is added. This is preferable for large scale systems as the residual chlorine will prevent recontamination. Usually bulk water treatment plants first dilute to HTH to make a 1% working solution at the rate of 14g HTH per liter of water. While testing to determine exact chlorine needs are preferable, the solution can be used at the dose rate of 8 drops/gallon, or for larger quantities, 1 part of 1% solution to 10,000 parts clear water. Either of these doses will result in 1 PPM chlorine and may need to be increased if the water wasn't already filtered by other means. When test kits are available, the WHO standard is a residual chlorine level of 0.2 to 0.5 mg/l after a 30 min. contact time. This may require as much as 5 mg/l of chlorine to be added to the raw water.

Iodine: Iodine's use as a water purification method emerged after WW2, when the US military was looking for a replacement for Halazone tablets. Iodine was found to be in many ways superior to chlorine for use in treating small batches of water. Iodine is less sensitive to the pH and organic content of water, and is effective in lower doses.

Some individuals are allergic to iodine, and there is some question about long term use of iodine. The safety of long-term exposure to low levels of iodine was proven when inmates of three Florida prisons were given water disinfected with 0.5 to 1.0 PPM iodine for 15 years. No effects on the health or thyroid function of previously healthy inmates was observed. Of 101 infants born to prisoners drinking the water for 122- 270 days, none showed detectable thyroid enlargement. However 4 individuals with preexisting cases of hyperthyroidism became more symptomatic while consuming the water.

Nevertheless experts are reluctant to recommend iodine for long term use. Average American iodine intake is estimated at 0.24 to 0.74 mg/day, higher than the RDA of 0.4 mg/day. Due to a recent National Academy of Science recommendation that iodine consumption be reduced to the RDA, the EPA discourages the use of iodized salt in areas where iodine is used to treat drinking water. Iodine is normally used in doses of 8 PPM to treat clear water for a 10 minute contact time. The effectiveness of this dose has been shown in numerous studies. Cloudy water needs twice as much iodine or twice as much contact time. In cold water (Below 41° F or 5° C) the dose or time must also be doubled. In any case doubling the treatment time will allow the use of half as much iodine

These doses are calculated to remove all pathogens (other than Cryptosporidium) from the water. Of these, giardia cysts are the hardest to kill, and are what requires the high level of iodine. If the cysts are filtered out with a microfilter (any model will do since the cysts are 6 μm), only 0.5 PPM is needed to treat the resulting water. Water treated with iodine can have any objectionable taste removed by treating the water with vitamin C (ascorbic acid), but it must be added after the water has stood for the correct treatment time. Flavored beverages containing vitamin C will accomplish the same thing. Sodium thiosulfate can also be used to combine with free iodine, and either of these chemicals will also help remove the taste of chlorine as well. Usually elemental iodine can't be tasted below 1 PPM, and below 2 PPM the taste isn't objectionable. Iodine ions have an even higher taste threshold of 5 PPM. Note that removing the iodine taste does not reduce the dose of iodine ingested by the body.

Sources of Iodine:

Tincture of Iodine: USP tincture of iodine contains 2% iodine and 2.4% sodium iodide dissolved in 50% ethyl alcohol. For water purification use, the sodium iodide has no purification effect, but contributes to the total iodine dose. Thus it is not a preferred source of iodine, but can be used if other sources are not available. 0.4 cc's (or 8 drops) of USP tincture (2% iodine) added to a liter of water will give the 8 mg/l (same as 8 PPM). If the iodine tincture isn't compounded to USP specs, then you will have to calculate an equal dose based on the iodine concentration.

Lugol's solution: Contains 5% iodine and 10% potassium iodide. 0.15 cc (3 drops) can be added per liter of water, but 3 times more iodine is consumed compared to sources without iodide. Betadyne (povidone iodine): Some have recommended 8 drops of 10% povidone iodine per liter of water as a water treatment method, claiming that at low concentrations povidone iodine can be regarded as a solution of iodine. One study indicated that at a 1:10,000 dilution (2 drops/liter), there was 2 PPM iodine, while another study resulted in conflicting results. However, at 8 drops/liter, there is little doubt that there is an antimicrobial effect. The manufacturer hasn't spent the money on testing this product against EPA standard tests, but in other countries it has been sold for use in field water treatment.

Kahn-Vassher solution: By adding a sufficient amount of iodine crystals to a small bottle, an almost unlimited supply of saturated iodine solution can be produced. As long as crystals remain in the bottle, the solution is saturated. Concentration of the iodine is dependent of temperature, either condition at ambient temperature can be assumed, or commercial models such as Polar Pure incorporate a liquid crystal thermometer to determine dose. One criticism of this method is the chance of decanting iodine crystals into the water being treated. This isn't that much of a problem as iodine is very weakly toxic, but the Polar Pure incorporates a collar into the neck of the bottle to help prevent this. Another disadvantage to this method is that the saturated iodine solution must be kept in glass bottles, and is subject to freezing, but this is hardly an insurmountable problem. Freezing, of course, doesn't affect the crystals. Use the commercial Polar Pure bottle, and refill it as necessary with USP crystals.

During a crisis, or extended camping trips, microfilter the water first, so a much lower dose of iodine is needed. With the Polar Pure bottle, dosage information is provided. Otherwise a 1 oz bottle can be used to carry the solution. The bottle is filled with water after use. At the next use, 1/2 of the supernatant (15 cc) is poured off into a liter of water. At 68° F, this will yield a dose of 9 mg/l. To use this method with a microfilter to get a 0.5 PPM concentration, either large batches of water need to be treated (1/2 oz to 4.5 gallons would be 0.5 PPM), or a TB syringe or medicine dropper can be used to measure doses. A USP medicine dropper should give 20 drops per ml. Iodine can also be dissolved in alcohol to make a solution of known concentration. No commercial products re recommended, but a pharmacy could compound one for you, or you could do it yourself. One suggested formula is 8g iodine/100 cc ethyl alcohol which yields enough solution to disinfect 250 gallons of water. At the rate of 0.1 cc (2 drops)/liter to give a concentration of 8 mg/l. Tetraglycine hydroperiodide (e.g. Potable Aqua): This is the form of iodine used by the US military for field treatment of water in canteen sized batches. Usual dose in one tablet per quart of water to give a concentration of 8 mg/l. Two tablets are used in cloudy or cold water or contact time is doubled. The major downside of this product is that the product will lose its iodine rapidly when exposed to the air. According to the manufacturer, they have a near indefinite life when sealed in the original bottle, but probably should be discarded within a few months of opening. The tablets will change color from gun metal gray to brown as they lose the iodine, and you should see a brown tint to the water after treating.

Iodine Resin Filter: Some commercial microfilters incorporate an iodine resin stage to kill viruses and bacteria, without putting as much iodine in the water as if it had been added to the raw water. A few products rely exclusively on an iodine resin stage. The downside of these filters is their fragile nature, dependency of effectiveness on flow rate and the inability to identify when they need to be discarded. If you are going to use one where the water is known to be contaminated with viruses, then one of the better known brands such as the PUR or Sweetwater Viraguard is recommended. More than one pass through the filter may be necessary in cold weather.

Resins do have the advantage of producing less iodine in the water for the same antimicrobial effect as for the most part, they only release iodine when contacted by a microbe. The downside is that physical contact between the microbe and the resin is needed.

Silver: Silver has been suggested by some for water treatment and may still be available outside the US. Its use is currently out of favor due to the EPA's establishment of a 50 ppb MCL (Maximum Contaminate Level) limit on silver in drinking water. This limit is set to avoid *argyrosis*, a cosmetic blue/gray staining of the skin, eyes, and mucous membranes. As the disease requires a net accumulation of 1 g of silver in the body, one expert calculated that you could drink water treated at

50 ppb for 27 years before accumulating 1 g. Silver has only be proven to be effective against bacteria and protozoan cysts, though it is quite likely also effective against viruses.

Silver can be used in the form of a silver salt, commonly silver nitrate, a colloidal suspension, or a bed of metallic silver. Electrolysis can also be used to add metallic silver to a solution. Some evidence has suggested that silver deposited on carbon block filters can kill pathogens without adding as much silver to the water. Katadyn markets a silver based water treatment product called Micropur. The manufacturer recommends a 2 hr contact time at a dose of 1 tab per liter and states the product is "For the disinfection and storage of clear water. Reliably kills bacterial agents of enteric diseases, but not worm eggs, ameba, or viruses. Neutral to taste... insure protection against reinfection for 1-6 months."

Potassium Permanganate: Potassium Permanganate is no longer commonly used in the developed world to kill pathogens. It is weaker than the alternatives, more expensive, and leaves an objectionable pink or brown color. If it must be used, 1 gram per liter would probably be sufficient against bacteria and viruses (no data is available on its effectiveness against protozoan cysts.

Hydrogen Peroxide: Hydrogen Peroxide can be used to purify water if nothing else is available. Studies have shown of 99 percent inactivation of poliovirus in 6 hr with 0.3 percent hydrogen peroxide and a 99% inactivation of rhinovirus with a 1.5% solution in 24 minutes. Hydrogen Peroxide is more effective against bacteria, though Fe^{+2} or Cu^{+2} needs to be present as a catalyst to get a reasonable concentration-time product.

Coagulation/Flocculation agents: While flocculation doesn't kill pathogens, it will reduce their levels along with removing particles that could shield the pathogens from chemical or thermal destruction, and organic matter that could tie up chlorine added for purification. 60-98% of coliform bacteria, 65-99% of viruses, and 60-90% of giardia will be removed from the water, along with organic matter and heavy metals.

Some of the advantages of coagulation/flocculation can be obtained by allowing the particles to settle out of the water with time (sedimentation), but it will take a while for them to do so. Adding coagulation chemicals such as alum will increase the rate at which the suspended particles settle out by combining many smaller particles into larger floc which will settle out faster. The usual dose for alum is 10-30 mg/liter of water. This dose must be rapidly mixed with the water, then the water must be agitated for 5 minutes to encourage the particles to form flocs. After this at least 30 minutes of settling time is need for the flocs to fall to the bottom, and them the clear water above the flocs may be poured off.

Most of the flocculation agent is removed with the floc, nevertheless some question the safety of using alum due to the toxicity of the aluminum in it. There is little to no scientific evidence to back this up. Virtually all municipal plants in the US dose the water with alum. In bulk water treatment, the alum dose can be varied until the idea dose is found. The needed dose varies with the pH of the water and the size of the particles. Increase turbidity makes the flocs easier to produce not harder, due to the increased number of collisions between particles.

Treatments requiring electricity:

Ozone: Ozone is used extensively in Europe to purify water. Ozone, a molecule composed of 3 atoms of oxygen rather than two, is formed by exposing air or oxygen to a high voltage electric arc. Ozone is much more effective as a disinfectant than chlorine, but no residual levels of disinfectant exist after ozone turns back into O2. (one source quotes a half life of only 120 minutes in distilled water at 20° C). Ozone is expected to see increased use in the US as a way to avoid the production of trihalomethanes. While ozone does break down organic molecules, sometimes this can be a disadvantage as ozone treatment can produce higher levels of smaller molecules that provide an energy source for microorganisms. If no residual disinfectant is present (as would happen if ozone were used as the only treatment method), these microorganisms will cause the water quality to deteriorate in storage. Ozone also changes the surface charges of dissolved organics and colloidally suspended particles. This causes microflocculation of the dissolved organics and coagulation of the colloidal particles.

UV light: Ultraviolet light has been known to kill pathogens for a long time. A low pressure mercury bulb emits between 30 to 90 % of its energy at a wave length of 253.7 nm, right in the middle of the UV band. If water is exposed to enough light, pathogens will be killed. The problem is that some pathogens are hundreds of times less sensitive to UV light than others.

The least sensitive pathogens to UV are protozoan cysts. Several studies show that Giardia will not be destroyed by many commercial UV treatment units. Fortunately these are the easiest pathogens to filter out with a mechanical filter. The efficacy of UV treatment is very dependent on the turbidity of the water. The more opaque the water is, the less light will be transmitted through it. The treatment units must be run at the designed flow rate to insure sufficient exposure, as well as insure turbulent flow rather than plug flow. Another problem with UV treatment is that the damage done to the pathogens with UV light can be reversed if the water is exposed to visible light (specifically 330-500 nm) through a process known as photoreactivation. UV treatment, like ozone or mechanical filtering leaves no residual component in the water to insure its continued disinfection.

Any purchased UV filter should be checked to insure it at least complies with the 1966 HEW standard of 16 mW.s/cm^2 with a maximum water depth of 7.5 cm. ANSI/NSF require 38 mWs/cm^2 for primary water treatment systems. This level was chosen to give better than 3 log (99.9%) inactivation of Bacillus subtillis. This level is of little use against Giardia, and of no use against Crypto. The US EPA explored UV light for small scale water treatment plants and found it compared unfavorably with chlorine due to 1) higher costs, 2) lower reliability, and 3) lack of a residual disinfectant.

Home Made Berkey Water Filter

What if your home does not afford us much space for water storage? A contingency water plan might include stormwater holding ponds near your home. However, standing water supplied by runoff from parking lots or other questionable sources will need filtering to remove the variety of contaminants present in the water. The best option for this situation is the proven Berkey water filter. Berkey filters are gravity filters that use cleanable micro-permeable ceramic filter elements. These filters are extremely effective, long-lasting and require no electricity. The only drawback is that they are expensive, and you can save about $175-200 or more by making your own.

You can construct a filter equivalent in performance to the Imperial Berkey that sells for about $300 with a total cost around $122. You will need the following:

- two 5-gallon food grade buckets (from Lowes for $5 each)
- two lids for the buckets (Lowes for $1.50 each)
- a pair of Black Berkey filter elements (ordered on EBay for $99 which included free shipping and a free Sport Berkey filtered bottle)
- a food grade spigot (the kind used for large coffee pots or water coolers is perfect. Try www.jamesfilter.com for $10)

Drill two 1/2" holes in the bottom of the upper bucket and two matching holes in the lid of the lower bucket.

Drill a 3/4" hole in the side of the lower bucket toward the bottom. Make sure that the hole is up just far enough for the spigot to clear when the filter is sitting on a flat surface Assemble the lower bucket by installing the spigot and the lid with holes. Install the filter elements in the upper bucket through the holes in the bottom.

Assemble the filter by placing the upper bucket on the lower. Be sure to line up the holes so the tubes extend through the lid of the lower bucket. Place the remaining lid on top. To use the filter, fill the upper bucket with water and wait. If you are starting with dry elements, it will take quite a while before the water starts dripping into the lower bucket. It takes up to several hours for the clean water to drain into the lower bucket. This process can be sped up considerably by frequently topping off the water in the upper bucket. This maintains maximum pressure on the elements.

Notes:

- The specifications of the Black Berkey elements can be found here: http://berkeywater.com/BerkeyLight/BB_Purification_Elements.html
- There are a number of ways to make this even cheaper: Use free buckets from a grocery store bakery or restaurant. Super Sterasyl elements can be substituted for the Black Berkey elements.
- The filter can be made considerably larger by using any two stacking containers suitable for water, trash cans or 30-gallon water barrels for instance. The flow rate can also be increased by adding more filter elements.
- The filtered solids remain on the outside of the filter elements and will eventually interfere with the rate of flow. Therefore, it is important to prefilter through a dense cloth if your source water is particularly cloudy. The elements can be scrubbed clean with a plastic scouring pad. The Black Berkey elements last for about 3000 gallons each (6000 gallons for the pair).

XIII Emergency Sanitation

Care and Use of Water Supplies

The first priority is always to safeguard your water. If you are asked to shut off the service valve that controls the water supply to your home, or if the taps do not flow following a disaster, turn off all the water outlets. These include taps or faucets, valves on pipes supplying float controlled equipment such as flush toilets, air cooling equipment, and heating equipment. Then when the water comes on again your home will not be flooded as these flotation devices sometimes stick after they have been allowed to dry out.

Turn off the gas or electricity that supplies your hot-water heater after closing your home water service valve, or when your water supply is interrupted for any other reason. Otherwise, if the limited supply of water remaining in your hot-water storage tank continues to be heated, an explosion may occur. Also, if no more water can reach the tank, continued heat will soon muddy its contents through oxidation and make the water useless for washing or drinking purposes.

If your water service is cut off following terrorist attack or other natural disaster, do not try to telephone or otherwise communicate with your local water department or water company. Once service is restored, the water from your faucets may have a strong chlorine taste. Don't worry, this is a sign that extra precautions are being taken for your safety.

Safeguarding Food

It is especially important to be sanitary in the storing, handling, and eating of food to avoid digestive upsets or other more serious illnesses. Be sure to:

- Keep all food in covered containers.
- Keep cooking and eating utensils clean. Diarrhea may result from dish soap that is not thoroughly rinsed from dishes.
- Keep all garbage in a closed container or dispose of it outside the home when it is safe to go out. If possible, bury it. Avoid letting garbage or trash accumulate inside the shelter, both for fire and sanitation reasons.
- Wash hands and utensils frequently.
- Prepare only as much food as will be eaten at each meal.
- Paper cups and plates, paper towels and napkins are helpful if the water supply is cut off.
- Refrigerators and home freezer units should be kept closed as much as possible once the services they depend on are cut off. The food they contain will keep loner if you plan your meals well in advance so that you won't have to open the doors any more than necessary. If the gas or electric service is not restored within 12 hours, eat or cook the most perishable items in your refrigerator before they spoil. If foods show signs of decomposition, discard them before they contaminate other foods that keep better.
- Food will keep in home freezer units after they are shut off for varying periods depending on the amount and kind of food, the temperature at which it was kept, and the construction of

the freezer. Frozen meats and other frozen foods can be preserved for later use by cooking them soon after they have thawed or by quick refreezing before they have completely thawed.

Official instructions regarding food will be issued locally in the event of an emergency. These instructions will tell you the type of disaster and its effect upon milk and other foods. Follow official instructions closely. Don't listen to rumors, and don't pass them on to others.

Laundry and Cleaning Supplies

During times of emergency it is critical that sanitation be strictly observed in the cleaning of clothing, bedding materials, and all kitchen and food preparation utensils. Chemical supplies fall into a few groups: soaps for washing and laundry and disinfectants. Some useful agents to stock include the following:

Supply	Use	Notes
Clorox Bleach	Disinfects water	Degrades after 6 months
Ammonia	Strong antiseptic	Household ammonia is a solution of NH_3 in water, it breaks up grime.
Purell	**PURELL(r)** is an alcohol-based instant hand sanitizer which kills "99.99%" of most common germs that may cause illness in as little as 15 seconds. Its active ingredient is ethanol.	Transmission of disease can but reduced significantly by washing hands.
Vinegar	White vinegar is often used as a household cleaning agent. Because it is acidic, it can dissolve mineral deposits from glass, coffee makers, and other smooth surfaces.	For most uses dilution with water is recommended for safety and to avoid damaging the surfaces being cleaned. vinegar (5% acetic acid) showed the strongest bactericidal activity against all strains tested, which was attributed to its high acetic acid content
Baking Soda, Bread Soda	Sodium Bicarbonate A paste made from sodium bicarbonate and a 3% hydrogen peroxide solution can be used as an alternative to commercial non-fluoride toothpastes, and sodium bicarbonate in combination with other ingredients can be used to make a dry or wet deodorant.	Sodium bicarbonate is primarily used in baking where it reacts with other components to release carbon dioxide, which helps dough rise.
Calcium Hypochlorite	Disinfects water – usually pools	Can kill beneficial intestinal bacteria.

		Use as last resort.
Detergent	In most household contexts, the term *detergent* by itself refers specifically to *laundry detergent* or *dish detergent*, vs *hand soap* or other types of cleaning agents. Most detergent is delivered in powdered form.	Most commonly, "detergent" refers to mixtures of chemical compounds including alkylbenzenesulfonates, which are similar to soap but are less affected by "hard water."

Sanitize vs. Disinfect:

- **Sanitizers** kill 99.999 percent of bacteria within 30 seconds. e.g. purell, germ-X hand sanitizers. 63% Ethyl Alcohol.
- **Disinfectants** kill even more bacteria than sanitizers do, but not necessarily within 30 seconds. e.g. Bleach, LYSOL® Disinfectant Spray, Clorox Disinfecting Kitchen Cleaner

Household ammonia (3 to 10 percent aqueous NH_3) and bleach (5 percent NaClO) are two of the most common cleaning agents. Combining them releases chloramine gas.

$$NH_4OH + NaOCl \rightarrow NaOH + NH_2Cl + H_2O$$

When inhaled, chloramines react with the moisture of the respiratory tract to release ammonia (NH_3), hydrochloric acid (HCl), and oxygen free radicals. Typically, exposures to low concentrations of chloramines produce only mild respiratory tract irritation. Bleach can react violently with hydrogen peroxide and produce oxygen gas.

EMERGENCY TOILETS & GARBAGE DISPOSAL

What will you do if your toilet stops flushing and you can't get anyone to take your garbage away? If an emergency causes your toilets or garbage service to stop working you MUST find a way to safely dispose of the human waste (sewage) and garbage yourself. **If you don't, you will soon be spending most of your time and energy treating sick people, including *yourself*.**

The three most important things to do are:

1. Bury or store all garbage and human waste at least 100 feet away from water wells or open water.

2. Keep flies, roaches and animals out of the sewage and garbage;

3. Wash or clean your hands whenever you handle something dirty and BEFORE you handle anything that you will be putting into your mouth or someone else's mouth.

TOILETS

#1 - If the toilet bowl and seat in your home are still usable (not wrecked) scrub the bowl clean using one part of laundry bleach to ten parts of water (10:1). When clean, drain the bowl and dry it.

Line the bowl with a plastic or paper bag. Line the inside of the first bag with a sturdy plastic bag and lay the toilet seat on it to keep it open. Use the toilet as you normally do. After every use, sprinkle the waste with the bleach/water solution mentioned above or cover it with a layer of sawdust, wood shavings, lime, dry dirt, grass clippings, etc. Limiting the liquids that go into the bowl will make it easier to change the bags. When the bag is full or you can't stand the smell anymore, carefully tie the top of the bag tightly closed, remove it and replace with another bag. Dispose of the waste using the instructions below. Other chemicals can be used in place of liquid chlorine bleach:

HTH (calcium hypochlorite), which is available at swimming pool supply stores and is intended to be used in solution. Following the directions on the package it can be mixed and stored.

Caution: *Do not use calcium hypochlorite to disinfect drinking water as it kills all the beneficial bacteria in the intestinal tract and thus causes mild diarrhea. Portable toilet chemicals, both liquid and dry, are available at recreational vehicle (RV) supply stores. These chemicals are designed especially for toilets which are not connected to sewer lines. Use according to package directions. Powdered, chlorinated lime is available at building supply stores. It can be used dry. Be sure to get chlorinated lime, not quick lime which is highly alkaline and corrosive.*

Caution: *Chlorinated products which are intended to be mixed with water for use can be dangerous if used dry. You may also use powdered laundry detergent, Lysol, Pinesol, ammonia, or other household cleaning and disinfecting products*

#2 - If your toilet bowl is not usable, use a five gallon bucket, wooden box or some other container sturdy enough to sit on. Sit the seat from your toilet on the bucket or make one from layers of heavy cardboard glued together, two boards laid across the top with a gap between them or cut a seat from plywood. Line with bags as outlined in #1 above. Dispose of the full bags using the instructions below.

#3 - If the emergency will only last for a day or two, you can use "cat holes" outside. These are small, onetime personal use holes you dig in the ground and squat over. The hole should be deep enough to cover your waste at least six inches deep when filled. Do not do this any closer than 100 feet from open water or water wells or the germs in the sewage will get into the water.

#4 – If the emergency will last more than a week and your toilet or bucket commode no longer will do the job you need to make a latrine. Use a shovel or posthole diggers to dig a pit four to six feet deep and about one foot wide. Place a bucket, box, barrel or anything with a hole in it that you can sit on over the pit. Whatever you use must cover the pit tightly so that flies cannot get in while no one is using it. The seat and box must be cleaned regularly with the bleach water solution mentioned above and kept tightly covered when not in use. When the pit fills to within eighteen inches of the top, fill the hole in with clean dirt and mound it over. Cover the mound to keep animals from digging it up.

DISPOSING OF WASTES: All wastes must be buried **no closer than 100 feet** from the nearest open water or water well or the germs will get into the water. Buried wastes must be covered with at least eighteen inches of dirt and protected from animals digging it up.

GARBAGE is trash that has food or anything else in it that would make attract insects, rats and other animals. It should not be allowed to accumulate where these pests can get into it. If garbage service is expected to resume in a few days then dry garbage should be tightly sealed in bags or kept in tightly covered garbage çans. Liquid wastes that don't have a lot of fat in them can be poured out outside if kept more than 100 feet away from open bodies of water and water wells. Liquids that do have a lot of fat should be buried to prevent attracting flies and roaches.

If garbage service is out for more several weeks and you are unable to store it, then it should be buried. Garbage should be buried no closer than 100 feet from open water or water wells. Crush containers to make them smaller. Garbage must be covered by at least eighteen inches of dirt. If burial is not possible then it will have to be burned. To burn garbage you must use a metal barrel with holes in the bottom and a grate or screen over the top to act as a spark arrester to prevent wildfires. Only dry garbage should be burned. Wet garbage should be buried.

If you have a baby in your home, it is best to keep an ample supply of disposable diapers on hand for emergency use. If these are not available, emergency diaper needs can be met by lining rubber pants with cleansing tissue, toilet paper, scraps of cloth, or other absorbent materials. To help insure proper sanitation it is imperative that you store a sufficient supply of disposable diapers, disposable wipes, and plastic garbage can liners. Change infants and toddlers regularly and keep them clean. Dispose of the soiled diapers in the plastic garbage can liners and keep them tightly sealed when not in use to help prevent the spread of disease. Be sure to wash your own hands regularly when working with infants (especially after each diaper change). Typhoid fever, amoebic dysentery, diarrhea, infectious hepatitis, salmonella and giardiasis are diseases that spread rapidly in times of emergency and threaten all, yet are all diseases that can easily be controlled by simply following the rules of good sanitation.

Disposal of Garbage and Rubbish

Garbage may sour or decompose. Rubbish (trash) will not, but offers disposal problems in an emergency. Garbage should be drained before being placed in storage containers. If liquids are strained away, garbage may be stored for a longer period of time without developing an unpleasant odor. After straining, wrap the garbage in several thicknesses of old newspapers before putting it into your container. This will absorb any remaining moisture. A tight-fitting lid is important to keep out flies and other insects. Final disposal of all stored garbage and refuse can be accomplished in the following manner, provided there is no danger from radioactive fallout:

1. All stored garbage should be buried if collection service is not restored and if unpaved yard areas are available—keep a shovel handy for this purpose. Dig a hole deep enough to cover it with at least 18-24 inches of dirt, which will prevent insect breeding and discourage animals from digging it up.

2. Other rubbish may be burned in open yard areas (if permission is granted by authorities under existing conditions) or left at dumps established by local authorities. Cans should be flattened to reduce their bulk. Do not deposit ashes or rubbish in streets or alley ways without permission. Such material may interfere with the movement and operation of firefighting and other emergency equipment.

XIV Store Food or Starve

A guide to food storage

People need to store food not only for their sake, but for everyone else as well. Who wants to decide which of their kids have to go hungry when their friends and unprepared kin come knocking on your door. Every individual who takes care of themselves and their families benefits society by not becoming a burden. Don't expect the Feds to come by to hand you your ration of government issued cheese. You could be in for a long wait. Wait too long, and you may end up with a greenstained mouth from eating grass, like the poor Irish during the potato famine in the mid 1800's. Or seriously reevaluate your aversion to cannibalism. Compared to those desperate methods, dumpster diving comes off as luxury cuisine.

The points you want to look for your storage food are, in order of importance:

1 No need for refrigeration.
2 High nutritious value per volume
3 Long shelf life, between 1-5 years.
4 That they don't need water
5 That they don't need cooking

This will usually take you to canned meats, canned tuna, canned vegetables, dried pasta, dehydrated soups, chocolate, milk powder, marmalades, soups, rice and dried beans. Canned food is excellent when it comes to long shelf life. Most of the time they are already hydrated, so they don't need water, and you can eat them out of the can. Just watch out not to dent the can, if this happens air may get inside and ruin it. If you have a dent or bump in a can, consume it fast. Also remember that once the can is opened, you have to remove the food from the can.

Avoid Refrigerators Become independent from the refrigerator, because continuous power supply isn't guaranteed. However, freeze as much as many perishables as you can, because it lasts longer, practically indefinitely, and because if the lights go out a large mass of frozen food will last for hours, even a day or two. The more mass of food you have frozen the longer it will hold. The survivalist, especially the urban one, should try to rely as little as possible on the refrigerator. Canned food and freeze dried food is your best friend.

Anyone who has been a while without fresh fruit knows that after some time your health starts to suffer. That's why you should try to have some fresh food to supplement you storage food. Not much, just 2 or 3 fruit trees in your garden and a small orchard would help. You don't have to feed out of this, you just need a little fresh vegetables or fruit every once in a while.

A favorite canned food is tuna. It lasts forever, it's full of proteins, and no matter how often you eat it, it always tastes good. Besides you can combine it with frozen vegetables or rice. Canned fruits and vegetables are also good, but they have much less vitamins than the fresh ones, and you lose most of it unless you drink the liquid they come in. Dried pasta may need a lot of water to cook, but it's one of the best ways to store carbs in convenient to use form. Flour or wheat can also be stored in large quantities and is nutritious, but requires more preparation to consume.

Minimum Food Needs

An adult needs a minimum 2,500 calories a day. More if you are physically active. This translates to about two pounds of food, plus a gallon of potable ("drinkable") water. To get started, follow this cardinal rule; Store what you eat, and eat what you store. Do not expect to suddenly acquire a taste for powered eggs or a jalapeno-spiced chili MRE in a long-term disaster. If you have children, they will be even more reluctant to eat such stuff. The next rule is not go into debt by spending thousands of dollars for pre-packaged foodstuffs. It defeats the purpose if you have to eat your food supply because you have no money left after buying it.

Begin building your food storage by buying 2–3 extra items every time you shop at the grocery store. A few cans here, some bags and boxes there, and it will begin to add up. Look for sales, two-for-one specials, and coupon items. Set aside some space, and put the oldest stuff in front, and the newest in back. Rotate from back to front as you use it. If you have food items that are going to expire soon that you don't have time to eat, donate them to a local food pantry for Karma points. There. You now have established a simple but effective short term food storage system. Everything from here on will expand upon it.

The next step is to create a larger, stable environment to preserve your food supply over the long haul. Regardless if you live in a country mansion or a studio apartment, you need the following conditions to preserve food:

- Keep it airtight
- Keep it cool
- Keep it dark
- Keep it dry
- Keep it protected

Food Storage

Given current uncertainties, a one-year minimum emergency food supply does not seem excessive. When the emergency is upon us, the time of preparation has passed." You can do a lot if you start early. Unfortunately, "early" might have been yesterday. Now you need a reasonable plan to get food supplies that will store well and don't cost too much. You've probably already realized that buying up extra cans of soup at the grocery store is a really stupid way to spend your preparedness money. You need a better plan. Every $10 you spend at the store might feed a person for a few days. You need more leverage, where you can spend $10 and feed a person for a few weeks.

Our food supply is more fragile than people think. Grocery stores don't stock weeks of food anymore. Most keep only 72 hours of food on the shelves, -stocked based on just-in-time delivery of food supplies. If the trucks stop rolling during a crisis, the store shelves will be emptied almost immediately. In fact, expect a shortage of mainstay items like milk and bread to occur similar to what happens before an approaching hurricane hits. Those who are aware of the problem, but who haven't already made preparations, will engage in a last-minute rush to buy a few extra supplies.

Without transportation, farmers can't get their crops to the wholesalers or food processing facilities. Food is heavy, generally speaking, and it requires trucks and trains to move it around — a literal ARMY of trucks and trains, weaving their way from city to city, optimized and prioritized by computers. If the computers freeze, the whole transportation infrastructure will shut down. Transportation also depends heavily on fuel, which means the oil-producing countries in the Middle East have to be able to produce the oil that gets refined into diesel fuel here in America. So, in other words, your food supply depends on Saudi Arabia being alive and well. Do you trust the people in charge in Saudi Arabia, Iraq, Iran, and Kuwait with your life? If you don't make preparations now, you're trusting them by default.

In short, you need to be prepared.

Buy extra, use FIFO

Start now by buying more food than normal when you're out shopping, and set it aside. Use the "first in, first out" rule to eat your older supplies first. Keep rotating your supplies so you never abandon food "way in the back."

Buy ingredients, not prepared foods

Ingredients such as salt, honey, oatmeal and wheat will last a lot longer than prepared foods like TV dinners, cereals, and food mixes. Naturally, as you purchase food ingredients, you'll want to practice actually using them! And remember the basics. For example, if you purchase a bag of wheat, how exactly do you plan to make flour out of it? Plans in a survival book describe throwing some wheat in a coffee can and pounding it into flour with a blunt stick. But do you want to make just a few cups of flour after ten of fifteen minutes of noisemaking?

Once you pick reasonable foodstuffs, you still need proper storage. Dry food packed in paper, cardboard boxes, or plastic are subject to oxygen spoilage over time. One solution is to repackage dry food items using food grade Mylar bags. These bags are an inexpensive method for those on a budget to customize their food storage to their personal needs and taste. Mylar is an excellent air and moisture barrier. It is said one can jump on a filled sealed bag and it won't pop. But they need protection against punctures and gnawing vermin—hence they need to be stored in a protective container.

The recommended base foods for long-term storage are wheat, oats, legumes, pasta, honey/sugar, and salt. These will easily last 20-30 years if packed and stored properly. Flour and dry milk are more finicky, and have a shelf life of only 5–10 years. If you or members of your family suffer from Celiac disease, and cannot consume gluten type foods such as wheat, substitute white rice instead. Avoid brown rice for long-term storage, as it contains oils that break down over time that causes it to spoil. Supplement your long term food with canned goods, MRE's and others sundries. The eventual goal is to build a diverse storage of food for health, variety, and if necessary, portability.

BARE-MINIMUM-Food Storage Requirements

Food storage requirements for 1 adult male for 1 year Approximately 2,300 calories per day. (695lbs total) *This will keep you fed, but leave you hungry.*

TOTAL FOOD PER DAY = 24.65 Ounces

Grains (400lbs)

Unless your family already eats 100% whole wheat homemade bread, white flour should be used in the transition process to whole wheat. Adding rye flour (10%) helps make wheat bread a more complete protein. Dent corn is used to make tortillas.

Beans & Legumes (90lbs)

Black beans cook quickly, make a good salad complement with a vinaigrette dressing over them. Soybeans can be used to make soy milk and tofu, a protein food you should be prepared to make. Familiarize yourself with sprouting techniques. Learn how to make wheat grass juice - the best vitamin supplement you can use.

Milk-Dairy products (75lbs)

Milk powder can be used to make cottage cheese, cream cheese and hard cheeses. Ideally your milk should be fortified with Vitamins A & D. When reconstituting aerate to improve flavor (special mixing pitchers can accomplish this). Whole eggs are the best all-purpose egg product. Powdered sour cream has a limited shelf life unless frozen.

Meats / Meat substitute (20lbs)

Use meat in soups, stews and beans for flavor. Freeze dried is the best option for real meat. Textured Vegetable protein is the main alternative to freeze dried meats.

Fats / Oils (20lbs)

This group can boost the calories one is getting from food storage products, and supply essential fatty acids.

Sugars (60lbs)

Store your honey in 5 gallon pails. Candy and other sweets can help with appetite fatigue.

Fruits / Vegetables (90lbs)

Some fruits and vegetables are best dehydrated, others freeze dried (strawberries & blueberries). Fruits are a nice addition to hot cereal, muffins, pancakes and breads.

Auxiliary foods (weight varies)

Vanilla extract improves the flavor of powdered milk. The production of tofu requires a precipitator such as nigari, epsom salt, calcium chloride or calcium sulfide (good calcium source). Learn how to make and use wheat gluten (liquid smoke adds good flavor). Chocolate syrup and powdered drink mixes help with appetite fatigue. Vitamins and protein powders will boost the nutrition levels of foods that may have suffered losses during processing.

Note:

- For an average adult Female - multiply the weight by 0.75
- For children ages 1-3 multiply by 0.3, 4-6 multiply by 0.5, 7-9 multiply by 0.75
- For adults engaged in manual labor multiply by 1.25-1.50

Do you REALLY have a year's supply?

Just how big is a Year's Supply of food? Here are some rule of thumb minimums for each adult:

- **400 lbs**. Grains (17.5oz / day)
- **60 lbs**. Beans (2.6oz / day)
- **10 quarts** Cooking oil (0.87oz / day)
- **60 lbs**. Honey (2.63oz / day)
- **8 lbs**. Salt (0.35oz / day)
- **16 lbs** Powdered milk (0.70oz / day)
- **14 gallons** of drinking water (for 2 weeks)

So, just how much is this? Two 5 gallon buckets will hold about 75lbs of wheat, rice or other grains. This means you need *11 buckets of grain* for each person in your family. If you store all your grains in #10 cans...

- **Wheat, Rice, Corn, etc..** You would need 64 cans or 10.5 cases per person.
- **Pasta** You would need 32 cans or 5.25 cases per person.
- **Rolled oats** These are lighter but bulkier, so they require more storage containers and space. You would need 124 cans or 21 cases person.
- **Beans** A 25 lb bag of beans will about fit in a single 5 gallon bucket, with a little space over, so 2 buckets would hold a one person supply, or 12 -13 # 10 cans or about 2 cases.

Daily Food

Dividing 400lbs by 365days, equals out to 1.09589lbs, or just over 1 lb of grain, per person, per day. That is approximately 2 cups of unground grain to cover your breakfast lunch and dinner.

Dividing 60lbs by 365, this works out to 0.16 lbs of beans per day, or 2.6 oz—approximately ¾ cup. The other foods listed would also need to be used in limited amounts.

This is not much food. Get the basics, then immediately begin to add more kinds of grain, soup mix, canned and/or dehydrated vegetables and fruit, etc to add variety and provide more than the minimal survival diet. As an example, the minimum recommended amount of grain, when ground and prepared will yield about 6 small biscuits or a plateful of pancakes. It's enough to keep you alive, but a far cry from being satisfied and not hungry.

One Year Food Supply

GRAINS
(400 lbs per adult)
Barley
Cereal
Corn (meal or Dent)
Cous Cous
Flour (4lb/can)
Millet
Multi grain soup mix(5lb/can)
Oats, rolled quick(3lb/can)
Oats, rolled regular(3lb/can)
Popcorn
Rye
Sprouting Seeds
Wheat(6lb/can)
White Rice(6lb/can)

_____

PASTAS
Macaroni(3lb/can)
Noodles
Spaghetti(4lb/can)

_____

MILK / DAIRY
(75 lbs per adult)
Brick cheese
Canned Milk
Canned sour cream
Cheese spreads
Condensed milk
Dried cheese
Dried eggs
Infant formula
Non-dairy creamer
Non-fat dry milk(4lb/can)
Powdered cheese
Powdered sour cream

_____

JUICES/BEVERAGES
(25 lbs per adult)
Apple juice
Apricot nectar
Baby strained juices
Cocoa drink mix(4lb/can)
Cranberry juice
Dried juice mix(6lb/can)
Grapefruit juice
Grape juice
Kool-aid
Lemonaid
Orange juice
Pineapple juice
Plum juice
Prune juice
Punch crystals
Soft drink mixes
Soft drinks
Tomato juice
V-8 juice

_____

FATS / OILS
(20 lbs per adult)
Butter
Cooking oil
Lard
Margarine
Mayonnaise
Olive Oil (extra virgin)
Peanut butter
Powdered butter
Powdered margarine
Powdered shortening
Salad dressing
Shortening
Bacon
Beef
Beef jerky

Chicken
Clams
Corned beef
Crabmeat
Deviled meats
Fish
Ham
Hamburger
Lamb
Lunch meats
Mutton
Pepperoni
Pork
Tuna
Salmon
Sandwich spreads
Sardines
Sausage
Shrimp
Spam
Treet
Turkey
TVP- Textured vegi Protein
Veal
Venison jerky
Vienna sausage

_____

AUXILIARY FOODS
Baking powder
Baking soda
Cake mixes
Calcium supplement
Casserole mixes
Chow mein noodles
Cookies
Cookie mixes
Cornstarch
Crackers

Cream of tartar
Hot roll mixes
Hydrated lime (for tortillas)
Instant breakfast
Instant yeast
Iron supplement
Marshmallows
MREs
Muffin mixes
Non perishable pet foods
Pancake mixes
Pastry mixes
Pectin
Pie crust mixes
Pie fillings
Pizza mixes
Plain gelatin
Rennin tablets
Salt
Sourdough starter
Survival bars
Tofu Solidifier
Vitamins and minerals
Whipped topping mixes

_____

FRESH FRUITS
90 lbs Dried, 370qts canned, 370Lbs
Apples (2lb/can)
Applesauce
Apricots
Peaches
Berries
Cherries
Coconut
Currants
Figs
Fruit cocktail
Grapefruit
Grapes
Mandarin oranges
Nectarines

Olives
Pears
Peaches
Pineapples
Plums
Prunes
Raisins
Tomatoes

_____

BEANS & LEGUMES
(90 lbs per adult)
Beans, pink(5lb/can)
Beans, pinto(5lb/can)
Beans, white(5lb/can)
Lentils
Nuts
Peas
Sprouting beans and seeds
Soybeans
Vegetables
Artichoke hearts
Asparagus
Beans
Beets
Broccoli
Brussels sprouts
Carrots (3lb/can)
Cauliflower
Celery
Corn-sweet
Green beans
Hominy
Mushrooms
Okra
Onions (2lb/can)
Parsnips
Peas
Peppers
Pickles
Potatoes, flakes (1.5lb/can)
Potatoes, pearls (3lb/can)
Pumpkins
Rhubarb

Rutabagas
Salsify
Sauerkraut
Soups
Spinach
Squash
Sweet potatoes (yams)
Tomatoes
Tomato powder
Turnips
Water chestnuts

_____

SPICES / CONDIMENTS
Almond extract
Allspice
Baking chocolate
Basil
BBQ sauce
Bouillon cubes / granules
Beef, chicken, onion, vegetable flavors
Cayenne pepper
Celery salt
Chili powder
Chives
Chocolate chips
Chocolate syrup
Cinnamon
Cloves
Cocoa
Coriander
Cumin
Curry
Dill weed
Garlic salt
Ginger
Gravy mixes
Herbs
Ketchup
Lemon extract
Lemon / lime juice
Liquid smoke

Marjoram	Salt (**5 lbs per adult**)	**SUGARS**
Maple extract	Sauce mixes	**(60 lbs per adult)**
Nutmeg	Seasoned salt	Corn syrup
Onion flakes	Spaghetti sauce	Hard candy
Onion salt	Soy sauce	Honey
Orange peel	Steak sauce	Jello
Oregano	Tarragon	Jelly or jam
Paprika	Thyme	Maple syrup
Pepper	Turmeric	Molasses
Poultry Seasoning	Vanilla extract	*Pudding, chocolate (5lb/can)*
protein supplement	Vinegar	*Pudding, vanilla (5lb/can)*
Sage	Worcestershire sauce	*Sugar (6lb/can)*
Salad dressings		

Monthly Food Storage Purchasing Calendar

We have tried to keep the costs down to between $25 and $35 per week. This might seem rather costly, but if you want to build a good food storage system in only one year, it will cost you more each week than if you spread out acquiring it over several years. Be certain to buy only items your family will use, and rotate and use the items in your storage throughout the year. Milk is an expensive item and prices keep soaring, so you might need to invest in a bit higher food storage bill to buy it right now.

The items in the first few months are basic essentials and are the most important to purchase and store.

It is vital to get *WATER - STORAGE* . If you don't have water, you will not be able to use many of the foods you have that are dehydrated or require water to cook. Many times in natural disasters, the electricity goes down and you will not be able to access your water. Sometimes the water is contaminated from flooding and cross-contamination from sewage. You will need water, at very least, you will need 3 days worth.

January
> **Week #1**
>> 1 case canned fruit
>> 2 #10 cans instant potatoes
> **Week #2**
>> 3 #10 cans dry milk
> **Week #3**
>> 3 #10 cans dry milk
> **Week #4**
>> 9 pounds yeast

Week #5

   Anything you have missed from above

February
Week #1

Water Storage Containers-buy either 55 gallon drums, 5 gallon water containers (available at all emergency preparedness stores and some super markets) and spigot, or start to save water in pop bottles and plastic juice containers. Also purchase 100 lbs. hard white wheat and three plastic storage buckets with tight fitting lids. Check out the local mills in your area for best prices.

Week #2 25 lbs of **sugar** or 20 lbs of **honey**

   5 lbs **salt** per person

   bucket opener

Week #3

   4 #10 cans **shortening** or 4 - 48 oz bottles **oil**

   2 #10 cans of **dry instant milk**

Week #4

   2 case **canned beans** (like refried pinto, black, kidney, white, pink etc.) or

   25 lbs **dry beans** (preferable) and bucket to store them in.

   50 lbs dried **corn or popcorn** (about $10.00 from a mill or food storage company)

      bucket to store it in. (Can be ground into cornmeal as well as for popcorn.)

March

(please note that many of these items are repeats because we want to be SURE you have enough of the essentials!)

Week #1 Enough **water** containers for 14 gallons per person in the family.

(This was mentioned last month-but we want to be sure you have this)

(Water is your most important item!)

If you didn't get enough containers last month, you can get them this month.

White Rice, at least 15 pounds per person in the family and if possible buckets to store it.

(Brown Rice goes rancid faster.)

Week #2

   2 jars **mayonnaise**

   1 gallon **oil**

   2 tubs **shortening**

Week #3

   25 pounds **sugar**

   1- 25 pound bag of **legumes** (pinto, lentils, white, pink etc.)

Week #4 Salt 5 more lbs

   2 bottles of **bleach**

   1 #10 can or 1 box of **dry milk.**

Week #5 Check your list for the last 8 weeks and purchase any items you fell short on.

These items are essential ones and you will need to be sure you have enough.

April
>   **Week #1**
>   >   100 pounds **wheat**
>   >   10 lbs. **brown sugar**
>
>   **Week #2** 2 #10 size cans **dried fruit** or 1 case **canned fruit**
>   >   1 pound **yeast**
>
>   **Week #3**
>   >   1 case **tuna or salmon**
>   >   2 #10 **cans milk**
>   >   3 lbs **sprouting seeds**
>   >   1 80 oz can Rumsford baking powder
>
>   **Week #4** 2 large jars **peanut butter** or
>   >   1 #10 can **peanut butter powder** (last longer)
>   >   2 cans **dried whole egg** (keep in a cool dry place)

May
>   **Week #1**
>   >   2 to 3 bottles of **multi-vitamins**
>   >   2 #10 cans of **rolled oats**
>
>   (if #10 cans are not available in your area, buy the largest packages available)
>   (in your local store, and also purchase a small bucket to store it in.)
>
>   **Week #2**
>   >   100 lbs. of **wheat**
>   >   3 buckets
>
>   **Week #3**
>   >   #10 can **margarine powder -** or shortening if marg. powder is unavailable
>   >   2 #10 cans **rolled oats**
>
>   (or equivalent, and a storage bucket)
>
>   **Week #4** 4 #10 cans **instant potatoes**
>   >   1 bottle **black pepper**

June
>   **Week #1**
>   >   2 cans dry milk, 2 boxes of Rennet
>
>   (used for making cottage cheese and other dairy products from dry milk.)
>   >   1 bottle lemon juice,
>   >   1 bottle vinegar. (also used in making dairy products from dry milk
>
>   **Week #2** 100 lbs wheat
>   >   25 lbs. white flour

Week #3 Baking soda (try bulk in places like Sam's Club or Cosco) Buy about 10 lbs.

25 lbs. or legumes (choose those you are willing to eat.

Remember you can sprout legumes and almost quadruple the nutritional value of them.

Buy one large box Knox or other gelatin to be used in place of eggs in baking.

Week #4 Tomato products (try to buy them by the case in normal size cans. Spaghetti sauce, Tomato sauce, and whole and chopped tomatoes. Buy a combination of flavored and not flavored tomatoes. Buy paste if you can get a good deal on it. It is less expensive to add water to paste to make

Sauce than it is just to buy sauce sometimes. *Buy three cases if possible*.)

Week #5 Be on the look-out for garden seeds that are NON- Hybrid. That way you can use the seeds from the plants you grow to grow a garden the next season. A good price for them is about $18-20 per can with about 10 varieties per can.

July

Week #1

200# wheat

(buckets to store it in if needed)

[keep filling pop bottles, Gallon syrup containers, etc. with water - basically no cost to this)

Week #2

20 lbs. Peanut butter

[keep filling those water containers]

Week #3

4 #10 cans shortening

2 # 10 cans dry milk

[keep filling water containers - make this a habit - when you empty something worthy of water storage, wash it and fill it right away]

Week #4 6 #10 cans dry milk [more water!]

August

Week #1

25# rice

25# sugar

1 # 10 can instant potatoes

5 lbs. salt

Week #2

1 case tuna or salmon or other meat

2 # 10 cans dry milk

Week #3

2 #10 cans dry milk

2 cans shortening

1 #10 can instant potatoes

Week #4 Note* In late August and early September, many stores have sales on canned fruits and vegetables. Ask your local store when these sales will be, and switch the weeks of this calendar as needed.

> 2 cases fruit
> 5 lbs. salt

Week #5

> 2 cases canned fruit
> 1 case misc. vegetables (green beans, peas, carrots, etc.)

September

Week # 1

> 5 - 12 cases canned fruit
> 1 case misc. vegetables

Week # 2

> 2 cases canned fruit
> 2 cans shortening

Week #3

> 2 cases fruit
> 1 case vegetables

Week #4

> 2 cans shortening
> 25# rice buckets to store rice if it did not come in #10 cans

October

Week #1

> 100 lbs. wheat and 3 buckets

Week #2

> 1 case tuna or other meat

Week #3

> 25 lbs. Sugar
> 2 large cans fruit juice powder

Week #4

> 3 #10 cans dry milk

Week #5

> 9 #10 cans potato flakes

November

Week #1

> 4 large jars peanut butter

Week #2

> 1 case canned fruit

15 pounds rice

Week #3

7 #10 cans shortening

Week #4

50 pounds rice and buckets to store

December

Week #1

100 lbs. wheat and 3 buckets

Week #2

1 large can fruit juice powder

3 large jars peanut butter

Week #3

3 #10 cans dry milk

Week #4

50 pounds of rice, oats, or barley buckets to store

Items needed for packaging food:

Food grade Mylar bags. The minimum should be 4.5mil thick bags in one-gallon size. These will hold about 4–6 lbs, depending on the bulk of the food products. Commercial vendors sell them online, along with other preparedness supplies. Their bags are 7mil thick. However, they only sell them in bulk, so 250 bags for $94 is probably more bags than you need.

500cc Oxygen absorber packets. It takes two of these for each one gallon, 11" x 13" or similar sized Mylar bags full of food. These packets come in a sealed bag with all the oxygen sucked out. If the bag is not flat, but puffy with air, the oxygen packets have been compromised. You will need a glass jar with a metal (not plastic) lid to store them after you open the bag. Or you can seal them in a Mylar bag. Ordinary plastic bags are no good for storing oxygen packets – they provide a poor air barrier. Oxygen packets will start to feel warm when activated by exposure to air. Take them out only when you have everything else all set to bag and seal. Make sure to close the lid to preserve the others.

5-gram silica gel desiccant. These absorb any residue moisture that may reside in your food, to prevent mold. Many who have stored food for years have experienced no problems *not* using desiccant packets, but you should put them in.

Sealer. This is a very expensive piece of equipment. It comes with a foot pedal, making it easier to seal bags. An alternative is using a hot iron set on wool or cotton (preferably not the wife's!) with a 2 x 4 piece of wood. Some find they can use conventional food sealers. But do your homework well, as it is for good reason that Mylar bags require industrial strength sealers compared to off-the-shelf food sealers.

Directions for sealing bags:

1   (Optional) Place two 5-gram silica gel packets at the bottom of the Mylar bag.

2   Pour flour, rice, grain, etc. in bag. This can be done single-handedly, but from experience, it is *so* much easier to have someone help holding the Mylar bag, as it is very slick and does not have a flat bottom to keep it upright. Flour and dry milk can be a pain because it "poufs" everywhere when poured in the bag. When it does, use a damp paper towel to clean up the inside of the top of the bags where it will be sealed together. Then apply a dry towel to remove any moisture. At this point, firmly bang the bag several times against the table to help settle the contents and reduce airspace between the food elements.

3   Place two 500cc oxygen packets on top of food. Be sure to keep the unused oxy packets sealed in an airtight container, so they will stay fresh.

4   Hold and pull tight both ends of the open bag, place in the sealer. Let the filled part of the bag drop down, to prevent food from coming up to opening and preventing a perfect seal. Hit the foot pedal. The seal bar will come down for 2–3 seconds to set the seal. You can add a second seal to each bag for good measure. Check the seal by attempting to peel the opening apart. If the seal is secure, you won't be able too. Also push on the bag and watch if any air leaks out. None should. For using an iron, place the Mylar bag opening on the 2 x 4, and press down. Some prefer to put a towel between the iron and the Mylar, but it's fairly hard to scorch a bag.

5   Use a permanent marker to write the on bag the date, the weight, and the description on the bagged food. Include the brand name of the food, in case you have any problems with it, or is recalled by the FDA. For things like powdered milk, tape the mixing instructions on the bag.

Mylar bags may be cut in half or smaller to store smaller portions. Filled Mylar bags are very stiff and rigid. The bagged food will be a bit awkward to store in round containers like buckets and trashcans. Stack fragile food like pasta on top of the heavier, bulkier bagged foods.

Large Mylar bags from vendors are available to store quantities up to 30 lbs in 5-gallon plastic buckets. Put one in, and fill up with the dry food product of your choice. Some recommend using dry ice on top of the food before sealing to displace oxygen in the bucket. If you can't find any dry ice in your area, put ten oxygen packets on top instead. Seal with a hot iron by pressing the Mylar against a 2 x 4 piece. Trim any excess from the sealed top edge of the bag with scissors to secure the Mylar bag into the bucket. Cover with a lid. Gamma screw-top lids seem to work best on buckets. They cost from $7–10 each, but are so much easier than popping and hammering lids off and on every time.

Other food storage methods include canning, both traditional glass jars and #10 metal cans. Dehydrating food is another valuable storage method.

A few more suggestions for building your food storage. Include fun foods to help break the monotony and uplift morale, such as hard candy, chocolate, powdered drinks, and dried fruit. Pick up some recipes on cooking the food you store, to add variety to your diet. When possible, supplement your food storage meals with garden vegetables, home grown sprouts, or ordinary dandelion leaves. Be careful of depending on a diet of MRE's. While they are portable and convenient for traveling, they are short on fiber, and can be hard on the digestive system, especially with children and the elderly. They also negatively affect those who are gluten intolerant.

THE SEVEN MAJOR MISTAKES IN FOOD STORAGE

There are seven serious problems that may occur trying to live on these basics:

1.) **VARIETY - Most people don't have enough variety in their storage.** Many people only store the 4 basic items mentioned earlier: *wheat, milk, honey, and salt.* Statistics show most of us won't survive on such a diet for several reasons.

   a. **Many people are allergic to wheat** and may not be aware of it until they are eating it meal after meal.
   b. **Wheat is too harsh for young children.** They can tolerate it in small amounts but not as their main staple.
   c. **We get tired of eating the same foods** over and over and many times prefer not to eat than to sample that particular food again. This is called *appetite fatigue.* Young children and older people are particularly susceptible to it.

Store *less* wheat than is generally suggested and put the difference into a variety of other grains, particularly ones your family likes to eat. Also store a variety of beans. This will add variety of color, texture and flavor. **Variety is the key to a successful storage program.** It is essential that you *store flavorings* such as tomato, bouillon, cheese, and onion.

Also, *include a good supply of the spices* you like to cook with. These flavorings and spices allow you to do many creative things with your grains and beans. Without them you are severely limited. One of the best suggestions is to **buy a good food storage cookbook.** Go through it and see what your family would really eat. Notice the ingredients as you do it. This will help you more than anything else to know what items to store.

2.) **EXTENDED STAPLES – Few people get beyond storing the four basic items,** but it is extremely important that you do so. *Never put all your eggs in one basket.* Store dehydrated and/or freeze-dried foods as well as home canned and store bought canned goods. Make sure you add cooking oil, shortening, baking powder, soda, yeast and powdered eggs. You can't cook even the most basic recipes without these items. Because of limited space we can't list all the items that should be included in a well balanced storage program. They are all included in the cookbook *The All New Cookin' With Home Storage* by Peggy Layton and Vicki Tate, as well as information on how much to store, and where to purchase it.

3.) **VITAMINS - Vitamins are important, especially if you have children,** since children do not store body reserves of nutrients as adults do. *A good quality multi-vitamin and vitamin C are the most vital.* Others may be added as your budget permits.

4.) **QUICK AND EASY - PSYCHOLOGICAL FOODS** Quick and easy foods help you through times when you are psychologically or physically unable to prepare your basic storage items. No cook foods such as freeze-dried are wonderful since they require little preparation. MRE's (Meals Ready to Eat), such as many preparedness outlets carry, canned goods, etc. are also very good.

Psychological Foods are the goodies - Jello, pudding, candy, etc. - you should add to your storage. These may sound frivolous, but people who have lived entirely on their storage for extended periods of time say these were the most helpful items in their storage to normalize their situations and make it more bearable. These are especially important if you have children.

5.) BALANCE - Time and time again families buy all of their wheat, then buy all of another item, and so on. Don't do that. It's important to **keep well-balanced as you build your storage.** Buy several items, rather than a large quantity of one item. If something happens and you have to live on your present storage, you'll fare much better having a one month supply of a variety of items than a year's supply of two to three items.

6.) CONTAINERS - Always store your bulk foods in food storage containers. Tons of food gets thrown away by survivalists because it was left in sacks, where it becomes highly susceptible to moisture, insects and rodents. If you are using plastic buckets make sure they are lined with a food grade plastic liner available from companies that carry packaging supplies. **Never use trash can liners** as these are treated with pesticides. Don't stack them too high. In an earthquake they may topple, the lids pop open, or they may crack. A better container is the #10 tin can which most preparedness companies use when they package their foods.

7.) USE YOUR STORAGE - One of the biggest problems with people storing food is their not knowing what to do with it. It's vital that you and your family become familiar with the things you are storing. You need to know how to prepare these foods. This is not something you want to learn under stress. Your family needs to be used to eating these foods. A stressful period is not a good time to totally change your diet. Get a food storage cookbook and learn to use these foods! It's easy to solve these food storage problems once you know what they are.

It's better to find out your food storage mistakes now while there's still time to make corrections, than wait until the last minute. It's relatively easy to take an existing basic storage system and add the essentials to make it livable, but you need to start somewhere. As you research cookbooks, make sure to include recipes that can be useful with what you have stored. The pioneers ate many of the same types of things you will want to store, but if you only have the 4 basics, there's very little variety possible. Adding just a few items it greatly increases your options, and the prospect of your family surviving on this diet. The good news is that the basic storage items you will gather are what most of the world has always lived on and will be be a return to good basic living with a few goodies thrown in.

COMMON STORAGE FOODS

A range of foods are suited for incorporation into home storage programs. There are several considerations you should keep in mind when deciding on what foods to include. The first is variety in the diet. This is of great importance but many do not give it adequate thought. Some simply buy however much wheat, corn, rice, or beans they think is necessary to meet their needs and leave it at that. Others rely on prepackaged decisions made for them by their storage food retailer who put together a "year's supply of food" to buy all at once. Either decision could possibly be a mistake.

There are many food storage plans one may use as a guide. Some are based on the so-called "Mormon Four" of wheat, milk, honey and salt, with as many additional foods as the planner found desirable. This Mormon plan was developed in the 1930's and we've learned a great deal about workable food storage in the decades hence. Among which are the food allergies that an unfortunate number of people in our society develop. One of the more common food allergens is wheat. Even more unfortunate is the fact that many who have such an allergy are unaware of it. They won't become aware until they try to live with whole grain wheat as a large part of their diet and their latent allergy reveals itself.

Another thing we have learned is that many adults suffer from an intolerance to the milk sugar lactose, especially those of certain ethnic backgrounds. For these reasons and more you should always make it a practice to store what you eat AND TO eat what you store, so that ugly surprises such as these do not arise after it's too late to easily avoid them.

A second reason to think about storing a wide variety of foods is appetite fatigue. There are those who think providing variety in the diet is relatively unimportant and that if and when the time comes they'll eat what they've got and that will be that. For healthy, well adjusted adults under ordinary circumstances or for those who have the vital survival mindset this might be possible without too much difficulty. However, the reason for having a home food storage program in the first place is for when circumstances aren't ordinary. Times of crisis produce stress - possibly physical, but always mental. If you are suddenly forced to eat a diet both alien and monotonous, it is going to add that much more stress on top of what you are already dealing with. If your planning includes the elderly, young children, and/or infants there is a significant risk they will quit eating or refuse to eat sufficient amounts of the right foods leaving them unable to survive.

This is not a trivial problem and should be given serious consideration. When it's wheat, day in and day out, wheat's going to start becoming unpopular fast. Far better to have a variety of foods on hand to forestall appetite fatigue and, more importantly, to use those storable foods in your everyday diet so that you'll be accustomed to eating them.

A post-WWII study by the British Food Ministry, found the people of England and Europe were more likely to reject unfamiliar or distasteful foods during times of stress than under normal conditions. Consider the positive aspects of adding variety and comfort foods to your storage program. Unless you are already familiar with and eating a particular type and brand of food do not put large quantities of it into your pantry until you – and preferably everyone who will be depending on that food – have eaten some of it first. It's not always as easy to pick up a new food as it may first appear. Differences between brands of foods alone can sometimes be enough to disappoint you when consumed. You'd hate to discover that you cannot abide a particular food item after you've brought home a case of Brand X.

GRAINS AND FLOURS

About Gluten:

As you read through the grain descriptions below you will come across frequent mention of "gluten". Gluten is a combination of proteins found in some grains which enables the dough made from them to rise by trapping the gases produced by yeast fermentation or chemical reaction of baking powder or soda. The amount of these proteins varies depending on the species of grain and varieties within a species. Some grains such as rice have virtually no gluten at all and will not produce a raised loaf by itself while others like hard winter wheat have a great deal and make excellent raised bread. As a general rule yeast raised breads need a fair amount of gluten to attain good dough volumes while non-yeast raised breads may need little or none at all. Whether gluten content is of importance to you will depend upon the end uses you intend for your grain. Some of the common and relatively uncommon types of grains are listed below.

AMARANTH: Amaranth is not a true cereal grain at all, but is a relative of the pigweeds and the ornamental flowers we call "cockscomb". It's grown not only for its seed, but for its leaves that can be cooked and eaten as greens. The seed is high in protein, particularly the amino acid lysine which is limited in the true cereal grains. It can be milled as-is, or toasted to provide more flavor. The flour lacks gluten, so is not suited for raised breads by itself, but can be made into any of a number of flat breads. Some varieties can be popped like popcorn, boiled and eaten as a cereal, used in soups, granolas, and the like. Toasted or untoasted, it blends well with other grain flours. NOTE: Like some other edible seeds, raw amaranth contains biological factors that can inhibit proper absorption of some nutrients. For this reason amaranth seeds or flour should always be cooked before consumption, whether for human food or animal feed.

BARLEY: Barley is thought by some to be the first grain intentionally cultivated by man. It has short, stubby kernels with a hull that is difficult to remove. Excluding barley intended for malting or animal feed, this grain is generally consumed directly by humans in two forms. Most common is the white, highly processed pearl barley with much of its bran and germ milled off along with its hull. It is the least nutritious form of barley. The second offering is called pot or hulled barley and it has been subjected to the same milling process as pearled, but with fewer trips through the polisher. Because of this, it retains more of the nutritious germ and bran, but does not keep as well as the more refined product without special packaging. Unless you are prepared to try to get the hulls off don't buy unhulled barley. Although it can be milled into flour, barley's low gluten content will not make a good loaf of raised bread. It can be combined with other flours that do have sufficient gluten to make leavened bread or used in flat breads. Barley flour and flakes have a light nutty flavor that is enhanced by toasting. Whole barley is commonly used to add thickness to soups and stews. Recently, a hull-less form has become available on the market through a few suppliers. This is whole grain barley with all of its bran and germ intact and should have the most nutrients of any form of this grain available.

BUCKWHEAT: Buckwheat is another of those seeds commonly considered to be a grain, but which is not a true cereal. It is, in fact, a close relative to the docks and sorrels. The "grain" itself is a dark, three cornered seed resembling a tiny beechnut. It has a hard, fibrous hull requiring a special buckwheat huller to remove. Here in the U.S., buckwheat is most often used in pancakes, biscuits and muffins. In Eastern Europe and Russia it is known in its toasted form as kasha. In the Far East, it's often made into soba or noodles. It's also a good bee plant, producing a dark, strongly flavored honey. The flour is light or dark depending on how much of the hull has been removed before grinding. Dark flour is much more strongly flavored than lighter flour, but because of the high fiber and tannin content of its hull, which can interfere with nutrient absorption, it is not necessarily more nutritious. Buckwheat is one of those foods with no middle ground in people's opinions — they either love it or they hate it. Like amaranth, it's high in lysine, an amino acid commonly lacking in the true cereal grains.

CORN (maize): Corn is the largest grain crop in the U.S., but is mostly consumed indirectly as animal feed or even industrial feedstock rather than directly as food. As one of the Three Sisters (maize, squash and beans) corn was the staple grain of nearly all of the indigenous peoples of the American continents before the advent of European colonization. This American grain has an amazing variety of forms. Major classes are the flint, dent, flour, and popcorns. To a certain extent, they're all interchangeable for milling into meal (sometimes known as polenta meal) or flour (very finely ground corn, not cornstarch). The varieties intended to be eaten as sweet corn (fresh green corn) are high in sugar content so do not dry or store well relative to the other corns but instead are usually preserved as a vegetable. There are a number of lesser corn varieties with specialized uses that do not lend themselves to direct food use, but these are seldom found in the open market. As a general rule of thumb, the flint varieties make better meal as they have a grittier texture than most other corns. If meal, hominy and hominy grits (commonly called just "grits") are what you are interested in then use the flint type if you can find a source. If you intend to make corn masa for tortillas and tamales, then the flour corns are what you want, but these are fairly uncommon on the commercial market so the dent corns are next best. Yellow dent seems to be the most commonly available and will work for almost any purpose except popping.

Popcorn is for snacks or used as a cold cereal after popping or can be ground into quite acceptable meal. It is difficult to hull popcorn with alkali treatment for making hominy (posolé, nixtamal) though your mileage may vary. Popcorn is one form of a whole grain available to nearly everyone in the U.S. It is so common a snack food, particularly at movie theaters, fairs, and ball games, that the smallest of towns will often have at least one business selling it cleaned, dried, and ready to pop in twenty-five or fifty pound bags. Popcorn is harder than other varieties of corn so if your mill is not of the heavy duty sort you may want to consider cracking the kernels into coarse pieces first then grinding into finer textured meal. The Family Grain Mill states that it should not be used to mill popcorn at all and the Back To Basics mill should not be used for any great quantity. All other manual and electric mills should mill popcorn without problem.

Once you've decided on your preferred corn type you may also be able to choose your preferred color. There are yellow, white, blue, red, and multicolored varieties. The yellow and whites are the most common by far with the blues, reds, and parti-colored varieties mostly being relegated to curiosities, though the blue and red corns have been gaining in popularity these last few years. These would be worth investigating if you can find a good source. It should be kept in mind that white corn does not have the carotene content (converts into vitamin A) of yellow corn. As vitamin A is one of the major limiting nutrients in long term food storage, any possible source of it should be utilized. For this reason you should be storing yellow rather than white corn. Additionally, much of the niacin content of corn is chemically bound up in a form not available for human nutrition unless it has been treated with an alkali. This is really of importance only if most of your sustained daily calorie intake will come from corn, but grits, hominy (posolé) or corn masa (for tortillas and tamales) are traditional uses of this grain and can go a long way toward increasing the number of recipes you can make with corn. .

Any grain as widely grown as corn is naturally going to be processed into many products. Here are a few suited for use in home storage programs:

Corn Meal (polenta meal): This is simply dry corn ground into a meal. Corn meal intended for polenta may be found in either a coarse or a fine grind. In the U.S. corn meal for making corn bread and most other uses is typically ground to a fairly fine meal. Very finely milled corn is often used for breading foods to be fried and is known as corn flour to distinguish it from coarser meals. This sometimes causes confusion because corn starch (see below)is also known as corn flour in Great Britain - a very different product and not really interchangeable.

The germ of the corn kernel contains about twice the oil content of wheat and is highly susceptible to rancidity once the kernel is broken in the milling process. Because of this most commercially available corn meal will have had the germ and hull removed to extend shelf-life then nutritionally enriched to make up for some of the vitamins and minerals lost with the grain germ. This is desirable for the miller and the grocer, but for the diner it comes at a cost of flavor and some of the nutrition of the whole grain. Some grocers may offer a whole grain corn meal that keeps the grain germ and bran which gives a superior flavored product and retains the full nutrition of the grain but makes for a more perishable commodity. If you go this route be sure of your product's freshness then store it in your refrigerator or freezer. The grocer's corn meal is mostly milled from yellow or white corn, but some suppliers are now offering blue or even red corn meals.

The flavor of the degerminated yellow and white meals are largely indistinguishable from each other, but blue and red corns are interestingly different. Might be worth investigating if you can find them. Storage life of degerminated corn meal is about one year in average conditions in store packaging and a good deal longer if you repackage it for long term storage. Whole grain meal is good for about four weeks on the shelf, months in the refrigerator, and several years in the freezer or if carefully put up in oxygen free packaging. If you have a grain mill, store your corn meal in the form of whole corn and milling it as needed, milling a few weeks worth of meal at a time then keeping it in the freezer until needed. The fresh whole grain meal has a much fuller corn flavor than the degerminated meal from the grocery store.

Hominy (posolé'): This is corn with the hull, and possibly the germ, removed. Hominy cooks faster than unhulled whole corn, is easier to digest, and in some circumstances the alkali peeled varieties can present a superior nutritional profile to whole corn. There are two methods of producing hominy: Mechanical dehulling in a wet milling process or by treating with one of a number of various alkalis such as industrial lye (sodium hydroxide), wood ash lye (mostly potassium hydroxides) or by using some form of lime (calcium hydroxide). Dry lye peeled hominy is now seldom found for sale, but canned white or yellow hominy is still common across the

Southern U.S. and many other areas as well as in Latin American groceries. Generally speaking hominy produced using lime is known by its Spanish name – posole' – but this will not always be clear on labels, lime peeled hominy is sometimes simply called hominy.

Whether this is important to you depends on the particular flavor you are trying to achieve in the dish you are preparing. Freshly hulled corn using the lime process that is to be ground to make masa (dough) for corn tortillas is called nixtamal. Dry posole' can be found in Latin American groceries or ordered from the Internet in nearly any color that corn offers. There's a world of things that can be done with hominy other than simply heating it up and serving with butter and salt. A few minutes spent searching the Internet will produce dozens of recipes using hominy as a major ingredient. It's an excellent ingredient in hearty soups and stews.

Hominy Grits: Usually just called "grits" this coarsely ground meal can be either simple whole corn ground coarse or corn that has been hulled in a process using a form of lye to make hominy then dried and coarsely ground. Grits produced from lye peeled corn typically cook faster, have a longer shelf life, and presents a different, possibly superior, nutritional profile than the whole grain product. Grits produced from whole corn take much longer to cook, have a short shelf life if not refrigerated or put up in special packaging, a superior flavor to the lye peeled product, and retains the nutrition of the whole grain. Very coarsely ground grits is also known as samp.

Hominy grits in the U.S. must be enriched like many other refined grain products and are now typically industrially produced. They are usually what you will find at your local grocers. Whole grain grits are primarily the product of grist mills making stone ground products and are often found in living history demonstrations, heritage fairs, pioneer day celebrations, and so on. Both yellow and white corns are commonly milled for grits and which one you should buy probably depends on what you ate growing up. If you're indifferent as to the color of your grits, buy yellow corn grits as the beta carotene content of yellow corn can be converted by our bodies into Vitamin A whereas white corn has none.

Masa Harina: In Spanish "masa" means "dough" and "harina" means "flour" which is a straight forward description of what masa harina is: A lime peeled corn that has been dried and milled into meal to be made into tortilla dough. It's flavor is distinctively different from either corn meal or hominy grits and is used in making tortillas, tamales, and many other Southwestern, Mexican, Central and South American dishes. Can often be found in mainstream grocery stores and grocers catering to a Latin American trade. Will store on the shelf for about a year and even longer if refrigerated or put up in good storage packaging. If you have a mind to try making your own tortillas you will save yourself much time and effort by using a tortilla press. These can be found in some groceries catering to a Latin American clientèle or ordered over the Internet.

Corn Starch: A common starch used as a thickener. Made by a roller milling process removing the hull and germ leaving behind a nearly pure starch. Storage life is indefinite if kept dry. In the United Kingdom and some other areas it is known as corn flour which occasionally causes confusion with very finely milled corn also known as corn flour here in the States. The two products are largely not interchangeable.

MILLET: Millet is an important staple grain in North China and India, but is little known in the U.S, where we mostly use it as bird feed. The grain kernels are very small, round, and usually ivory colored or yellow, though some varieties are darker. A lack of gluten and a rather bland flavor may account for the anonymity of this cereal. Millet has a more alkaline pH (and a higher iron content) than other grains which makes it very easy to digest. A major advantage of millet is that it swells a great deal when cooked and supplies more servings per pound than any other grain. When cooked like rice millet makes an excellent breakfast cereal. It has little gluten of its own, but mixes well with other flours. Adding whole millet kernels to the dough can add a pleasant crunch to your homemade breads.

OATS: Though the Scots and the Irish have made a cuisine of oats, it is mostly thought of in the U.S. as a bland breakfast food. Seldom found as a whole grain, it's usually sold processed in one form or another. Much like barley, the oat is a difficult grain to separate from its hull. Besides its longtime role as a breakfast food, oats make an excellent thickener of soups and stews and a filler in meat loafs and casseroles. Probably the second most common use for oats in America is in cookies and granolas. A little creative thought can really increase their culinary range. Listed below are the forms of oats found in the U.S. Rolled and cut oats retain both their bran and their germ.

Oat groats: These are whole oats with the hulls removed. They are not often found in this form, but can sometimes be had from natural food stores and some storage food dealers. Oats are not the easiest thing to obtain a consistent grind from so producing your own oat flour takes a bit of experience. If you have a roller mill or attachment you can produce your own oatmeal using whole oat groats.

Steel cut oats: Also known as Irish, pinhead or porridge oats. They are oat groats cut into chunks with steel blades. They're not rolled and look like coarse bits of grain. Steel cut oats can be found in many supermarkets and natural food stores. They take longer to cook than rolled oats, but retain more texture. They need oxygen free packaging to be kept at their best for long term storage.

Rolled oats: These are also commonly called old fashioned, thick cut or porridge oats. To produce them, oat groats are steamed and then rolled to flatten. They can generally be found wherever oats are sold. They take slightly longer to cook than do the quick cooking oats, but they retain more flavor, texture and nutrition. This is what most people will call to mind when they think of oatmeal.

Quick cooking rolled oats: These are just steamed oat groats rolled thinner than the old fashioned kind above so that they will cook faster. They can usually be found right next to the thicker rolled oats. Instant rolled oats: These are the "just add hot water" or microwave type of oat cereals and are not particularly suited for a storage program. They do, however, have uses in "bug out" and 72 hour food kits for short term crises.

Whole oats: This is with the hulls still on. They are sold in feed & seed stores and sometimes straight from the farmer who grew them. Unless you have some means of getting the hulls off, don't buy oats in this form. If you do buy from a seed supplier, make certain that they have not been treated with any chemicals that are toxic to humans.

QUINOA: Quinoa is yet another of the grains that is not a true cereal. It's botanical name is Chenopodium quinoa (pronounced "keen-wah"), and is a relative of the common weed Lambsquarter. The individual kernels are about 1.5-2 mm in size and are shaped rather like small flattened spheres. When quinoa is cooked, the germ of the grain coils into a small "tail" that lends a pleasant crunch when eaten. Some forms of this grain have a bitter tasting water soluble component that should be removed by a thorough washing unless this was already done by the processor as most of the quinoa sold in the U.S. apparently has. There are several varieties of quinoa that have color ranging from near white to a dark brown. The larger white varieties are considered superior and are the most common.

RICE: Rice is the most widely consumed food grain in the world with the U.S. being the leading exporter of this important staple, though we actually only produce about 1% of the global supply. The majority of the world's rice is eaten within five miles of where it was grown. Much like wheat and corn, rice comes in a number of varieties, each with different characteristics. They are typically divided into classes by the length of their kernel grains; **short**, **medium** and **long**.

Short grain rice: The short grain variety is a little softer and bit moister when it cooks and tends to stick together more than the longer rices. It has a sweeter, somewhat stronger flavor than long grain rice.

Medium grain rice: The medium grain variety is not very common in the States. It has flavor like the short variety, but with a texture more like long.

Long grain rice: The long grain variety cooks up into a drier, flakier dish than the shorter types and the flavor tends to be blander. It is the most commonly found size of rice on American grocery shelves.

Each of the above may be processed into brown, white, parboiled or converted, and instant rice. Below is a short discussion of the differences between the various types.

Brown rice: This is whole grain rice with only the hull removed. It retains all of the nutrition and has a pleasant nutty flavor. From a nutritional standpoint it is by far the best, but it has one flaw: The essential oil in the germ is very susceptible to oxidation and soon goes rancid. As a result, brown rice has a shelf life of only about six months unless given special packaging or storage. Freezing or refrigeration will greatly extend this. It's possible to purchase brown rice from long term food suppliers already specially packaged in air tight containers with an inert nitrogen atmosphere or you can do it yourself. In this kind of packaging, (if properly done), the storage life can be extended for several years.

Converted rice: Converted rice starts as whole rice still in the hull which undergoes a process of soaking and steaming until it is partially cooked. It is then dried, hulled and polished to remove the bran and germ. The steaming process drives some of the vitamins and minerals from the outer layers into the white inner layers. This makes it more nutritious than polished white rice, but also makes it more expensive. Its storage life is the same as regular white rice.

White rice: This is raw rice that has had its outer layers milled off, taking with it about 10% of its protein, 85% of its fat and 70% of its mineral content. Because so much of the nutrition is lost, white rice sold in the U.S. has to be "enriched" with vitamins to partially replace what was removed. It stores very well and is generally the cheapest form of rice to be found in the market place making it a very common storage food.

Instant rice: The type of rice is fully cooked and then dehydrated needing nothing more than the addition of water to reconstitute it. In a pinch, it's not even necessary to use hot water. It's not particularly suitable for inclusion in storage programs, but may have a place in "seventy-two hour" and other short-term emergency kits. The white variety is by far the most common, but in the last few years instant brown rice has made an appearance on the market.

RYE: Rye is well known as a bread grain in the U.S. It has dark brown kernels longer and thinner than wheat, but less gluten. Rye flours can be found in varying stages of refinement from dark whole grain flour to semi-refined medium to pale fully refined offerings. Bread made from this grain tends to be dense unless gluten is added (often in the form of a lot of wheat flour). German pumpernickels and Russian black breads, made with unrefined rye flour and molasses, are two of the darkest, densest forms of rye bread. Many sourdoughs are built upon a rye base with a resulting interesting, intense flavor.

SORGHUM: Sorghum is probably more widely known here in the States for the syrup made from the sweet juice squeezed from the stalks of some varieties of this grain. Also known as "milo", it is one of the principle cereal grains of Africa. Its seeds are somewhat round, a little smaller than peppercorns, of an overall brown color with a bit of red and yellow mixed in. The varieties called "yellow endosperm sorghum" are considered to have a better taste. It is a major feed grain in the Southwestern U.S. and is where the vast majority of the national production goes. Like most of the other grains, sorghum is low in gluten, but the seeds can be milled into flour and mixed with higher gluten flours or made into flat breads, pancakes or cookies. In the Far East, it is cooked and eaten like rice, while in Africa it is ground into meal for porridge. It's also fermented for alcoholic beverages.

TEFF: Easily the smallest of the grains, teff kernels are only about 1/32nd inch in diameter. The name itself means "lost" because if dropped on the ground, it's too small to recover. It's been very little known until recently, but has been a staple grain in Ethiopia for nearly five millennia. Small amounts are now being grown in South Africa and the United States. This grain ranges in color from reddish brown to near white. It has a protein content in the 10- 12% range, good calcium and a useful source of iron. It is traditionally used in making the Ethiopian flat bread "injera", but has no gluten content of its own. It'll combine well with wheat flour though and has something of a sweetish flavor.

TRITICALE: Triticale is a cross between durum wheat and rye. This youngest of grains combines the productivity of wheat with the ruggedness of rye and has a high nutrition value. The kernels are gray-brown, oval shaped larger-than-wheat and plumper than rye. It can be used in much the same way as either of its two parents. It will make a raised bread like wheat does, but its gluten is a bit weak so wheat flour is frequently added to strengthen it. Because of the delicate nature of its gluten, excessive kneading must be avoided.

WHEAT: The most widely consumed grain in the United States and along with rice and corn one of the three most widely grown in the world. Wheat is also one of the most intensively processed to turn into food of all the grains. It comes in a number of different varieties each more suitable for some purposes than others based on its particular characteristics. The most common classifications of these varieties are based on their respective growing season, hardness of kernel, and color of their bran layers - spring or winter, hard or soft, red or white.

The hard wheats have kernels that tend to be small, hard in texture, and with high protein (primarily gluten) contents. As a general rule, hard varieties have more protein than soft varieties. Yeast raised breads that need a lot of gluten are where it's at for the hard wheats.

The soft wheats have kernels tending to be larger, plumper and softer in texture than hard wheats. As their gluten content is lower they are primarily used in biscuits, pastries, quick breads, some pastas, and breakfast cereals where a higher gluten content would contribute an undesirable tougher texture. Soft wheats do not produce as fine a loaf of yeast raised bread as high gluten hard wheat, though it can still be used for yeast breads by combining with higher gluten flours or using methods suitable for its protein level. Many traditional European yeast raised breads are made with lower protein flours.

Durum wheat also has a very hard kernel and a high protein content, but of a somewhat different nature than the other hard wheats. Durum is not primarily used for breads but is instead consumed mostly in the manufacture of pasta where it lends its characteristic yellowish color to the finished product. There are some specialty breads that call durum/semolina flour so it can be used for bread making even if it's not best suited to the task. Winter wheats are planted in the Fall, over winter in the field, grow through the Spring and are harvested early the next Summer. Spring wheats are planted in the early Spring and are harvested the following Fall. Red wheats comprise most of the hard varieties while white wheats comprise most of the soft.

Recently, hard white wheats have been developed that are very suitable for yeast raised bread making. Some feel the hard white varieties make a better tasting whole wheat bread than the hard reds. When milled, whole grain hard white wheat flour looks somewhat like unbleached refined white flour in appearance. The hard red varieties, either spring or winter, are commonly chosen for storage programs because of their high protein content which should be no less than 12% with 14% or more being excellent. The hard white spring wheats are still relatively new and not yet as widespread but are steadily growing in popularity. They have the same excellent storage characteristics as the hard red wheats and should be selected with the same protein contents as well.

With so many different varieties of wheat it should come as no surprise that there are a number of different types of wheat flour offered to the home baker. Distinguishing between the array of products available through both retail grocery stores and commercial supply houses catering to bakers nearly requires the knowledge of a professional baker or a cereal chemist and would take up page after page to explain it all. Instead we will briefly cover only those flours or flour products that one can usually find in supermarkets in the U.S. and elsewhere. If you need more advanced knowledge in order to purchase through commercial or institutional food channels more information is available on the Usenet newsgroups rec.food.baking, sci.bio.food-science, or alt.bread.recipes where you may be able to get answers from professionals in the field.

All Purpose Flour: Of all the flours in the retail market allpurpose flour is the one most subject to major differences between brands, regions of the U.S., and/or other nations. This refined flour is typically made from a blend of hard and soft wheats with a protein content that can range from as low as 8% to as high as 12%. The regional brands of the Southern U.S. have traditionally been on the lower end of the protein scale. This is due to the fact that historically only soft wheats were grown in the South and the resulting flour was best used is in making biscuits and other types of non-yeast raised breads that did not require high gluten levels. The regional brands of the Northern U.S., and Canada are typically at the high end of the protein scale at or approaching 12%. This is because hard wheats are primarily northern grown and are well suited to making yeast raised breads which need higher gluten levels as were customarily made there. The national brands either differ by region or are in the 10-11% range in an effort to try to satisfy all markets.

In the U.S. all-purpose flour is enriched and can be had either bleached or unbleached and may possibly have small quantities of malt added as well (see below about enrichment, bleaching and malting). As the name implies all-purpose is meant to serve as a general all-around flour from which you can make anything from cakes and pie crusts to sandwich bread. So far as it goes you can, but it's a lot like one-size-fits-all clothing in that chances are it won't work as well for a given project as a flour milled with that particular use in mind. The lower protein all-purpose flours sold in the Southern U.S. will produce a more tender biscuit, cake, or pie crust than the higher protein all purpose flours of the Northern U.S. and Canada, but unless you use some special techniques (like how true French bread is made) it won't produce a very satisfying loaf of yeast bread.

The flours in 10-11% range try to strike a happy medium between the two, but still won't serve as well as flour produced specifically with a given end use in mind. If you want you put into your storage program I'd recommend going with the 10-11% flours and either plan on adding gluten as needed to make the best yeast raised breads or cornstarch to produce more tender cakes and pie crusts. In the United Kingdom and Canada all-purpose flour is oft times labeled as "plain flour", "top patent", "general purpose", or "family flour."

Bread Flour: A refined white flour with a higher protein (gluten) content than most all-purpose flours to achieve better performance in making yeast raised breads. Protein levels should be at least 12% with 13-14% better still. As this is a refined flour in the U.S. it will be enriched with added vitamins and iron, and can be found either bleached or unbleached. Because it is intended primarily for use in yeast raised breads this flour will usually have other additives such as small amounts of malt to improve yeast performance and vitamin C (ascorbic acid) to improve dough volume and texture. Some bread flours may also be treated with potassium bromate to improve gluten qualities, but concerns over possible toxicity of this additive is leading to its diminished use. A high gluten refined bread flour is commonly added to whole wheat doughs to strengthen them which can improve loaf rises and volume. Bread flour is most commonly used in the production of yeast raised breads, pizza crusts, and some specialty baked goods. In Great Britain bread flour is often labeled as "Strong Flour" meaning it has a high protein content.

Whole Wheat Flour: Real whole wheat flour should include 100% of the bran and germ so read your ingredient labels carefully to be sure this is so. This flour is mostly milled from hard red wheats, but whole grain hard white flour is available from some mills and will produce a bread that looks closer to refined white bread if that is what you are accustomed to eating. Protein contents can vary, but as most whole wheat flour is used in yeast bread making it should be at least 12% with 13-14% being better still. This is good because the bran and the germ can interfere with good gluten development as the dough is mixed and kneaded. Some do not mind this while others strengthen their flour by adding vital wheat gluten or high protein refined bread flours to achieve the rise and volume they are accustomed to in yeast breads.

Approximately 90% of the total protein of a kernel of wheat is gluten with the remaining 10% other proteins being mostly found in the grain germ. Refined flours have had the germ removed so a statement of protein content can be taken as an indication of that flour's suitability for making raised yeast breads. With whole wheat flours one must remember that ten percent of non-gluten germ proteins and judge that flour's protein content accordingly. Whole wheat flour milled from lower protein soft wheats may be offered as "whole wheat pastry flour" so be sure of what you are buying. Some whole-wheat flours are also enriched. Whole wheat flour may also be called "Graham Flour", sometimes simply "Stone Ground Wheat Flour" and in Great Britain, Canada, and Australia may be known as "Whole Meal Flour." In Britain there is also a "Brown Flour" which is midway between whole meal and white flour in that it retains about 85% of the wheat kernel rather than only the 72-75% that is typical of refined white flours.

The real disadvantage to storing whole wheat flour is that like other processed grain products that includes the oil rich germ it wants to go rancid. How fast this can happen depends upon temperature, moisture, etc, but four to six weeks is generally enough time for rancidity to become noticeable. One can, of course, package the flour in good containers with oxygen absorbers and the like, but better still would be to buy the flour in the form of whole wheat berries and mill them yourself. Baking with fresh, whole wheat flour is something of an art so the time to get good with it is right NOW while you can toss your failures to the chickens rather than having to eat them regardless because you can't afford to waste the food.

Vital Wheat Gluten: Sometimes labeled as simply "wheat gluten." This is the purified gluten of hard wheat extracted from flour. It is generally 75-80% protein and is used to strengthen weak or whole grain flours for making yeast raised breads or made into "seitan" a wheat protein meat substitute. Somewhat confusing the issue is "High Gluten Flour" which is available in some markets. Careful investigation is needed here because this flour can range from a mere high gluten bread flour (approx 14%) to a gluten enriched flour typically 40%+) all the way up to purified wheat gluten (75%+). Be clear as to what it is you're buying and if you're not certain contact the manufacturer. If your whole wheat bread is not rising for you as much as you'd like then an addition of a few spoonfuls of gluten or some high gluten flour may perk it up a bit.

Cake Flour: Typically the lowest protein content (6-8%) flour available to the home baker. This highly processed flour will make the tenderest cakes, cookies, and biscuits but performs poorly for yeasted breads. The flour is nearly always bleached (chlorinated) both to give it a bright whiteness and to improve its moisture holding capacity for cakes calling for a high ratio of sugars or fats. Unless you make a lot of cakes this is a rather specialized item to store.

Pastry Flour: Similar to cake flour, but generally slightly higher in protein, not chlorinated, and may be found bleached or unbleached. Used to produce tender pie crusts, biscuits, etc. Very similar to the regional all-purpose flours of the Southern U.S. Can also sometimes be found in a whole-wheat version as well. In Great Britain, Canada, and Australia may be known as "soft flour."

Semolina/Durum: Produced from durum wheat this flour is typically high in protein, 12% or more, enriched, unbleached with a distinctive pale yellow color. Texture depends largely on brand and can range from fairly coarse to bread flour fine. Most commonly used in the production of pastas, noodles, and couscous, but some specialty types call for semolina flour. May also be known as "alimentary flour", "macaroni flour", or "pasta flour." Farina, a coarse meal used as a breakfast cereal, is made from durum wheat.

Self-Rising Flour: This is ordinary refined and enriched all-purpose flour to which approximately 1.5 teaspoons of baking powder and 0.5 teaspoons of salt have been added to each cup of flour. This flour has its fans, but it's not well suited to long storage as the baking powder wants to go flat over time even with special packaging. Nor is it suited to making yeast raised breads. Most self-rising flours are in the mid to low end of the protein scale (8-10%) because this is where chemically leavened quick breads perform best to achieve good rises and textures. You can make your own self-rising flour by adding in the requisite amount of double acting baking powder and salt mentioned above rather than trying to store the ready-made product. Self-rising flour is sometimes known as phosphated flour (for the baking powder used in it) and in Great Britain, Canada, and Australia may be known as "self-raising flour" or "raising flour."

Instant Flour: This specialized flour product is also sometimes known as "shaker flour" for the shaker can in which it's usually found This is a low-protein flour in a granular form processed for easy and rapid dissolution into hot or cold liquids for making sauces, gravies, and batters. A fairly specialized item which any worthy cook can use ordinary flour to replace.

FLOUR TREATMENTS AND ADDITIVES

Flour milling companies (and home bakers) use a variety of additives and treatments in their flours to improve or suppress a particular quality in their product. If you read the package labels carefully you can discern quite a lot about what has and has not been done. Here are a few of the more common:

Enrichment: U.S. law (and some other nations) requires that refined flours which have had their bran and germ portions removed to be "enriched" by adding back a portion of the niacin, thiamin, riboflavin, folic acid, and iron that were lost in the refining process. Some milling companies go even further by adding vitamins A & D as well. There are various opinions about the value of this enrichment, but it's there. It has no affect on the taste, color, texture, caloric value, or baking qualities of the flour. Outside of the U.S. refined white flours may or may not be enriched so study your package labels carefully if this concerns you.

Bleaching: White bread and white cakes come by their snowy beauty thanks to bleaching. This is a process by which the yellowish carotenoid pigments that naturally occur in wheat are bleached white in order to improve the appearance of the flour and perhaps to change some of its physical characteristics as well.

This would occur naturally by itself were the refined flour allowed to sit around for several months, but it's an uneven process and time is money to the milling companies who cannot afford to have large stocks of product sitting around in their warehouses for long periods of time. Beyond making naturally off-white flour snowy in appearance bleaching can perform several other functions which the individual baker must decide if they are important to his needs. Until fairly recently much refined flour was also "bromated" using potassium bromate both to lighten the color, and to improve the qualities of the gluten.

Concerns over the toxicity of this chemical has led to its gradual decline or outright ban on its use. Other bleaching agents are now used such as chlorine gas, chlorine dioxide, benzoyl peroxide and possibly others as well. Flours treated in this fashion will often exhibit improved loaf volume, finer grain, and look better in the finished product. Cake flour is generally chlorinated not only whiten but also to improve its moisture holding ability when used in cakes with a high ratio of sugar and fat to flour. This bleaching also further tempers the already low gluten of the flour to produce the tenderest possible texture. For the folks who do not care to buy bleached flours, small amounts of ascorbic acid (vitamin C) are often added as a dough conditioner and yeast nutrient. Home bakers often add their own vitamin C to their breads when they make them for the same reasons. A mere 1/8 vitamin C to their breads when they make them for the same reasons. A mere 1/8 tsp of ascorbic acid per cup of flour is all that is necessary. All bleached flours must be so labeled in the U.S.

Malting: Many bread flours and some all-purpose flours will have small amounts of malt, malted barley flour, malt flour, or diastatic malt added to them. This additive improves the performance of the yeast by providing enzymes which speed the conversion of some of the flour starches into the digestible sugars the yeast use as fuel which can improve both the rise of the dough and the flavor of the finished product. The malt can also serve to improve the appearance of the bread when baked and lengthen its shelf life. You can add your own diastatic malt in the ratio of about 0.5-1.0 teaspoons for every three cups of flour.

Organic: This is flour produced and processed under the guidelines of the U.S. Department of Agriculture's Organic foods program. Most of the basic flour types (all-purpose, bread, pastry, etc.) can be found in organic forms though you may have to search a bit to find them.

Pre-Sifted: This is flour sifted at the mill before it was packaged. Supposedly this means you do not need to sift it again at home, but many feel that due to settling during transport and storage if the recipe calls for sifted flour it should be done again.

Other Additives: There are many other potential additives that you may potentially come across in flour which would require more space than is possible here to cover them. Most are for use within the commercial/industrial baking fields and you would need to contact the supplier to determine precisely what it is they can do for you.

STORING FLOUR PRODUCTS

As already mentioned above whole wheat flour wants to go rancid rather quickly after it has been milled. Once ground it will stay fresh for about four to six weeks sitting on your room temperature kitchen shelf. In a sealed container in the refrigerator the flour will stay good for a year or so. In the freezer it will keep for years. It is probably best to store your whole wheat flour in the form of wheat berries and only mill as much flour as you will use in a week or two and keep that in the refrigerator or freezer until you do. If for some reason you cannot do this then buy the freshest product you can and package it well in Mylar bags, glass jars, or metal cans with oxygen absorbers. Due to the fine texture of flour it will not gas flush very well at all. Even the refined white flours have limited shelf-lives.

In spite of what some would have you believe flour products are not "dead foods." The bran and germ may have been removed, but a minute portion of the germ oils will remain as well as the naturally occurring enzymes found in the grain. Refined white flour won't noticeably go off on you the way whole wheat flour will, but given sufficient time and exposure to heat and atmospheric humidity the protein content of the flour will slowly breakdown. Your first indications of trouble may be a slowly developing musty smell or degraded dough performance – poor rises and bad loaf volumes. In a sealed, air tight container you should easily achieve six months to a year at room temperatures. Sealed containers in the refrigerator or freezer will last for at least several years. If you want your white flour to stay at its best for the longest possible time then package it in Mylar bags, glass jars, or metal cans air tight with oxygen absorbers. At a decent storage temperature sealed in a low oxygen environment you should easily achieve five years of shelf life or more.

LEGUME VARIETIES

If you're willing to spend what it takes on preserved meats and dairy products it's not necessary to store legumes at all. But most people do choose to keep a selection of beans, peas, and lentils in their larders either for reasons of economy, because they like them, or both. There are few non-animal foods that contain the amount of protein to be found in legumes with the varieties commonly available in the U.S. ranging from 20%-35%. As with most non-animal proteins, they are not complete in themselves for purposes of human nutrition, but become so when they are combined with the incomplete proteins found in grains. This is why grains and legumes are so often served together the world around.

The legume family, of which all beans, peas, lentils, and peanuts are a part, is one of the largest in the plant kingdom. Because of this and the many thousands of years of cultivation and development that man has given them on several continents the variety of edible legumes available to us is huge. Both their appearance and their names are colorful and varied. They range from "adzuki beans", a type of soybean from the Orient, to "zipper peas", a common fieldpea here in the Southern U.S. Their color can range from a clean white, to deep red, dull green to flat black with thousands of mixtures and patterns in between.

In spite of this incredible variety, many legumes are largely interchangeable in cooking, although some dishes just wouldn't be the same if a different type were used. Below is a partial list of common legumes.

ADZUKI BEANS: These small, deep red beans are very popular in Japan, China and other Asian nations, but are not as well known in the U.S. They are actually a cousin of the soybean and are commonly used in producing sweet bean paste for Chinese buns and other dishes. Pressure cooking will sometimes impart a bitter flavor so they are best presoaked then boiled in the conventional fashion. Their flavor is somewhat milder than kidney or small red beans, but they can serve as an adequate substitute for either in chili and other dishes in which those beans are commonly used.

BLACK BEANS: Also known as "turtle beans", they are small, dark brownish-black and oval-shaped. Well known in Cuban black bean soup and commonly used in Central and South America and in China. They tend to bleed darkly when cooked so they are not well suited to being combined with other beans, lest they give the entire pot a muddy appearance. The skins of black beans also slip off easily so for this reason they are generally not recommended for pressure cooking for fear of clogging the vent. This can be lessened by not presoaking before cooking.

BLACK-EYED PEAS: Also known as "cowpeas" or "field peas" there are many varieties these peas eaten across the Southern United States, Mexico, and Africa with black-eyed peas being the most commonly known in the U.S. The coloring of field-peas is as varied as the rest of the legume family, with black-eyed peas being small, oval shaped with an overall creamy color and, of course, their distinctive blackeye. Dried field-peas cook very quickly and combine very tastily with either rice or cornbread and are often eaten as Hoppin' John every New Years for luck. They're also reputed to produce less flatulence than many other beans.

CHICKPEAS: Also known as the "garbanzo bean" or "cecci pea" (or bean), they tend to be a creamy or tan color, rather lumpily roundish and larger than dried garden peas. Many have eaten the nutty flavored chick-pea, even if they've never seen a whole one. They are the prime ingredient in hummus and falafel and are one of the oldest cultivated legume species known, going back as far as 5400 B.C. in the Near East. Chickpeas tend to remain firmer when cooked than other legumes and can add a pleasant texture to many foods. They are good in red spaghetti sauces in particular and are often used in Spanish cuisine in a tomato based sauce. Roasted brown then ground they have also served as a coffee substitute.

FAVA BEANS: Not as well known in the U.S. as in Europe and the Mediterranean favas are also known as "broad beans" or "horse beans" being broad in shape, flat and reddish brown in color. This is one of the oldest legume species in European cultivation, but it does require more effort to consume. The hull of the bean is tough and not conducive to being tenderized by cooking so is often peeled away. The skinless bean falls apart so is made into a puree. A small number of people with Mediterranean ancestry have a genetic sensitivity to the blossom pollens and undercooked beans, a condition known as "favism" so should avoid consuming them.

GREAT NORTHERN BEANS: A large white bean about twice the size of navy beans they are typically bean flavored and are frequently favored for soups, salads, casseroles, and baked beans. One of the more commonly eaten in the U.S. Milled into meal these mild flavored beans can be included in many baked goods as a protein booster or used to thicken soups and stews.

KIDNEY BEANS: Like the rest of the family, kidney beans can be found in wide variety. They may be white, mottled or a light or dark red color with their distinctive kidney shape. Probably best known here in the U.S. for their use in chili and bean salads, they figure prominently in Mexican, Brazilian and Chinese cuisine.

LENTILS: Lentils are an odd lot. They don't fit in with either the beans or the peas and occupy a place by themselves. Their shape is different from other legumes being roundish little discs with colors ranging from muddy brown, to green to a rather bright orangish-red. They cook very quickly and have a distinctive mildly peppery flavor. They are much used in Far Eastern cuisine from India to China. Next to mung beans they make excellent sprouts though their peppery flavor tends to strengthen somewhat so are best mixed with milder sprouts.

LIMA BEANS: In the Southern U.S., they are also commonly called "butter beans". Limas are one of the most common legumes, found in this country in all manner of preservation from the young small beans to the large fully mature type. Their flavor is pleasant, but a little bland. Their shape is rather flat and broad with colors ranging from pale green to speckled cream and purple. They combine very well with rice.

MUNG BEANS: Best known here in the States in their sprouted form, they are quite common in Indian and other Asian cuisines and are a close relative of the field peas (cowpeas). Their shape is generally round, fairly small with color ranging from a medium green to so dark as to be nearly black. They cook quickly and presoaking is not generally needed.

NAVY BEANS: Smaller than Great Northerns these petite sized beans are also sometimes knows as pea beans. They are the stars of Navy and Senate Bean Soups, favored for many baked bean dishes, and are most often chosen for use in commercial pork and beans. They retain their shape well when cooked. Ground into meal they can be added to many soups and stews without overpowering them.

PEANUTS (Groundnuts): The peanut is not actually a nut at all, but a legume. They are another odd species not much like the more familiar beans and peas. Peanuts have a high protein percentage and even more fat. Whatever their classification peanuts are certainly not unfamiliar to U.S. eaters. They are one of the two legume species commonly grown for oilseed in this country, and are also used for peanut butter, and boiled or roasted peanuts. Peanut butter (without excessive added sweeteners) can add body and flavor to sauces, gravies, soups, and stews. Many Central and South American, African, Chinese, and Thai dishes incorporate peanuts so they are useful for much more than just a snack food or cooking oil.

PEAS, GREEN OR YELLOW: More often found as split peas though whole peas can sometimes be had. The yellow variety has become somewhat uncommon but has a milder flavor than the green types which well lends them to blending inconspicuously into other foods. Probably best known in split pea soup, particularly with a smoky chunk of ham added. They are also used in Indian cuisine, especially dals. Whole peas need soaking, but split peas can be cooked as is. Split peas and pea meal makes an excellent thickener for soups and stews. Because splitting damages the pea, this more processed form does not keep for as long as whole peas unless given special packaging.

PINK AND RED BEANS: Related to the kidney bean these are smaller in size but similar in flavor. The pink bean has a more delicate flavor than the red. The are both often favored for use in chili and widely used across the American Southwest, Mexico, and Latin America. They can add nicely to the color variety in multibean soups.

PINTO BEANS: Anyone who has eaten Tex-Mex food has likely had the pinto bean. It is probably the most widely consumed legume in the U.S., particularly in the Southwestern portion of the country. Stereotypically bean shaped, it has a dappled pattern of tans and browns on its shell. Pintos have a flavor that blends well with many foods. When ground together with great northern or navy beans they make a great homemade version of falafel. When milled into a meal pintos will cook in mere minutes, making a near instant form of refried beans.

SOYBEANS: The soybean is by far the legume with the highest protein content in large scale commercial production and it's amino acid profile is the most nearly complete for human nutrition. Alongside the peanut it is the other common legume oilseed. The beans themselves are small, round, and with a multitude of different shades though tan seems to be the most common. Because of their high oil content, they are more sensitive to oxygen exposure than other legumes and precautions should be taken accordingly if they are to be kept for more than a year in storage, especially if they are to be processed for soymilk or tofu.

Although the U.S. grows a large percentage of the global supply, we consume virtually none of them directly. Most go into cattle feed, are used by industry, or exported. What does get eaten directly has usually been intensively processed. Soybean products range from soymilk to tofu, to tempeh, to textured vegetable protein (TVP) and hundreds of other forms. They don't lend themselves well to merely being boiled until done then eaten the way other beans and peas do. For this reason, if you plan on keeping some as a part of your storage program you would be well served to begin to learn how to process and prepare them now while you're not under pressure to produce. This way you can throw out your failures and order pizza, rather than having to choke them down, regardless.

DAIRY PRODUCTS

Got milk? Butter? Cheese? In the refrigerator, right? Dairy products are a great source of essential amino acids, vitamin D, and calcium, but in their usual forms found in the refrigerator case of your local supermarkets are perishable commodities. Fortunately, there are a number of dairy products that lend themselves to food storage.

DRY MILKS Dry, powdered milk is available in nearly as many varieties as the fresh fluid product. Most can be found on the shelves of your local supermarket while a few may have to come from rather more specialized suppliers. Skillfully and knowledgeably used they can vastly improve the quality of your food storage program.

NONFAT (skim): This is pasteurized skim milk reduced to a powdered concentrate and is found in two forms - regular and instant. They are both made from the same type of milk, but the instant variety has been given further processing to make it more easily soluble in water than regular dry milk. Both types have essentially the same nutrient composition. The regular variety is more compact, requires less storage space than the instantized variety, usually costs somewhat less, but is a little more difficult to reconstitute.

Instant dry milk is commonly available in nearly any grocery store. The regular type generally has to be sought out from baking and restaurant suppliers or storage food dealers. There is a retail brand by the name of "Milkman" that has a bit of fat content that makes it similar to 1% milk. The fat content means it should be stored like whole milk, described below. It takes 3.2 oz or about 3 tablespoons of instant nonfat dry milk added to 32 oz of water to make 1 quart of milk you can drink or cook with like fresh milk. Combining the dry milk with water at least several hours before you plan to use it gives it time to dissolve fully and to develop a fresher flavor. Shaking the fluid milk vigorously will incorporate air and will also help to improve flavor.

Add the powder to baked goods, gravies, smoothies, hot cereals, casseroles and meat loaf as a nutrition booster. It can also be used to make yogurt, cheese and most any cultured dairy product that does not require a high fat content. Several of the ways that we use dry milk powder is in making grits, oatmeal, and our favorite whole wheat bread. A few tablespoons of dry milk greatly improves the amino acid composition of any grain product.

FLAVORED NONFAT: This may be found packaged in a variety of forms from a low calorie diet drink (artificially sweetened) to the other end of the scale, as cocoa mix or malted milk. The key ingredient is the dry milk so buy and store these products accordingly.

WHOLE MILK: This is whole dry milk with all of its fat content (roughly 28% milkfat) and therefore has a shorter shelf life than nonfat. Other than that, it may be reconstituted and used in exactly the same way as nonfat dry milk. Dry whole milk can sometimes be found in the Hispanic foods area of grocery stores (Nido and Klim by Nestlé are two brands), natural or health food stores, and some storage food suppliers carry it as well as institutional and restaurant foods businesses. It can also sometimes be found where camping and outback supplies are sold. Because of the high fat content this form of dry milk really needs to be either vacuum sealed or packaged with oxygen absorbers in gas impermeable containers such as canning jars, Mylar bags, etc. Rotate and use dry whole milk within two years, less if not packaged for long-term storage.

BUTTERMILK: Dry buttermilk is for use in recipes calling for buttermilk. It can be reconstituted into liquid buttermilk, but it's not much like the fresh liquid product and is best used in baked goods. Since it has a slightly higher fat content than nonfat dry milk, it generally does not keep as long. If properly packaged it should keep for several years.

SOUR CREAM: Made from cultured sweet cream like the fresh product then dried and processed into a powder. Like the real thing it has a high milkfat content (25-28%) and should be stored like whole milk using vacuum sealing and/or oxygen absorbers and kept in a cool place. Mixed with the proper amount of cold water it can be reconstituted into a rich, thick product much like fresh sour cream and can be used in a similar manner or just used as a powder to add a tangy richness to many foods. Properly stored in oxygen free packaging and kept in a cool environment it is possible to achieve about a three year shelf life.

MILK SUBSTITUTES: There are a number of products on the market that purport to take the place of cow or goats milk. They range from soy "milk", rice or other grain "milks", and beverages based on milk components such as whey. If there is not a substantial fat content they may all be stored as you would nonfat dry milk. Those products with a significant fat content (above 1% by weight) should be stored as you would whole dry milk. Do keep in mind that nearly all of these products DO NOT have the same nutritional composition as either nonfat or whole milk. In storage food programs dairy products serve as important sources of high quality complete proteins, calcium, vitamin D and possibly vitamin A. If the milk substitute you're considering does not you'll need to find another adequate source of these important nutrients.

BUYING DRY MILK PRODUCTS

(**a**) - Be sure the dry milk you are buying has been fortified with vitamins A and D. Most all of the whole and nonfat dry milks come fortified with these two vitamins. The dry buttermilk does not come this way, at least the SACO brand does not. The flavored dry milks vary by manufacturer.

(**b**) - There should be no artificial colors or flavors. It may be illegal to add preservatives to any dry milk sold in the U.S. so a claim of "no preservatives" on the label is of no consequence. Other nations may be different, however.

(**c**) - "Extra Grade" on the label indicates the manufacturer has held to higher processing and quality standards and the milk is somewhat lower in fat, moisture and bacterial content, is more soluble, and has fewer scorched particles. There are still some manufacturers of dry milk that sell ordinary Grade A product, but they are becoming fewer.

(**d**) - If you'll be buying your milk in bulk from businesses such as restaurant and institutional foods suppliers be sure to specify "low-temperature spray process" dry milk. The high temperature process dry milks will not give you a very desirable product unless you intend to use it solely for baking.

(**e**) - Try to buy your dried milk in containers of a size that makes sense for the level of consumption in the household. Once it is opened, powdered milk has a short shelf life before undesirable changes in flavor and nutrient content occurs. If you buy large packages and do not use much at one time, consider breaking it down and repackaging into smaller containers at the time of purchase. Vacuum seal it in glass canning jars. (f) - As with any storage food you buy, try to deal only with reputable dealers. It is particularly important to do this with dry milk because of its short shelf life and sensitivity to storage conditions. Check expiration dates, then date and rotate packages.

STORING DRY MILKS

Dry milk products are highly sensitive to environmental conditions, particularly temperature and moisture. Their vitamins A and D are also photosensitive and break down rapidly if exposed to light. The area where your dry milk is stored should be kept as cool as possible. Air-conditioning or even refrigeration can greatly extend the nutrient shelf life. If the storage container is transparent or translucent then it should be put into a second container opaque to light or stored in a dark room.

Dry milk will absorb moisture and odors from the air so storage containers should be impervious to both air and moisture. The drier it can be kept, the better it will keep which makes the use of desiccants is an excellent idea. Oxygen also speeds decomposition so vacuum sealing or oxygen absorbers will decrease the available oxygen. Because of its fine powdery texture gas flushing with nitrogen or carbon dioxide generally yields poor results. If the dry milk you purchased was not packaged for long term storage then it should be repackaged right away. You can purchase the instant variety of dry skim, whole milk, and sometimes buttermilk powder at your local grocery and repack it at home.

One method is to pour the powder into clean, dry canning jars then vacuum seal them with a Tilia Foodsaver using the jar adapter then storing in the ubiquitous cool, dark place. They must be guarded against breakage, but they offer the advantage of not holding odors, thus allowing for reuse after cleaning. Since the glass is transparent they must be protected against light. Clean, sound plastic one and two liter soda bottles can also be used, but probably should be used just once since the plastic is somewhat permeable and will hold odors. If you have access to a can sealer, #10 cans make wonderful storage containers for dry milk, particularly if used in conjunction with O2 absorbers.

SHELF LIFE OF DRY MILKS

According to the makers of SACO Mix'nDrink Instant Pure Skim Milk, their Mix'n Drink will keep its nutrition value for up to about two years if kept cool and dry, and the only vitamins that actually decrease over time are the vitamins A and D. These are not shelfstable vitamins and are sensitive to heat and light. A good rule of thumb to follow is that the vitamins A and D will dissipate at a rate of about 20% every year if stored properly. The less the milk is exposed to, the better the vitamins will keep. A freezer could extend the shelf life, as long as the powder does not get moisture in it.

Putting a time limit on the Mix'nDrink, for rotation purposes, dates it at about two years after the date of purchase. After opening a package of dry milk, transfer the powder to a tightly covered glass or metal container (dry milk can pick up odors from plastic containers) and keep it in the refrigerator. Unsealed nonfat dry milk keeps for a few months; dry whole milk for a few weeks.

CANNED FLUID MILKS AND CREAMS

Preserved liquid milk comes in a number of forms, none of which are very similar to each other. The most common are as follows:

CANNED MILKS: These are commonly called UHT milks (Ultra High Temperature) for the packaging technique used to preserve them. They come in the same varieties as fresh liquid milks: Whole, 2%, 1% and skim. Even whipping creams can be found in UHT packaging (Grand Chef - Parmalat), though this may be offered only in the commercial and restaurant trade. In the U.S. they all have vitamin D added. The lesser fat content milks do not keep as long as whole milk and their use by dates are correspondingly shorter term. This milk is packaged in aseptic laminated paper cartons. It has the same composition as fresh milk of the same type, and can be stored at room temperature because of the special pasteurizing process used. The milk has a boiled flavor, but less so than evaporated milk. The dates are usually for approximately six months. The milk is still usable past its date, but the flavor soon begins to go stale and the cream separates. With a six-month shelf life this type of canned milk naturally requires a much faster rotation cycle than other types. Several companies sell flavored milks (chocolate, etc.) in this packaging, usually in the smaller single-serving sizes. UHT milk makes excellent yogurt, losing the boiled flavor.

EVAPORATED MILK: Made from fresh, unpasteurized milk using a vacuum-heating process that removes 60% of the water, the concentrate is heated, homogenized, and in the States, vitamin D is added. It is then sealed in cans and heated again to sterilize the contents. Some brands may have other nutrients and/or chemical stabilizers added so read can labels closely. A mixture of one part water and one part evaporated milk will have about the same nutritional value as an equal amount of fresh milk. It does not taste like fresh milk but many do not find the flavor to be disagreeable. Both whole and skim milk varieties are available with the higher fat content type having the best storage life. The typical recommended storage time is six months. There is generally no date or use by code on evaporated milk. Some grocers along with health food stores carry canned, evaporated goat's milk, in a similar concentration.

SWEETENED CONDENSED MILK: A less processed product than evaporated milk. It starts with pasteurized milk combined with a sugar solution. The water is then extracted until the mixture is less than half its original weight. It is not heated because the high sugar content prevents spoilage. It's very rich as well: 8 oz contains 980 calories. Obviously with a greatly reduced water content and a high sugar level it won't taste like fresh milk but it does have many uses in cooking. Some use condensed milk to cream their coffee. This type too is available in whole and skim varieties. A fairly new entry into the sweetened condensed milk field is Dulce de Leche a popular dessert item in Latin America. It's basically sweetened condensed milk that has been heated to the point that the sugar begins to brown which produces a rich tasting caramel dessert. In the past you had to make it yourself, but now it can be purchased ready-made in the can. It is often fund in the canned/dry milk areas or the Hispanic/ethnic foods areas of many grocery stores. Although it is often hard to find, the condensed milk can label should have a stamped date code which indicates the date by which it should be consumed. Condensed milk may thicken and darken as it ages, but it is still edible.

CANNED CREAM: Apparently in the U.S. only the Nestlé company produces canned creams, both being imports. One is "Media Crema" produced in Mexico with a pull-top can and the other is "Table Cream" produced in Australia in a standard (as in use an opener) can. There is a slight difference in preservatives and thickeners, but basically both are a shelf stable light cream which can be used in any way that you would use fresh light cream. The shelf-life for these products seems to be in excess of two years in any decent storage environment. Like the Dulce de Leche above they can be found either in the dry/canned milk areas or the Hispanic/ethnic areas of your grocery store.

BUTTER

Butter can be found in several forms each with their particular strengths and weaknesses.

BUTTER POWDER: Probably the easiest to find of the shelf-stable butters the powder is a moisture free product consisting of butter fat condensed on milk solids generally with added antioxidants. It can be reconstituted by mixing with water to make a spread similar to whipped butter, but it cannot be used for frying or other applications requiring high heat that would burn the milk solids. Most butter powders have something of a milky taste due to the additional milk solids necessary to create the powder, but many do not find this objectionable. Because it is a powder (lots of surface area) with a high fat content it needs good packaging to keep it at its best. Vacuum sealing and/or oxygen absorbers will work well if you are doing your own packaging.

CLARIFIED BUTTER (GHEE): Another form of butter suitable for storage programs is clarified butter or ghee as it is known in India. This is fresh, unsalted butter gently heated to drive off the moisture with the remaining fat poured off of the butter solids. It can be purchased commercially but most choose to make it themselves. As it's essentially pure butterfat with no water there is little to spoil so will keep for years in a glass jar protected from oxygen, heat, and light. A good source of fat calories and useful in cooking, but maybe not something you'd want to spread on a biscuit.

CANNED BUTTER: For those whom only the real thing will do it's now possible to find shelf stable real butter. It seems mostly to be sold in those nations where home refrigeration is not as common as it is here in the U.S. One of the few U.S. importers of shelf stable canned is Bruce Hopkin's Internet Grocer (http:// www.internet-grocer.com). His product is Red Feather brand canned butter from New Zealand. It is salted though not as heavily as most salted butter in the U.S. The manufacturer claims an eighteen month shelf-stable storage life though they do advise keeping it in a cool, dry place. Like all butter it will liquefy it allowed to warm too much. Each can contains twelve ounces (equivalent to about three sticks of butter) and once opened should be handled like any other butter.

CHEESE

There are a number of shelf-stable cheese products that are suited for storage programs. Each of them have particular strengths or weaknesses for given uses. The basic forms storage cheeses can take are:

CANNED CHEESE: Actually, it's "Pasteurized Processed Cheddar Cheese Product" but it's the closest thing to a shelf-stable real cheese. It's another one of those products produced for use in countries where home refrigeration is scarcer than it is here in the U.S. One of the few brands available in the States is made by Kraft's Australian division whose product most resembles a mild white cheddar or perhaps an American cheese. A U.S. source for this cheese is again Bruce Hopkin's

Internet Grocer (http://www.internetgrocer.com). It comes in an eight ounce can and the manufacturer claims it will keep "indefinitely" at any reasonable storage temperature.

DRIED GRATED CHEESES: These are the familiar grated dry Parmesan and Romano cheeses, possibly others as well. They're generally a coarse dry powder, low or nonfat, and often with a fair amount of salt. Kept dry, cool, and dark they'll keep as they come from the store for several years though to get the maximum possible shelf life you should vacuum seal them in glass. Usually fairly expensive for the amount you get but as they're also strongly flavored a little will go a long way.

These are the familiar grated dry Parmesan and Romano cheeses, possibly others as well. They're generally a coarse dry powder, low or nonfat, and often with a fair amount of salt. Kept dry, cool, and dark they'll keep as they come from the store for several years though to get the maximum possible shelf life you should vacuum seal them in glass. Usually fairly expensive for the amount you get but as they're also strongly flavored a little will go a long way.

SAUCES AND SOUPS: These are products such as Cheez Whiz, Campbell's Cheddar Cheese Soup, chip dips and related. They're not really cheese, but a mixture of cheese, milk, flour, and other ingredients. Depending on what your end uses may be they can provide a cheese flavor, calories, and a degree of protein, fat, and calcium. In any decent storage conditions they'll keep for several years at least. Aerosol cheese is an abomination that will not be discussed here.

POWDERED CHEESE: Used in products such as boxed macaroni and cheese, au gratin potatoes, snacks, and the like, this is basically cheese that has had its moisture removed leaving behind mostly protein, fat, a fair amount of calcium and various flavoring and coloring compounds (naturally occurring or added) along with a fair amount of salt. It can't really be melted, but it can add a nice cheese flavor where a real cheese texture is not needed. There are also cheese powder blends, typically a mixture of cheese powder, food starch, whey, milk solids and other noncheese ingredients. It has less fat than true cheese powder, about the same protein, but less calcium. You can make it yourself with dry milk and cornstarch so there's little point in not getting real cheese powder. Cheese powder will keep for many years in sealed metal cans kept at cool temperatures. You'll probably have to get it from restaurant foods suppliers or order it from storage foods dealers. It's high fat content means that it needs low-oxygen packaging.

EGGS

The noble fruit of the hen, eggs play an important role in the kitchen arts. Unfortunately, outside of regular runs to the store to buy fresh eggs or keeping your own hens they're problematical to store. There are two basic ways to keep eggs for those times when fresh eggs may be hard to come by. One is to preserve them in the shell, a process which must be done at home as there are no commercial sources of preserved shell eggs. The second is to buy dry, or powdered, eggs.

DRY EGGS

Dry eggs are generally available in four different forms – whole eggs, egg whites, egg yolks, and as a mix for making scrambled eggs and omelets. Which you should buy depends on how you expect to use them. As a general rule dry eggs reconstitute more easily when mixed with warm (not hot) water. Mixing the dry powder with other dry ingredients before adding liquids also increases the ease by which they can be reconstituted. Allowing the eggs to sit a few minutes before using improves water adsorption.

WHOLE EGGS: This is everything but the shell and the water. Usually found in the form of a somewhat clumpy, eggy smelling yellow powder. Typically one tablespoon of whole egg powder mixed with two tablespoons of water will equal one large fresh egg. Can be used to make most anything you'd make with fresh eggs though they seem to work better in baking rather than as scrambled eggs or omelets. Whole egg powder is commonly used in baking mixes of all kinds, but plain powdered eggs are rarely for sale in any grocery. Fortunately, they're easy to come by from mail order suppliers. A #10 can of powdered eggs is quite a lot so give some thought as to how fast you might use them and either order smaller cans, repackage an opened can into smaller containers, or plan on eating eggs often.

EGG WHITES: Nearly pure protein, egg white powder can add a high-protein boost to anything you put it in. The powder itself is whitish in color and not as clumpy as whole egg powder. When properly reconstituted it will whip into meringue like fresh egg whites and can be used in producing angel food and sponge cakes. Dry egg whites are often found in the baking section of many supermarkets. One brand name is "Just Whites" by Deb El. Powdered egg whites are also available from many mail order suppliers.

EGG YOLKS: High protein, high fat, and a source of lecithin (a natural emulsifier). Egg yolk powder can add richness and flavor to any number of foods, used to make custards, sauces, noodles, even mayonnaise. Not generally as easy to find as whole eggs and whites, but can be mail ordered. Being pure yolks this powder has a high fat content and most be appropriately packaged to achieve a good shelf life.

EGG MIX OR SCRAMBLING MIX: Typically a mix of whole egg powder, nonfat milk powder, oil, and salt. Used for making scrambled eggs, omelets, or general egg cookery. This mix does offer a degree of convenience but you can easily make it yourself and save the trouble of having to store it as a separate product.

STORING DRY EGGS All dry egg products are exceedingly sensitive to moisture and will go off quickly if allowed to become the least bit damp. Whole eggs, egg yolks, and egg mix have high fat contents which make them very sensitive to oxygen. Use vacuum sealing in glass jars or oxygen absorbers in conjunction with some other form of high barrier property packaging to keep these products at their best. If you bought quality products, packaged them well in oxygen free packaging, and put them away in a good storage environment then whole eggs, egg yolks, and egg mix should be able to achieve at least a three year shelf life, possibly more. Egg whites will easily achieve five years. Naturally, if you're packaging your eggs in any sort of transparent or translucent packaging then they should be stored in a dark place.

SUGAR, HONEY AND OTHER SWEETENERS

There are a wide number of sugars to be found for purposes of sweetening foods. Fructose is the primary sugar in fruit and honey; maltose is one of the sugars in malted grains; pimentose is found in olives, and sucrose is what we know as granulated or table sugar. Sucrose is a highly refined product made primarily from sugar cane though sugar beets still contribute a fair amount of the world supply. Modern table sugar is now so highly refined as to be virtually 100% pure and nearly indestructible if protected from moisture. Powdered sugar and brown sugar are simple variations on granulated sugar and share its long life. Liquid sweeteners do not have quite the longevity of dry sugars. Honey, cane syrup, molasses, corn syrup and maple syrup may crystallize or mold during long storage. These syrups are chemically not as simple as table sugar and therefore lose flavor and otherwise break down over time.

GRANULATED SUGARS:

Buying refined sugar is a simple matter. Select a brand you know you can trust, be certain the package is clean, dry and has no insect infestation. There's little that can go wrong with it.

GRANULATED: Granulated sugar does not spoil, but if it gets damp it will grow lumpy or turn into a sugar rock. If it does, it can be pulverized into smaller pieces and used. Granulated sugar can be found in varying textures, coarser or finer. "Castor/caster sugar" is a finer granulation than what is commonly sold as table sugar in the U.S. and is more closely equivalent to our super fine or berry sugar.

POWDERED, CONFECTIONERS, ICING: All names refer to the same kind of sugar, that is white granulated sugar very finely ground. For commercial use there is a range of textures from coarse to ultra-fine. For home consumption, what is generally found is either Very Fine (6X) or Ultra-Fine (10X), but this can vary from nation to nation. Not all manufacturers will indicate the grind on the package. Sugar refiners usually add a small amount of cornstarch to prevent caking which will make it undesirable for use in sugar syrups or solutions where clarity is needed. Powdered sugar is as inert as granulated sugar, but it is even more hygroscopic and will absorb any moisture present. If it soaks up more than a little it will cake and become hard. It's difficult to reclaim hardened powdered sugar, but it can still be used like granulated sugar where clarity in solution (syrups) is not important.

BROWN, LIGHT & DARK: In the United States brown sugar is generally refined white sugar that has had a bit of molasses or sugar syrup and caramel coloring added to it. Dark brown sugar has more molasses which gives it a stronger flavor, a darker color and makes it damp. Light brown sugar has less molasses which gives it a milder flavor, a blonder color and is slightly dryer than the dark variety. Light brown sugar can be made by combining one fourth to one third white sugar to the remainder dark brown sugar and blend thoroughly. Both varieties need to be protected from drying out, or they will become hard and difficult to deal with. Nor do you want to allow them to become damper than what they already are. There are dry granulated and liquid brown sugars available, but they don't have the same cooking qualities as ordinary brown sugars. They also don't dry out and harden quite so readily either.

RAW, NATURAL, TURBINADO & OTHERS: In recent years, refiners have realized there is a market for less processed forms of cane sugar in the U.S. so have begun to sell these under various names and packaging. None of them are actually raw sugar as it is illegal to sell in the States due to the high impurities level in the truly raw product. All will have been processed to some degree, perhaps to remove the sticky surface molasses or to lighten the color, but will not have been subjected to the full refining and whitening processes of ordinary white table sugar. This leaves some of the natural hue and a strength of flavor that deepens with the color. All of these less refined sugars may be stored and handled like brown sugar.

Outside of the United States it is possible to buy cane sugars from the truly raw product with all of the detritus remaining from the cane juice extraction process up through various stages of refinement much like we have here in the United States. Many can be found with names such as "muscavado", "jaggery" (usually a raw palm or date sugar), "demerara", "succanat," and others. Colors will range from quite dark to blonde and may or may not be sticky with molasses. Generally the darker the color the stronger the flavor will be. In spite of any impurities they can be stored like brown sugar since their sugar content is high enough to inhibit most microbial growth.

STORING GRANULATED SUGARS

All granulated sugars have basically the same storage requirements. They need to be kept in air tight, insect and moisture proof containers. For powdered, and granulated sugar you might want to consider using some desiccant in the storage container if your local climate is damp. Since brown sugars and raw sugars are supposed to be moist, they do not need desiccants. Shelf life is indefinite if kept dry, but anything you intend to eat really should be rotated occasionally. Time has a way of affecting even the most durable of foods. Brown sugar that is six years old when removed from storage may be fine, other than the molasses settling somewhat toward the bottom.

HONEY

Honey may be the oldest sweetener known to man- its use predates recorded history. Remains of honey have been found in the Egyptian pyramids. This product of honeybees is typically sweeter than granulated sugar by a factor of 25%-40% depending upon the specific flowers from which the bees gathered their nectar. This means a smaller amount of honey can give the same amount of sweetening as sugar. The source flowers also dictate the flavor and the color as well. Honey color can range from very dark (nearly black) to almost colorless. As a general rule, the lighter the color and the more delicate the flavor, the greater the price the honey will bring. As you might expect, since honey is sweeter than table sugar, it also has more calories as well — an average of twenty two per teaspoon compared to granulated sugar's sixteen. There are also trivial amounts of minerals and vitamins in the bee product while white sugar has none. Honey is not a direct substitute for table sugar however, its use in recipes may call for a bit of alteration to make them to turn out right.

Although the chance is remote, raw honey may also contain minute quantities of *Clostridium botulinum* spores so should not be fed to children under one year of age. Raw honey is OK for older children and adults. Honey comes in a number of forms in the retail market and all with somewhat different storage characteristics:

WHOLE-COMB: This is the bee product straight from the hive. It is the most unprocessed form of honey, being large pieces of waxy comb floating in raw honey. The comb itself will contain many unopened honey cells.

RAW: This is unheated honey that has been removed from the comb. It may contain bits of wax and other small particles.

FILTERED: This is raw honey that has been warmed slightly to make it easier to filter out small particles and impurities. Other than being somewhat cleaner than raw honey it is essentially the same. Most of the trace amounts of nutrients remain intact.

LIQUID/PURE: This is honey that has been heated to higher temperatures to allow for easier filtering and to kill any microorganisms. Usually lighter in color, this form is milder in flavor, resists crystallization and generally clearer. It stores the best of the various forms of honey. Much of the trace amounts of vitamins, however, are lost.

SPUN, CRYSTALLIZED or CREAMED: This honey has had some of its moisture content removed to make a creamy spread. It is the most processed form of honey. It keeps quite well. Also available in various flavors.

BUYING HONEY

Much of the honey sold in supermarkets has been blended from a variety of different honeys and some may have even had other sweeteners added as well. Like anything involving humans, buying honey can be a tricky business. It pays to deal with individuals and brands you know you can trust. In the United States you should buy products labeled U.S. GRADE A or U.S. FANCY if buying in retail outlets. However, be aware there are no federal labeling laws governing the sale of honey, so only honey labeled pure is entirely honey and not blended with other sweeteners. Honey grading is a matter of voluntary compliance which means some producers may be lax in their practices. Some may also use words like "organic", "raw", "uncooked" and "unfiltered" on their labels, possibly to mislead. Fortunately, most honey producers are quite honest in their product labeling so if you're not certain of who to deal with, it is worthwhile to ask around to find out who produces a good product. Honey may also contain trace amounts of drugs used in treating various bee ailments, including antibiotics. If this is a concern to you, then it would be wise to investigate with your local honey producer what they may have used.

STORING HONEY

Honey is much easier to store than to select and buy. Pure honey won't mold, but may crystallize over time. Exposure to air and moisture may cause color to darken, flavor to intensify and may speed crystallization as well. Comb honey doesn't store as well liquid honey so you should not expect it to last as long. Storage temperature is not as important for honey, but it should not be allowed to freeze or exposed to high temperatures if possible. Either can cause crystallization and heat may cause flavor to strengthen undesirably. Filtered liquid honey will last the longest in storage. Storage containers should be opaque, airtight, moisture and odorproof. Like any other stored food, honey should be rotated through the storage cycle and replaced with fresh product.

If crystallization does occur, honey can be reliquified by placing the container in a larger container of hot water until it has melted. Avoid adding water to honey you intend to keep in storage or it may ferment. Avoid storing honey near heat sources or petroleum products (including gasoline/diesel engines), chemicals or any other odor-producing products which may infuse through plastic packaging.

RAW HONEY AND BOTULISM

Honey contains very, very small amounts of the bacteria that cause botulism. For adults, this seldom causes problems. Our immune system is capable of dealing with small numbers of even nasty bacteria, they do it all the time. The problem is when we get large numbers of bacteria, or when our immune system is damaged or not yet developed. That is where the problem with honey comes in. Some people used to use honey to sweeten milk or other foods for infants. Infants immune systems sometimes cannot handle the bacteria that cause botulism, and, of course, those infants became seriously ill. So pediatricians now advise strongly against using honey for children under a certain age.

Yes, raw honey can contain the temperature resistant spores of Clostridium botulinum, the bacterium that causes botulism. The organism is a strict anaerobe, meaning that it only grows in the absence of molecular oxygen. The problem with infants and honey is that the small, intestinal tract of an infant apparently is sufficiently anaerobic to allow the spores to germinate into actively growing C. botulinum organisms. Essentially, the infant serves the same role as a sealed, airtight, contaminated can of beans as far as the organisms are concerned. There in the infant's body the bacteria secrete the dangerous toxin that causes the symptoms of botulism. There have been quite a few documented infant deaths due to honey. Most pediatricians recommend no honey for the first year.

HONEY OUTGASSING

Q: My can of honey is bulging. Is it safe to use?

A: Honey can react with the can lining to release a gas especially when stored over a long period of time. Honey's high sugar content prevents bacteria growth. If there is no sign of mold growth, it is safe to eat.

CANE SYRUPS

CANE SYRUP: Seldom found in supermarkets pure cane syrup is a sweet symbol of the U.S. Deep South. Produced by boiling down the extracted juice of the sugarcane in much the same fashion as sorghum and maple syrups are produced. The best syrup is clear with a dark amber color and a smooth intense flavor. Cane syrup usually has to be purchased from roadside stands, living history recreations, farm festivals, or state and county fairs. Some syrup makers will add small quantities of lemon juice or corn syrup to deter crystallization. Flavored cane syrups can sometimes be found, but are usually a sign of inferior syrup .

MOLASSES: A by-product of sugar refining, molasses is generally composed of sugars such as glucose that are resistant to crystallization, browning reaction products resulting from the syrup reduction process, and small amounts of minerals. Flavor can vary between brands, but is usually strong and the color dark and opaque. Sulfured molasses can sometimes be found but its intense flavor is unappealing to most. Brands labeled as 'blackstrap molasses' are intensely flavored.

SORGHUM SYRUP: This is produced in the same manner as cane syrup, but sweet sorghum cane, rather than sugar cane, is used. Sorghum tends to have a thinner, slightly sourer taste than cane syrup. Good syrup should be a clear dark amber with a smooth flavor. It can sometimes be found in the supermarket, but more often is found in the same types of places as genuine sugar cane syrup.

TREACLE: This sweetener comes in varying colors from a rather dark version, similar to, but not quite the same as blackstrap molasses, to paler versions more similar to golden syrup. If you cannot find it in your store's syrup area check in their imported foods section. All of the above syrups are generally dark with a rich, heavy flavor.

GOLDEN SYRUP: This syrup is both lighter and paler in color than any of the above four, more similar to what we would call a table syrup here in the U.S. Can usually be found in the same areas as treacle above.

TABLE SYRUP: There are many table syrups sold in supermarkets, some with flavorings of one sort or another such as maple, various fruits, butter, etc. A close examination of the ingredients list will reveal mixtures usually of cane syrup, cane sugar syrup or corn syrup along with preservatives, colorings and other additives. Table syrup usually has a much less pronounced flavor than molasses, cane or sorghum syrup or the darker treacles. Any syrup containing corn syrup should be stored as corn syrup.

STORING CANE SYRUPS

All of the above syrups, except for those having corn syrup in their makeup, have the same storage characteristics. They can be stored on the shelf for about two years and up to a year after opening. Once they are opened, they are best kept in the refrigerator to retard mold growth. If mold growth does occur, the syrup should be discarded. The outside of the bottle should be cleaned of drips after each use. Some pure cane and sorghum syrups may crystallize in storage, but this causes no harm and they can be reliquified using the same method as for honey. Molasses or other sugar refining by-products won't usually crystallize, but will dry into an unmanageable tar unless kept sealed .

CORN SYRUP Corn syrup is a liquid sweetener made by breaking down cornstarch into its constituent sugars through an enzyme reaction. Available in both a light and a dark form, the darker variety has a flavor similar to molasses and contains refiners syrup (a by-product of sugar refining). Both types often contain flavorings and preservatives. It is commonly used in baking and candy making because it does not crystallize when heated. Corn syrup is common in the U.S., but less so elsewhere. Corn syrup stores poorly compared to other sweeteners and because of this it often has a best if used by date on the bottle. It should be stored in its original bottle, tightly capped, in a cool, dry place. New unopened bottles can be expected to keep about six months past the date on the label and sometimes longer. After opening, keep the corn syrup four to six months. These syrups are prone to mold and to fermentation so be on the lookout for bubbling or a mold haze. If these present themselves, throw the syrup out. You should wipe off any drips from the bottle after every use.

MAPLE SYRUP Maple syrup is produced by boiling down the sap of the maple tree (and a lot of it too) collected at certain times in the early Spring until it reaches a syrup consistency. This is slightly sweeter than table sugar and is judged by much the same criteria as honey: Lightness of color, clarity and taste. Making the syrup is energy and labor intensive so pure maple is generally expensive. Maple flavored pancake syrups are usually mixtures of corn and cane sugar syrups with either natural or artificial flavorings and should be kept and stored as corn syrups. New unopened bottles of maple syrup may be kept on a cool, dark, shelf for up to two years. The sweetener may darken and the flavor get stronger, but it is still usable. After the bottle has been opened, it should be refrigerated. It will last about a year. Be careful to look out for mold growth. If mold occurs, discard the syrup.

FATS AND OILS

All oils are fats, but not all fats are oils. They are similar to each other in their chemical makeup, but what makes one an oil and another a fat is the percentage of hydrogen saturation in the fatty acids of which they are composed. The fats which are available to us for culinary purposes are actually mixtures of differing fatty acids so for practical purposes we'll say saturated fats are solid at room temperature (70ºF, 21º C) and the unsaturated fats we call oils are liquid at room temperature. For dietary and nutrition purposes fats are generally classified as saturated, monounsaturated and polyunsaturated, which is a further refinement of the amount of saturation of the particular compositions of fatty acids in the fats.

BUYING AND STORING OILS AND FATS

There is a problem with storing oils and fats for the long term and that is they want to go rancid. Rancid fats have been implicated in increased rates of heart disease, arteriosclerosis and are carcinogenic (cancer causing) so are best avoided whenever possible. Oxygen is eight times more soluble in fat than in water and it is the oxidation resulting from this exposure that is the primary cause of rancidity. The less saturated a fat is, the faster it will go bad. This may not be readily apparent at first because vegetable oils have to become several times more rancid than animal fats before our noses can easily detect it. An extreme example of rancidity is the linseed oil (flaxseed) that we use as a wood finish and a base for oil paints. In a matter of hours the oil oxidizes into a solid polymer. This is very desirable for wood and paint, very undesirable for food.

Because of this difficulty in storing fats and oils for any long period of time many books and articles on the subject of food storage make only passing mention of them. This is unfortunate because fat contains nine calories to the gram compared to the four calories contained by either carbohydrates or protein. This makes fat a valuable source of concentrated calories that could be of real importance if faced with a diet consisting largely of unrefined grains and legumes. Small children, infants, nursing mothers, and the elderly may not be able to consume the volume of food necessary in the course of a day to get all of the calories they need to avoid weight loss and possible malnutrition. Additionally, fats play an important role in our perception of taste and texture and their absence would make many foods more difficult to prepare and consume.

Furthermore, a small amount of dietary fat is necessary for our bodies to properly absorb fat soluble vitamins like A,D,E and K. Long term storage of fats may be problematical, but it is not impossible. There are some general rules you can follow to get the most life out of your stored cooking oils and fats:

#1 - Exposure to oxygen, light and heat are the greatest factors to rancidity. If you can, refrigerate your stored oil, particularly after it's been opened. If possible, buy your oils in opaque, airtight containers. If you purchase it in plastic, particularly clear plastic, then transfer it to a gas impermeable glass or metal container that can be sealed airtight. If you have a means of doing so, vacuum sealing the storage container is an excellent idea as it removes most of the air remaining inside, taking much of the oxygen with it. Transparent glass and plastic containers should be stored in the dark, such as in a box or cabinet. Regardless of the storage container, it should be stored at as cool a temperature as possible and rotated as fast as is practical. All other considerations being equal, oils and fats with preservatives will have a greater shelf life than those without, provided they are fresh when purchased.

#2 - Unless they have been specially treated, most unopened cooking oils have a shelf life of about a year to a year and a half, depending upon the above conditions. Some specialty oils such as sesame and flax seed have shorter usable lives. If you don't use a lot, try to not buy your fats in big containers. This way you won't be exposing a large quantity to the air after opening, to grow old and possibly rancid, before you can use it all up. Once opened, it is an excellent idea to refrigerate cooking fats. If it turns cloudy or solid, the fat is still perfectly usable and will return to its normal liquid, clear state after it has warmed to room temperature. Left at room temperatures, opened bottles of cooking oils can begin to rancid in anywhere from a week to a couple of months, though it may take several more months to reach such a point of rancidity that it can be noticeably smelled.

#3 - Although darker colored oils have more flavor than paler colored, the agents that contribute to that flavor and color also contribute to faster rancidity. For maximum shelf life buy paler colored oils.

EXTENDING SHELF LIFE BY ADDING ANTIOXIDANTS

If obtaining the maximum possible shelf life in your cooking fats is important to you, it is possible to add antioxidant preservatives to the fat you have purchased. Used in conjunction with a gas impermeable container, either opaque in color or stored in a dark place, and cool storage temperatures (70° F 21°C or less) then shelf life can be extended to about five years, possibly longer. The antioxidant in question is Butylated HydroxyToluene (BHT). It is often used in the food industry to slow the development of offflavors, odors and color changes caused by oxidation, mostly in foods with significant fat contents. BHT is on the U.S. Food and Drug Administration's Generally Recognized As Safe (GRAS) list as a common preservative. The FDA limits the use of BHT to 0.02% or 200 parts per million (ppm) of the oil or fat content of a food product. The directions below will be for the FDA limit. BHT is available over the counter in the retail trade, typically found in health or natural foods stores or vitamin and nutritional supplement from various suppliers on the Internet.

To get the best results you will need the freshest oil you can find. Purchasing from a large, busy supermarket will usually suffice. You'll also need containers that are gas impermeable such as glass jars, or metal cans. There may be plastic containers with high gas barrier properties that will also serve. It is important that your containers be food grade, clean, dry and dust-free. In keeping with the FDA's GRAS guidelines you want to add 5.3mg of BHT crystals per fluid ounce of oil or fat. If you're using a scale calibrated in grains, such as a reloading powder scale, you may use the following table.

HT in grains OIL BHT in milligrams

- grain 1 fl oz 5.3 mg
- 0.7 grain 8 fl oz (1 cup) 42.4 mg
- 1.3 grain 16 fl oz (1 pint) 84.8 mg
- 2.6 grain 32 fl oz (1 quart) 169.6 mg
- 5.2 grain 64 fl oz (1/2 gal) 339.2 mg
- 10.3 grain 128 fl oz (1 gallon) 678.4 mg

NOTE: The grain weight measurements have been rounded up to the nearest tenth grain since most powder scales will not accurately measure less than one-tenth of a grain.

IMPORTANT NOTE: If you are using a reloading powder scale, be sure the balance pan is clean and the balance has been calibrated recently with a reliable set of check weights.

Remove the BHT crystals from their gelatin capsules and weigh them, if you're going to. Once you have the appropriate amount, add the crystals to a pint or so of the oil, shaking vigorously. It may take several hours for the preservative to dissolve completely. Bringing the oil up to a warm, NOT HOT, temperature will speed the process. Once completely dissolved, pour the antioxidant laden oil into the rest of the oil and mix thoroughly. Once mixed, the oil can then be poured into its storage containers leaving approximately 1/2 inch of headspace. If you have a vacuum sealer the jars or cans may be vacuum sealed to remove most of the oxygen laden air from the container, otherwise just seal the lid. Store in a cool place and if using transparent jars, be certain to put them in a larger container such as a box to keep the contents in the dark. Don't forget to label and date the jars. No amount of preservatives that can be added to your stored fats will substitute for proper storage and rotation.

Don't sit on your oil supply for years without rotating it. ***A little bit rancid is a little bit poisonous..***

COOKING ADJUNCTS

Baking powder is a combination of an acid and an alkali with starch added to keep the other tw0 ingredients stable and dry. The powder reacts with liquid by foaming and the resulting bubbles of carbon dioxide can aerate and raise dough. Almost all baking powder now on the market is double acting, meaning it has one acid that bubbles at room temperature and another acid which only reacts at oven temperatures. Unless a recipe specifies otherwise, this is the type to use. Don't expose baking powder to steam, humid air, wet spoons, or other moisture. Store in a tightly lidded container for no more than a year. Even when kept bone dry it will eventually loses its potency. To test its strength, measure 1 tsp powder into 1/3 cup hot water. The mixture should fizz and bubble furiously. If it doesn't, throw it out.

For those concerned with aluminum in the diet, the Rumford brand has none and there may be others.

BAKING SODA

This gritty powder is sodium bicarbonate also known as sodium acid bicarbonate ($NaHCO_3$), a mild alkali. When combined with an acid ingredient such as buttermilk it is used in baking to leaven quick breads and other baked foods working in the same manner as baking powder. It can also be used to make hominy. When combined with an acid ingredient, the bicarbonate reacts to give off carbon dioxide bubbles which causes the baked goods to rise. If kept well sealed in an air and moisture-proof container its storage life is indefinite. If kept in the cardboard box it usually comes in, it will keep for about eighteen months. Do keep in mind that baking soda is a wonderful odor absorber. If you don't want your baked goods tasting of whatever smells it absorbed then keeping it in an airtight container is a good idea.

HERBS AND SPICES It is difficult to give exact instructions on how best to store culinary herbs and spices because there are dozens of different seeds, leaves, roots, barks, etc., we call an herb or a spice. There are, however, some general rules that may be followed to best preserve their flavors. All spices, particularly dried, are especially sensitive to heat, air, moisture, and light. Room temperature is satisfactory for storage but refrigeration or freezing is even better. Whatever you do they should be kept away from heat sources. It is common for the household spice cabinet or shelf to be located over the stove, but this is really about the worst possible place to keep herbs and spices even if it is convenient. Dark opaque glass is best for storage, but failing that, keeping a tightly sealed glass container in a dark place is next best. The cellophane packets some products come in won't do. Tightly sealed metal containers will work as well. Even dense plastic will do, but glass is best.

Where possible, buy spices whole. Whole nutmegs will keep their flavor far longer than ground nutmeg, the same for other seeds and roots. You'll have to use a grater, grinder or whatever, but the difference in flavor is worth it. If you buy spices in bulk containers (which is certainly cheaper) consider transferring some into smaller containers and keeping the larger one tightly sealed in a cool, dark place. This will prevent unwanted light and air from continually getting in and playing havoc. Keep large jars of reserve spices in vacuum sealed jars with smaller jars of ready spices kept in the kitchen. There are many mail order or online suppliers of bulk herbs and spices- try Penzey's (http://www.penzeys.com).

SALT Storage life for salt is indefinite. So long as you do not let it become contaminated with dirt or whatever, it will never go bad. Over time, iodized salt may turn yellow, but this is harmless and can still be used. Salt is rather hygroscopic and will adsorb moisture from the air if not sealed in an airtight container. If it does cake up, it can be dried in the oven and then pulverized again with no harm done. All salt, however, is not the same. Salt comes in a number of different varieties, and very little of what is produced in the U.S. is intended for use in food. The rest of it, about 98%, has other uses. Therefore, it is important to be certain the salt you have is intended for human consumption. Once you are satisfied it is, you should then determine its appropriateness for the tasks to which you might want to set it to. Below is a list of some of the available salts:

TABLE SALT: This is by far the most widely known type of salt. It comes in two varieties; iodized and non-iodized. There is an ingredient added to adsorb moisture so the salt will stay free flowing in damp weather. This non-caking agent does not dissolve in water and can cause cloudiness in solutions if sufficiently large quantities are used. In canning this won't cause a problem since little per jar is used. For pickling, though, it would be noticeable. If you are storing salt for this purpose, you should be sure to choose plain pickling salt, or other food grade pure salt such as kosher salt. In the iodized varieties, the iodine can cause discoloration or darkening of pickled foods. For folks in areas that are historically iodine deficient a store of iodized salt for table consumption should be kept.

CANNING SALT: This is pure salt and nothing but salt. It can usually be found in the canning supplies section of most grocery stores. This is the preferred salt for most food preservation or storage uses. It is generally about the same grain size as table salt.

KOSHER SALT: This salt is not really, in itself, kosher, but is used in "kashering" meat to make the flesh kosher for eating. This involves first soaking the meat then rubbing it with the salt to draw out the blood which is not-kosher and is subsequently washed off along with the salt. The cleansed meat is then kosher. What makes it of interest for food storage and preservation is that it is generally pure salt suitable for canning, pickling and meat curing. It is of a larger grain size than table or canning salt, and usually rolled to flake the grains for easier dissolving. Frequently it is slightly cheaper than canning salt and usually easier to find in urban/suburban areas.

NOTE: Not all brands of kosher salt are exactly alike. Diamond Crystal Kosher Salt is the only brand that I'm aware of that is not flaked, but still in its unaltered crystal form. The Morton brand of Coarse Kosher Salt has "yellow prussiate of soda" added as an anti-caking agent but unlike other anti-caking agents it does not cause cloudiness in solution. Morton even gives a kosher dill pickle recipe on the box.

Whether flaked or in its unaltered crystal form, kosher salt takes up more volume for an equivalent amount of mass than does canning salt. If it is important to get a precise amount of salt in your pickling or curing recipe you may want to weigh the salt to get the correct amount.

SEA SALT: This type of salt comes in about as many different varieties as coffee and from many different places around the world. The "gourmet" versions can be rather expensive. In general, the types sold in grocery stores, natural food markets and gourmet shops have been purified enough to use in food. It's not suitable for food preservation, though, because the mineral content it contains (other than the sodium chloride) may cause discoloration of the food.

ROCK or ICE CREAM SALT: This salt comes in large chunky crystals and is intended primarily for use in home ice cream churns to lower the temperature of the ice filled water in which the churn sits. It's also sometimes used in icing down beer kegs or watermelons. It is used in food preservation by some, but none of the brands label it as food grade nor do they specifically mention its use in foods so avoid using it for this purpose.

SOLAR SALT: This is also sometimes confusingly called "sea salt". It is not, however, the same thing as the sea salt found in food stores. Most importantly, it is not food grade. It's main purpose is for use in water softeners. The reason it is called "solar" and sometimes "sea salt" is that it is produced by evaporation of sea water in large ponds in various arid areas of the world. This salt type is not purified and still contains the desiccated remains of whatever aquatic life might have been trapped in it. Those organic remains might react with the proteins in the foods you are attempting to preserve and cause it to spoil.

HALITE: For those of us fortunate enough to live where it is warm, halite is the salt that is used on roads to melt snow and ice. It, too, is not food grade and should not be used in food preservation. This form of salt is also frequently called rock salt, like the rock salt above, but neither are suitable for food use.

SALT SUBSTITUTES: These are other kinds of metal salts such as potassium chloride used to substitute for the ordinary sodium chloride (NaCl) salt we are familiar with. They have their uses, but should not be used in foods undergoing a heated preservation processing, as they can cause the product to taste bad. Even the heat from normal cooking is sometimes sufficient to cause this.

VINEGAR

There is vinegar and then there is vinegar and it is not all alike. The active ingredient in all vinegars is *acetic acid,* but how the sour stuff was made can vary widely. The most common vinegar is *white distilled* which is actually diluted distilled acetic acid and not true vinegar at all. It keeps pretty much indefinitely if tightly sealed in a plastic or glass bottle with a plastic cap. The enamel coated metal caps always seem to get eaten by the acid over time. It is usually about 5-6% acetic acid and for pickling it is the type most often called for.

The next most common is *apple cider vinegar* which is available in two varieties. A cider *flavored* distilled acetic acid type and a *true cider vinegar* fermented from hard cider. Either will store indefinitely at room temperature until a sediment begins to appear on the bottom.

Nondistilled vinegar will sometimes develop a cloudy substance. This is called a *mother of vinegar* and it is harmless. As long as the liquid does not begin to smell foul it can be filtered out through cheesecloth or a coffee filter and rebottled in a clean container. The mother can even be used to make more vinegar. If it begins to smell bad, however, it's gone over and should be tossed out.

The more exotic *wine, balsamic, malt, rice* and other vinegars can be stored like cider vinegar. Age and exposure to light and air, however, eventually begin to take their toll on their delicate flavors. Tightly capped in a cool, dark cabinet or refrigerator is best for their storage.

YEAST

Yeast is just not a product you can stow away and forget about until you need it in a few years. After all, this single celled microscopic fungus is a living organism so if it's not alive at the time you need it, you'll get no action. When we incorporate yeast into our bread dough, beer wort or fruit juice it begins to ferment madly (we hope) and produce several by-products. If you're baking, the by-product you want is carbon dioxide which is trapped by the dough and subsequently causes it to rise. In brewing or vintning what is wanted is the ethyl alcohol and, if the drink is to be carbonated, the carbon dioxide as well. Almost all yeasts used for these purposes are in the same genus (Saccharomyces or sugar fungi), but several different species or strains within species have evolved and some are more suitable for a particular task than others. It's entirely possible to use grocery store bread yeast to brew beer or ferment wine, but the flavor may leave a great deal to be desired. It's also possible to use yeast from ale brewing to make bread, the results are pretty much indistinguishable from bread yeast.

Types of Baking Yeasts

Leaving aside the brewing and vintning yeasts we will concentrate on bread yeast. It comes in two generally available forms; *compressed* or *fresh yeast* and *dried yeast* which is further broken down into *active dry yeast* and *rapid acting* also known as *rapid rise* or *bread machine yeasts*. Although both of the dry yeasts are in the same species they come from different genetic strains with different performance characteristics and are processed somewhat differently from each other.

COMPRESSED (FRESH) YEAST: Compressed yeast is only partly dried (about 70% moisture), requires refrigeration and keeps even better in a deep freezer. If kept in an air- and moisture-tight container to prevent desiccation this type of yeast will keep for a year in the freezer (0ºF, –17ºC or less), but only about two weeks in the refrigerator. Unless your kitchen is quite chilly it will not keep on the shelf. It should not have a mottled color or a sour odor. Compressed Yeast is generally available in 0.6-ounce and 2-ounce foil-wrapped cakes. For traditional baking, dissolve compressed yeast in warm (90°-95°F, 32°-35ºC) liquids. A 0.6- ounce cake will leaven up to 4 cups of flour (about a pound). A 2-ounce cake will leaven about 12 cups or roughly three pounds of flour.

ACTIVE DRYYEAST: A granular powder with about an 8% moisture content, active dry yeast can be found in either single use foil packets or vacuum packed foil covered one pound 'bricks'. In general bread making active dry yeast is typically dissolved in water (105º-115ºF, 40º-46ºC) along with an equal amount of sugar to give it time to resuscitate and actively begin growing before being mixed into the dry ingredients. Bread machines, however, are often different in this regard and you should follow the directions your particular machine's manufacturer gives. Mine calls for putting the dry yeast atop the other dry ingredients completely out of contact with the liquid ingredients until the machine mixes them together. One envelope (roughly 2 ¼ teaspoons) is sufficient to leaven about four cups or roughly one pound of flour.

RAPID ACTING & BREAD MACHINE YEAST: A more finely granulated powder with a lower moisture content than standard active dry yeast the rapid acting version is designed to raise bread as much as fifty percent faster. This lends it to the 'quick' or 'rapid' cycles of many bread machines that eliminate one rise cycle of the bread dough to facilitate faster production. This form of yeast is also generally mixed with a small amount of ascorbic acid which acts as a dough conditioner to give improved rise performance. Rapid Acting yeasts often perform poorly in recipes calling for long fermentation periods. Because of its finer granulation it does not need to be dissolved in liquid first and should be added to the dry ingredients instead. In the case of bread machines follow the manufacturer's directions. One envelope (roughly 2 ¼ teaspoons) is sufficient to leaven about four cups or roughly one pound of flour.

Interchanging Yeast Types

Can fresh, active dry, and rapid acting yeasts be used interchangeably?

Yes, to a certain extent. To substitute Rapid Acting yeasts for Active Dry yeasts reduce the amount of Rapid Acting used by 25% from the amount of Active Dry the recipe calls for then add the dry yeast to the dry ingredients before mixing. To substitute Active Dry for Rapid Acting increase the amount of Active Dry by 25% over what the recipe calls for of Rapid Acting yeast and dissolve in warm water (105º-115ºF, 40º-46ºC) with an equal amount of sugar before mixing in with the dry ingredients. Once 0.6 ounce cake of fresh, compressed yeast is roughly equivalent to one pack of active dry yeast (2 1/4 teaspoons) or to about 1 3/4 teaspoons of Rapid Acting yeast.

NOTE: Substituting one yeast type for another can be done, but will oft times require a bit of tweaking. If at all possible use the yeast type specified in the recipe. If you can't be prepared to make adjustments where necessary.

PROOFING YEAST: Although it's generally not necessary anymore if you are concerned that your yeast may be dead due to age or poor storage conditions any type of yeast can be tested for viability by *proofing*. This is nothing more than mixing a small amount of the yeast with an equal amount of sugar in warm water 105º-115ºF, 40º-46ºC for dried; 90º-95ºF, 32º-35ºC for fresh.

Within about five to ten minutes active yeast will become bubbly and begin to expand (at normal room temperature). Yeast which only slowly becomes active can still be used, but you will have to use more. If there is no activity at all, the yeast is dead and should be tossed. If you've stored your yeast in half-way decent conditions, or better yet in the freezer, proofing will usually not be necessary.

NOTE: Rapid Acting yeast loses its fast rising capabilities if dissolved in liquid for proofing, and will require two complete rises like standard active dry yeast.

STORINGYEAST: All of the dry yeasts will last for months on the shelf, until the expiration date which should be clearly stamped on the package. If packaged in an air/moisture tight container and kept in the freezer it may last for several years though one year is the general recommendation most often found among various authorities. The larger packs of yeast should be transferred to an air and moisture tight container after opening. A canning jar with a decent lid will suffice. There is another means of providing leavening for breads besides buying yeast from a grocery store and that is by using a sourdough starter.

INFANT FORMUAL

While not universal, it's safe to say that most folks interested in food storage are planning for families, real or as yet hypothetical. Many of these families will include children under the age of two. Very young children have nutritional requirements that are different from adults and require somewhat different preparations than adults or even older children. If at all possible, it's best for children up to the age of six months to be breast fed by their mothers and up to the age of one year breast milk should contribute a significant portion of the child's nutritional intake. Indeed, breast feeding can supplement a child's diet in an important way until age two. Even the American Academy of Pediatrics now recognizes and recommends this. For the preparedness-minded breast feeding makes particularly good sense as mama can consume a far wider range of storable foods than a baby can, and she can produce from those foods a nutrition source perfectly suited to her child. To promote this end here is the contact information for the largest and best known breast feeding support group.

La Leche League International

1400 N. Meacham Road

Schaumburg, IL (USA) 60173-4808

Phone (847) 519-7730 or 1-800-LALACHE (US) Fax (847) 519-0035

E-mail: LLLHQ@llli.orgWeb: http://www.lalecheleague.org

They can help you to find local chapters of the League in your area and point out useful books and sources of information.

ALTERNATIVES TO BREASTFEEDING

If breastfeeding should not be a viable option you'll need to find another source of infant nutrition. WE STRONGLY RECOMMEND AGAINST USING HOME-MADE INFANT FORMULAS AS A SOLE SOURCE OF NUTRITION FOR A BABY. If you know you're going to have a nursing infant on your hands, if and when the balloon should go up, you should take steps in advance of the crisis to put away a suitable food supply for the child. Young children have nutritional needs that are different from those of adults or even older children. Lacking human breast milk, you should put by a store of commercially made infant formula. Evaporated milk, dry milk, sweetened condensed milk, goat's milk and all the rest can be an important supplement for children over the age of six months, particularly over one year of age. For children under six months of age these products simply do not contain sufficient amounts of the appropriate nutrients to provide adequate nutrition when used as the sole source of sustenance. As for soy milk, there are considerable important differences in soy nutritional content compared to cow's milk which is to say nothing of human milk. Soy milk alone is simply not nutritious enough to serve as a sole source of nutrition for children under the age of six months and should not be used as more than a supplement for children over six months of age. This does not apply to commercially made soy protein infant formula which is a very different product than soy milk.

SELECTING AND FEEDING AN INFANT FORMULA

If the child is already familiar, you probably already know which formula you need to put away. Unless instructed against doing so by your doctor, make sure the formula has iron in it. The problems of iron in formulas from the nineteen fifties and sixties have long ago been solved and young children very much need this nutrient. If you feel the need to store formula in advance for a child not yet on the scene (or who is only a contingency to plan against) try storing one of the *cow's milk based lactose-free formulas*. Two brand names that work well are "Lactofree" from Mead Johnson and "Similac Lactose Free" from Ross Laboratories. Lactose is the sugar found in milk and an inability to properly digest lactose is the most common source of infant formula feeding= problems. Of course, there is the remote chance the child could have a true allergy to cow's milk protein, but the child could be allergic to soy protein too. It's been known to happen for a child to be allergic to both at the same time. There is no absolute certainty in preparedness, but you can plan for the most likely problems which is why you should be storing lactose free cow's milk formula.

Unless you store only disposable bottles and "ready to feed" formula, don't forget that both reconstituting formula from dry powder or liquid concentrates and washing feeding equipment requires the use of clean, safe drinking water. You'll need to carefully examine your water storage in this regard.

STORING INFANT FORMULAS AND BABY FOODS

Storing infant formula and baby food is easy. Infant foods are one of the few areas in which the (US) Federal government regulates shelf life labeling. All containers of infant formula and baby food should have a clear "best used by" or similar date somewhere on the container which is generally longer than a child will require such food. Unopened containers of formula should be stored the same way you would keep dry milk, in a dark, cool, dry place and used before the date on the container is reached. Opened containers of dry formula powder should be used within one month of opening and the contents should be kept bone dry, cool and in the dark. If it hasn't been needed by the time the expiration date begins to near it's an excellent idea to donate the infant formula to a nursing infant or organization like a food bank that can put it to use before it expires. There's too much valuable high quality nutrition in infant formula to allow it to go to waste.

XV   Meals Ready to Eat

Pros and Cons of Freeze-Dried, Dehydrated, MRE, Food Bars, & Basic Commodities.

Freeze-Dried / Instant

- Very low moisture Most expensive food storage option
- Very lightweight Most items require water to prepare
- Long shelf life Items are bulkier than if dehydrated
- Reconstitutes quickly
- Retains original shape, texture,
- color after reconstitution
- Best way to dry meat items

Dehydrated (most items)

- Low moisture Requires water to prepare
- Lightweight Some items take a long time to reconstitute
- Long shelf life Some items lose taste after reconstitution
- No waste Dehydration process can affect nutritional value
- Not easily spoiled Some items have poor visual appeal

MRE (Meals Ready to Eat)

- Can be eaten right from pouch without preparation Taste of MREs considered poor by some
- Requires no water to prepare Artificial additives added in many recipes
- Can be heated for hot meal by many methods Expensive considering actual food received
- Convenient to use Many entrees more like sauces & require
- Familiar foods available additional quality carbohydrates for a filling
- No mixing or blending required meal
- Entrees alone will not supply adequate nutritional value
- Because of foil pouch, they are susceptible to puncture Can be heavy if larger quantities need to be transported

Emergency food bars

- Compact – convenient Limited nutritional value
- Low cost Not a satisfying substitute for a hot meal
- 5 year shelf life Not adequate for prolonged use
- Can take exposure to high heat

Grains, Beans, Basic Commodities

- Very familiar Not generally appropriate for shorter term
- Low cost Very heavy weight emergencies

- Long storage life Requires large quantities of water and fuel
- Traditional basic foods to prepare
- Good nutritional value More time consuming to prepare
- Many sproutable seeds, grains, and beans increase Time is required to adapt to basic commodity nutritional value oriented diet For higher calorie requirements a fairly large quantity of nutritional value grains/beans must be consumed when eaten exclusively.

MREs: MEALS, READY TO EAT

This category includes more than the modern day military rations known by the above acronym, but also their civilian equivalents which are marketed by two of the major U.S. military MRE contractors, and a number of other products in the civilian market that fit better into this category than any other. Over the last several years the number of self-contained meals available in either the new style flexible pouches or old fashioned metal cans has greatly increased. We will cover only those meals that also include some form of self-contained heating device to warm the food to serving temperature. This allows one to have a hot meal yet needing no equipment other than a spoon to eat with. Whether you buy self-heating meals or supply the heat yourself to non-self heating meals you should investigate the offerings your local grocer may now be carrying. They have great potential for those situations where cooking food would be difficult or impossible.

U.S. MILITARY MREs

The Meal, Ready to Eat (MRE) is the current U.S. military field ration for those times when troops are out of contact with their regular mess facilities. In the early 1980's they replaced the older C & K-rations that had honorably served since the Second World War. These new rations represented a major leap forward in food preservation technology by disposing of the heavy, unwieldy metal can and replacing it with the much lighter, flexible "retort pouch." These pouches are beefier cousins of the aluminized Mylar bag used in long-term food storage and are basically constructed the same way. A thick outer layer of tough polyester film, a thin middle layer of aluminum foil for its excellent gas barrier properties, and an inner layer of food safe polypropylene film to allow heat sealing. Food is placed in the pouch then specially heat processed for preservation which renders it microbiologically shelf-stable, fully cooked, and ready to eat.

What's in an MRE?

From the Defense Logistics Agency Subsistence we find this:

The twenty-four different varieties of meals can be seen in the menu table. Components are selected to complement each entrée as well as provide necessary nutrition. The components vary among menus and include both Mexican and white rice, fruits, bakery items, crackers, spreads, beverages, snacks, candy, hot sauce, and chowmein noodles for the pork chow mein entrée. The fruits may be applesauce, pears, peaches, pineapple, or strawberry. The bakery items include a fudge brownie, cookies, fruit bars, a toaster pastry, and pound cake in flavors of lemon, vanilla, orange, pineapple, and chocolate mint. Each meal also contains an accessory packet. The contents of one MRE meal bag provides an average of 1250 kilocalories (13 % protein, 36 % fat, and 51 % carbohydrates). It also provides 1/3 of the Military Recommended Daily Allowance of vitamins and minerals determined essential by the Surgeon General of the United States. (http://www.dscp.dla.mil/subs/rations/meals/mres.htm)

All of which is then placed inside of a heavy plastic pouch and sealed. Being field rations they had to be designed to take considerable punishment in packs, air drops, and other forms of abuse remaining safely intact until consumed. By and large they do just that. All of this sounds rather attractive to the person interested in emergency preparedness and they are. So much so, in fact, that several years ago the U.S. military finally said "enough!" to the continuing losses of their rations to the civilian market and banned any further civilian sale. All new MRE complete ration packs now bear the words "U.S. Government Property. Commercial Resale Is Unlawful." This did slow the loss rate somewhat, but anyone that wants the real thing can still get them from military personnel they may know, at gun shows, some military surplus shops, or via E-Bay. Whether you should do this is up to you, but there are a couple of cautions here:

#1 – Being a back channel acquisition chances are you have no way of knowing the storage history of what you're buying. Maybe it's been sitting in some nice cool warehouse since it was produced or maybe it bounced around in the back of a deuce-and-a-half in the Nevada desert for a month last summer. If you don't know where it's been how can you estimate how much useful shelf life it may have left?

#2 – Make sure what you're buying really is a military MRE or MRE component. Some of the civilian commercial products can look remarkably similar, but are not quite the same. Know what you're looking at and make it clear with the person you're buying from that you want genuine military issue (if that's what you want).

MRE Heaters: These devices will either come with your MRE at the time of purchase or they can be bought separately. They contain a small amount of salt, magnesium, and iron and when you add a small amount of water they undergo a flameless chemical reaction that will heat an 8 oz MRE entrée by roughly 100° Fahrenheit (37°C) in about ten minutes. As water is what starts the reaction it is imperative the heaters be kept dry until used. If stored in an area of high humidity the heaters can undergo a slow reaction leading to degraded performance later or even complete failure over time. As a part of the chemical reaction the heaters release small amounts of hydrogen gas which is generally harmless but large numbers of heaters in a damp, sealed storage area could conceivably present a danger. This is unlikely unless you're storing many cases of heaters. In such an event keep them in an air tight storage container with some desiccant. While any MRE can be eaten cold these heaters can certainly improve the palatability of the food. Lacking a heater you can simply boil the individual retort pouches in water for a few minutes, lay them in the sun to warm, or tuck them in your shirt. The one thing you should not do is expose them to direct flame.

For more detailed information on U.S. military, civilian, some foreign military MREs, and other rations please see the excellent MRE Info website at http://www.mreinfo.com/index.html

U.S. MILITARY MRE SHELF LIFE

Much discussion has gone into how long one should keep MREs on hand before rotating them out of stock. In this regard they're no different than any other type of preserved food. The longer you keep them on hand the more unpalatable and non-nutritious they will become with heat playing a large role in shortening their useful lifespan. The short answer to the shelf-life question (from http://www.dscp.dla.mil/subs/rations/meals/mres.htm) is simply "The shelf life of the MRE is three (3) years at 80 degrees F. However, the shelf life can be extended through the use of cold storage facilities prior to distribution." Of course, that's at 80° Fahrenheit (27°C). What if your storage temperature is different? Then you need the storage life chart that was developed by the U.S. Army's NATIC Research Laboratories which basically says that at a given storage temperature an MRE will remain palatable for so many months as illustrated below:

Storage Temperature Shelf Life

- 120° F (49°C) 1 month
- 110° F (43°C) 5 months
- 100° F (37°C) 22 months
- 90° F (32°C) 55 months
- 80° F (27°C) 76 months
- 70° F (21°C) 100 months
- 60° F (15°C) 130 months +

Note: As with any other stored food, time and temperature have a cumulative effect. For example, storage at 100° F. for 11 months moved to 70°F(21°C) would lose one half of the 70°F. storage.

A complete shelf-life chart for all U.S. military rations may be found here:

http://www.dscp.dla.mil/subs/subsbo/qapubs/table.pdf

U.S. CIVILIAN MREs (WORNICK, SOPAKCO, OTHERS?)

Except for contract overruns on individual components actual military MREs, especially complete MRE ration packs, are not legal for sale on the civilian market. Recognizing there was a civilian market for such rations both Wornick and Sopakco through its Crown Point, limited, subsidiary brought out similar products for commercial sale. Their complete civilian ration packs are not precisely the same as their military cousins, but the individual components are usually produced on the same production lines. Because there are no legal restrictions on their sale these civilian MREs are easier to find and are generally available in three basic forms –individual components, complete ration packs, and multi-serving tray packs meant for group feeding. Exact menus vary over time, usually being a subset of whatever the companies are producing for the military at the time of their production so I'm not going to try to address specific menus.

Some of the typical differences between military and civilian MREs are:

- *Menu choice.* Military MREs presently have twenty four different menu choices. Their civilian equivalents are currently limited to twelve.
- *Ration heaters.* These are standard with military MREs, but you may have to pay extra to get them with the civilian equivalents.
- *Total amount of food.* Many of the civilian offerings contain less total food than military MREs, typically in the form of fewer side items. One notable difference is that fewer of the civilian rations contain the little Tabasco packets than their military counterparts.
- *The spoon.* The spoons in the civilian packets are not the same as in the military rations. The civilian spoon is white plastic while the military spoon is brown and of a longer length which makes it easier to get to the bottom of the pouches without getting food on your fingers.

For more detailed information on U.S. military, civilian, and some foreign military MREs, and other rations please see the excellent MRE Info website at

http://www.mreinfo.com/index.html

U.S. CIVILIAN MRE SHELF LIVES

One would think that the shelf lives of U.S. military and civilian MREs would be the same, but are they? If you look at the manufacturer's websites for what they say about their civilian equivalent rations we find:

How long will these products last?

SOPAKCO Packaging uses an estimated shelf life figure of "3-5 years, plus or minus" for its MREtype pouched food products. Actual shelf life may vary from this estimate. A key factor effecting actual shelf life is the temperature of the storage environment. Storage at temperatures higher than 85F (85 degrees Fahrenheit) may shorten the shelf life of MRE-type food products. On the other hand, lowering the storage temperature will help extend the products' shelf life. This effect is common to most processed food products. The shelf life figures given below for MRE's are based on studies conducted by the U.S. Army's NATIC Research Laboratories. This study was conducted by NATIC without participation of the MRE manufacturers. As such, SOPAKCO Packaging cannot verify the test procedures used by the NATIC labs, nor do we adopt these shelf life figures as a guarantee of any sort. The data is useful, though, as a general indication of the effects of storage temperatures on the shelf life of MRE-type food products

.

Temperature (Fahrenheit): 100º 90º 85º 80º 75º 70º 60º

Storage Life in Months: 22 55 60 76 88 100 130+

The above storage data and time periods were based on "acceptable taste" measures, which is a subjective standard that may vary among each individual. Test participants were asked to indicate which products they were presented would be rated to still be of "acceptable taste". Responses were noted, and average values were calculated to yield the data above. The above data does not indicate the maximum useful life of MRE food products. The NATIC study noted that nutritional value and product safety value of the products often extended far beyond these time points.

Again, SOPAKCO Packaging in no way adopts the NATIC shelf life figures as any form of express or implied guarantee of the actual shelf life of its MRE food products. This information is provided as a general indication of the effects of storage temperature on MRE-type packaged foods.

Long Life Food Depot (The Wornick Company's civilian sales agent)

From http://www7.mailordercentral.com/longlifefood/Faq.asp#heaterpouches

How long do MRE products last - what is their Shelf Life

We guarantee our MRE products to last 5 years from the date of sale, in a room temperature environment (70 deg. F), no matter what the production date. Of course, the production date is visible on all our entrees and on most side dishes, desserts, and other components. The production date is a four digit number(date code) on each item, example "2156." In this example the 2 represents the year 2002 (a "3" would represent 2003, etc.), the 156 represents the 156th day of the year. See the top of the individual box or look on pouch for the Date Code. At this time nearly all of our MRE products were manufactured between 2002 and 2003and have always been kept in a climatecontrolled warehouse to ensure freshness. The official MRE Shelf Life Chart, created by the Army's Natick Research Lab, gives the whole picture and explains why we are prepared to guarantee our products for 5 years from date of sale. It is clear that the wholesomeness of the products extends well beyond 5 years. A more complete discussion of MRE Shelf LIfe, is here:

http://www.longlifefood.com/mre.html#Shelflife

MRE Shelf Life:

A main concern in the development and testing of rations for our armed forces has always been SHELF LIFE. An amazing amount of research has been done in the development of the retort pouch and the MRE to determine the exact length of time and the exact conditions under which it is safe to store the entrees and the side dishes. The main thing we have to work with is the shelf life chart (shown below) compiled by the Army's Natick Research labs. This gives a very good overview and summary of all the findings gathered from all the testing of MRE products. However, it leaves many questions unanswered. Here are additional facts and observations we have gathered about MRE shelf life:

1) The shelf life ratings shown in the chart below were determined by taste panels, panels of "average" people, mostly office personnel at the Natick labs. Their opinions were combined to determine when a particular component or, in this case, the entire MRE ration, was no longer acceptable.

2) The shelf life determinations were made solely on the basis of taste, as it was discovered that acceptable nutritional content and basic product safety would extend way beyond the point where taste degradation would occur. This means that MREs would be safe and give a high degree of food value long after the official expiration of the products as determined by taste.

3) MRE pouches have been tested and redesigned where necessary according to standards much more strict than for commercial food. They must be able to stand up to abuse tests such as obstacle course traversals in field clothing pockets, storage outdoors anywhere in the world, shipping under extremely rough circumstances, 100% survival of parachute drops, 75% survival of freefall air drops, severe repetitive vibration (1 hour at 1 G vibration), 7,920 individual pouch drops from 20 inches, and individual pouches being subjected to a static load of 200 lbs for 3 minutes.

4) Freezing an MRE retort pouch does not destroy the food inside, but repeated freezing increases the chances that the stretching and stressing of the pouch will cause a break in a layer of the laminated pouch. These pouches are made to withstand 1,000 flexes, but repetitive freezing does increase the failure rate by a small fraction of a percent.

Both company's refer to the NATIC shelf-life chart with qualifiers *"The NATIC study noted that nutritional value and product safety value of the products often extended far beyond these time points."* and *"This means that MREs would be safe and give a high degree of food value long after the official expiration of the products as determined by taste."* Neither state how much or what kinds of nutrition would remain once the food goes beyond its recommended shelf life, but it can be safely assumed the most sensitive nutrients (notably vitamins A and C among others) will have significantly declined. Old food is not likely to be attractive food, nor will it give long term nutrition, but if it's all you've got it'll still be safe to eat it.

BRITISH/CANADIAN MREs

These are basically MREs little different in form than the American made product but made by companies in these respective nations. Shelf-life is the same. Menu choices reflect British/Canadian tastes, of course. Company contact information can be found in the Suppliers Section. One minor difference seems to be with the Hot Pack company of U.K./Canada in that they claim their ration heaters are somewhat larger than the ones packaged with U.S. MREs From the company's web site:

Will defrost ice or snow for drinking water. Will heat 300 g (10.6 oz.) of food or water from room temperature to 80°C (178°F) in 12 minutes. Will provide a source of heat for up to forty five minutes after activation. Is sometimes reusable for a limited heat cycle (dependent on how much of the heating element was exhausted in the first cycle). The chemical reaction is totally safe. When water is added to the heater, the mixture bubbling away inside the sleeve (magnesium hydroxide) is a pharmaceutical chemical used by doctors to treat stomach acidity. Food grade ingredients are used in the manufacturing of the heater. Once activated, the heater will keep hot for approximately 45 minutes. It can be used as a body warmer or to heat a drink after heating the meal.

OTHER SELF-HEATING READY TO EAT TYPE PRODUCTS

As one might expect once the bugs were worked out of retort pouch and flameless ration heater technologies the manufacturing companies that produce them would try them on the civilian market. This has been a little slow in coming, mostly because in the modern day 'fresh is best and refrigeration is cheap' world their market segment is somewhat small, but they are arriving. At the time of this writing there are several products now available, some of them quite new.

HEATERMEALS

HeaterMeals are a type of MRE in casual clothing. Like the rations above they are a retort pouch preserved meal with its own built in heater. The heater itself is the same technology as the MRE heaters (the company makes them for the military), but a little different in form, to include having its own self-contained water to start the heating reaction. The meals themselves aren't packaged with the idea of rough handling in mind, but they'll keep well on the shelf.

The meals themselves come in two basic forms: An entrée pack with the heater, seasoning packet and cutlery A complete meal pack with the heater, entrée, seasoning packet, cutlery, side items like fruit, snack, and dessert, and a bottle of water to drink. If you're not having to use them under rough field conditions they represent a self-heating, completely self contained meal. These meals can be ordered from the manufacturer, a number of dealers which are listed on the company website, or you can often find them at truck stops, some supermarkets, sporting goods stores, and other such businesses. Shelf life info for HeaterMeals was found at:

http://www.heatermeals.com/faq.html#shelflife

What is the shelf-life of HeaterMeals and HeaterMeals Plus Meals?

HeaterMeals are a high quality canned food, so storage is easy. HeaterMeals Dinner entrees do not require refrigeration, and are shelf-stable for approximately 2 years. HeaterMeals entrees come with a "Please use by" date stamped on each box. This date is two years after we package the meals, as this is the optimum time to eat your HeaterMeals. The HeaterMeals Breakfast "Pancakes, Syrup & Sausage Links" and all HeaterMeals Plus meals have a one year shelf-life. HeaterMeals dinner entrees are designed to safely store (at 80 degrees Fahrenheit) for at least two years; three years or more, if stored at a temperature of 60°F or cooler. The shelf-life of HeaterMeals can be even longer; and the unique packaging of the entree and water pouch permits freezing for unlimited storage.

HOT CANS – UNITED KINGDOM

In the United Kingdom there is another entry in the self heating meal field. This is the Hot Can from Hot Can UK, Limited. It's an interesting blend of old and different new tech in that the food itself is contained in a run-of-the-mill pop-top metal can, but the food can is contained in a sealed larger can filled with calcium oxide (quicklime) and a separate water capsule. When needed the self-contained water capsule is pierced with the provided tool allowing moisture to seep into the dry quicklime below and the food can pop-top is removed. In twelve to fifteen minutes the can will have heated to 65°-70° Celsius and remains at that temperature for roughly forty five minutes which means once you've finished the food inside you can quickly rinse the can and heat something else, perhaps a beverage. There are a variety of meals available from the company, each weighing about 400 grams (roughly 14 ozs). Shelf life is "Three years from manufacturing date, or as indicated on printed bottom end of can." The heater itself releases no harmful or dangerous gasses and if for some reason you should break one open and spill some of the quicklime on yourself it can simply be washed off again with water. Company contact information can be found in the Suppliers Section. Hot Cans are probably also available through retail dealers in the U.K. and elsewhere.

ALPINEAIRE INSTANT – SELF HEATING MEALS

New on the market from AlpineAire is their entry into the self-heating meal arena. Uses the same retort and flameless heater technology as MREs but in different packaging. Snap the bottom of the package and in eight minutes your entrée is hot and ready to go. They're rather pricey at a suggested retail of $8.95 for a mere 240 calories worth of vegetarian food. Still, it's a start and with time they may both lower the price and increase the menu choices. Alpineaire advises an eighteen month shelf life for this particular product line. They may be ordered directly from AlpineAire or through their many stocking dealers.

MOUNTAIN HOUSE MOUNTAIN OVEN

Mountain House isn't really offering a true Meal, Ready to Eat since you still have to add water to their freeze dried/dehydrated food, but I'm including it here since it's close. Basically, what they're offering is their own version of a flameless ration heater and some new packaging of a few of their entrees that allows the pouches to be put into their heaters to be warmed. They call their heater a "Mountain Oven" though they really don't bake anything, just warms things up. To use their heater you dissolve one of the furnished salt tablets in a plastic bottle that comes in the kit. Place a "heat activation pad" in the bottom of the insulated over pouch then pour the salt water on it. Open up the food pouch, pour in the required amount of water then put the pouch inside the insulated bag and zip it closed (the outer bag is vented). Twenty minutes later the food should be about 100° F. (38°C) hotter than when you started. Each Mountain Oven kit is good for five uses. At a suggested retail of $11.99 per kit that's about $2.40 per use which makes it rather pricey compared to the ordinary MRE heaters already on the market which can usually be purchased for about a buck apiece or less. Still, like the AlpineAire entry it's a start and with time they may come down in price and perhaps be easier to use as well. The Mountain Oven kits can be ordered from Mountain House directly or purchased from one of their many dealers as they are distributed.

RATION BARS

U.S. Coast Guard approved lifeboat ration bars are not common storage foods. Nevertheless they have a specific use important enough to warrant inclusion in personal preparedness programs. As many involved with emergency preparedness discover, finding foods capable of being stored for long periods of time under harsh conditions that will remain both palatable and nutritious is a real undertaking.

This is especially a problem with vehicle emergency kits where interior temperatures in the Spring, Summer, or Fall may exceed 120°F (50°C) for hours at a time each day. Very little in the way of anything usefully edible will survive such sustained temperatures for long before it breaks down, becomes unpalatable, with most or all of its nutrients damaged or destroyed. This is a problem not only for those of us trying to build vehicle emergency kits but also for mariners needing to provision life boats that might be exposed to anything from desert temperatures to arctic climates.

In reaction to this and a number of other marine emergency preparedness needs most of the world's maritime nations met to develop the Safety Of Life At Sea (SOLAS) conventions, one of which concerns itself with emergency provisions for lifeboats. In the United States responsibility for implementing the SOLAS regulations falls to the U.S. Coast Guard and they have developed guidelines by which manufacturers must abide in order to become Coast Guard approved suppliers of life boat rations. Among the guideline requirements are:

- Lifeboat rations must be capable of withstanding long periods of high temperatures or sub freezing weather without significant deterioration;
- must not increase bodily water needs with high protein or salt levels yet provide sufficient calories to keep the body from burning its fat reserves which also increases bodily water needs;
- be compact in size and lightweight;
- be sufficiently palatable that injured or ill passengers would be able to eat them;
- not constipate nor cause diarrhea;
- use packaging that is sufficiently durable to withstand rough conditions.

Those manufacturers that meet these guidelines can submit their products for approval to be placed on the U.S. Coast Guard Equipment List 160.046 - Emergency Provisions for Merchant Vessels which may be found here: http://www.uscg.mil/hq/g-m/mse/equiplists/160046.pdf Each of these companies produces lifeboat rations. In the U.S. the two most commonly available product lines are the Mainstay Emergency Food Ration and the Datrex Red (or White) or Blue ration. The Mainstay rations are lemon flavored and available in 1200, 2400, and 3600 calorie packages. The Datrex rations are coconut flavored and available in 2400 (red or white ration) or 3600 (blue ration) calorie packages. As per regulations both have a five year shelf life. Each package from either company has been tabletized and subpackaged to make it easier to serve them out in controlled portions. Both are primarily composed of complex carbohydrates, fairly low protein, enriched with extra vitamins and minerals then vacuum sealed in heavy aluminized plastic pouches similar to military MREs.

Flavors are noted above, textures are similar to a fairly dense pound cake. For the relative few days a vehicle or similar emergency kit is intended to get you through they'll get the job done and not turn into something nasty after a few months of hot weather. In the cool times of the year when vehicle interiors do not climb into oven temperature ranges food options increase considerably with some form of military or civilian equivalent MRE being well suited to the task. Something to consider if you're building emergency kits or bug-out bags.

XVI Storage Containers

WHAT IS FOOD GRADE PACKAGING?

Q: *OK, I'm ready to start my storage program. What should I put the food in?*

A: You should use food grade packaging for storing anything you intend to eat. A food grade container is one that will not transfer noxious or toxic substances into the food it is holding. If you are uncertain whether a package type is food grade you can contact the manufacturer. Ask if that particular container is (US) FDA approved meaning that it is safe for food use. When inquiring be sure to specify the characteristics of the food you are storing; wet, dry, strongly acidic or alkaline, alcoholic or a high fat content. A container that is approved for one of the above types of food may not be approved for another.

The major functions of a food storage container are to:

1) Protect its contents from outside environmental influences such as moisture, and oxygen, but possibly also heat or cold, light, insects and/or rodents as well.

2) Prevent damage during handling and shipping.

3) Establish and/or maintain microbiological stability. The container should not allow microorganisms such as fungi and bacteria from outside the container to come into contact with its contents. This is of critical importance to wet-pack foods such as canned vegetables, fruits and meats.

4) Withstand the temperatures and pressures it will be exposed to. This is necessary if the contents are to be pasteurized or sterilized, either immediately before or after filling. It must not have any structural failures nor release any noxious or toxic breakdown chemicals into the food it contains. This is the reason why purpose built canning jars are recommended for home canning and mayonnaise jars aren't. The former are made heavier to withstand high temperatures and handling whereas the latter are not and have an increased risk of breakage if used for that purpose. Virtually all containers used in home food preservation involving exposure to high temperatures are made of glass or metal, with the exception of some specialized "heat & seal" type of plastic bags. Glass can be used with any food type providing it is clean and in sound condition but the lids, particularly the liner inside the lid, may not be so you'll need to investigate suitability.

Metal cans are more specialized. They must be intended for food use and must also have a lining or coating of the inside that is suitable for the pH level of the food it will be in contact with. If the foods are not subjected to some form of heat processing before or after packaging your selection of container types for home use is a great deal larger. Virtually any kind of clean, sound glass jar can be used and many types of new metal containers. Several sorts of plastics have become popular. These various kinds of plastics are each suited for different purposes, making selection a more complex task.

WHERE DO I FIND FOOD GRADE CONTAINERS?

Food grade packaging is everywhere. Every time you go into the grocery store you are surrounded by it. Many well known companies such as Tupperware and Rubbermaid manufacture and sell empty packaging for the express purpose of containing repackaged foods. The kinds of containers you are interested in and the types of foods you want to put in those containers will dictate where you need to look for a particular packaging system. For food storage purposes, most folks are usually interested in five and six gallon plastic pails, certain recycled plastic containers such as soda or juice bottles, glass jars from half pint to gallon sizes, metal containers such as the institutional sized #10 cans, and Mylar or other high barrier property plastic bags. Those are the containers most often used, but virtually anything that can protect foods from outside environmental influences, safely contain something you're going to later eat and have a volume capacity large enough to be worthwhile may be used. A number of food storage retailers sell plastic buckets, Mylar bags and a few even sell new #10 cans with lids. It may also be possible to purchase #10 cans through dealers such as *Lehman's Hardware, Cumberland General Store* or *Home Canning Specialty and Supply.*

Plastic five gallon buckets are widely available, but only if you purchase them through a company catering to a food related trade will you likely be able to tell if they're safe to keep food in. If you can locate a customer service number for the manufacturer of a container that interests you call them and ask. Many times manufacturers will make products that are FDA approved and sell them as general purpose containers, but you need to ask to be sure.

Packaging supply houses have large FDA approved packaging lines. Some require minimum orders and others don't. The cost of shipping the containers will probably play a major role in your decision making. If you are going to package a great deal of food all at once, perhaps for a group, some of the companies that require minimum purchases may save you a fair amount of money and supply packaging you might otherwise have a difficult time finding.

For glass jars, don't overlook flea markets, yard sales, thrift shops and similar places. Canning jars can sometimes be had for very little. Delicatessens, sub shops and restaurants of all sorts can be a source of one gallon glass jars formerly containing pickles, peppers, etc. If the lids are still in good condition, they are well suited to bulk storage and can be reused over and over. Beekeeping supply houses also sell new buckets for bulk honey storage.

Metal cans, by and large, are not reusable for food storage, but some companies might be able to sell you new cans. The traditional single use #10 can is only the beginning of what might be available with a little looking. Gallon sized or larger cans with double friction lids (like paint comes in) make excellent storage containers and some companies make them food safe. One gallon and larger cans with wide diameter screw caps are available from some companies as well. You might have seen some of these holding edible oils, soy sauce, honey and other liquid food. If they come with a cap that will seal air tight they would be well suited for bulk storage of grains and legumes, particularly if they come in a four to six gallon size.

Pick up your local phone book, log on to your favorite search engine or head to your local public library and explore the possibilities. Make it clear that what you want must be FDA approved and be up front about how many you need or can deal with. If one company won't deal with you, try another.

PLASTIC PACKAGING

Before we can discuss plastic packaging it is necessary to understand what is the substance we call "plastic." Plastics are produced from basic polymers called "resins", each of which have differing physical properties. Additives may be blended in for color or to modify particular properties such as moldability, structural rigidity, resistance to light or heat or oxidation. Additionally, it is common for several different kinds of plastic to be laminated together each performing a particular desired task. One might offer structural rigidity and the other might be more impermeable to the transfer of gasses and odors. When bonded together a rigid, gas impermeable package can be made.

Whether that package is safe for food use will depend on the exact nature of the additives blended into the plastic. Some of them, notably plasticizers and dyes, can migrate from the packaging material into the food it's containing. This may be exacerbated by the food it's in contact with especially if it is high in fat, strongly acidic, or alcoholic in nature. Time and temperature may also play a prominent role in the migration of plastic additives into food. For this reason, the (US) FDA assesses the safety of packaging materials for food contact and conducts toxicological studies to establish safety standards. Only plastics that are FDA approved for a particular food type should be used for direct contact with that food.

Being FDA approved, however, may not be the entire story. It must still be determined whether the particular plastic in question has the physical properties that would make it desirable for your purpose. As mentioned above each base resin has somewhat differing physical properties that may be modified with additives or combined by laminating with another plastic or even completely unrelated materials such as metal foils.

An example of this is "Mylar", a type of polyester film. By itself, it has moderate barrier resistance to moisture and oxygen. When laminated together with aluminum foil it has very high resistance and makes an excellent material for creating long term food storage packaging. One or more other kinds of plastic with low melting points and good flow characteristics are typically so that the aluminized Mylar can be fashioned into bags or sealed across container openings. The combined materials have properties that make them useful for long term storage that each separately do not have.

The most common plastic that raises suitability questions is High Density Polyethylene (HDPE). It's used in a wide array of packaging and is the material from which most plastic five and six gallon buckets are made. It has a moderate rigidity, a good resistance to fats, oils, moisture and impacts, a fair resistance to acids, but is a relatively poor barrier to oxygen. Whether it is suitable for your purpose depends on how sensitive to oxygen your product is and how long you need it to stay in optimal condition.

Foods such as whole grains are not particularly delicate in nature and will easily keep for years in nothing more than a tightly sealed HDPE bucket. Most legumes are the same way, but those that have high fat contents such as peanuts and soybeans are more sensitive to O2. Other foods such as dry milk powder might only go a year before deleterious changes are noticed. If that milk were sealed in an air-tight aluminized Mylar bag with the oxygen inside removed, the milk would keep for much longer. Better still would be to seal the milk in a metal can or glass jar. HDPE alone can be used for long term storage with one or more of the following precautions to keep a high food quality: The food should either be put on a shorter rotation cycle than packaging also using a second gas barrier such as Mylar; be periodically opened and re-purged or fresh absorbers should be inserted.

Another common plastic used in food storage is polyethylene terephthalate commonly known as PETE or PET plastic. Used to make soda, juice, and some water bottles among other products it is available for recycling into food storage containers in nearly every home. Properly cleaned and with intact screw-on lids PETE plastic containers will serve for keeping nearly any kind of food providing the containers are stored in a dark location. PETE has good barrier properties against oxygen and moisture and when used in combination with oxygen absorbers presents a complete dry-pack canning system in itself. About the only drawbacks to PETE plastics are that they are nearly always transparent to light, container volumes typically are limited to a gallon or less, and when used in conjunction with oxygen absorbers the sides will flex sufficiently to make stacking difficult though you could simply lay them on their sides.

There are other plastics and plastic laminates with good oxygen and moisture barrier properties that are suited for long term food storage, but they are not as easy to find, though some used containers might be available for reuse.

HOW DO I GET THE ODOR OUT OF PICKLE BUCKETS?

As vinegar is the primary smell in pickles and it's acidic in nature, use a base to counteract it. First scrub the bucket well, inside and out, with dish detergent. Then fill the buckets with hot water and dissolved a cup of baking soda in each. Stir well, get the bucket as full as you can and put the top on. Put the bucket in the sun to keep it warm so the plastic pores stay open as much as possible. In a couple of days come back and empty the buckets. Rinse them out, fill with warm water again and add about a cup of bleach and reseal. Put back in the sun for another couple of days. Empty out and let dry with the tops off. Generally this will eliminate the vinegar smell as well as many other smells.

METAL CANS   Metal cans and glass jars being heat resistant, can both be used for heat processed, wet-pack foods and for nonheat treated dry pack canning. Relative to glass jars though, metal cans have several disadvantages for the do-it yourselfer. They are hard to come by, and they need specialized equipment to seal them that can be difficult to locate. The greatest flaw which makes them unpopular for home canning is they can only be used once. As the commercial canning industry is not interested in reusing the containers, metal cans make great sense for their purposes. The cans are both cheaper (for them) and lighter than glass jars. This adds to the economy of scale that makes canned foods as cheap as they are in the grocery store.

For home canning, glass jars are better because even the smallest towns have at least one business that carries pressure and boiling water canners along with jars, rings and lids. With metal cans, a sealer is also necessary which usually has to be ordered from the manufacturer or a mail-order distributor.

Tin cans are not really made of tin. They're actually steel cans with a tin coating on the inside and outside. Some kinds of strongly colored acidic foods will fade from long exposure to tin so an enamel liner called "R-enamel" is used to forestall this. Certain other kinds of food that are high in sulfur or that are close to neutral in pH will also discolor from prolonged contact with tin. For those foods, cans with "C-enamel" are used.

The excellent food preservation book, *Putting Food By* Chapter 6 has a section on the use of metal cans for wet packed foods as does the *Ball Blue Book*.

Probably the most common use of metal containers is the #10 cans . This is not the only way metal containers may be used though and there are various food grade metal containers available of sufficient volume to make them useful for food storage. They usually have double friction lids similar to paint cans or screw caps like jars that can achieve an air-tight seal. If you can find them with a sufficient volume capacity they can be of real use for storing bulky foods such as grains, legumes and sugar. Smaller cans of a gallon or less would be useful for storing items like dry milks.

If properly sealed, metal cans have a far higher barrier resistance to gasses such as oxygen, CO_2, and nitrogen than any plastic. Although they can hardly be considered portable the use of clean metal drums (not garbage or trash cans), either themselves food grade or used with food grade liners, is also a possibility. A fifty five gallon drum of grain will weigh several hundred pounds, but may make for a much easier storage solution than multiple buckets. The advantage of using such a large container is that a great amount of a single product can be kept in a smaller amount of space and fumigating or purging the storage atmosphere would be simpler. The disadvantages are the difficulties of moving it and rotating the stock in the drum. If using oxygen absorbers make sure the drum you want to use is capable of making an air-tight seal, otherwise you should stick with carbon dioxide fumigation.

POOLING RESOURCES:

Although the purchase of a can sealer and metal cans for home use is not generally economically feasible for most people, one method can make it practical. This is by pooling community resources to purchase the equipment and supplies. It may even not be necessary to form your own community to do this; there may already be local groups who might be found through the Cooperative Extension. By sharing the cost of the equipment and purchasing the cans in bulk quantities, they are able to enjoy the advantages of metal cans and professional equipment over plastic containers while minimizing the disadvantages of cost.

PREVENTING EXTERIOR CORROSION OF CANNED GOODS

Some areas have difficulty storing metal canned goods for long periods of time. This is usually caused by high humidity or exposure to salt in a marine environment. If this is a problem, it is possible to extend the life of metal cans by coating their outsides. This is sometimes used on boats here in like Florida, especially when loading for a long trip. There are at least five methods that can be used to do this, but for cans that require a can opener only the paraffin or mineral oil methods should be used.

PARAFFIN METHOD: Using a double boiler, paraffin is melted and brushed on the clean, unrusted cans. Be certain to get a good coat on all seams, particularly the joints. If the can is small enough, it can be dipped directly into the wax. Care must be taken to not cause the labels to separate from the cans. Do not leave in long enough for the can contents to warm. **MINERAL OIL METHOD**: Use only food grade or drug store (medicinal) mineral oil. Wipe down the outside of each can with only enough oil to leave a barely visible sheen. Paper labels will have to be removed to wipe underneath with the contents written on the outside beforehand with a marker or leave the under label areas uncoated. Even with a barely visible sheen of oil the cans will tend to attract dust so you will need to wipe off the can tops before opening.

PASTE WAX METHOD: Combine 2-3 oz. of paste or jelly wax with a quart of mineral spirits. Warm the mixture CAREFULLY in its container by immersing it in a larger container of hot water. DO NOT HEAT OVER AN OPEN FLAME! Stir the wax/spirits thoroughly until it is well mixed and dissolved. Paint the cans with a brush in the same manner as above. Place the cans on a wire rack until dry. B: A light coating of ordinary spray silicone may be used to deter rust. Spray lightly, allow to dry, wipe gently with a clean cloth to remove excess silicone.

CLEAR COATING: A clear type of spray or brush on coating such as Rustoleum may be applied. This is best suited for larger resealable cans, but will keep them protected from corrosion for years.

GLASS JARS

Compared to metal cans, glass jars are very stable, although they obviously don't take being banged around well. Fortunately the cardboard boxes most jars come in are well designed to cushion them from shocks. The box also has the added bonus of keeping damaging light away from food.

The major advantage of glass jars is they are reusable. For wet-pack canning the lids should be replaced, but the rings can be reused until they finally rust away or become too dented to use. For dry pack canning even the lids may be reused nearly indefinitely if you're careful in removing them. Ball lids seem to work better than Kerr, especially for vacuum sealed dry pack canning. The red sealing compound Ball uses seems to more reliably achieve a seal than the gray compound Kerr uses.

The bottom line, it is seldom practical strictly in terms of dollars and cents to wet-pack your own food in jars. When you count the cost of your equipment, including the jars, rings, lids and all the rest, along with a not inconsiderable amount of personal time, the cost of purchasing or growing your produce, you'll almost always come out ahead to buy food canned for you by the commercial canning industry.

That said, forget about the strict bottom line and examine more closely why you want to put up your own food. For many, gardening is a pleasure and they have to have something to do with the food they've grown! There's also the fact that for many, you simply cannot buy the quality of the food you can put up for yourself. The canning industry tries to appeal to a broad spectrum of the general public while you can put up food to your own family's specific tastes. Home canning is not so much about saving money as it is about satisfaction. You get what you pay for. If home canning appeals to you, please a good resource is the rec.food.preserving FAQ where much good information about methods and techniques may be found. Dry-pack canning using glass jars, on the other hand, may well make a great deal of economic sense.

It is usually far cheaper per pound to purchase dry foods in bulk quantities, but often unsuitable to store it that way. Breaking the food down into smaller units allows for easier handling and exposes a smaller quantity to oxygen and moisture before it can be eaten. Of course, packaging used for doing this can be made of many different materials, but glass is often the easiest and most convenient to acquire and use. Used containers are often free or of little cost. One source of gallon sized glass jars are sandwich shops and restaurants that use pickles, peppers and other sandwich condiments. There are also half-gallon canning jars, though they are sometimes difficult to find. Both Ball and Kerr make these jars, have a local hardware order them.

MYLAR BAGS

The word "Mylar" is a trademark of the DuPont Corporation for a special type of polyester film. Typically made in thin sheets, it has a high tensile strength and is used in a wide variety of industrial settings. In food storage, particularly for the long term, it is commonly found as a laminate with Mylar as the top layer, a very thin aluminum foil in the middle and one or more other types of plastic films on the bottom acting as sealant plies. This laminate combination possesses a high resistance to the passage of oxygen, carbon dioxide, nitrogen, other gasses, water vapor, and light which is what makes it valuable for our purposes. Unfortunately, it has a poor puncture resistance so must be used as an interior liner for more puncture resistant containers rather than as a standalone package.

Food grade aluminized Mylar complies with US FDA requirements and is safe to be in contact with all food types except alcoholic. For food use, Mylar is most commonly available as pre-made bags of various sizes. Flat sheets or rolls of the material might also be found from which bags could be fashioned as well.

When Mylar bags are used by the storage food industry they are generally for products sealed in plastic buckets. The reason for doing this is the High Density Polyethylene (HDPE) from which the pails are made is somewhat porous to gasses. This means that small molecules, such as oxygen (O_2), can slowly pass through the plastic and come into contact with the food inside. The problem is further compounded if oxygen absorbers are used, as the result of their absorbing action is to lower the air pressure inside the container unless it has first been carefully flushed with an inert gas such as nitrogen. How fast this migration activity will occur is a function of the specific plastic formulation, its wall thickness and the air pressure inside the container. In order to gain the maximum possible shelf life a second gas barrier, the Mylar bag, is used inside the pail.

Whether the use of these bags is necessary for your home packaged storage foods depends on how oxygen sensitive the food item is and how long you want it to stay at its best. If the container is made of a gas impervious material such as metal or glass then a second gas barrier inside is not needed. If it is HDPE or a plastic with similar properties and you want to get the longest possible storage life (say 10+ yrs for grain) then Mylar is a good idea. If you're going to use the grain in four to five years or less then it is not needed. Provided the oxygen has been purged from the container in the first place, either with a proper flushing technique, or by absorption, there will not have been sufficient O2 infiltration to seriously impact the food. Particularly oxygen sensitive foods such as dry milk powders that are to be kept in plastic containers for more than two years would benefit from the use of Mylar. Naturally, storage temperature and moisture content is going to play a major role as well.

There is also the question of the seal integrity of the outer container. If you are using thin walled plastic buckets in conjunction with oxygen absorbers the resulting drop in air pressure inside the pail may cause the walls to buckle. If this should occur, there would be a risk of losing seal integrity, particularly if the buckets are stacked two or more deep. If the food was packed in Mylar bags with the absorbers inside this would keep the vacuum from seriously stressing the container walls. Better still would be not to have the problem at all by either using containers of sufficient wall thickness or flushing with inert gas before sealing. Heavy wall thickness is one reason why the six gallon Super Pails have become so widespread. It should be noted that Mylar is not strongly resistant to insect penetration and not resistant at all to rodents. If mice chew through your buckets, they'll go right through the bags.

HOW DO I USE MYLAR BAGS?

Sealing food in Mylar bags is a straight-forward affair, but it may take a bit of practice to get it right, so purchase one or two more bags than you think you'll need in case you don't immediately get the hang of it.

#1 - The bags typically sold by storage food dealers look rather large when you compare them to the five or six gallons buckets they are commonly used in. That extra material is necessary though if you are to have enough bag material left over after filling to be able to work with. Unless you are sure of what you are doing, don't trim off any material until after the sealing operation is completed.

#2 - Place the bag inside the outer container and fill with the food product. Resist filling it all the way to the top. You need at least an inch or so below the bucket rim left open to get the lid to seat completely. If you'll be using desiccants and oxygen absorbers together place the desiccant on the bottom of the bag before filling.

#3 - When the pail seems to be full, gently thump it on the floor a few times to pack the product and reduce air pockets. Add any makeup food necessary to bring level back to where it should be.

#4 - Take the bag by the corners and pull out any slack in the material so that all sides can be pulled together evenly. Place your oxygen absorbers inside if you are going to use them. Now place a board over the top of the bucket and fold the bag end down over it keeping it straight and even. Place a piece of thin cotton fabric such as sheet or t-shirt material over the edge of the bag mouth. Using a clothes iron set on the cotton, wool or high setting run it over the cloth-covered Mylar about a half-inch from the edge for about twenty seconds or so until it seals. You'll probably have to do the bag in sections. Temperature settings on irons vary so experimenting on a leftover strip to find the right setting is a good idea.

#5 - When you've done the entire bag, allow it to cool, then try to pull the mouth of the bag open. If moderate pressure doesn't open it, fold the bag down into the pail until you feel the trapped air pillowing up against the material and wait to see if it deflates. If it stays buoyant, your seal is good. You can seal on the bucket lid at this point or take the further step to vacuum or gas flush the bag.

Once a seal has been obtained the bags can be left as-is, vacuum sealed or gas flushed. To obtain the most efficient oxygen removal the bags can be first drawn down with a vacuum pump and then purged using an inert gas.

Vacuum Sealing Mylar Bags

Once you have obtained a good seal on the bag, pulling a vacuum on the contents is straight forward. First you'll need something to make a vacuum with. This can be either a regular vacuum pump, a vacuum sealer such as the Tilia Food Saver or even the suction end of your household vacuum cleaner. The end to be inserted into the bag will need to be of fairly small diameter in order to keep the hole in the Mylar from being any larger than necessary. This means that if you use a vacuum cleaner you'll need to fashion some form of reduction fitting. One such is a plastic film canister with a hole drilled in the bottom and a piece of plastic tubing epoxied in place.

Cut a hole into the Mylar bag on a corner, making the opening only just large enough to admit the vacuum probe. Insert the nozzle and using a sponge, or something similar, push down on the material over the probe to make a seal. Now draw down a vacuum on the bag. When it's drawn down as much as possible, run a hot iron diagonally across the cut corner resealing the bag.

Gas Flushing Mylar Bags

Flushing with inert gas works essentially like vacuum sealing except that you're putting more gas into the bag rather than taking it out. You'll want to keep the entry hole small, but don't make a seal around it as above. Beyond that, follow the directions as given in the *Section - CO2 and Nitrogen*. When you feel that the bag has been sufficiently flushed, run the iron across the corner as above to seal.

Flushing with dry ice can also be done, but it is important to wait until the frozen carbon dioxide has completely sublimated into gas before making the final seal otherwise the bag will burst like an overfilled balloon.

REUSING OR RECYCLING PACKAGING

In an effort to save money or because new packaging may be hard to come by, it is common for many people to want to re-use previously used containers. There is nothing wrong with this, but it is sometimes more complicated than using new containers would be. Here are some general rules if you have an interest in doing this.

#1. Do not use containers that have previously contained products other than food. There are two risks this can expose you to. The first is that the particular package type may not have been tested for food use and may allow the transfer of chemicals from the packaging into your food. The second is that all plastics are porous to some degree. Small amounts of the previous contents may have been absorbed by the packaging material only to be released into your food, particularly if it is wet, oily or alcoholic.

#2. Previously used containers should only be used with foods of a similar nature and exposed to similar processes. This means that if a container previously held a material high in fat, such as cooking oil, then it should not be used to store a strong acid such as vinegar. Nor should a container be exposed to extreme conditions, such as heat, if the original use of the package did not subject it to that treatment. An exception to this is glass which is covered below. Generally speaking, dry, non-oily, non-acidic or alkaline, non-alcoholic foods may be safely contained in any food safe container. An example of this is keeping grains and legumes in HDPE buckets formerly containing pickles.

#3. Glass may be used to store any food provided it is in sound condition and has only been used to store food previously. The lid or cap that seals the jar, however, is subject to the cautions given above. Glass jars not specifically made for home canning, either boiling water bath or pressure canning, have a significant risk of breakage if used for that purpose.

#4. Porous packaging materials such as paper, cardboard and Styrofoam should not be reused. Their open texture can trap food particles and are difficult to adequately clean. Packaging formerly holding raw meats, seafoods, or egg products are particularly at risk.

#5. Containers previously holding odorous foods may trap those odors and transfer them to foods later stored. Pickle flavored milk leaves a lot to be desired. Foods such as dry milk powders, fats and oils, flours and meals will absorb any odors seeping from your container material. Be sure to get the smell out before you fill them.

CARBON DIOXIDE AND NITROGEN

Carbon dioxide (CO_2) and nitrogen (N_2) are commonly used in packaging both fresh and shelf-stable foods, in order to extend their shelf lives. Fresh foods are outside the scope of this work so attention will be focused on those foods suitable for use in storage programs. The most common use of these gasses is for excluding oxygen (O_2) from the atmosphere contained inside of a storage container (called head gas). When head gas oxygen levels can be dropped below 2% the amount of undesirable oxidation reactions in stored foods can be greatly decreased resulting in longer shelf lives.

Actually achieving this is not a simple matter when limited to the equipment and facilities typically available in the home. Still, with careful technique and proper packaging materials it is possible to achieve useful results. In order for either gas to be used most effectively it is should be contained inside of packaging with high barrier properties to prevent outward diffusion over time or allowing oxygen to infuse in.

Examples of this kind of packaging are aluminized Mylar or other high barrier property plastics, metal cans or glass jars. Buckets made of HDPE plastic are relatively poor gas barriers and will, over time, allow oxygen to infuse into the container. In order for foods to be kept for their maximum shelf lives the containers would need to be re-purged every three to four years. Foods that are particularly oxygen sensitive, such as dry milk powders, should not be stored in HDPE without a secondary gas barrier. It is possible to use HDPE buckets alone when gas purging if a shorter rotation period is used. An example would be using wheat in four to five years instead of the eight to ten that would be achievable if a high barrier container were used.

Purging efficiency can be greatly improved when used with a vacuum device. By first drawing down the head gas of the container and then flooding with the purging gas much more oxygen can be removed. Repeating the process once more will improve removal efficiency even more. If a true vacuum pump is not available, the suction end of a home vacuum cleaner can be made to serve and still achieve useful results.

With careful technique, oxygen levels can be dropped to between 0.5-2%. Finely textured materials such as grain flours and meals, dry milk powders, dry eggs, and similar textured foods will purge poorly and are better packaged with oxygen absorbers.

A less common, but important use for carbon dioxide is fumigation. This is killing or retarding insect life contained in a product. Many chemical fumigants are available to do this but are not thought desirable by many who have foodstuffs they want to put into storage. CO_2 is not as certain as the more toxic fumigants, but it can be made to work and will not leave potentially harmful residues behind. It is possible for nitrogen to work in a similar manner, but it must be in a head gas concentration of 99%+ whereas carbon dioxide can be effective over time at levels as low as 3%. The precise amount of time necessary for the gas to do its work will vary according to the specific insect species and its growth stage along with the temperature and humidity level of the product being fumigated. In general, the more active the growth stage and the warmer the temperature the more effective CO_2 is in killing weevil infestations. The gas also exhibits bacterial and fungal inhibiting properties, but for our purposes this will be of little moment since all foods should be too dry to support such growth in the first place.

The procedure for fumigating foodstuffs with carbon dioxide is precisely the same as the one used in purging oxygen from storage containers mentioned below. The only change is that for the fastest effectiveness the sealed container should be left in a warm place for a week or so before moving it into its final storage location. The gas is still effective at cooler temperatures, but because insect life is slowed by lower temperatures the carbon dioxide takes longer to complete its mission.

NOTE: Both Mitsubishi Gas-Chemical, maker of the Ageless line of oxygen absorbers, and Multisorb, manufacturer of the FreshPax D 750 absorbers, state that their products should not be used in a high carbon dioxide environment. There are absorbers that will work well in high carbon dioxide atmospheres but they require an external moisture source which would make them difficult to use for our purposes.

Dry Ice

Using dry ice to displace oxygen from food storage containers is straightforward. To get the best results it is recommended that all foodstuffs and packaging materials be put in a warm location for a few hours before beginning the purging process. The reason for this is that the cold CO_2 sublimating from the dry ice will be denser than the warmer, lighter oxygen containing air. The cold gas will tend to stay on the bottom, gradually filling the container and pushing the warm air out the top.

When you first pick up your dry ice from the supplier, put it in a moisture proof container so that air humidity will be less able to condense and freeze on it. The sublimating gas will prevent you from achieving a tight seal, but you can slow down the water ice accumulation.

Gather your containers and any interior packaging materials. Break off a piece of dry ice of sufficient size for the volume to be purged. One pound of dry ice will produce about 8.3 cubic feet of carbon dioxide gas so approximately two ounces per five gallon bucket will do. Wipe off any accumulated water frost which should look whiter than the somewhat bluish frozen gas. Wrap in a paper towel to keep foodstuffs out of direct contact. Place in the bottom of the container that will actually contain the food, i.e. the bag. Fill the package with the food product, shaking and vibrating while doing so to achieve the maximum packing density. If a vacuum process is not to be used then place the lid on the container, but do not fully seal. If a liner bag is being used then gather the top together or heat seal and cut off a small corner. This is to allow the air being purged to escape as it is pushed upward by the expanding gas from the dry ice. Do not move or shake the container while the ice is sublimating so as to minimize turbulence and mixing.

After about two hours feel the bottom of the container immediately below where you put the ice. If it's not still icy cold complete the seal. Check the container every fifteen minutes or so to be sure that a pressure build up is not occurring. A small amount of positive pressure is OK, but do not allow the container to bulge. If a vacuum process is used then cut off a corner of the bag and insert the probe or place the container in the vacuum chamber. Draw a vacuum and when it has reached the desired point shut it off, but do not allow air back inside. When the dry ice has finished sublimating, seal the container. If a slightly larger piece of dry ice is used this process may be repeated once more to improve oxygen removal. Watch for pressure signs as above.

NOTE: It is natural for some grains and legumes to absorb carbon dioxide when stored in an atmosphere with high levels of the gas. This will result in a drop in head space air pressure much like using oxygen absorbers will cause as they absorb oxygen. Precautions should be taken in thin walled containers against buckling and possible loss of seal integrity. When the food products are removed from the container they will release the adsorbed CO_2 and suffer no harm.

WARNING: Dry ice is extremely cold (about –110° degrees F.) and can cause burns to the skin with prolonged contact. Because of this you should wear gloves whenever handling it. Also, dry ice evaporates into carbon dioxide gas, which is why we want it. CO_2 is not inherently dangerous, we breathe it out with every breath we exhale, but you should make sure the area where you are packing your storage containers is adequately ventilated so the escaping gas will not build to a level dangerous enough to asphyxiate you.

IMPORTANT NOTE: Because dry ice is very cold, if there is much moisture (humidity) in the air trapped in the container with your food, it will condense. Try to pack your containers on a day when the relative humidity is low or in an area with low humidity, such as in an air-conditioned house. Use of a desiccant package when using dry ice to purge storage containers may be a good idea.

DRY ICE SUPPLIERS

Dry ice may be found at ice houses, welding supply shops, some ice cream stores, meat packers or you could look in your local phone book under the headings "ice", "dry ice" or "gasses". If you are still unable to locate a source, contact your local hospital and ask to speak to the laboratory manager. Ask where the hospital gets the dry ice they use to ship biological specimens. You may be able to use the same source. You may also want to check out Dry Ice Info.com (http://www.dryiceinfo.com) and click on the directory link to find a dry ice retailer in your area. While you're there check out some of the other uses for dry ice on the site. It's an interesting place.

OXYGEN ABSORBERS

WHAT IS AN OXYGEN ABSORBER?

Oxygen absorbers are a relatively recent food storage tool whose arrival has been a real boon to the person wanting to put up oxygen sensitive dry foods at home. The packets absorb free oxygen from the air around them and chemically bind it by oxidizing finely divided iron into iron oxide. This removes oxygen from being available for other purposes such as oxidative rancidity and respiration by insects, fungi or aerobic bacteria. The practical upshot of all this is that by removing the free oxygen from your storage containers, you can extend the storage life of the foods inside. Not all foods are particularly oxygen sensitive but for those that are the absorbers truly simplify getting the job done. The absorbers themselves have only a relatively short life span, roughly about six months from the time they were manufactured for the types that do not need an external moisture source. They don't suddenly become ineffective all at once, it's just at that point you will begin to notice (if you can measure it) that the absorbers no longer soak up as much as they would when they were new. Better to use them while they're fresh.

HOW ARE OXYGEN ABSORBERS USED?

In order to make the best use of your absorbers you need to know three things:

#1 – *Is the food I want to put by particularly oxygen sensitive for the time I want to keep it in storage?* Whole grains that have not been polished or hulled such as wheat, corn, and rye are not especially oxygen sensitive. If you intend to use them up in five years or so, there's no great advantage to using oxygen absorbers, unless used to deter weevil infestations. The same for most beans and peas. Processed or high fat grains and legumes such as oats, barley, brown rice, soybeans, peanuts and split peas would benefit from their use if they are to be kept for more than a year. Whole grain products such as whole wheat flour and rolled oats would as well. Refined grain products such as white rice, white flour, degerminated cornmeal will keep fine for a year or so, possibly longer, without oxygen absorbers if kept dry and protected from weevils. Dry milk, dry eggs, dry meats, and many kinds of dehydrated foods and any kind of freeze dried foods would benefit from oxygen absorbers. Foods with an easily transferable fat content should not be used with oxygen absorbers, nor should they be used with foods that are high in moisture or with free liquids in the storage container. These should be preserved using pressure or boiling water bath canning as appropriate.

#2 – *Will the packaging I want to use seal airtight and is the packaging material itself a good gas barrier?* Obviously if the container won't seal air tight you're wasting your time trying to use oxygen absorbers but the barrier properties of a container stump many folks. Canning jars with good lids, properly sealed #10 (or other size) cans, properly sealed Mylar bags, PETE plastics with appropriate lids or caps, military surplus ammo cans with good gaskets, and many other types of packaging will seal air-tight and provide good barrier properties against oxygen infusing through the packaging material. Nonlaminated flexible plastic packaging (bags, sheets, etc.), HDPE plastic buckets and any kind of nonlaminated paper or cardboard container have poor gas barrier properties. "Poor" is a relative term, though, and if you're going to use the food up in two or three years, even oxygen sensitive foods can be kept in unlined HDPE buckets if you use an appropriately sized absorber and make sure the bucket is well sealed. You'll be using the food before sufficient oxygen has been able to infuse through the walls of the container to make a significant impact.

#3 – What is the volume of the container and how much air volume remains after I've filled it with food? This is important to know if you want to make the most efficient use of your absorbers and be certain your food is adequately protected. Taking the question in two parts, here is how to determine the answer:

A. Absorber capacity is rated by the amount of oxygen in milliliters that each will absorb so you'll need to know what the volume of your container is in milliliters. The table below gives conversions between common U.S. container sizes and their milliliter equivalents.

Pint jar	(16 fl oz)	475 milliliters
Quart jar	(32 fl oz)	950 milliliters
Half-gallon jar	(64 fl oz)	1,900 milliliters
#10 can	(112 fl oz)	3,300 milliliters
One gallon jar	(128 fl oz)	3,800 milliliters
Five gallon pail	(640 fl oz)	19,000 milliliters
Six gallon pail	(768 fl oz)	22,800 milliliters
Fifty-five gallon drum	(7,040 fl oz)	208,175 milliliters

Fluid ounces x 29.57 = milliliters = cubic centimeters

Now multiply the volume of your container times the 21% (0.21) of the atmosphere that oxygen constitutes and you'll come up with the volume of oxygen, in milliliters, that your container holds when it's empty.

An example: A quart jar (32 ozs) is approximately 950 milliliters in volume. Multiply 950 x 0.21 (21%) and you get 199.5 milliliters of oxygen in an empty quart jar. This leads to the second half of the above question.

B. Determining remaining air volume in a container that has been filled can be difficult. Foods vary widely in their density and porosity from flour, which will pack tightly to elbow macaroni which is mostly air even if you pack it to just short of crushing. The following are three rough and ready rules that can be used and will work.

i> Foods that have a lot of open space between the food particles (called *intersitial space*) such as macaroni, pasta, instant dry milk, instant potato flakes, many coarsely chunky dehydrated foods, cold cereals, etc. should use *one half* the container volume as the remaining air space. Using the example above with the quart jar, there would be approximately 100 milliliters of oxygen remaining.

ii> Foods that pack more densely such as non-instant milk, dry eggs, flours and meals, grains with small kernels, dehydrated foods with fine particles and the like should use *one-third* the container volume as the remaining air space. Using the example above, there would be 66 milliliters of oxygen remaining.

iii> Alternatively, you could do what many of the commercial storage food packagers do and use the *entire container volume.* This is not as efficient as more closely determining remaining air volume but it does add certainty that your absorbers will soak up all available free oxygen and still leave some capacity to deal with any microscopic leaks or infusion through the packaging material.

NOTES:

#1 — Both Multisorb and Mitsubishi corporations advise that their oxygen absorbers should not be used in a high carbon dioxide environment. This is apparently for reasons that the absorbers will also absorb carbon dioxide as well as oxygen and may run out of capacity before all of the oxygen in the container has been absorbed.

#2 — If you do choose to use oxygen absorbers in packing your food, give some consideration to the sturdiness of your containers. In doing its job the absorber is going be removing the 21% of the atmosphere that oxygen constitutes. Since nothing is replacing the absorbed gas, this will leave the storage container with a lower atmospheric pressure inside than outside. If the container is sufficiently sturdy this pressure differential will be of little consequence. For containers with thinner walls the pressure drop could cause them partially collapse or buckle, particularly if other containers are stacked upon them. Should this occur, the entire stack could fall causing one or more to burst.

Metal cans and glass jars should have no problems, but some plastic buckets made of HDPE have relatively thin walls which can buckle when the internal air pressure drops. To deter this, a liner bag of Mylar or other high gas barrier plastic should used. Heavier walled buckets won't need a liner unless you're trying to achieve the maximum possible shelf life. Seal the absorbers inside of the liner bag so that the pressure drop with not stress the walls of the container. Other containers should probably be tested or first flushed with an inert gas (N2) before the absorber is sealed in.

#3 — If the pack of absorbers you need to open contains more than you are going to use in fifteen minutes or so, you should minimize exposure of the remaining packets. This can be done by heat sealing the bag they came in with an iron after expelling as much air as possible or better yet by vacuum sealing the bag. You can also put the remaining absorbers in as small a jar or metal can as they will fit in and closing with an air tight lid.

#4 — The chemical reaction that absorbs the oxygen releases minor amounts of heat. This heat release is trivial in an individual packet but if they are piled one atop another as you're using them they can warm each other and speed the absorptive reaction. This costs you capacity lost to open room air so it's best to spread the packets in immediate use out on a tray so they lay atop each other.

#5 — If absorbers are sealed in a package with desiccants some thought should be given to how low the relative humidity will become. Silica gel will reduce humidity to approximately 40% which should not interfere with the absorbers oxidation reaction. Other desiccants, however, are capable of reducing relative humidity to very low levels. This might adversely affect your absorber's ability to carry out its mission by removing moisture from the absorber package that is necessary to sustain the oxidation reaction. If you do use desiccants and oxygen absorbers in the same package, place the desiccant on the bottom, fill the package and then place the oxygen absorber on top of the food before sealing.

MOISTURE IN PACKAGING AND FOOD STORAGE

WHY MOISTURE IS IMPORTANT

Moisture in inappropriate amounts and places is damaging to food. Because of this, much effort is put into reducing the water content of dry foods in order to prolong their shelf lives. Once it is reduced to the desired level the product can then be packaged for storage. Unfortunately, merely reducing moisture content is not always sufficient. Environmental conditions can play a role as well. There are four mechanisms by which environmental conditions may cause a moisture problem in your food storage:

1. - The air trapped in the container with the food may have held sufficient humidity to raise the moisture content of the food to undesirable levels.

2. - Even if the water vapor content wasn't too high, a falling temperature level may cause the trapped humidity to reach its dew point causing water to be squeezed out of the air to condense on your food much the same way as dew forms on your lawn on cool mornings after a warm, humid night. This can be a particular problem if the condensation is localized– say, only the portion of the food next to the walls of the container – resulting in excessive moisture in that local area even though the contents as a whole would be at a satisfactorily low moisture level.

3. - The seal of the container may not be sufficiently tight enough to prevent moisture laden air from leaking in.

4. - The packaging material itself may be porous to water vapor to one degree or another. All paper, wood and cardboard has this fault. Depending upon their particular physical properties some plastics do as well. Metal and glass containers have excellent barrier properties though their seals may not.

The solution for moisture problems is multi-faceted.

1 - Make sure the product to be stored is at an appropriate water content for that particular foodstuff. Beans and grains store well at a 10% moisture level, but milk powders, dried eggs and dehydrated or freeze dried foods should be lower for best results. As a general rule, nearly any dry food will store well at moisture contents between 3%-10% with the lower the better. Don't get carried away with this though. Extreme low moisture levels (below 3%) can make some foods difficult or impossible to reconstitute and damage the viability of seeds. Ideally, the dry foodstuffs you have on hand will have no more than a 10% moisture content. If they do not then you will need to reduce moisture to a level appropriate for the kind of food you are storing.

One of the following methods might be of use in lowering moisture content.

A - The least involved is to wait until the driest time of year for your location making sure there is plenty of free air circulation around the food product. If this doesn't suit, then turn your air conditioning on a little high. Bring in your buckets, lids, and the storage food. Let everything sit in a well-ventilated place where it's going to get plenty of cool, dry air from the A/C (avoid anywhere near the kitchen or bathroom areas, as they put out a lot of moisture). Stir the food frequently to maximize moisture loss. A few days of cool, constant air flow and low humidity ought to dry things out. Due to its odor absorptive nature, don't do this with any dried milk products or other powdered foods, flours or meals. This method works best with coarse particles such as grain, legumes and dried foods.

B - Warm, dry air can also be used to lower moisture content and works well if you have large quantities of grains and legumes. This is similar to what is used on farms for drying harvested grain. You'll need a source of forced, warm, not hot, air. Place the grain in a drum or barrel and blow the heat from the bottom so that the warm and the moisture it will carry can exit from the top. It's important to not let the bottom product get too hot. You should also monitor the top, center of the drum to be certain the product there is not getting damp from the moisture escaping other areas. Stirring occasionally may be necessary. Some have used an old, drum style vacuum cleaner that puts out fairly warm exhaust air and it works pretty well. Do be sure to clean the vacuum thoroughly so you don't blow the grain full of dust.

C - If the above methods won't do or you have powdery foods to dry, you can put the food and a large quantity of desiccant (see below) in a storage container. The desiccant should be in its own container placed on top of the food and the container lid sealed on. After about a week, unseal and check the desiccant. If it's saturated, change it out with dry desiccant and reseal. Continue to do this until the contents are sufficiently dry. If it doesn't become saturated the first time, change it anyway before sealing the bucket permanently to deter saturation in storage. If your food products are sufficiently dry you can pack them in storage containers using the packaging method of your choice and have a reasonable expectation of your food staying in good condition. Whether you will need to use a desiccant will be dependent upon the conditions discussed below.

2 - Try to package your goods in a dry atmosphere and do not allow extreme temperature swings in storage areas. Warm temperatures and a high relative humidity when a container is sealed means the air trapped inside the container will have a high dew point. This will lead to condensation should storage temperatures fall below that dew point. An example of this would be a container sealed on a day that was 70º F and 40% relative humidity. At that temperature the relative humidity would be quite reasonable for all but the most moisture sensitive food. However, should the temperature fall to 44º F the capacity of the air to hold water vapor would have dropped to the point that it could not contain what was sealed in at 77º F and the excess would be squeezed out to condense on the food, i.e. – it will grow moister. Possibly the food will be able to absorb this moisture without harm and then again, it may not.

3 - Use appropriate packaging materials and make certain it is sealed correctly. If you are going to consume them in four to five years, storing grains, beans and peas in unlined HDPE buckets at normal humidities is fine. If you want to keep them at their best for many years beyond that, the plastic the pail is made of is too porous to water vapor for best results and should have an interior liner of a material with better barrier properties. Dry milk powders should not be kept for more than a year in unlined HDPE, but can be kept for much longer in #10 metal cans, glass jars or Mylar bags. Naturally, even the most highly resistant packaging material is useless if its seal isn't good so be sure you use good technique when making closures. Lastly, you may wish to consider using a desiccant if good humidity control at the time of of packing is difficult or if the storage area is in a high humidity environment or if the packaging material does not have sufficiently high barrier properties.

NOTE: There has been some confusion in the past over the appropriate use of desiccants in food storage. Any desiccants you may seal in your storage containers (if you use them) are not for lowering the moisture content of the foods therein, but for moderating any shifts in moisture levels caused by those factors mentioned above. If the food you want to put up is too high in moisture for good storage this needs to be dealt with BEFORE you seal the packaging.

An example would be 10lbs of wheat with a 15% moisture content. That's too high for safe storage and needs to be lowered, preferably to 10% or less. To lower the moisture content of that grain to 10% you need to remove the 5% excess. 5% of 10lbs is eight ounces of water. Good dry silica gel (one of the most common desiccants) will hold 40% of its mass in moisture so to soak up that extra water you would need 20 ounces of silica gel – quite a large amount – all to remove that 5% excess moisture in ten pounds of grain. Fifty pounds of grain at that same moisture level would require 100 ounces or six and a quarter pounds of silica gel. Clearly no practical amount of desiccant you can put inside your storage packaging will do for you what should have been done before the food was put by. Desiccants can be used for lowering food moisture content, but this will involve rotating packages of desiccant in and out of the foodstuff until the desired moisture content has been reached. Once the package is sealed any desiccant you leave inside should be there to control moisture fluctuations or to guard against moisture infiltration from the outside.

WHAT IS A DESICCANT?

A desiccant is a substance with strong hygroscopic properties, meaning it will soak up water vapor from the surrounding air. A number of different substances are capable of doing this, but only a relative few of them are of practical use and fewer still are going to be readily available to the average person. Before elaborating on the different types that might be useful for our purposes it's necessary to explain how to choose a desiccant. The U.S. military has done much of the best research on the use of desiccants in packaging and have largely set the standards by which they are judged. Each type of desiccant has temperature and humidity ranges where it performs best and particular physical and chemical characteristics that may need to be considered in relation to what you propose to do with them. The most applicable standard for home food storage defines a unit of desiccant as the amount of desiccant that will adsorb at least 6 grams of water vapor at 40% relative humidity at 77º F (25º C).

Desiccant Needed to Adsorb 6 Grams of Water Vapor

Desiccant Type	Mass (weight) of Desiccant Needed
Silica Gel	15 grams
Indicating Silica Gel	75 grams
Montmorillonite Clay	24 grams
Calcium Oxide (quicklime)	21.5 grams
Calcium Sulfate (gypsum, Drierite)	60 grams
Wood	43 grams

In order to maximize surface area to obtain optimal adsorption, desiccants are manufactured in granular or powder forms. This presents a problem of keeping the desiccant, which may not be safe for direct contact with food, out of the product while still allowing sufficient air flow for it to carry out its task. Manufacturers call this "dusting" and deal with it by packaging the adsorbent in materials such as uncoated Tyvek, a spunbonded high-density polyethylene material produced by the Dupont Corporation. Unfortunately, uncoated Tyvek may not be available at retail, just the coated variety such as is used in postal envelopes. Second best, is two or more layers of coffee filter paper securely sealed over the mouth of the container holding the desiccant. You can also make "cartridges" of filter paper for use in narrow necked containers such as two-liter bottles using ordinary white glue. Getting a good seal all the way around requires some care in execution. Brown Kraft (butcher paper) may be used as well. For coarse granular materials tightly woven fabrics might serve the purpose providing the seams are tightly stitched.

TYPES OF DESICCANTS SILICA GEL

The most commonly known and used desiccant is silica gel which is a form of silica dioxide ($SiO2$), a naturally occurring mineral. It will work from below freezing to past the boiling point of water, but performs best at room temperatures (70-90º F) and high humidity (60-90%). Its performance begins to drop off over 100º F, but will continue to work until approximately 220º F. It will lower the relative humidity in a container to around 40% at any temperature in its range until it is saturated. Silica gel will absorb up to 40% of its weight in moisture. Some forms are approved by the FDA for direct food use (check with your supplier to be sure). It recharges easily (see below in the indicating silica gel text) and does not swell in size as it adsorbs moisture.

INDICATING SILICA GEL In the retail trade, the most common form of silica gel is indicating silica gel composed of small white crystals looking much like granulated sugar with pink or blue colored crystals scattered throughout. This is ordinary silica gel with the colored specks being coated with cobalt chloride, a heavy metal salt. When the gel has absorbed approximately eight percent of its weight in water the colored crystals will turn from blue to pink making an easy visual indicator of whether the gel has become saturated with moisture. *Because cobalt is a heavy metal,* **indicating silica gel** *is not food safe and should be kept from spilling into anything edible.*

The indicating silica gel will still adsorb up to 40% of its weight in water vapor like the nonindicating type will but once it has gone past the 8% level and the crystals have turned pink there is no way to tell how close it is to saturation. This isn't necessarily a problem, you'll just have to treat like the other non-indicating desiccants and either weigh it to determine adsorption or use a *humidity indicator card*. These cards are made to show various humidity ranges and can be had from many desiccant and packaging suppliers.

When saturated, both varieties of silica gel can be dried out and used again. This is done by heating the crystals in an oven at a temperature of no more than 300° F (149° C) for approximately three hours approximately three hours or until the crystals turn blue. Dehydrating the desiccant may also be accomplished by heating in a microwave oven. Using a 900 watt oven heat the crystals for three minute intervals until the color change occurs. The exact amount of time necessary will depend upon the oven wattage. Spreading the desiccant in a broad pan in a shallow layer will speed the process. Heating to 325° F (149°C) or more, or using a microwave oven over 900 watts can damage the gel and render it unable to absorb moisture. If your desiccant is packaged in Tyvek, do not heat above 250° F (121° C) or you could damage the material. This leaves a fairly narrow temperature window since silica gel will not begin to desorb moisture below 220° F (104° C). It's a good idea to use a reliable oven thermometer to check your oven temperature as the thermostats in home ovens are often off by more than twenty five degrees. Start with the packets in a cold oven and raise the temperature to 245° F (118° C), keeping it there for twenty four hours. Spread the packets so they are not touching and keep them at least 16 inches from any heating elements or flames so that radiant heat does not damage the packaging. Tyvek should not be microwaved.

HOW DO I USE DESICCANTS?

Before you get to this point you should have already used the charts above and determined how much of the particular desiccant you're interested in you need for the size of the storage containers you'll be using. Once you know that you're ready to put them it into use. Although they perform different functions, desiccants and oxygen absorbers are used in a similar fashion. They both begin to adsorb their respective targets as soon as they are exposed to them so you want to only keep out in the open air as much desiccant as you are going to use up in fifteen minutes or so.

If you'll be using oxygen absorbers in the same package, place the desiccant on the bottom of the package and the oxygen absorber on the top. This is to keep the desiccants from robbing needed moisture from your oxygen absorbers which will hinder their operation. If your desiccant is pre-packaged, that's all there is to it, put it in the package and seal it up. If you have purchased bulk desiccant you'll first need to make your own containers. You can use indicating silica gel for practically everything.

You can scrounge clear plastic pill bottles, such as aspirin bottles or small plastic jars. Fill the bottle with the desiccant (remember to dry the gel first) and then use a double thickness of coffee filter paper carefully and securely tied around the neck of the bottle to keep any from leaking out (remember the indicating type of silica gel is not food safe). The paper is permeable to moisture, but it's tight enough not to let the crystals out. You can use several winds of plain cotton string for this as both adhesive tapes and rubber bands have a way of going bad over time which might allow the cap to come off spilling the desiccant into the food.

For containers that have openings too narrow to use a desiccant container such as described above you can make desiccant packets with the same filter paper. One easy way is to wrap at least a double layer of paper around the barrel of a marker pen and use a thin bead of white glue to seal. Slide the packet off the pen and allow to dry. When ready, fill with the necessary amount of desiccant. You can then fold the top over twice and tie with string or staple closed. Take care that the top is closed securely enough not to allow any desiccant to leak out. Virgin (not recycled) brown Kraft paper can be used to make the packets with as well. The above method will also work other desiccants, subject to whatever precautions the individual type may have.

IMPORTANT NOTE: The indicating form of silica gel (has small blue or pink specks in it) is not edible so you want to use care when putting together your desiccant package to insure that is does not spill into your food.

WHERE DO I FIND DESICCANTS?

Try buying indicating silica gel at Wal-Mart in their dry flower section where it is sold in one and five pound cans for flower drying. It is also sold the same way in crafts stores and other department type stores that carry flower arranging supplies. You can also buy it from many other businesses already prepackaged in one form or another to be used as an adsorbent. The desiccant found packaged this way may be rather expensive, so shop carefully.

There are a number of Internet sources available which will probably provide your best route for finding what you want. Businesses carrying packaging supplies sometimes also sell desiccants. Some businesses commonly receive packets or bags of desiccants packaged along with the products they receive. Montmorillonite clay in bags as large as a pound are sometimes shipped with pianos coming in from Japan. Small packets of silica gel seem to be packed in nearly everything. Naturally, any salvaged or recycled desiccant should be of a type appropriate for use with the product you want to package. It is possible to make your own desiccants using gypsum from drywall and maybe Plaster of Paris. Calcium oxide can also be produced from limestone (calcium carbonate) or slaked or pickling lime (calcium hydroxide) by roasting to drive off the adsorbed water and carbon dioxide, however clear instructions on how to go about this aren't available. Please do keep in mind that calcium oxide (quicklime) is caustic in nature and is hazardous if handled incorrectly.

DIATOMACEOUS EARTH

WHAT IS DIATOMACEOUS EARTH? Diatomaceous earth is a naturally occurring substance partially comprised of the fossilized remains of diatoms. Diatoms are microscopic sized hard shelled creatures found in both marine and fresh waters. The diatom shells are covered in sharp spines that make them dangerous to exoskeletal insects, but not to animals with internal skeletons. The spines of the diatom skeletons pierce the soft body tissues of insects between their hard exoskeletal plates and it is through these numerous microscopic wounds that the insect loses bodily moisture to the point of desiccating and dying. Creatures with internal skeletons such as humans, cattle and pets have means of resisting such damage and are not harmed. Thus, it is possible to mix a small amount of DE into your stored grains and beans to deter insect infestations without having to remove the dust again before you consume them. *Diatomaceous earth works in a purely physical, not chemical, manner thus has no chemical toxicity.*

As neat as this sounds, in the limited number of controlled studies it seems that DE is not as effective in controlling food storage insects as properly used freezing techniques, fumigation with carbon dioxide (dry ice) or sealing in air-tight containers with oxygen absorbers. This is primarily for reasons that most of the insects that cause a problem in grain storage are hard-shelled weevils which have only a limited amount of soft tissue exposure. Use DE for controlling ants and roaches in areas where you feed animals and bedding areas. Still, some folks want to use DE in their food storage so the following information is provided.

WHERE DO I FIND D.E. AND WHAT TYPE SHOULD I BUY?

IMPORTANT NOTE: There are two kinds of diatomaceous earth to be found on the market and only one of them is suitable for use as an insecticide in your stored grains. *The type you DO NOT WANT FOR FOOD USE is sold by swimming pool suppliers as a filtering agent.* DE to be used for filtering has been subjected to a heat treatment that dramatically increases its crystalline silicate content which makes it unsuitable for use with your foodstuffs. *The diatomaceous earth that is needed for use in food storage has not been heat treated and has a crystalline silica content of no more than 1-1.5%.* It is commonly sold in hardware and garden stores as an "organic pesticide" and is available from a number of storage food dealers. A few of these suppliers are listed in the *Resources* section.

You can usually purchase DE from your local hardware store and have no concerns about its safety. However, some local suppliers keep their DE in the same area as their chemical pesticides. This causes some concern about possible contamination and you may not want to use DE from these sources. Since the actual amount of DE (by weight) that is necessary to protect grains is fairly small, order yours from suppliers who will guarantee their product is *food grade* as stipulated by the US FDA. This will insure you receive a product that has no deleterious contaminants and is safe to use.

HOW DO I USE D.E. IN FOOD STORAGE?

To use, you should mix thoroughly one cup (8 fl ozs) of DE to every forty pounds of grain, grain products or legumes. This works out to approximately one cup of DE to every five gallon bucket of food you want to treat. You need to make certain that every kernel is coated so it is better to do the mixing in small batches where you can insure more even coating. Both the grain and the DE should be quite dry when doing the mixing otherwise you'll get an uneven distribution.

WARNING: DE is a powdery dust which you need to take steps to keep out of your lungs and eyes. A paint or hardware store filter mask and a pair of goggles will do the job. It's a good idea to do the actual mixing outside in a slight breeze otherwise you'll get DE all over everything. Even whole wheat flour dust can cause lung irritation if you breathe in a sufficient amount. Being inactive and usually covered in a hard shell, DE works poorly on insect eggs or pupae. It has more effectiveness on larvae and adult insects with a fair amount of soft tissue exposure.

SPOILAGE

INSECT INFESTATIONS PESTS OF STORED GRAINS, LEGUMES AND DRY FOODSTUFFS

Insect infestations can occur in a wide variety of foodstuffs such as flours, meals, pastas, dried fruits or vegetables, nuts, sweets, whole grains, beans, sugars, TVP, jerky, bird seed and pet foods.

Naturally, the best way to deal with an insect infestation is not to have one in the first place. Try to purchase your goods from suppliers who are clean and who turn over their inventory quickly so the products you purchase will be less likely to have bugs.

When you buy foodstuffs examine them closely to be sure they are insect free. Check for any packaging or use by dates to insure their freshness. Don't shake the package, most adult insects will be found in the top couple of inches of the product and shaking the package will mix them into the contents disguising their appearance. If the package does turn out to be infested, return it for replacement.

If not already packaged for storage when you buy them transfer your foods into air- and moisture-tight containers so they cannot be invaded after you have brought them home.

With sufficient time, some adult and larval insect forms can penetrate paper, cardboard and thin plastic packaging. Storage containers should be glass, metal, or heavy plastic with tight fitting lids. As with everything in food storage, you should use older packages before newer ones and opened packages before unopened ones.

Storage areas should be kept clean. Don't allow grain, flour, beans, bits of pasta or other food particles to accumulate on shelves or floors. Cracks and crevices should be sealed or otherwise blocked. Except for sticky spills, vacuuming is the best method of cleaning as soap and water can wash food particles into cracks.

Insects may also get their start in chairs, sofas and carpets where food is dropped and not cleaned up. Don't forget to replace the filter bag on the vacuum as some insects can survive and reproduce in the bag.

Bags of dry pet food and bird seed can harbor insect infestation. Decorative foodstuffs such as ears of colorful Indian corn, colored beans and hard squashes can carry insects that may infest your edible food. Even poison baits can harbor flour beetles.

CONTROL OF INSECT INFESTATIONS

Should you find that in spite of buying fresh products and using careful packaging techniques you have an insect infestation, you can try some of the following steps:

1. If the food is too heavily infested to try to save it should be disposed of as soon as possible. Remove from the kitchen or food storage area immediately so as to not infest other foods.

2. Large bugs can be sifted or winnowed out if the food's not too heavily infested and you want to try to save it. Then treat by placing into a deep freezer at 0º F (-18º C) for three to seven days depending upon the size of the package. Refrigerator freezers usually do not freeze low enough to effectively kill all of the life stages of insects, but if left there, will slow their development. If freezing is not workable then the product could be spread on baking sheets and heated to 150º F for fifteen to twenty minutes, cooled and repackaged. This will shorten shelf life so heat treated foods should be consumed shortly thereafter.

3. The surface areas where the food containers are stored can be treated with an insecticide. This is not a replacement for clean storage habits and good containers, but is rather a supplement. This will not control insect infestations already in your stored foods. Spray the shelf surface with 0.5% chlorpyrifos (Dursban), 1% propoxur (Baygon), 0.5 percent diazinon, or 0.25 percent resmethrin. You can find any of these in the hardware store in ready to apply packages. If a sprayer isn't feasible then they can be applied with a paint brush. Allow the solution to dry thoroughly. Cover the shelves with clean, untreated shelf paper then put properly packaged foods back on shelves. READ THE PRODUCT LABEL FOR SAFETY INFORMATION CONCERNING CHILDREN AND PETS. Household bleach, Lysol and other sterilizers will not control insect infestation, though they can be used for mold, mildew and algae. You may continue to find some insects after the cleanup is finished. This could be for several reasons. It may be they escaped from the packages they were infesting and did not get cleaned up. There may be more packages infested than were originally found or, there may be hiding places in the storage area that need attention. Once you have carefully eliminated all food sources, the bugs should disappear in a few weeks.

MOLDS IN FOOD Molds are fungi like mushrooms and yeast. Also like mushrooms, they reproduce by releasing spores into the air that land on everything, including your food and food storage containers. If those spores begin to grow, they create thin threads that spread through their growing medium. These threads are the roots of the mold fungus, called *mycelium*. The stalk of a mold fungus is the portion above or on the surface of the food. It produces the spores and gives the mold its color. We've all seen examples of this when we discover a dish of something or other left too long in the refrigerator only to become covered in a mold fuzz.

Molds can grow anywhere they have a growing medium (their food), sufficient moisture and warmth. Some can even grow at refrigerator temperatures, albeit more slowly than they would if it were warmer. These fungi can also withstand more salt and sugar than bacteria, which is why you sometimes find mold in jellies and jams with their high sugar content and on dry cured products like ham or bacon with their high salt content.

In the past, a slight amount of mold was commonly felt to be harmless and the food consumed anyway. For molds that were intentionally introduced, such as the mold in bleu cheese, this is fine.

For the unintentional molds, it could possibly be a serious error in judgment. These Unwanted molds could be producing toxic substances called *mycotoxins* which can be very bad indeed. Mycotoxins are produced around the root or mycelium of molds and these mold roots can penetrate deeply into the food. Mycotoxins can survive for a long time and most are not destroyed by cooking. The molds probably best known for this dangerous spoilage are the various *Aspergillus* species which produces a mycotoxin known as *aflatoxin*, but there are other dangerous fungi as well, such as the *Fusarium* molds. Both of the above affect grains and some legumes.

IMPORTANT NOTE: In wet pack foods such as your home canned goodies, molds can do something else as well, possibly with lethal consequences. If they find their way into wet pack acid foods canned by the boiling water bath method, whether by reasons of improper procedure or contamination after the fact, they can consume the natural acids present in the food. The effect of this is to raise the pH of the food in the container, perhaps to the point that it becomes possible for spores of *Clostridium botulinum*, better known as *botulism*, to become active and reproduce. For this reason, moldy wet pack foods should be *safely* discarded. This most deadly kind of food poisoning has an entry of its own in the bacterial spoilage section. Molds in low acid foods canned by the pressure canning method are equally dangerous and should also be discarded in a safe manner.

MINIMIZING MOLDS

You can do a number of things to minimize unwanted mold growth in your kitchen, food storage areas and refrigerators. Generally it is the refrigerator that is going to collect the most fungal growth. This can be dealt with by washing the inside every couple of months with a tablespoon of baking soda dissolved in a quart of warm water. Rinse clean and allow to dry. The black mildew that grows on the rubber door gaskets and other places can be dealt with by wiping down with a solution of three tablespoons of household bleach in a quart of water using a soft bristle brush for this. A really bad case will not bleach back to a white color, but will instead turn pink or red after the bleach has carried out its disinfection mission.

The rest of the kitchen can be kept mold free by keeping the area clean, dry, and spraying occasionally with a product such as Lysol. Patches of mold can be eliminated with the bleach solution used on the refrigerator doors.

Try not to purchase more fresh food than you'll be able to eat in a short period of time. This will keep you from having to deal with the moldy remains that didn't get eaten. If food does go moldy, don't sniff it. This is a good way to give yourself respiratory difficulties if you are at all susceptible to mold allergies. Moldy food should be disposed in such a manner that you're animals and children won't be able to get into it. Mycotoxins are every bit as bad for your animals as they are for you.

Obviously, you don't have to throw out everything that shows a spot of mold on it. Some foods can be safely dealt with and still partially saved if they show signs of fungal growth. Below is a set of guideline from M. Susan Brewer, Ph.D., R.D., a specialist in food safety. Her articles and works are found in many state university extension services publications lists. *If the food shows even a tiny mold spot, follow these guidelines:*

1. Hard or firm foods with tiny mold spots can be trimmed; cut away the area around the mold (at least an inch) and rewrap in clean wrap. Make sure that knife does not touch the mold.

TRIM:

- Hard Cheese (Cheddar, Swiss, etc.)
- Bell Peppers, Carrots, Cabbage
- Broccoli, Cauliflower, Brussels Sprouts
- Garlic, Onions
- Potatoes, Turnips
- Zucchini
- Apples, Pears

2. Soft foods such as cheese slices, cream cheese, sour cream and yogurt should be thrown away.

TOSS:

- Soft Cheeses, (Mozzarella, Brie, etc.)
- Sour Cream, Yogurt, Cottage cheese
- Bacon, Hot dogs, Sliced lunch meats
- Meat pies
- Opened canned ham
- Most left-over food
- Bread, Cakes, rolls, flour, pastry
- Peanut butter
- Juices, berries
- Jam, Jellies, Syrups
- Cucumbers, Tomatoes
- Spinach, Lettuce, other leafy vegetables
- Bananas, Peaches, Melons
- Corn-on-the-cob
- Stored nuts, whole grains, rice

MOLDS IN CANNED GOODS

If good equipment and proper technique are used, it is unlikely goods. If you do have such, there was either a flaw in the procedure used, or something affected the jar or can after the fact to break its seal. In any event, once the food has molded, it is past saving and should be discarded in such a way that children and animals will not be able to get into it. The most likely home canned products to show mold growth are jams and jellies sealed with paraffin wax. There are a number of points in the canning process where this can occur:

(1) In the time after the jar is taken out of its boiling water bath, but before it is filled.

(2) In the time between when the jar is filled and covered with the melted wax.

(3) When the wax cools, if it pulls away from the side of the jar, leaving an opening for the mold to get in.

(4) If bubbles form in the paraffin, which break and leave holes.

For these reasons most canning authorities no longer recommend using this technique. If you must do so, the jars should be boiled for at least 10 minutes before the jelly is poured. The filled and wax capped jars should then be covered with some sort of protective lid. The book, *Putting Food By* has excellent instructions on this or see the applicable section of the *rec.food.preserving FAQ*.

MOLDS IN GRAINS AND LEGUMES

It has long been known that eating moldy grain is bad for your health with the ugly consequences of eating ergot infected rye being a well known example. It has only been about thirty years, though, that intensive study has been carried out on other species of grain fungi and their respective mycotoxins. Fortunately, for those of us in the U.S., the USDA and the various state departments of agriculture go to a great deal of trouble to detect grain and legumes infected with these toxic fungi. In some of the less developed countries, the citizenry are not so lucky. It is good to have something of an understanding of what one should do to prevent mold growth in ones stored grains and to have an idea of what to look for and ask about when purchasing grains and legumes.

The one fungal group that has caused the most commotion in recent history are the various *Aspergillus* species of molds. Under certain conditions with certain grains, legumes, and to a lesser extent, nuts, they can produce a mycotoxin called *aflatoxin*. This is a serious problem in some parts of the world, most especially in peanuts, occasionally in corn. Documented deaths in the United States from aflatoxicity are hard to find, but other nations have not been so fortunate. What makes aflatoxin worrisome in this country is that it is also a potent carcinogen (cancer causing agent).

In addition to the Aspergillus molds, there is also a large family of molds known as *Fusarium* which can produce mycotoxins of their own, none of which do you want to be eating directly or feeding to your food animals where you will get the toxins back indirectly when the animal is slaughtered and eaten.

The Federal and state governments continuously monitor food and forage crops entering the marketplace. Those products found to be contaminated with mold or mycotoxins are not allowed to be sold for food. Once purchased however, the responsibility is yours to keep your food safe from mold growth. If you have already found mold growth in your whole grains, meals, flours or other grain products, they should be discarded. Most mycotoxins are not broken down or destroyed by cooking temperatures and there is no safe way to salvage grain that has molded.

PREVENTING MOLD GROWTH IN STORED GRAINS AND LEGUMES

The easiest method to prevent mold growth in your stored grains and legumes is to keep them too dry for mold to grow. The Aspergillus and Fusarium molds require moisture contents of 18% and above to reproduce. This is subject to some variability, but in all grains and soybeans, they must have a moisture content of that level. If you are storing raw (not roasted) peanuts, in the shell or shelled, you want to get the moisture content to less than 8% as peanuts are particularly susceptible to mold growth. The recommended moisture content for all other grain and legume storage is no more than 10%. Please see part Grains and Legumes for a method to determine moisture content. At 10% moisture, there is simply too little water for fungi to grow.

BACTERIAL SPOILAGE

Like the fungi, bacteria are everywhere, in the water, soil, air, on you, your food and your food storage containers. Fortunately, the vast majority of the bacteria we encounter are relatively harmless or even benign and only a few represent a danger to us and our stored foods. Bacteria can be much more difficult to kill than molds and insects. Some are capable of continued growth at temperatures that would kill other spoilage organisms. When conditions are such that they are unable to grow, some bacteria can go dormant and form spores. These spores can be quite hardy, even to the point of surviving boiling water temperatures. In order to grow, bacteria must have water, some species needing as little as a 20% moisture content. For properly packaged dry grains, legumes, powdered milk and other low moisture foodstuffs bacterial spoilage will never be a problem as their moisture levels should be too scant to support growth

WARNING: It is in wet pack canned goods (where the container has free liquid in it) and fresh foods we must be the most concerned about spoilage bacteria. It is here that a little bad luck and a moment's inattention to what you are doing could kill or seriously injure you or some other person who eats the foods you've put by. In both home-canned and commercially-canned goods, IF THE CAN IS BULGING, LEAKING, SMELLS BAD, OR SPEWS LIQUID WHEN YOU OPEN IT THEN THROW IT OUT! But, throw it out safely so that children and animals cannot get into it.

BOTULISM

Clostridium botulinum is one of the oldest life forms on this planet dating from a time before the Earth had an abundant oxygen atmosphere. Like the gangrene bacteria, it is an anaerobic organism meaning it lives and grows only in the absence of free oxygen. When conditions are not suitable for growth the bacteria can form durable seed like spores which are commonly found in the soil. This means that *C. botulinum* can be brought into your life on raw produce, tools, hands or anything else that came into contact with dirt. To further complicate matters, botulinum spores are extremely heat-hardy. The bacteria itself can be killed by a short exposure to boiling water (212º F AT SEA LEVEL PRESSURE), but its spores cannot. To kill them, the food product and container must be exposed to temperatures of 240º F (AGAIN AT SEA LEVEL PRESSURE) for a long enough period of time to allow all of the food in each container to come completely up to the proper temperature. Only a pressure-canner can reach the necessary temperature.

It's not the bacteria or its spores which are directly deadly, but the toxin the bacteria creates when it grows and reproduces. In its pure form, botulism toxin is so potent that a mere teaspoon would be enough to provide a fatal dose to hundreds of thousands of people. It is this lethality that is why every responsible book on home canning, food preservation and food storage hammers constantly on the need for care in technique and method and why spoilage must be taken seriously.

Like any other life form *Clostridium botulinum* must have suitable conditions for its growth to become a danger. One of the most important of these is water - the botulism bacterium needs moisture in the 35% range to grow making it a danger only in improperly processed high moisture foods. Another requirement is suitable pH, which is the measure of acidity or alkalinity in a substance and is measured on a scale of 1-14. Anything above 7 is considered alkaline and everything below 7 is considered acid. If the acidity of your wet pack food is BELOW pH4.6 then *C. botulinum* is unable to grow.

Keep in mind that in foods pH is not necessarily stable and could possibly change if other spoilers like mold are able to grow. If the product should change to a lesser acidity than pH4.6 your previously botulinum proof food may start allowing the lethal spoiler to grow (see *molds in canned goods*). This is why it is vital to use proper technique, even for acid foods like tomatoes. It has been found that when this Ph shift occurs, *C. botulinum* can become active producing its lethal toxin and the bacterium also produces minute amounts of acid which can lower the pH of the poisoned food back into what should have been the safe zone had the pH not jumped up and allowed the bacteria to grow. Again and again — use good technique and pay attention to what you are doing.

Unlike fungal mycotoxins Botulinum toxin can be destroyed by boiling food briskly in an open vessel for fifteen minutes. Because of this, if your canned food shows any safety problems you should follow this procedure. If the food shows even the slightest mold growth, keep in mind that mycotoxins are not for the most part broken down by heat and dispose of the food safely. Read the *Ball Blue Book* or most especially the book *Putting Food By* for in depth information on this subject.

ENZYMATIC ACTION IN FOOD SPOILAGE

Every living organism uses enzymes of many sorts in its bodily functions as part of its normal life cycle. Enzymes are used in creating life. After death, enzymes play a role in the decomposition of once living tissue. The enzymes in a tomato help it to ripen and enzymes produced by the tomato and whatever fungal and bacterial spoilers are on it cause it to decay.

Fortunately, slowing down or stopping the action of a food's enzymes is much easier than slowing or stopping some of the bacterial spoilers mentioned above. Enzymes are most active in a temperature range between 85-120º F and begin to be destroyed when the temperature goes above 140º F. Cold also slows down the action of enzymes, which is why fresh tomatoes last longer in the refrigerator than they do on the kitchen table. Most enzymatic action also requires moisture to occur. In foods stored at 10% moisture or less, there is not enough moisture for most enzymes to be active.

RECOMMENDED FOOD STORAGE TIMES At 70° F.

Food Keep the Product Storage Tips
- Baking powder Till can date Sealed & bone dry
- Baking soda 2 years Sealed & dry
- Biscuit, brownie, muffin mix 9 months Sealed, cool, dry, weevil proofed
- Bouillon, cubes or granules 2 years Sealed, cool and dry
- Cake mixes,

- Regular 9 months Sealed, cool, dry, weevil proofed
- Angel food 1 year Sealed, cool, dry, weevil proofed
- Canned food,
- Metal can, Non-Acidic 2 years Cool & Dry
- Metal Can, Acidic 12-18months Cool & Dry
- Glass jars 2-3 years Dark, Cool & Dry
- Chocolate, semi-sweet or unsweetened, bars or chips 18 months Cool and dark
- Chocolate syrup 2 years Cool & tightly sealed
- Cocoa, powder or mixes 8 months Sealed and cool
- Coffee creamers, powdered 9 months Sealed and cool
- Cornmeal 1 year Keep dry & weevil proofed
- Cornstarch 18 months Keep dry
- Crackers 3 months Keep dry & weevil proofed
- Flour, Refined white 8-12 months Dry & weevil proofed,
- Whole wheat 4-6 weeks Refrigerate/freeze for longer shelf life
- Frostings, Canned 3 months Cool
- Mix 8 months Dry and cool
- Fruits, dried 6-12 months Cool, sealed, weevil proofed
- Gelatin, all types 18 months Protect from moisture
- Grains, whole 2 years Dry and weevil proofed
- Hominy, hominy grits,
- masa harina 1 year Dry and weevil proofed
- Honey 2 years Cool, tightly sealed, dark
- Jellies, jams, preserves 2 years Dark, cool, tightly sealed.
- Molasses & syrups 2 years Tightly sealed
- Mayonnaise 6 months Cool & dark
- Milk, Condensed or evaporated 1 year Turn over every 2 months
- Non-fat dry 6 months Bone dry and cool
- Nuts, Vacuum canned 1 year Cool and Dark
- Other packaging 3 months Cool and dark – better Refrigerated
- In shell 4 months Cool, dry & dark, better refrigerated or frozen
- Pancake mix 6-9 months Dry and weevil proofed
- Pastas (macaroni, noodles, etc) 2 years Dry and weevil proofed
- Peanut butter 6-9 months Sealed, cool, dark
- Peas and beans, dry (not soybeans) 2 years Dry and weevil proofed
- Potatoes, instant 6-12 months Dry and weevil proofed
- Pudding mixes 1 year Cool and very dry
- Rice, White 2+ years Dry and weevil proofed
- Brown 3-6 months Dry & weevil proofed, better refrigerated or frozen
- Flavored or herb 6 months Sealed, dry and weevil proofed
- Salad dressings 10-12 months Sealed, dark, cool. Better refrigerated
- Salad oils 6 months Sealed, dark, cool. Better refrigerated
- Sauce and gravy mixes 6-12 months Cool and dry

- Shortening, solid 1 year Cool, dark, tightly sealed.
- Soup mixes 1 year Cool, dry, and weevil proofed
- Sugar, Brown 2 years Tightly sealed, Dry.
- Confectioners 18 months Tightly sealed, Dry.
- Granulated 2+years Dry
- Syrups (corn syrup based) 8-12 months Sealed and cool
- Vegetables, dried 1 year Cool, dark, dry, weevil proofed
- Vinegar 2+ years Sealed

Storage Life of Dehydrated Foods

Determining the storage life of foods is at best an inexact science **as there are so many variables. These range from the condition your food was in when you first purchased it and includes many other factors. This information should be used as a general guide only, and should not be followed "as the gospel truth" because your results may be different.**

Four Factors that affect food storage:

Factor #1: The Temperature: Temperature has more to do with how long well dried foods store than anything else. The USDA states, *"Each 5.6 C. (10.08F) drop in temperature doubles the storage life of the seeds."* Obviously, there is a limit as to how far this statement can be taken. However you can expect it basically holds true from room temperature down to freezing. No doubt, the inverse could also be considered true. *"Each 5.6C. (10.08F) rise in temperature halves the storage life of seeds."* This theory holds true for non-garden seeds as well.

Storage Life Differences Depending on Temperature

Constant Storage Temp in degrees Storage life in Years

- 39.76 40
- 49.84 30
- 59.92 20
- 70.00 10
- 80.08 5
- 90.16 2.5
- 100.24 1.25

Note: the above chart is not for a specific food but shows the relationship between temperature and storage life.

The bottom line is even with the very best packaging methods, if you are planning on storing your food in a warm environment, it will only last a fraction of the time it would last if stored in a cool, dry place. You can expect good storage life if your storage temperature is at 60 degrees F or below. Optimum storage temperature is at 40 degrees F or less. It is important you also find a place where the temperature remains constant. Frequent temperature changes shorten storage life. If you don't have a cool place for your food storage, plan on rotating your storage quickly enough to prevent food loss.

Factor #2: Product moisture content:

By looking at the USDA nutritional tables, dry beans, grains, and flours contain an average of 10% moisture. Although it is very difficult and unnecessary to remove all moisture from dry foods, it is imperative that any food be stored as dry as possible. Foods with excess moisture can spoil right in their containers. This is an important consideration when packing food with dry ice as moisture condenses and freezes on the outer surface of the dry ice. For long term storage, grains should have a moisture content of 10% or less. It is also important to know that you cannot dehydrate foods at home that reach these levels. Food that is dried to a moisture level of 10% moisture crisply snap when bent. Those of you who dehydrate foods at home know dehydrated foods from your dehydrator are quite pliable when bent, especially fruits. These will not store well long term.

Factor #3: Atmosphere the product is stored in:

Foods packed in air don't store as well as in oxygen free gasses. This is because air contains oxygen which oxidizes many of the compounds in food. Bacteria, one of several agents which make food go rancid also needs oxygen to grow. Food storage companies have a couple of different processes for removing the oxygen:

- **Displacing the oxygen:** This is done by purging out all the air in the product with an inert gas. Nitrogen is almost always used because it is the most inert gas known. People doing their own packing occasionally use dry ice which gives off carbon dioxide gas, and probably works just about as well.
- **Absorb the oxygen:** Oxygen absorber packets do just that. Air contains about 78% nitrogen and 21% oxygen, leaving about 1% for the other gasses. If the oxygen is absorbed, what remains is 99% pure nitrogen in a partial vacuum. If oxygen absorber packets are used, care must be taken to use a storage container that can stand some vacuum. If it's not air tight, air will be sucked into your container as the oxygen is absorbed, reintroducing more oxygen that must be absorbed. Before long, the oxygen absorbers will have absorbed all the oxygen they can. Obviously, your product won't be oxygen free under these circumstances.
- **Seeds store better in nitrogen.** On the other hand, seeds you plan on sprouting, such as garden seed, or seeds set aside for growing your own sprouts store better in air. For this reason Walton cans their garden seed packs in air. Oxygen absorbers also contain a minute amount of moisture to activate the absorber. Sometimes, with the heat generated by the absorber, they can cause sweating if you use glass bottles or Tupperware type containers.

Factor #4: The container the product is stored in:

To get the best storage life out of your product it must have a hermetic (air tight) seal. Containers that do this well are:

- #10 Cans (Use only cans that are enamel lined, otherwise your food flavor will be tainted by the steel it comes in contact with. An enamel lined can also prevent the inside of the can from rusting.)
- Sealable food storage buckets
- Sealable food quality metal (lined) or plastic drums.

Whatever container you use, be sure it is food grade as your product can be tainted with whatever the container is made from. Plastic sacks are not good air tight containers, for even if they are sealed, the relatively thin plastic breathes,' allowing air to pass through. Paper sacks are of course even worse. There is some concern as to how good a seal is made by the lids on plastic buckets used by food storage companies. Manufacturer studies show an extremely small amount of air transfer. This amount is so small, however, that it can be considered a hermetic seal. It has also been found that the lids can be re-used several times without dramatically degrading the performance of the seal.

People who purchase products from food storage providers are often concerned about receiving their buckets bulging or with one side collapsed in. Collapsed buckets occasionally occur when ordering from Walton's as the elevation of their packing facility is above 6,000 feet. As the buckets are shipped to a lower elevation, the increased ambient air pressure can sometimes push in one side. If a side is popped in, it is a great indication that the bucket is indeed sealed. And this also holds true for buckets that might be under a slight amount of pressure. If either condition concerns you, crack the lid to equalize the air pressure. You can do this without seriously degrading the storageability of the product within the bucket. Remember to re-seal the lid after doing this.

Bulging cans:

Some bulging cans that are returned to suppliers held mixes that contained baking powder or soda. It is believed that occasionally the extremely small amount of moisture found in the product interacts over time with the baking powder or soda and creates a small amount of carbon dioxide gas. Oxygen absorbers can also react with the baking powder causing the cans to bulge. These cans have been sent off for bacteria analysis and and in each case came back negative.

STORAGE LIFE NOTES ABOUT SPECIFIC FOODS:

The Soft Grains

Barley Hulled or Pearled, Oat Groats, Rolled Oats, Quinoa Rye.

Soft Grains have softer outer shells which don't protect the seed interior as well as hard shelled seeds and therefore won't store as long. Hermetically sealed in the absence of oxygen, plan on a storage life of 8 years at a stable temperature of 70 degrees F. They should keep proportionately longer if stored at cooler temperatures.

The Hard Grains

Buckwheat, Corn, Dry Flax, Kamut, Millet, Durum wheat, Hard red wheat, Hard white wheat, Soft wheat, Special bake wheat, Spelt, Triticale.

The Hard Grains all store well because of their hard outer shell which is nature's near perfect container. Remove that container and the contents rapidly deteriorate. Wheat, probably nature's longest storing seed, has been known to be edible after scores of years when stored in a cool dry place. As a general rule for hard grains, hermetically sealed in the absence of oxygen, plan on a storage life of 15-20 years at a stable temperature of 70 degrees F. They should keep proportionately longer if stored at cooler temperatures.

Beans

Adzuki Beans, Blackeye Beans, Black Turtle Beans, Garbanzo Beans, Great Northern, Kidney Beans, Lentils, Lima Beans, Mung Beans, Pink Beans, Pinto Beans, Small Red Beans, Soy Beans.

As beans age they lose their oils, resist water absorption and won't swell. Worst case, they must be ground to be used. Storing beans in nitrogen helps prolong the loss of these oils as does cool temperatures. Hermetically sealed in the absence of oxygen, plan on a storage life of 8-10 years at a stable temperature of 70 degrees F. They should keep proportionately longer if stored 10-20 degree F cooler temperatures.

Dehydrated Vegetables

Broccoli, Cabbage, Carrots, Celery, Onions, Peppers, Potatoes.

Dehydrated vegetables store well if hermetically sealed in the absence of oxygen. Plan on a storage life of 8-10 years at a stable temperature of 70 degrees F. They should keep proportionately longer if stored at cooler temperatures.

Dehydrated Dairy Products

Cheese Powder, Cocoa Powder, Powdered Eggs, Butter/margarine Powder, Powdered Milk, Morning Moo, Whey Powder.

Dehydrated Dairy Products generally store very well if stored dry in hermetically sealed containers with the oxygen removed. Plan on a storage life of 5 to 10 years if stored at a stable temperature of 70 degrees F. They should keep, probably 5 years longer, if stored at cooler temperatures. One exception is Morning Moo. As a new whey based product, it hasn't been tested for long term storage. Plan on rotating this product after 5 years. Our dairy powders (excluding our sour cream powder) contain no fat, an agent that markedly decreases the storage life of dairy products.

Flours and Other Products made from Cracked / Ground Seed.

All Purpose Flour, Bakers Flour, Unbleached Flour, White Flour, Whole Wheat Flour, Cornmeal, Mixes, Refried Beans, Cracked wheat, Germade, Gluten, Wheat flakes.

After seeds are broken open their outer shells can no longer protect the seed contents and seed nutrients start to degrade. Don't try to store unprotected flours longer than a year. Hermetically sealed in the absence of oxygen, plan on a storage life of 5 years at a stable temperature of 70 degrees F. They should keep proportionately longer if stored at cooler temperatures. Note: Granola is not a long storing food because of the nuts. They contain high concentrations of oil which go rancid over the short term. Expect granola to last about 6-9 months.

Pasta

Macaroni, Noodles, Ribbons, Spaghetti.

Pasta will store longer than flour if kept dry. Hermetically sealed in the absence of oxygen, plan on a storage life of 10 - 15 years at a stable temperature of 70 degrees F. Pasta should keep proportionately longer if stored at cooler temperatures.

Dehydrated Fruit

Fruit doesn't keep as well as many dehydrated items. Hermetically sealed in the absence of oxygen, plan on a storage life of 10-15 years at a stable temperature of 70 degrees F. They should keep proportionately longer if stored at cooler temperatures.

Honey, Salt and Sugar

Honey, Salt and Sugar should keep indefinitely if stored free of moisture. Watch out for additives in the honey. It is possible to buy honey with water and sugar added. This honey generally doesn't crystallize like pure 100% honey does when stored for a long time. If there are additives, there is no saying how long it will last.

Peanut Butter Powder

Peanut Butter Powder will not store as long as wheat flour. Hermetically sealed in the absence of oxygen, plan on a storage life of 4-5 years at a stable temperature of 70 degrees F. It should keep proportionately longer if stored at cooler temperatures.

Brown and White Rices

Brown and white rices store very differently. Brown rice is only expected to store for 6 months under average conditions. This is because of the essential fatty acids in brown rice. These oils quickly go rancid as they oxidize. It will store much longer if refrigerated. White rice has the outer shell removed along with those fats. Because of this, white rice isn't nearly as good for you, but will store longer. Hermetically sealed in the absence of oxygen, plan on a storage life for white rice of 8-10 years at a stable temperature of 70 degrees F. It should keep proportionately longer if stored at cooler temperatures. Stored in the absence of oxygen, brown rice will last longer than if it was stored in air. Plan on 1 to 2 years. It is very important to store brown rice as cool as possible, for if you can get the temperature down another ten degrees, it will double the storage life again.

Garden Seed or Sprouting Seed

All viable seeds are hibernating tiny living plants that only need moisture and warmth to sprout. And much like a chick in an egg, all the nutrients this little life needs to spring into existence is contained within its shell. Like boiling an egg, heating a seed will kill that little life within it.

However, unlike an egg, a seed can withstand cold temperatures. As seeds usually remain edible after the life within it dies, we must use different criteria when determining sproutable seed storage life. And again the big deciding factor is temperature. Plan on a storage life of 2 to 3 years at a stable temperature of 70 degrees F. They should keep proportionately longer if stored at cooler temperatures. And remember, you want to store all of these seeds in air. Packed in nitrogen, the viability of some seeds will last longer than others. This is still to a large degree an unexplored science, and therefore we recommend you store all the seeds you plan on sprouting in air. Alfalfa is a unique seed as it actually germinates better if the seed is 2 or 3 years old. Most any sample of alfalfa contains 'hard' seed and 'soft' seed. Soft seed germinates within two days while hard seed germinates in about a week. The problem is, by the time the soft seed sprouts are ready to harvest, the hard seed may not have germinated yet. As storage time draws on, the hard seed turns into soft seed. Older seed germinates closer together. Stored in cool conditions, alfalfa seed should have a good percentage of germination up until it is 8 years old.

Total Vegetable Protein

Total Vegetable Protein, made from soy beans, has an unusually long storage life. Hermetically sealed in the absence of oxygen, plan on a storage life of 15-20 years at a stable temperature of 70 degrees F. meat substitute should keep proportionately longer if stored at cooler temperatures.

Yeast

Yeast, a living organism, has a relatively short storage life. Keep yeast in the original metal foil storage containers. If the seal remains intact, yeast should last 2 years at 70 degrees F. However it is strongly recommended that you refrigerate it, which should give you a storage life of 5 years. Frozen yeast should store for a long time.

DRYING FRUITS AND VEGETABLES

Food drying is one of the oldest methods of preserving food for later use. It can either be an alternative to canning or freezing, or compliment these methods. Drying foods is simple, safe and easy to learn. With modern food dehydrators, fruit leathers, banana chips and beef jerky can all be dried year round at home.

How Drying Preserves Food

Drying removes the moisture from the food so bacteria, yeast and mold cannot grow and spoil the food. Drying also slows down the action of enzymes (naturally occurring substances which cause foods to ripen), but does not inactivate them. Because drying removes moisture, the food becomes smaller and lighter in weight. When the food is ready for use, the water is added back, and the food returns to its original shape. Foods can be dried in the sun, in an oven or in a food dehydrator by using the right combination of warm temperatures, low humidity and air current. In drying, warm temperatures cause the moisture to evaporate. Low humidity allows moisture to move quickly from the food to the air. Air current speeds up drying by moving the surrounding moist air away from the food.

Drying foods out-of-doors

Sun Drying

The high sugar and acid content of fruits make them safe to dry in the sun. Vegetables and meats are not recommended for sun drying. Vegetables are low in sugar and acid. This increases the risks for food spoilage. Meats are high in protein making them ideal for microbial growth when heat and humidity cannot be controlled. To dry in the sun, hot, dry, breezy days are best. A minimum temperature of 86°F is needed with higher temperatures being better. It takes several days to dry foods out-of-doors. Because the weather is uncontrollable, sun drying can be risky. Also, the high humidity in the South is a problem. Humidity below 60 percent is best for sun drying. Often these ideal conditions are not available when fruit ripens. Fruits dried in the sun are placed on trays made of screen or wooden dowels. Screens need to be safe for contact with food. The best screens are stainless steel, Teflon coated fiberglass or plastic. Avoid screens made from "hardware cloth." This is galvanized metal cloth that is coated with cadmium or zinc. These materials can oxidize, leaving harmful residues on the food. Also avoid copper and aluminum screening. Copper destroys vitamin C and increases oxidation. Aluminum tends to discolor and corrode.

Outdoor Drying Rack

Most woods are fine for making trays. However, do not use green wood, pine, cedar, oak or redwood. These woods warp, stain the food or cause off-flavors in the food. Place trays on blocks to allow for better air movement around the food. Because the ground may be moist, it is best to place the racks or screens on a concrete driveway or if possible over a sheet of aluminum or tin. The reflection of the sun on the metal increases the drying temperature. Cover the trays with cheesecloth to help protect the fruit from birds or insects. Fruits dried in the sun must be covered or brought under shelter at night. The cool night air condenses and could add moisture back to the food, thus slowing down the drying process.

Solar Drying

Recent efforts to improve on sun drying have led to solar drying. Solar drying also uses the sun as the heat source. A foil surface inside the dehydrator helps to increase the temperature. Ventilation speeds up the drying time. Shorter drying times reduce the risks of food spoilage or mold growth.

Homemade Solar Dryer

Pasteurization

Sun or solar dried fruits and vine dried beans need treatment to kill any insect and their eggs that might be on the food. Unless destroyed, the insects will eat the dried food. There are two recommended pasteurization methods:

1. **Freezer Method -** Seal the food in freezer-type plastic bags. Place the bags in a freezer set at 0°F or below and leave them at least 48 hours.

2. **Oven Method -** Place the food in a single layer on a tray or in a shallow pan. Place in an oven preheated to 160°F for 30 minutes. After either of these treatments the dried fruit is ready to be conditioned and stored.

Drying Foods Indoors

Most foods can be dried indoors using modern dehydrators, convection ovens or conventional ovens. Microwave ovens are recommended only for drying herbs, because there is no way to create airflow in them.

Food Dehydrators

A food dehydrator is a small electrical appliance for drying food indoors. A food dehydrator has an electric element for heat and a fan and vents for air circulation. Dehydrators are efficiently designed to dry foods quickly at 140°F. Food dehydrators are a relatively new item and are available from department stores, mail-order catalogs, natural food stores, seed catalogs and garden supply stores. Costs vary from $40 to $350 or above depending on features. Some models are expandable and additional trays can be purchased later. Twelve square feet of drying space dries about a half-bushel of produce.

Oven Drying

Everyone who has an oven has a dehydrator. By combining the factors of heat, low humidity and air flow, an oven can be used as a dehydrator. An oven is ideal for occasional drying of meat jerkies, fruit leathers, banana chips or for preserving excess produce like celery or mushrooms. Because the oven is needed for every day cooking, it may not be satisfactory for preserving abundant garden produce. Oven drying is slower than dehydrators because it does not have a built-in fan for the air movement. (However, some convection ovens do have a fan). It takes about two times longer to dry food in an oven than it does in a dehydrator. Thus, the oven is not as efficient as a dehydrator and uses more energy.

To Use Your Oven - First, check the dial and see if it can register as low as 140°F. If your oven does not go this low, then your food will cook instead of dry. Use a thermometer to check the temperature at the "warm" setting. For air circulation, leave the oven door propped open two to six inches. Circulation can be improved by placing a fan outside the oven near the door. CAUTION: This is not a safe practice for a home with small children. Because the door is left open, the temperature will vary. An oven thermometer placed near the food gives an accurate reading. Adjust the temperature dial to achieve the needed 140°F. Drying trays should be narrow enough to clear the sides of the oven and should be 3 to 4 inches shorter than the oven from front to back. Cake cooling racks placed on top of cookie sheets work well for some foods. The oven racks, holding the trays, should be two to three inches apart for air circulation.

DRYING FRUITS

Dried fruits are unique, tasty and nutritious. Begin by washing the fruit and coring it, if needed. For drying, fruits can be cut in half or sliced. Some can be left whole. See the table "Drying Fruits at Home" later in this publication for specific directions for preparing each fruit. Thin, uniform, peeled slices dry the fastest. The peel can be left on the fruit, but unpeeled fruit takes the longer to dry. Apples can be cored and sliced in rings, wedges, or chips. Bananas can be sliced in coins, chips or sticks.

Fruits dried whole take the longest to dry. Before drying, skins need to be "checked" or cracked to speed drying. To "check" the fruit place it in boiling water and then in cold water. Because fruits contain sugar and are sticky, spray the drying trays with nonstick cooking spray before placing the fruit on the trays. After the fruit dries for one to two hours, lift each piece gently with a spatula and turn.

Pretreating the Fruit

Pretreatments prevent fruits from darkening. Many light-colored fruits, such as apples, darken rapidly when cut and exposed to air. If not pretreated, these fruits will continue to darken after they have dried.

For long-term storage of dried fruit, sulfuring or using a sulfite dip are the best pretreatments. However, sulfites found in the food after either of these treatments have been found to cause asthmatic reactions in a small portion of the asthmatic population. Thus, some people may want to use the alternative shorter-term pretreatments. If home dried foods are eaten within a short time, there may be little difference in the long- and short-term pretreatments.

Sulfuring - Sulfuring is an old method of pretreating fruits. Sublimed sulfur is ignited and burned in an enclosed box with the fruit. The sulfur fumes penetrate the fruit and act as a pretreatment by retarding spoilage and darkening of the fruit. Fruits must be sulfured out-of-doors where there is adequate air circulation. (For more information contact your county Extension office.)

Sulfite Dip - Sulfite dips can achieve the same long-term anti-darkening effect as sulfuring, but more quickly and easily. Either sodium bisulfite, sodium sulfite or sodium meta-bisulfite that are USP (food grade) or Reagent grade (pure) can be used. To locate these, check with your local drugstores or hobby shops, where wine-making supplies are sold. Directions for Use - Dissolve 3/4 to 1 1/2 teaspoons sodium bisulfite per quart of water. (If using sodium sulfite, use 1 1/2 to 3 teaspoons. If using sodium metabisulfite, use 1 to 2 tablespoons.) Place the prepared fruit in the mixture and soak 5 minutes for slices, 15 minutes for halves. Remove fruit, rinse lightly under cold water and place on drying trays. Sulfited foods can be dried indoors or outdoors. (This solution can be used only once. Make a new one for the next batch.)

Ascorbic Acid - Ascorbic acid (vitamin C) mixed with water is a safe way to prevent fruit browning. However, its protection does not last as long as sulfuring or sulfiting. Ascorbic acid is available in the powdered or tablet form, from drugstores or grocery stores. One teaspoon of powdered ascorbic acid is equal to 3000 mg of ascorbic acid in tablet form. (If you buy 500 mg tablets, this would be six tablets). Directions for Use - Mix 1 teaspoon of powdered ascorbic acid (or

3000 mg of ascorbic acid tablets, crushed) in 2 cups water. Place the fruit in the solution for 3 to 5 minutes. Remove fruit, drain well and place on dryer trays. After this solution is used twice, add more acid.

Ascorbic Acid Mixtures - Ascorbic acid mixtures are a mixture of ascorbic acid and sugar sold for use on fresh fruits and in canning or freezing. It is more expensive and not as effective as using pure ascorbic acid.

Directions for Use - Mix 1 1/2 tablespoons of ascorbic acid mixture with one quart of water. Place the fruit in the mixture and soak 3 to 5 minutes. Drain the fruit well and place on dryer trays. After this solution is used twice, add more ascorbic acid mixture.

Fruit Juice Dip - A fruit juice that is high in vitamin C can also be used as a pretreatment, though it is not as effective as pure ascorbic acid. Juices high in vitamin C include orange, lemon, pineapple, grape and cranberry. Each juice adds its own color and flavor to the fruit.

Directions for Use - Place enough juice to cover fruit in a bowl. Add cut fruit. Soak 3 to 5 minutes, remove fruit, drain well and place on dryer trays. This solution may be used twice, before being replaced. (The used juice can be consumed.)

Honey Dip - Many store-bought dried fruits have been dipped in a honey solution. A similar dip can be made at home. Honey dipped fruit is much higher in calories.

Directions for Use - Mix 1/2 cup sugar with 1 1/2 cups boiling water. Cool to lukewarm and add 1/2 cup honey. Place fruit in dip and soak 3 to 5 minutes. Remove, drain well and place on dryer trays.

Syrup Blanching - Blanching fruit in syrup helps it retain color fairly well during drying and storage. The resulting product is similar to candied fruit. Fruits that can be syrup blanched include apples, apricots, figs, nectarines, peaches, pears, plums and prunes.

Directions for Use - Combine 1 cup sugar, 1 cup light corn syrup and 2 cups water in a saucepot. Bring to a boil. Add 1 pound of prepared fruit and simmer 10 minutes. Remove heat and let fruit stand in hot syrup for 30 minutes. Lift fruit out of syrup, rinse lightly in cold water, drain on paper toweling and place on dryer trays.

Steam Blanching - Steam blanching also helps retain color and slow oxidation. However, the flavor and texture of the fruit is changed.

Directions - Place several inches of water in a large saucepot with a tight fitting lid. Heat to boiling. Place fruit not more than 2 inches deep, in a steamer pan or wire basket over boiling water. Cover tightly with lid and begin timing immediately. See below for blanching times. Check for even blanching half way through the blanching time. Some fruit may need to be stirred. When done, remove excess moisture using paper towels and place on dryer trays.

Drying the Prepared Fruit

Whichever drying method you choose-sun drying, solar drying, oven drying or dehydrator drying-be sure to place the fruit in a single layer on the drying trays. The pieces should not touch or overlap. Follow the directions for the drying method you choose and dry until the food tests dry.

Approximate drying times are given below. Food dries much faster at the end of the drying period, so watch it closely.

Determining Dryness of Fruits

Since dried fruits are generally eaten without being rehydrated, they should not be dehydrated to the point of brittleness. Most fruits should have about 20 percent moisture content when dried. To test for dryness, cut several cooled pieces in half. There should be no visible moisture and you should not be able to squeeze any moisture from the fruit. Some fruits may remain pliable, but are not sticky or tacky. If a piece is folded in half, it should not stick to itself. Berries should be dried until they rattle when shaken.

After drying, cool fruit 30 to 60 minutes before packaging. Packaging food warm can lead to sweating and moisture buildup. However, excessive delays in packaging could allow moisture to re-enter food. Remember, if you have dried fruit in the sun, it must be pasteurized before it is packaged.

Conditioning Fruits

When dried fruit is taken from the dehydrator or oven, the remaining moisture may not be distributed equally among the pieces because of their size or their location in the dehydrator. Conditioning is a process used to equalize the moisture and reduce the risk of mold growth. To condition the fruit, take the dried fruit that has cooled and pack it loosely in plastic or glass jars. Seal the containers and let them stand for seven to ten days. The excess moisture in some pieces will be absorbed by the drier pieces. Shake the jars daily to separate the pieces and check the moisture condensation. If condensation develops in the jar, return the fruit to the dehydrator for more drying. After conditioning, package and store the fruit.

DRYING VEGETABLES

Vegetables can also be preserved by drying. Because they contain less acid than fruits, vegetables are dried until they are brittle. At this stage, only 10% moisture remains and no microorganism can grow.

Preparing Vegetables

To prepare vegetables for drying, wash in cool water to remove soil and chemical residues. Trim, peel, cut, slice or shred vegetables according to the directions for each vegetable in the chart below. Remove any fibrous or woody portions and core when necessary, removing all decayed and bruised areas. Keep pieces uniform in size so they will dry at the same rate. A food slicer or food processor can be used. Prepare only as many as can be dried at one time.

Pretreating Vegetables

Blanching is a necessary step in preparing vegetables for drying. By definition, blanching is the process of heating vegetables to a temperature high enough to destroy enzymes present in tissue. Blanching stops the enzyme action which could cause loss of color and flavor during drying and storage. It also shortens the drying and rehydration time by relaxing the tissue walls so moisture can escape and later re-enter more rapidly. Vegetables can be water blanched or steam blanched. Water blanching usually results in a greater loss of nutrients, but it takes less time than steam blanching.

Water Blanching - Fill a large pot 2/3 full of water, cover and bring to a rolling boil. Place the vegetables in a wire basket or a colander and submerge them in the water. Cover and blanch according to directions. Begin timing when water returns to boiling. If it takes longer than one minute for the water to come back to boiling, too many vegetables were added. Reduce the amount in the next batch.

Steam Blanching - Use a deep pot with a tight fitting lid and a wire basket, colander or sieve placed so the steam will circulate freely around the vegetables. Add water to the pot and bring to a rolling boil. Place the vegetables loosely in the basket no more than 2 inches deep. Place the basket of vegetables in the pot, making sure the water does not come in contact with the vegetables. Cover and steam according to the directions.

Cooling and Drying the Prepared Vegetables

After blanching, dip the vegetables briefly in cold water. When they feel only slightly hot to the touch, drain the vegetables by pouring them directly onto the drying tray held over the sink. Wipe the excess water from underneath the tray and arrange the vegetables in a single layer. Then place the tray immediately in the dehydrator or oven. The heat left in the vegetables from blanching will cause the drying process to begin more quickly. Watch the vegetables closely at the end of the drying period. They dry much more quickly at the end and could scorch.

Determining Dryness of Vegetables

Vegetables should be dried until they are brittle or "crisp." Some vegetables would actually shatter if hit with a hammer. At this stage, they should contain about 10 percent moisture. Because they are so dry, they do not need conditioning like fruits.

DRYING FRUIT LEATHER

Fruit leather is a tasty, chewy, dried fruit product. Fruit leathers are made by pouring puréed fruit onto a flat surface for drying. When dried, the fruit is pulled from the surface and rolled. It gets the name "leather" from the fact that when puréed fruit is dried, it is shiny and has the texture of leather.

Leather From Fresh Fruit

* Select ripe or slightly overripe fruit.

* Wash fresh fruit or berries in cool water. Remove peel, seeds and stem.

* Cut fruit into chunks. Use 2 cups of fruit for each 13" x 15" inch fruit leather. Purée fruit until smooth.

* Add 2 teaspoons of lemon juice or 1/8 teaspoon ascorbic acid (375 mg) for each 2 cups of light colored fruit to prevent darkening.

* Optional: To sweeten, add corn syrup, honey or sugar. Corn syrup or honey is best for longer storage because it prevents crystals. Sugar is fine for immediate use or short storage. Use 1⁄4 to 1⁄2 cup sugar, corn syrup or honey for each 2 cups of fruit. Saccharin-based sweeteners could also be used to reduce tartness without adding calories. Aspartame sweeteners may lose sweetness during drying.

Leathers From Canned or Frozen Fruits

* Home preserved or store bought canned or frozen fruit can be used.

* Drain fruit, save liquid.

* Use 1 pint of fruit for each 13" x 15" leather.

* Purée fruit until smooth. If thick, add liquid.

* Add 2 teaspoons of lemon juice or 1/8 teaspoon ascorbic acid (375 mg) for each 2 cups of light colored fruit to prevent darkening.

* If desired, sweeten as directed above for leathers from fresh fruit.

* Applesauce can be dried alone or added to any fresh fruit purée as an extender. It decreases tartness and makes leather smoother and more pliable.

Drying the Leather

For drying in the oven or sun, line cookie sheets with plastic wrap. In a dehydrator, use plastic wrap or the specially designed plastic sheets that come with the dehydrator. Pour the leather onto the lined cookie sheets or tray. Spread it evenly to a thickness of 1/8 inch. Dry the fruit leather at 140° F until no indentation is left when you touch the center with your finger. This could take about 6 to 8 hours in the dehydrator, up to 18 hours in the oven and 1 to 2 days in the sun. While still warm, peel from the plastic wrap. Cool and rewrap in plastic and store.

PACKING AND STORING DRIED FOODS

After foods are dried, cool them completely. Then package them in clean moisture-vapor-resistant containers. Glass jars, metal cans or freezer containers are good storage containers, if they have tight-fitting lids. Plastic freezer bags are acceptable, but they are not insect and rodent proof. Fruit that has been sulfured or sulfited should not touch metal. Place the fruit in a plastic bag before storing it in a metal can. Dried food should be stored in a cool, dry, dark place. Most dried fruits can be stored for 1 year at 60° F, 6 months at 80° F. Dried vegetables have about half the shelf-life of fruits. Fruit leathers should keep for up to 1 month at room temperature. To store any dried product longer, place it in the freezer.

USING DRIED FOODS

Dried fruits can be eaten as is or reconstituted. Dried vegetables must be reconstituted. Once reconstituted, dried fruits or vegetables are treated as fresh. Fruit leathers and meat jerky are eaten as is. To reconstitute dried fruits or vegetables, add water to the fruit or vegetable and soak until the desired volume is restored. (See the chart on rehydrating dried food, for the amount of water to add and minimum soaking time.) Do not over-soak the food. Over-soaking produces loss of flavor and a mushy, water-logged texture. For soups and stews, add the dehydrated vegetables, without rehydrating them. They will rehydrate as the soup or stew cooks. Also, leafy vegetables and tomatoes do not need soaking. Add enough water to cover and simmer until tender. CAUTION! If soaking takes more than 2 hours, refrigerate the product for the remainder of the time.

Rehydrating Dried Foods

Product	Water to Add to 1 Cup Dried Food (Cups)	Minimum Soaking Time (Hours)
Fruits*		
Apples	1 1/2	1/2
Pears	1 3/4	1 1/4
Peaches	2	1 1/4
Vegetables**		
Asparagus	2 1/4	1 1/2
Beans, lima	2 1/2	1 1/2
Beans, green snap	2 1/2	1
Beets	2 3/4	1 1/2
Carrots	2 1/4	1
Cabbage	3	1
Corn	2 1/4	1/2
Okra	3	1/2
Onions	2	3/4
Peas	2 1/2	1/2
Pumpkin	3	1
Squash	1 3/4	1
Squash	1 3/4	1
Spinach	1	1/2
Sweet Potatoes	1 1/2	1/2
Turnip Greens and other greens	1	3/4

* *Fruits – Water is at room temperature.*

** *Vegetables – Boiling water used.*

INCREASE SHORT-LIFE SUPPLY WITH VACUUM SEAL JARS

As you work to build your short-life food storage, you should begin to consider techniques to help extend the shelf life of your food. The longer it will last, the more you can store. In addition to freezing, dehydrating, canning, smoking, pickling, and storing in a dark, cool place, simply removing the oxygen from food will make it last much longer. *foodsaver.com*

Many are familiar with vacuum bag sealers that allow you to suck the air out and seal it shut. Freezing food this way can extend its life up to five times. It also dramatically reduces or eliminates freezer burn. Many aren't aware of what else their sealers can do though. Many models come with a utility port where you can connect attachments, such as a jar sealer. An inexpensive but powerful addition to your preservation toolkit, vacuum sealing jars should become part of your cooking and food storage routine.

Are you tired of raisins going stale and brown sugar going hard? Suck the air out! Vacuum sealing is not a substitute for canning, but it is an effective way to prolong the life of food. Jellies, mustard, spices, nuts, rice, flour, and dried fruits and vegetables are just a few examples of what you can store, prolonging shelf life years and years. The jar sealer fits on your own Ball® and Kerr® Mason jars and comes in wide and regular mouth sizes.

First, wash your jars, lids, and rings in hot, soapy water. The wide-mouth jars are preferred for this type of storage as they are much easier to get things in and out of and easier to clean. Next, fill the jars. Use a glove so that you don't leave the moisture and oils from your hands on the food. Leave one inch of space between the food and the top of the jar.

Connect the utility hose to the vacuum sealer and then engage the lock. Now place a lid on top of the jar. Do not attempt to seal with the ring. You can use it later to prevent the lid from getting knocked, but it is not necessary with jar sealing.

Then, connect the other end of the hose to the jar attachment and press the attachment down firmly over the top of the jar. Your vacuum sealer should have a special button for sealing canisters. Once the vacuum stops, pull the hose out of the attachment to release the pressure. You can then remove the attachment from the jar by pulling directly upward. Don't forget to disengage the lock on the sealer once you are finished. Once you are done, you will have jars of food ready for the shelves. Open the sealed jars by placing a teaspoon between the edge of the lid and the highest part of the threads on the bottle opening and prying down.

Store a jar of each item in the kitchen pantry and the rest goes in the store room. Remember, this is food that you are eating regularly and rotating. You are only sealing it to prolong its shelf-life. Keep your sealer on your counter. Use it every day. There is no danger or harm in resealing your jars again and again.

KEEP YOUR FOOD STORED PROPERLY

Freeze dried food is commonly found in emergency food storages. What could be done to make it last longer?

Freeze dried food is the one that lost 98 percent of water. This food does not have any bacteria or insects on it. That is why this food has a very long shelf life. But freeze dried food still have one enemy left. And this enemy is oxygen. If your freeze dried food does not contact with oxygen, it could last for more than 30 years. This means that even in 25-30 years these food products will taste the same way and have the same nutritional value. Even beyond this period of time these food products will be safe to eat, but they might taste or look differently.

Oxygen absorbers are the common way to extend the shelf life of your freeze dried foods. They are materials that actively react with oxygen. They combine with oxygen and therefore remove it from the environment. Iron powder and iron carbonate are usually used in oxygen absorbers. They are very effective. Oxygen absorbers react with oxygen until they are fully oxidized. This means they cannot react with oxygen any more. That is why you need to make sure your oxygen absorbers are properly sealed before you used them. If you want to use oxygen absorbers for your freeze dried food, just put them in the container of food before it is sealed. This way oxygen absorber will absorb all the oxygen that gets into the container over the period of storage. And no oxygen will be left to react with the food.

There are two major types of oxygen absorbers on the market. One of them requires moisture to work. It is usually used for storing bread and meats which contain some moisture. And another type of absorber contains their own moisture and therefore could be used for storing dried foods. You need to understand that any vacuum container will let some air inside over the years. Even if it is a top quality container. That is why oxygen absorbers are needed. They are able to absorb oxygen that is present in the air initially during the packing process. And afterwards they will also be able to absorb oxygen from the air that leaks in over time. Oxygen absorbers will allow to greatly extend the shelf life of your dried foods. And this means you will be able to save some money on your food storage program. Nitrogen packing is another common way of fighting oxygen in foods. Here the container is packed in a nitrogen environment or is flushed with nitrogen. This means that containers are filled with nitrogen, but not air. And this in turn means they have no oxygen inside initially.

MASTER FOOD LIST

6 GRAIÑ PANCAKE MIX
6 WAY ROLLED GRAIN, 6 TYPES
OF GRAIN
9 GRAIN CRACKED CEREAL
ALFALFA FOR SPROUTING
ALFALFA, POWDER
ALFALFA, CUT
ALMONDS, RAW
ALLSPICE (JAMAICAN) POWDER
ALLSPICE (JAMAICAN) WHOLE
AMARANTH, ORGANIC
ANISE (STAR), WHOLE
ANISE SEED, WHOLE
APPLE FLAKES, PEACH
FLAVOR,DEHYDRATED
APPLE FLAKES, STRAWBERRY FLAVOR
APPLE SLICES,
APPLESAUCE, DEHYDRATED
ARROWROOT POWDER
BAKING POWDER,
BAKING SODA,
BANANA SLICES, DEHYDRATED,
BARBECUE SPICE BLEND GROUND
BARLEY FLAKES
BARLEY FOR SPROUTING
BARLEY, HULLED,
BARLEY, HULLESS WAXY
BARLEY, PEARL
BASIL (EGYPTIAN) - CUT
BASIL (SWEET CALIFORNIA), CUT
BAY LEAVES, CUT
BAY LEAVES, WHOLE
BEANS, BLACK, BULK, FREEZE DRIED
BEANS, 10-BEAN MIX,
ANASAZI BEANS
BEANS, AUZZUKIE
BEANS, BABY LIMAS,
BEANS, BLACK EYED,
BEANS, BLACK TURTLE,

BEANS, GARBANZO,
BEANS, GREAT NORTHERN WHITE,
BEANS, GREEN, DEHYDRATED,
BEANS, KIDNEY,
BEANS, LARGE LIMA,
BEANS, MUNG,
BEANS, NAVY, BULK, DEHYDRATED,
BEANS, PINK,
BEANS, PINTO,
REFRIED BEANS
REFRIED BEANS W/CORN OIL
BEANS, SMALL RED
BEANS, SMALL WHITE, NAVY
BEANS, SOY,
BEANS, SPROUTING, AUZZUKIE,
BEANS, SPROUTING, GARBANZO,
BEANS, SPROUTING, MUNG,
BEANS, SPROUTING, SOY,
BEE POLLEN
BOUILLON, BEEF
BOUILLON, CHICKEN
BROCCOLI, DEHYDRATED
BUCK WHEAT, HULLED,
BURDOCK ROOT CUT
BUTTER POWDER,
BUTTERMILK POWDER
CABBAGE
CABBAGE SEED,
CAJUN SPICE BLEND, GROUND
CAKE MIX, GINGERBREAD (ADD WATER)
CAKE MIX, BROWNIE (ADD WATER)
CAKE MIX, CARROT (ADD WATER)
CAKE MIX, DEVIL'S FOOD
CAKE MIX, LEMON
CAKE MIX, POUND CAKE (ADD WATER)
CAKE MIX, SPICE
CAKE MIX, SWISS CHOC (ADD WATER)
CAKE MIX, WHITE
CAKE MIX, YELLOW

CAKE, FUNNEL (ADD WATER)
CARAWAY SEED
CARDAMOM (DECORTICATED) WHOLE
CARDAMOM (WHOLE GREEN PODS)
CARDAMOM (GROUND)
CAROB (ROASTED), POWDERED
CARROT DICES, DEHYDRATED,
CAYENNE (40 HEAT UNIT) DOMESTIC
CAYENNE (60 HEAT UNIT) IMPORTED
CAYENNE (90 HEAT UNIT)
CELERY
CELERY SEED - GROUND
CELERY SEED - WHOLE
CHAMOMILE TEA BAGS
CHEESE SAUCE, DEHYDRATED, BULK
CHEESE, CHEDDAR, DEHYDRATED, BAG
CHIA SEEDS (FOR SPROUTING)
CHICKWEED
CHILI BLEND, GROUND
CHILI PEPPERS, GROUND
CHILI, CRUSHED
CHINESE FIVE SPICE,
CHIVES, CUT
CHOCOLATE CHIPS, MILK CHOCOLATE
CHOCOLATE CHIPS, SEMI SWEET
CILANTRO CUT
CINNAMON CHIPS, SMALL CUT
CINNAMON POWDER
CINNAMON STICKS, 1 INCH,
CLOVES (SMALL VERY FRAGRANT)
CLOVES POWDER
COCOA MIX
COCOA MIX CHOCOLATE MINT TRUFFLE
COCOA MIX MINT
COCOA MIX, ORANGE CREME
COCOA FOR COOKING,
COCONUT (UNSWEETENED) - MEDIUM
CORIANDER SEED, GROUND
CORIANDER SEED, WHOLE
CORN MEAL, BAG
CORN, SWEET, DEHYDRATED
CORN, WHOLE YELLOW, PAPER BAG
CORN, YELLOW GRIT-HOMINY POLENTA

CORNSTARCH
CORN SYRUP SOLIDS
CREAM OF TARTAR
CUMIN SEED, GROUND
CUMIN SEED, WHOLE
CURRY POWDER, HOT BLEND
CURRY POWDER, REGULAR BLEND
DILL SEED, WHOLE
DILL WEED, (DOMESTIC) CUT
DOUGH ENHANCER, NATURAL
DRESSING, 1000 ISLAND
DRESSING, BLEU CHEESE,
DRESSING, OUR HOUSE DRESSING
DRINK BASE, APPLE CIDER, INSTANT,
DRINK MIX, APPLE, DEHYDRATED,
DRINK MIX, CHERRY,
DRINK MIX, FRUIT PUNCH
DRINK MIX, GRAPE,
DRINK MIX, HOT CIDER,
DRINK MIX, LEMONADE,
DRINK MIX, ORANGE,
DRINK MIX, PEACH
DRINK MIX, PINK LEMONADE,
DRINK MIX, STRAWBERRY,
DRINK MIX. TOFU
DRINK, APPLE, W/FRUIT JUICE
DRINK, PEACH, DEHYDRATED, BG
EGG MIX, DEHYDRATED,
EGG WHITES, DEHYDRATED,
EGGS, WHOLE
FAJITA SEASONING,
FENNEL SEED, POWDER
FENNEL SEED, WHOLE
FENUGREEK SEED, WHOLE
FLAVOR CRYSTALS, MAPLE, NATURAL &
ART
FLAVOR CRYSTALS, VANILLA, NATURAL
& AR
FLAVOR CRYSTALS, WALNUT, NATURAL
& AR
FLAX SEED,
FLOUR, ALL PURPOSE,
FLOUR, BAKERS BLEND HIGH PROTEIN

FLOUR, WHOLE WHEAT	KELP POWDER
FLOUR, WHOLE WHEAT RED	KAMUT
FLOUR, UNBLEACHED,	LECITHIN GRANULES
FLOUR, UNBLEACHED, HARD WHITE	LEMON GRANULES
FLOUR, UNBLEACHED-RED	LEMON JUICE POWDER (INSTANT)
FLOUR, UNBLEACHED-WHITE	LEMON PEEL CUT
FRANKINCENSE	LEMON PEPPER BLEND, GROUND
FROSTING MIX, CHOCOLATE	LENTILS, 100 LB BAG
FROSTING MIX, FUDGE	LICORICE MINT BLEND (TEA) NO
FRUCTOSE,	CAFFEINE
FRUIT BLEND (TASTY TEA) NO CAFFEINE	LICORICE ROOT POWDER
FRUIT BLEND TEA BAG	LICORICE SPICE BLEND (TEA) CAFFEINE
FRUIT GALAXY, DEHYDRATED BAG	FREE
FRUIT WHIRLS	LICORICE STICKS
GARLIC (DOMESTIC),	MACE, GROUND
GARLIC GRANULES (CALIFORNIA)	MACARONI & CHEESE
GARLIC POWDER (DOMESTIC)	MAPLE LEAF
GARLIC MINCED	MARGARINE POWDER,
G EL CAPS -00-	MARJORAM, CUT
GELATIN, CHERRY,	MEAT TENDERIZER, SEASONED,
GELATIN, LEMON,	MEAT TENDERIZER, UNSEASONED,
GELATIN, LIME,	MICROWAVE POPCORN CINCH BUTTER
GELATIN, ORANGE,	MILK, INSTANT, NON FAT DRY,
GELATIN, PEACH,	MILK, REGULAR, NON FAT DRY,
GELATIN, RASPBERRY,	MILLET,
GELATIN, STRAWBERRY,	MILLET, HULLED,
GERMADE,	MIX, BELGIAN WAFFLE
GINGER ROOT PIECES, 1/4 IN PIECES	MIX, BLUEBERRY MUFFIN
GINGER ROOT POWDER	MIX, BROWNIE
GINSENG POWDER	MIX, BUTTERMILK BISCUIT
GOTU KOLA POWDER	MIX, CHEASECAKE
GRANOLA, 25 LB BAG	MIX, CHOCOLATE CHIP COOKIE
GRAVY MIX, BROWN,	MIX, COOKIE, CHOCOLATE CHIP
GRAVY MIX, CHICKEN,	MIX, FUDGE BROWNIE
GRAVY MIX, TURKEY,	MIX, HONEYWHEAT BREAD & ROLL
GRAVY, COUNTRY STYLE,	MIX,SCONES
GREEK SEASONING, GROUND	MIX, WHITE FROSTING,
HERB MIX (SALT SUBSTITUTE)	MOLASSES, HOME MADE,
HONEY, CLOVER	MRE, COMPLETE MEAL,
HONEY, CREAMY WHIPPED	MRE, APPLESAUCE
HONEY, COX'S (CREAMED)	MRE, BEEF FRANKFURTERS
ITALIAN SEASONING, CUT	MRE, BEEF RAVIOLI
ITALIAN SEASONING, GROUND	MRE, BEEF STEAK (CHUNKED & FORMED)

MRE, BEEF TERIYAKI
MRE, CHEESE SPREAD
MRE, CHEESE TORTELLINI
MRE, CHERRY BEVERAGE POWDER
MRE, SOLID CHICKEN BREAST PATTIES
MRE, CHICKEN NOODLE
MRE, CHICKEN SALSA
MRE, CHILI MACARONI
MRE, CHOCOLATE COVERED COOKIES
MRE, COCOA
MRE, CRACKERS
MRE, HAM SLICES
MRE, LEMON POUND CAKE
MRE, MEAT LOAF W/BROWN ONION
GRAVY
MRE, MEXICAN RICE
MRE, OATMEAL COOKIE BAR
MRE, PASTA VEGETABLE
MRE, PASTA & VEGETABLE ALFREDO
SAUCE
MRE, PEANUT BUTTER
MRE, PORK W/RICE
MRE, PORK CHOW MEIN
MRE, ESCALLOPED POTATO W/HAM
MRE, POTATO STICKS
MRE, SPAGHETTI
MRE, GRILLED TURKEY BREAST &
POTATOES
MRE, TURKEY BREAST & POTATOES
MRE, WESTERN BEANS
MRE, WHITE RICE
MUFFIN, BLUEBERRY
MUFFIN, CORN,
MUNG BEANS (FOR SPROUTING)
MUSHROOM SLICES, DEHYDRATED,
MUSTARD SEED (BROWN) WHOLE
MUSTARD SEED (YELLOW) POWDER
MUSTARD SEED (YELLOW) WHOLE
MYRRH GUM PCS
NOODLES, EGG
NUTMEG, GROUND
NUTMEG, WHOLE
OAT BRAN,

OAT GROATS,
OATS
OIL, 100% CANOLA FRYING OIL,
ONION, CHOPPED
ONION, GRANULES
ONION, POWDER, DOMESTIC
ORANGE PEEL GRANULES
ORANGE SPICE
OREGANO (GREEK), CUT
OREGANO (MEXICAN), CUT
OREGANO (MEXICAN), GROUND
OREGANO (MEXICAN), WHOLE,
PAN D'ARCO (CUT)
PANCAKE MIX, 6 GRAIN
PANCAKE MIX, BLUEBERRY
PANCAKE MIX, BUTTERMILK,
PANCAKE OLD FASHIONED,
PAPRIKA GROUND
PARSLEY FLAKES (CALIFORNIA)
PARSLEY HERB POWDER
PASTA, EGG NOODLES,
PASTA, LASAGNA, WIDE CUT,
PASTA, MACARONI, JUMBO SHELL,
PASTA, MACARONI, LARGE SHELL,
PASTA, MACARONI, ELBOW,
PASTA, MACARONI, SALAD,
PASTA, MACARONI, SMALL ELBOW
PASTA, MACARONI, SMALL SHELL,
PASTA, MACARONI, WHOLE WHEAT
PASTA-PIZZA SAUCE MIX
PASTA, SPAGHETTI,
PEACH SLICES
PEACH FLAVOR APPLE SLICES
PEANUT BUTTER POWDER,
DEHYDRATED
PEAS, ALASKAN
PEAS, BLACK EYED,
PEAS, SPLIT GREEN,
PEAS, SPLIT YELLOW,
PEAS, SWEET GARDEN, DEHYDRATED
PEAS, WHOLE GREEN,
PEPPER (BLACK) 1/4 CRACKED
PEPPER (BLACK) TABLE GRIND

PEPPER (WHITE), FINE GROUND
PEPPERCORNS (BLACK), WHOLE
PEPPERMINT, DOMESTIC
PEPPERMINT TEA BAGS
PEPPERS (GREEN BELL)
PICKLING SPICE BLEND, WHOLE
POPCORN, RABBIT EARS,
POPPY SEED
POPPY SEED, (BLUE), WHOLE
POTATO DICES, DEHYDRATED
POTATO FLAKES, DEHYDRATED,
POTATO GRANULES,
POTATO SLICES, DEHYDRATED,
POTATO, HASHBROWNS, DEHYDRATED,
POULTRY SEASONING, GROUND
PSYLLIUM HUSKS
PUDDING, BANANA, ADD MILK/INST
PUDDING, BUTTERSCOTCH, MILK/INS *
PUDDING, CUSTARD
PUDDING, CHOCOLATE, MILK/COOK *
PUDDING, CHOCOLATE, MILK/INST *
PUDDING, COCONUT, MILK/INST *
PUDDING, LEMON, MILK/INST *
PUDDING, TAPIOCA
PUDDING, VANILLA, ADD MILK/INST *
PUDDING, VANILLA, MILK/COOK
PUMPKIN PIE SPICE,
PUMPKIN SEEDS, SHELLED
QUINOA,
RADISH SEED,
RADISH SEED, (FOR SPROUTING)
RAISINS, SELECT
RAISINS, GOLDEN
RASPBERRY LEAF
RED CLOVER SEEDS (FOR SPROUTING)
RICE, BASMATI BROWN-ORGANIC
RICE, BROWN, LONG GRAIN
RICE, PAR BOILED
RICE, WHITE, LONG GRAIN
ROSE HIP POWDER
ROSEMARY, CUT
ROSEMARY, GROUND
ROSEMARY, WHOLE

RYE FLAKES, PAPER BAG
RYE, PAPER BAG
SAGE, FINE POWDER
SAGE, RUBBED
SAGE, WHOLE
SALAD SUPREME SEASONING
SALT
SAUCE, AU JUS INSTANT
SAUSAGE SEASONING,
SESAME SEED (NATURAL) WHOLE
SHEPHERDS PURSE
SHORTENING POWDER, DEHYDRATED
SLIPPERY ELM POWDER
SOUP BASE, BEEF FLAVOR
SOUP BASE, CHICKEN FLAVOR,
SOUP BASE, CREAM, NON DAIRY
SOUP MIX, ABC,
SOUP MIX, BEEF BARLEY
SOUP MIX, OLD FASHIONED,
SOUP, AU-JUS SAUCE
SOUP, BEEF, BARLEY, VEGETABLE
SOUP, BEEF NOODLE
SOUP, BEEF FLOVORED STEW
SOUP, CHICKEN NOODLE, (GREAT
FLAVOR)
SOUP, CORN CHOWDER BASE, MAKES
SOUP, CREAM OF CHICKEN, MAKES
SOUP, CREAM OF MUSHROOM, MAKES
SOUP, CREAM PEA CHOWDER, MAKES
SOUP, CREAMY CHEDDAR CHWD,
SOUP, CREAMY POTATO
SOUP, FRENCH ONION SOUP,
SOUP, ITALIAN TOMATO/VEG,
SOUP, MINESTRONE,
SOUP, MOUNTAIN STEW BLEND
SOUP, NE CHOWDER BASE,
SOUP, OLD FASHIONED SOUP MIX
SOUP, ORIGINAL CREAM SOUP BASE
SOUP, VEGETABLE BEEF #
SOUR CREAM POWDER
SOUTHERN BUTTERMILK BISCUIT MIX
SOUTHERN CORNBREAD II (YELLOW)
SOY SAUCE,

SPEARMINT SPICE BLEND (TEA) NO
CAFFEIN
SPELT, (ORGANIC)
SPINACH FLAKES
SUGAR, BROWN,
SUGAR, POWDERED,
SUGAR, WHITE
SUNFLOWER SEED, RAW,
SWEET POTATO
SYRUP, APRICOT,
SYRUP, BLUEBERRY,
SYRUP, BOYSENBERRY,
SYRUP, NATURAL BUTTER FLAVOR,
SYRUP, STRAWBERRY,
SYRUP, LIGHT CORN,
T.V.P. BACON FLAVORED,
T.V.P. BEEF FLAVORED, DEHYDRATED
T.V.P. CHICKEN FLAVORED,
T.V.P. IMAGIC BARBECUE MIX
T.V.P. IMAGIC BBQ FLAVOR,
T.V.P. IMAGIC SLOPPY JOE MIX
T.V.P. IMITATION HAM FLAVOR
CHIPLETS
T.V.P. PEPPERONI, IMITATION FLAVOR
T.V.P. SAUSAGE FLAVOR
T.V.P. TACO BEEF FLAVOR
T.V.P. ULTRA-SOY, MINCED, NATURAL
FLAVOR

TACO SEASONING, GROUND
TAPIOCA PEARLS (MEDIUM) WHOLE
TARRAGON (CALIFORNIA), CUT
TEA STRAINER(S)
THYME, GROUND
THYME LEAVES
TOMATO POWDER, DEHYDRATED,
TUMERIC POWDER
VALERIAN ROOT CUT
VALERIAN ROOT POWDER
VANILLA EXTRACT
VEGETABLE FLAKES, MIXED
VEGETABLE SOUP BLEND
VEGETABLE STEW BLEND
WHEAT BRAN, PAPER BAG
WHEAT FLAKES, WHITE,
WHEAT GERM
WHEAT, CRACKED,
WHEAT, GOLDEN 86,
WHEAT, HARD RED STORAGE,
WHEAT, HARD WHITE,
WHEAT, SOFT WHEAT,
WHEAT, VITAL GLUTEN,
WHEAT, WHITE, GOLDEN
WHEY,
WHITE CREAM SAUCE
WHITE PEPPER, WHOLE
YEAST, INSTANT

XVII Gardening

SEED LIST

Eventually you will need to start raising your own food. To do this, you will need seeds, but not the kind of seeds you buy at the store. Why? Because those are hybrid seeds, and most hybrid seeds have no capacity to reproduce. Hybrid seeds are a cruel trick played out on humanity. Seeds are God's gift to mankind, and for corporations and marketing people to purposely create seeds that can't produce offspring seems criminal. Yet this is exactly what goes on every day, all over the world. It's all about protecting patents and "profits."

Well, those profits might get you killed if you're dumb enough to go along with the mainstream and buy hybrid seeds. You need non-hybrid seeds. These are genetically-pure seeds, grown for hundreds or thousands of years, that consistently produce viable offspring. One of the few places to get a complete garden-package of non-hybrid seeds at an affordable price: the Ark Institute. Buy their non-hybrid seed package and store it away as if it were gold. If civilization breaks down, these seeds may be the key to your survival and prosperity. While everyone else is scratching their heads wondering why their green beans won't sprout, you'll be reaping a huge harvest of self-proliferating, nonhybrid fruits and vegetables.

When you buy the non-hybrid seed package from the **Ark Institute**, you'll receive these seeds:

- Asparagus
- Green Bush Beans
- Yellow Bush Beans
- Red Kidney Beans
- White Navy Beans
- Pinto Beans
- Sweet Green Peas
- Snow Peas
- Red Beets
- White Sweet Corn
- Yellow Sweet Corn
- Spring Broccoli
- Fall Broccoli
- Red Cabbage for Salads
- Cabbage for coleslaw/kraut
- Early Carrots
- Mid-Season/Late Carrots
- Salad Cucumbers
- Pickling Cucumbers
- Eggplants
- Butterhead Lettuce
- Red Lettuce
- Mildew-resistant Cantaloupe
- Summer Oak Leaf Lettuce
- Basil
- Spanish Onions
- Red Onions
- Yellow Onions
- Scallions
- Green/Red Sweet Pepper
- Long Yellow Sweet Peppers
- Cayenne Hot Pepper
- Pie Pumpkins
- Giant Radish
- Spinach
- Canning/Catsup Tomato
- Yellow Summer Squash
- Zucchini Summer Squash
- Butternut Squash
- Acorn Winter Squash

- Solid Salad/Canning Tomato
- Italian Plum Tomato
- Large Salad Tomato
- Heirloom Slicing Tomato
- Flour/Meal Corn

- Wheat
- Drought-resistant Cantaloupe
- Romaine Lettuce
- Parsley

During World War II, every family was encouraged to plant a victory garden to provide fresh fruits and vegetables at home so that fuel and other commercially grown food resources could be directed elsewhere. It is time to re-visit that tradition. Below are five tips for planting your own survival garden. Whether the food shortage reaches crises level, or not, growing your own produce is a fun pastime that produces nutritious and money-saving food. You can then save the money you did not have to spend on fresh produce to use in case of a true recession.

1. When growing your own food, cover the basics. There is a reason that the Aztecs grew beans and corn. Together, those two plants provide all of the essential amino acids not produced by the human body that are necessary for healthy growth and protein production. When planning your garden, choose a variety of plants that provide different nutrients. Think about the rainbow-and try to grow a plant in every color. That is a simple way to ensure that you grow plants that provide a variety of vitamins and minerals.

2. Start slowly. As with an exercise plan, if you take on too much in the beginning, you will get discouraged and quit. A garden that is no bigger than 4 feet X 12 feet will allow you to start strong and produce a lot of food, but will not be too large to handle

3. Use natural fertilizers for the best results. When growing your own produce, you will want to harvest the most nutritious food possible. Natural and seaweed based fertilizers contain a variety of micronutrients not found in synthetically produced fertilizers.

4. Learn how to can, dry and preserve your extra food. Not only will you have the luxury of eating your own tasty tomatoes in the middle of winter, should disaster strike, you will be well-prepared.

5. Invest in your soil. The number one most important aspect of growing your own food is having healthy soil. Using natural fertilizers helps maintain soil fertility because the natural fertilizer components will not harm soil organisms. Regularly adding thoroughly composted organic matter will help your soil maintain its fertility. Managing your own compost bin will also help you save money because you will have a way to re-use, rather than toss, food scraps.

The "Three Sisters Garden" Originally developed by the native people of North America, this garden may indeed be *"The Original Survival Garden"* because it was the main means of sustenance for the majority of native North American People. A Three Sisters Garden is a fairly simple proposition to plant. Basically the three sisters garden is laid out as follows,

- Build a round bed slightly hilled about 4-8 feet in diameter
- For the first year make sure to add some high nitrogen fertilizer for the corn
- Plant 6-8 corn plants in a circle about 6-8 inches apart
- Give the corn plants about 2-3 weeks to begin growing

- Now plant 12-14 pole bean plants about 6 inches outside of your corn plants
- Now after the beans get started plant about 6-7 squash plants about 12-15 inches outside of your beans.
- As the plants grow encourage the pole beans to climb up the corn stalks and the squash vines to cover the ground between your corn and beans

The result is a highly productive symbiotic garden. The beans produce nitrogen for the corn and the corn allows the beans a natural trellis and the squash shades the ground and conserves water.

The best soil test you can run is to go to your garden spot and turn over a spadeful of dirt. If the shovel won't go in because there's a web of tree roots, relocating is a good idea. If it's just rocky, that's not so bad. Rocks actually contribute fertility to soil. It's the finer stuff we really want to study. If your soil is really good it will be black and loose, kind of like devil's food cake with worms in it. High in organic matter, full of living things, based on sand and clay or the remains of some ancient dust storm. You might even have rich soil based on volcanic ash--some of the best agricultural land is just that, a disaster ameliorated by time and persistent living things. Flood plains are the most popular places traditionally, refertilized and rebuilt layer by layer during the inevitable Spring catastrophes.

Chances are very good that you won't have soil like that. In modern housing developments the top layer of soil is often scraped away before houses are built. Many locations were forest land until just recently, and forest soils are often thin to begin with and virtually disappear down to the subsoil when the trees go away. Probably you'll have land that's partly subsoil and partly fill dirt, and if you plant corn in it without any help you'll get corn that is about a foot high. Most soil will need immediate assistance if you expect a garden from it.

The solution is pretty much the same no matter if it's clay or sand or something else: add organic material. As it decays, dead matter like tree leaves or grass and weeds that are plowed under becomes food for worms, who distribute fertilizer pellets on the surface and open up deep airways. Encourage life, and the soil gets better year by year.

GROWING AND USING SPROUTS

Sprouts are great to eat for everyday living and especially so in an emergency situation. Typical foods set aside for storage are traditionally low or nonexistent in vitamin C and many of the B vitamins. Yet it is exciting to know the seeds from those same storage foods can be sprouted to give a rich source of these important nutrients. Sprouts are an excellent source of vitamin C and also contain many good B vitamins. And you probably won't find a less expensive way to get these vitamins than from low calorie sprouts. Green leafy sprouts are also a good source of vitamin A. Sprouts are a good source of fiber, protein, and contain enzymes that aid digestion. In addition, sprouting destroys the seed's natural preservative enzymes that inhibit digestion.

Different kinds of seeds you can sprout: (This list gives the popularly sprouted seeds and is not all inclusive as you can sprout almost any kind of seed.)

Generally eaten raw:

Alfalfa, radish, mung bean, sunflower, clover, cabbage.

Generally cooked:

Kidney, Pinto and other miscellaneous beans.

Eaten raw or cooked:

Lentils, Soy beans, green peas and wheat. (In addition, all the sprouts that are generally eaten raw can be easily cooked.) Alfalfa: Alfalfa, one of the most popular sprouts, is a good source of vitamins A, B, C, D, E, F, and K and is rich in many minerals, as well as many enzymes needed for digestion.

Radish sprouts are high in vitamin C and potassium and have a rich flavor.

Wheat is high in Vitamins B, C, and E and has three times the vitamin E of dry wheat. Wheat also has many minerals.

Mung Beans: These should be sprouted under pressure to produce long and juicy sprouts. Mung bean sprouts are an excellent source of protein, vitamin C, A and E, along with many minerals.

Green Pea sprouts are rich in many of the B vitamins and vitamin C. Green pea sprouts make a rich addition to any green salad.

Soybeans: An extremely rich source of protein and vitamins A, B, C and E. Soybeans are rich in minerals and lecithin. They can be sprouted under pressure like mung beans.

Kidney beans, pinto beans and miscellaneous beans: They are a good source of vitamin C, many of the B vitamins and many minerals. Sprouting these beans also changes their indigestible carbohydrates to digestible carbohydrates, greatly reducing the intestinal gas they otherwise cause.

Lentils: Rich in protein, vitamin C and the B vitamins. They have a mild ground pepper flavor.

Buckwheat: Makes a great salad green. High in vitamins A, B, C and D.

Sunflower: Rich in vitamins B, D, and E, many minerals, and Linoleic Acid, the W6 EFA.

Do Not eat tomato, peppers or potato sprouts as they are poisonous.

Growing Sprouts:

Sprouts are easy to produce and require no special equipment or knowledge. All that is required to produce sprouts is seeds, moisture, warmth, darkness and maybe 10 minutes of your time every day. Methods vary from high tech production to something as simple as quart jar or a cloth covered pan. Perhaps the simplest method is to take your seeds, place them in a quart jar, and cover them with water to start the process.

Seed amounts to use per quart jar:

1/2 Cup Seeds: Wheat, All Beans, Rye, Oats, Rice, Sunflower, Lentil, Hulled Buckwheat, and Garbanzo Beans. **2 Tablespoons:** Alfalfa, radish, clover, cabbage.

Be aware that seeds soak up 2 or 3 times their dry volume in water. After they have absorbed all the water they are going to absorb (2-12 hours depending on the size of the seed), drain the water off, rinse them, and put them in a dark, warm place, with the bottle upside down and tipped up against a corner so water can drip out. Of course you need to put something under the bottle to catch the dripping water. Use a lid that permits air to move in and out of the jar. You can use a thin cloth, a nylon stocking, or anything you have that's handy. Fasten it down around the opening of the jar using an elastic or bottle ring. After the seeds have stopped draining, if you are sprouting very small seeds like alfalfa, cabbage or radish seeds, roll the bottle, coating the outer wall of the bottle with seeds. Leave the bottle on its side in the dark. Room temperature is best for growing sprouts, around 70 degrees F. Rinse the seeds twice a day, being sure to drain them well. (Do not neglect to rinse them. They will sour and be useless.) Within two days your seeds should begin sprouting.

For sprouts you are going to cook, let the sprout grow only as long as the seed. For sprouts you will eat raw (except wheat) let them grow up to 2-3 inches. Expose mature alfalfa, wheatgrass, buckwheat or sunflower sprouts to indirect sunlight for 4-5 hours. As they turn dark green their vitamin A content dramatically increases. (This is an important step, for if you don't, your sprouts will have only about 1 percent of this vitamin's RDA. Don't expose bean sprouts to sunlight as this will give them an unpleasant bitter taste.) When your sprouts have grown to the desired length, rinse them again, then put them in a sealed container with something to absorb the water on the bottom and store them in the refrigerator.

Sprouting mung beans under pressure. Place soaked beans in a small colander inside another container. Place several layers of burlap over the top of the seeds, then place a 3-5 pound bag of marbles or small stones on top of this. Water every two or three hours to ensure adequate moisture (this prevents the root systems from over developing in their search for water). Keep them in the dark at all times or they will turn bitter as they begin to green. When they are 2 to 3 inches long, remove them from the colander and refrigerate.

Using your sprouts After sprouts reach their peak, they immediately begin to lose their vitamin C. Because of this, don't attempt to store sprouts longer than a week. Only grow small quantities of sprouts that can be used in a short period of time. If you plan on getting many of your vitamins from sprouts, it would be a good idea to have one or two small batches of sprouts growing all the time.

Cook sprouted beans using the same recipes you normally use. Sprouted beans cook in 2/3rds the time of unsprouted beans. Heat kills a percentage of the vitamins and enzymes gained by sprouting, so simmer or steam slowly depending on your recipe, and don't cook longer than necessary.

You can sprout a mixture of seeds to make great green salads all by themselves. You can also

- use raw sprouts in just about anything:
- Blended in drinks.
- Added to bean or lettuce salads.
- Mixed with already cooked breakfast cereals.
- Wrapped in tortilla or taco shells and smothered in your favorite sauce.
- Added to soups and stews just before eating.
- Sprout filled Won Tons.

- Put into sandwiches.

Raw sprouts are so versatile that they can also be thrown into just about anything then cooked:

- Breads and biscuits.
- Soups.
- Pancakes.
- Eggs and omelets.
- Oatmeal or cracked wheat.
- Sauces.
- Mexican or Chinese foods.
- Potato Patties.
- Casseroles.
- Dips.
- Meatloaf.
- Any vegetable.
- Stir fried all by themselves.
- Even desserts. Really, the sky's the limit.

When cooking sprouts, it is better to steam or stir fry them than to boil them and discard the water. You only lose 20-30 percent of the vitamin C compared to 60 percent.

How much sprouting seed you should store and tips on purchasing.

It is suggested that if you plan to get all your vitamins from sprouts alone, that you store up to 125 lbs of a variety of seeds per year per person. If you have other sources for your vitamins, it is suggested you have 30 lbs of seeds set aside for sprouts to be eaten raw, and 30 lbs of sprouts intended to be cooked per year per person.

Many specialty companies exist that deal exclusively in sprout seed. Usually these seeds cost several times more than other seeds of the same type. One study shows that mung beans sold exclusively for sprouting cost 4.5 times more than regular mung beans. Yet 99 percent of the time the cheaper seed will sprout and grow as quickly as the more expensive seed. It is the web page author's opinion that it is a waste of money to buy 'sprouting seed' over regular seed. Before purchasing a large amount of storage seed intended for sprouting, purchase a small amount and test it to see if it sprouts well.

Do not attempt to store your sprouting seed for more than 5 years unless it is stored in a cool (at least 60-65 degrees F) dry place. If you are storing large seed, it may be packed in the absence of oxygen. Seed may last up to 15 years stored in this way. As your seeds get old they will take longer to sprout, and you will progressively get more seeds that won't sprout. The key again is rotate, rotate, rotate.

Use several different kinds of sprouts to find what you like before purchasing a large quantity of seed. Do not purchase seeds intended for anything except human consumption. Many seeds processed by farmers and gardeners for planting have been **treated with fungicide and or insecticide** agents and are very **poisonous**. These seeds are usually, but not always dyed red. If in doubt, ask.

XVIII Storage Space

Where To Hide All That Food Storage!

Storage space got you down? Do you feel as though you are tripping over your food storage? Never fear - there is a light at the end of the storage tunnel! Storage space seems to be a never ending problem these days. Many new homes are built with terrific vaulted ceilings, great views, and NO storage space!!! Older homes can also have a shortage of space. With a little creative thinking, and some planning, Saints can have space to store the important things in your life.

The first thing that must be done, (and this is the very hardest part) is that you must de-junk your home. Saints are all packrats to a certain extent. At a speech regarding the de-junking of our homes, the presenter asked how many people present had a watch at home that did not work. Every single person in the room held up his hand. Do YOU have one of these treasures in your home? (Be honest, now!) We all have things in our homes that were once priceless treasures, but have now become a nuisance. Get rid of them! There are probably a million suggestions of ways to de-junk. Choose one that fits with your life style. A book that can help you with this is Clutter's Last Stand: It's time to de-Junk Your Life by Don Aslett. Check your local library for other books on this subject.

Once you have gotten rid of some of the non-essentials, you must become creative. Stand in each room of your home and take a good look around.

- Is there storage space that is currently not being utilized?
- Is there space that is being used inefficiently?
- Are there shelves that could be built taller?
- Are there shelves that are deep that are only filled partially?
- Making efficient use of the storage space you already have may net you enough new space to store quite a bit.
- There are a lot of nice, new plastic storage containers on the market that may help you
- store things more easily, and stack them a bit deeper. Sturdy cardboard boxes can also
- help. Grocery stores will generally give you fruit boxes if you ask.

Learn to be creative with space

- Build your own couches using a basic toybox type design. Purchase thick foam rubber, and make cushions to go on top of the boxes. The hollow bottoms have lots of extra space.
- Check whether the cupboards have space above them. Modify them so your kitchen cupboards go all the way to the ceiling.
- Utilizes the space under your stairs.
- An upstairs bedroom built into the attic space might have some space (under the eaves) for additional storage. Build small doors into the wall to put something.

- Put shelves on the walls to keep things up off the floor. By building shelves you can move miscellaneous family items out of prime food-storage space, to store more food. In many cases, your best food-storage space is full of things that could be stored elsewhere.
- **Check for hollow spaces between walls**. It might not be a huge space, but enough to provide some more storage. Take the paneling off that portion of the wall, and put a cupboard door on. Cupboard doors are not expensive, nor are they difficult to install. Now you have a storage closet where non-existed originally.
- If your house isn't built on a concrete slab, you might have a great space to store things in the crawl space under your floor. Even in the heat of summer, this space is cool and can store potatoes, and foods that are in air-tight containers.
- **Use garbage cans as bedside tables.** This is done by purchasing regular garbage cans at a discount store. New ones are recommended because they have no odd smells or dirt attached! One sheet of plywood is then used to cut two circles four to five inches bigger in diameter than the top of the can. The lids to the garbage cans are not used. Let the kids use them as shields when they play. Place the plywood circles over the top of the garbage cans, and then cover your new bedside tables with nice round covers (called "table rounds") that coordinate with your bedspread. Nobody will know that your lovely bedside tables are actually garbage cans! This provides wonderful food storage space for some of the items that need to be stored in bulk, such as beans or wheat.
- **Don't forget the space under your beds!** Lots of food items can be stored in the small spaces under your beds. Salt, peanut butter, cans of potato flakes, canned vegetables, and cans of shortening can all be stored easily under the beds. They are also easily accessible.
- **Look at your closets.** Is there room on the floor of the closet? There are many commercial closet storage systems on the market that can help you more efficiently use your space, or build your own for less expense. Five gallon buckets can be stored on the floor of the closet, and a board put across the top of them to make a handy shelf for shoes and boots. Does the space in the top of the closet go all the way to the ceiling? Five gallon buckets could be stored up there as well, just don't store heavy things in them. This may be a good place to store tissue, paper towels, or toilet paper. Laundry detergent buckets make terrific storage containers for such items.
- **Struggling with a tiny dining area?** Build your own benches with hollow bottoms (the toy box design again). Put colorful cushions on top, and then use your own dining room table. Benches generally seat more people than traditional chairs. Now the entire family can fit in a small dining area, and you have extra storage space as well.
- **Take apart your bed frame** and use buckets, about 12-16 to hold up the bed. It will be a little higher than before, but it looked fine. Or use #10 cans in boxes that the fit in 6 at a time. Stack those under the bed. Also, you can stack those three high and put a table cloth over it for a nice little table in the Living Room or Family room. You can also put food storage in the kids room, in their closet on the floor. Not many little kids use all their closet space."

Don't let storage problems scare you! You are smarter than the things you own! A little creativity and elbow grease can go a long way toward providing more storage space in your home.

XIX Health, Fitness & Hygiene

What about medical care? How do people get treated for injuries or illnesses after the collapse?

If you have private health care you may be ok, but if you don't have the money for it (probably cash) you will have problems.

Obamacare isn't going to help you either, in fact this unfunded healthcare system is one of the reasons we are headed towards economic Armageddon. Forget about hospitalization, you'll die because of an infection. They won't have supplies and even sterile needles could be hard to get in a public hospital. If you don't have private health you have a foot in the grave.

At the root of the problem is the inexorable advance of subsidized healthcare which is swamping the entire economic system with unaffordable costs. The volume of services per Medicare patient increased by 50 percent between 2000 and 2010. Part of this is due to the rising cost of advanced, life-extending medicine, which contributes to the actuarial nightmare of Medicare and Social Security systems that were designed back when the average life expectancy was fifteen years less.

A lot of the increase comes from "defensive medicine," extra tests and procedures designed to stave off malpractice suits. Obamacare does absolutely nothing to alleviate these costs. Instead, it will make them worse, since it includes provisions that will dramatically increase the demand for medical services, such as forcing insurance companies to cover pre-existing conditions. Much of this new demand will come from younger patients eager to use the "free" benefits from their government-mandated health insurance, shifting resources away from the elderly, who are logically the heaviest consumers of medical services. As for malpractice reform… well, you didn't see any trial lawyers weeping at the passage of Obamacare.

Preventive Maintenance

If the healthcare delivery system is headed towards overpriced chaos, then you have only one real option: don't get sick! Visit you doctor NOW. Get yourself fixed. Talk to your doctor a lot. Never stop yourself from asking questions. Adopt that as a general philosophy and you'll end up learning a little about everything. Mechanics, doctors, policemen, you can always learn something new from people with skills.

Visit the dentist and make sure your mouth is in perfect conditions. Nothing is worse than having toothache and no one available to take care of it. Remember that doctors and dentists may not be as available in your future as they are now.

As a survivalist, and as a smart person, you should try to know a little about everything, Always be curious. Buy comprehensive first aid and drug reference books (not CDs, what happens when the power is out?). Some books to consider:

- The American Red Cross First Aid and Safety Handbook
- American Medical Association Handbook of First Aid and Emergency Care

- The Pill Book
- The PDR Family Guide to Prescription Drugs

Consider Lasik eye surgery to take care of your sight problems. The advantage of laser eye surgery isn't limited to not needing glasses. (which can break and would be nearly impossible to replace in a shutdown) People react to you in a different way. Humans are after all instinctive animals. Bad guys will look at you as a weaker person if you wear glasses. Maybe they don't know that at a conscious level, but they do react differently, it's the way things are.

Old people and women are especially vulnerable. After old people and women and children, come small framed people, the smaller you are, the weaker you look, the more likely you are to be chosen as a victim by a bad guy. This may be cruel, but it is the way it works. A young man with a well formed body, broad shoulders, muscled arms and a "don't f*** with me" face, is less likely to be a victims of small time thieves. Even if you are in one of the disadvantaged categories, you can improve your chances with general fitness.

WORKING OUT

Working out 3 times a week, for a couple of hours will keep you in shape. It could be as simple as working out at home with a bench and some weights. Try to compliment aerobics with your weight lifting. Being in shape will also make you less prone to diseases, such as high pressure, heart problems, and will boost your immune system in general.

Running belts and bicycles are also good.

Research the subject and make your own routine, join a gym and talk to a professional if possible. Whatever you do, the idea is to have a fit, healthy body. No use sniper shooting at 100 yards if you have a gut that hangs half way to the floor and you can't run that same distance without needing an oxygen mask. After some time you'll start to enjoy working out, your stamina and morale will definitely increase, and you'll start looking forward to exercise. The survivalist that spends 3 hours a week on his gun skills and no time at all on his own body is not doing things right. Imagine if you have to run away from a riot/gunfight/attack while carrying your beer belly, or fighting bare handed against someone that has surprised you.

MARTIAL ARTS

Working the boxing bag is good exercise, it works most muscles if done right, and you'll have a much more powerful punch. Keep in mind that a bag is no replacement for a sparring partner and that the bag does not faint nor does it punch back.

Both men and women should know how to fight bare handed. You don't have to be Bruce Lee or Mike Tyson, just know how to throw a decent punch and cover your face. Take some kind or martial art classes. Try Judo. This is both for the exercise as well as self defense, both of which affect your health.

Practicing defensive moves is useful, especially if you spar with someone who knows what they are doing. Practice as you would fight in real life. Getting chocked isn't nice, but you get to know what you are working with and know how effective it actually is.

Medicine

Find an online Canadian pharmacy to supplement or even replace your local pharmacy. The Canadian online pharmacies don't seem to be overly particular about having prescriptions, especially if it is for standard prescriptions and not for high powered painkillers.

If you take drugs regularly try to have at least a year's worth of your medication. Medicines may be hard to get and expensive. If there is medication that has a substantial impact on your health, such as insulin, blood sugar testing, and syringes for diabetics or anti seizure medications for epileptics, blood pressure meds etc., talk with your doctor and pharmacist about your concerns for long term supplies and long term storage of such medications for extended emergencies. It doesn't hurt to ask. Those with less common ailments like Parkinsonism who need special medicines should stock pile as much medicines as they can. Apart from the regular 1st aid kit stuff you usually have at home, concentrate on Ibuprofen and antibiotics, both for children and adults.

Antibiotics are precious in a long term collapse. Diversify your stock of antibiotics. The body will adapt if you always use the same ones, making that particular antibiotic ineffective, especially in small children. Keep at least two different kinds of antibiotics – save some every time you get a prescription. Lung infections are particularly dangerous.

Prescription medications can be the most difficult part of survival stockpiling. They can be hard to get in quantity, but without certain medications patients would die or become ill in short order. The U.S. Air Force performed a study to determine the shelf life of its inventory of medications. It seems the Air Force was concerned about having to dump and restock millions of dollars worth of pharmaceuticals after the stated expiration date. The study proved that even though they were given a date of shelf life, many of them maintain their stability, safety and potency up to as much as an additional 107 months past their expiration dates.

With a handful of exceptions — notably nitroglycerin, insulin and some liquid antibiotics — most drugs are probably as durable as those tested for the military. Most drugs degrade very slowly, in all likelihood, you can take a product you have at home and keep it for many years, especially if it's in the refrigerator. Every time you visit the Doctor or Dentist for whatever reason any unused antibiotics should quickly find their way into your stockpile of survival meds.

Hygiene

Preventing sickness may be a life and death matter in a collapse because of the absence of medical help, either by unavailability or because of cost.

Sometimes the simplest things make the most difference. One of these is simple hand washing, something that can help prevent disease which you can ill afford in stressed circumstances. Hand washing has been shown to cut the number of child deaths from diarrhea (the second leading cause of child deaths) by almost half and from pneumonia (the leading cause of child deaths) by one-quarter. There are five critical times in washing hands with soap and/or using of a hand antiseptic related to fecal-oral transmission:

- after using a bathroom (private or public)
- after changing a diaper

- before feeding a child

- before eating

- before preparing food or handling raw meat, fish, or poultry, or any other situation leading to potential contamination

To reduce the spread of germs, it is also better to wash the hands and/or use a hand antiseptic before and after tending to a sick person. For control of staphylococcal infections in hospitals, it has been found that the greatest benefit from hand-cleansing came from the first 20% of washing, and that very little additional benefit was gained when hand cleansing frequency was increased beyond 35%. Washing with plain soap results in more than triple the rate of bacterial infectious disease transmitted to food as compared to washing with antibacterial soap. Comparing hand-rubbing with alcohol-based solution with handwashing with antibacterial soap for a median time of 30 seconds each showed that the alcohol hand-rubbing reduced bacterial contamination 26% more than the antibacterial soap. But soap and water is the more effective than alcohol-based hand rubs for reducing H1N1 influenza A virus and Clostridium difficile spores from hands.

Another hygiene issue to remember is that keeping a clean, ventilated house goes a long way when it comes to preventing diseases. This is hard when the city is full of filth and there are cockroaches and rats everywhere but it can be done. In a full economic collapse, some people will literally sleep and eat with rats. Cockroaches will be a problem too, but you can keep them controlled with poisons that you place around the house. Stock up on rat and cockroach poison. If services are bad in general, the garbage collectors may not come by. Once, they go on strike for a week (much less areas they they go months without collecting) you could see rats running around the piles of garbage that people throw on the streets spreading disease all over the city.

XX   Basic First Aid

First, this is not a First Aid book, it is a survival book just meant to get you started. Please take some Red Cross courses or other first aid training.   However, if this is the only book you have handy to survive immediate life threatening trauma, the following are some techniques to at least give you a chance to avoid total mental paralysis.

Keep a first aid kit and any other special medicine you may need handy.

While kit contents will vary, the basic first aid kit should include the items listed below. Most drugstores, outdoors or camping type stores should carry basic first aid kits. If you can't buy one with these contents, pick up a few supplies and create your own:

- Assorted adhesive bandages. Bandages can also be made from clean rags, disposable diapers and sanitary napkins. Dressings can be held in place by neck ties, cloth belts, nylon stockings, and plastic bags.
- Antibiotic ointment for dressing wounds (Neosporin)
- Gauze pads
- Iodine/Alcohol or similar prep pads
- Butterfly bandages
- Adhesive tape (1/2 inch and 1 inch wide rolls)
- Pain relievers to reduce swelling as well as relieve pain (Tylenol, Aspirin, Ibuprofen, Children's pain reliever)
- Mylar space blanket for warmth and to prevent shock

The more advanced medical kit will include the following items in addition to those listed in the intermediate kit:

- Special bandages, such as conforming, trauma and field dressings
- Rubbing alcohol for sterilization
- Hydrogen peroxide to wash and disinfect wounds
- Betadine
- Scissors
- Forceps
- Scalpels
- Hemostats
- Sterile sutures, in several sizes
- Wound probe
- Mouth to mouth shield
- Instant hot packs
- Instant cold packs

- Prep pads
- Eye pads
- Sponges
- Cotton balls
- Burn treatments
- Dental tools
- Splint materials
- Cold remedies
- Colloidal silver

And don't forget to include an in-depth first aid manual or basic surgical guide.

If you have children, are elderly, or take care of individuals with special medical problems, remember to add whatever extra items you think might be appropriate.

If you are child-bearing, or have experience in labor and delivery, it might be a good idea to store a birthing kit.

STOP BLEEDING

Regardless how severe, all bleeding can be controlled. If left uncontrolled, bleeding may lead to shock or even death. While you're performing the steps for controlling bleeding, you should also be calling for an ambulance to respond. Most bleeding can be stopped before the ambulance arrives at the scene.

The first step in controlling a bleeding wound is to plug the hole. Blood needs to clot in order to start the healing process and stop the bleeding. Just like ice won't form on the rapids of a river, blood will not coagulate when it's flowing.

The best way to stop it is to...stop it. Put pressure directly on the wound. If you have some type of gauze, use it. Gauze pads hold the blood on the wound and help the components of the blood to stick together, promoting clotting. If you don't have gauze, terrycloth towels work almost as well.

If the gauze or towel soaks through with blood, add another layer. *Never* take off the gauze. Peeling blood soaked gauze off a wound removes vital clotting agents and encourages bleeding to resume.

Gravity makes blood flow down easier than it flows up. If you hold one hand above your head and the other at your side, the lower hand will be red while the higher one is pale.

Step two to control bleeding uses this principle. Elevate the wound above the heart. By elevating the wound, you slow the flow of blood. As the blood slows, it becomes easier to stop it with direct pressure. Remember, it must be *above the heart* and you must *keep direct pressure on it*.

Pressure points are areas of the body where blood vessels run close to the surface. By pressing on these blood vessels, blood flow further away will be slowed, allowing direct pressure to stop bleeding.

When using pressure points, make sure you are pressing on a point closer to the heart than the wound. Pressing on a blood vessel further from the heart than the wound will have no effect on the bleeding.

Common pressure points:

- Arm between shoulder and elbow - brachial artery
- Groin area along bikini line - femoral artery
- Behind the knee - popliteal artery

When should you apply a tourniquet? The simple answer: almost never. Tourniquets severely restrict or occlude blood flow to the arm or leg to which they are applied. Using a tourniquet to stop bleeding has the potential to damage the entire arm or leg. Patients have been known to lose limbs from the use of tourniquets.

Often, if a tourniquet doesn't cause a loss of function on the extremity which has it, then it probably wasn't applied correctly. Applying a tourniquet is a desperate move - only for the most dire emergencies where the choice between life and limb must be made.

Using a tourniquet requires wrapping a cravat (non stretchy material like terry cloth or linen) around an extremity and tightening it with the use of a windlass stuck through the bandage.

The tourniquet should be tightened until the wound stops bleeding. If there is any bleeding at the wound after placing a tourniquet, then the tourniquet must be tightened.

When a tourniquet is applied, it is important to note the time of application and write that time down somewhere handy. The best bet is to write the time on the patient's forehead with a water-proof marker.

Once bleeding is controlled, take steps to treat the victim for shock.

TREAT SHOCK

Uncontrolled bleeding may lead to a condition known as shock. Shock is essentially a decrease in blood flow to the brain and other important organs. Untreated, shock from bleeding will almost always cause death.

The most important step in treating shock is to control bleeding. However, if the victim is already showing signs of shock, it's important to take the necessary steps to stabilize the victim until help arrives.

Here's How:

1. Make sure the victim is breathing. If not, begin rescue breathing.
2. Before any other treatments for shock are done, bleeding must be stopped.
3. If you do not suspect a neck injury, lay the victim on their back (supine) and elevate the legs. If you suspect a neck injury, do not move the victim. Car and other vehicle accidents often lead

to neck injuries. Neck injuries are also common in falls, especially falls from a height taller than the victim.

4. Keep the victim warm.

5. Continue to check on the victim. If the victim stops breathing, begin rescue breathing. If the victim vomits, roll the victim to one side and sweep the vomit from his or her mouth with your fingers.

DIARRHEA

Diarrhea is a condition that leads to frequent, loose or watery stools. Those with it don't absorb nutrients or water properly. Use these general treatments when the cause of diarrhea isn't known or can't be treated itself.

Time Required: 24 to 72 hours

Here's How:

1. **Avoid dehydration**. Drink lots of clear fluid -- no alcohol or caffeine. Milk will usually prolong diarrhea, but it might help provide nutrients for folks with very mild cases. For moderate to severe cases, use an electrolyte solution like Gatorade or Pedialyte.

2. **Eat probiotic yogurt**. These active cultures can ease the symptoms of some types of diarrhea and shorten their duration.

3. **Try the BRAT diet**: bananas, rice, apples or applesauce, and dry toast. This diet is often suggested for kids, but adults can eat it as well. It's not necessary to restrict kids or adults to this diet, but adding these foods may help shorten episodes of diarrhea.

4. **Avoid diarrhea medications**, unless the doctor tells you to take them. The function of diarrhea is to rid the body of bad bugs. Often the only way to get better is to suffer through the loose stools.

5. The following cases require **seeking emergency treatment**:
   - Vomiting or diarrhea in a newborn under 3 months (call as soon as it starts)
   - Kids older than 3 months vomiting for more than 12 hours
   - Diarrhea lasting more than 3 days
   - Bloody, black, or oily looking stools
   - Abdominal pain that doesn't get better with a bowel movement
   - Dehydration symptoms including dizziness, weakness or muscle cramps
   - Fever, along with diarrhea, of more than 101 in adults or 100.4 in kids
   - Recent travel outside the country (Traveler's Diarrhea)
   - People you've eaten with complaining of diarrhea
   - Diarrhea after starting a new medication

XXI Cardiopulmonary Resuscitation

Cardiopulmonary resuscitation (CPR) is a lifesaving technique useful in many emergencies, including heart attack or near drowning, in which someone's breathing or heartbeat has stopped. Ideally, CPR involves two elements: chest compressions combined with mouth-to-mouth rescue breathing. However, what you as a bystander should do in an emergency situation really depends on your knowledge and comfort level.

The bottom line is that it's far better to do something than to do nothing at all if you're fearful that your knowledge or abilities aren't 100 percent complete. Remember, the difference between your doing something and doing nothing could be someone's life. Here's advice from the American Heart Association:

- Untrained. If you're not trained in CPR, then provide hands-only CPR. That means uninterrupted chest compressions of about 100 a minute until paramedics arrive (described in more detail below). You don't need to try rescue breathing.
- Trained, and ready to go. If you're well trained, and confident in your ability, then you can opt for one of two approaches:
  1. Alternate between 30 chest compressions and two rescue breaths.
  2. Just do chest compressions. (Details described below.)
- Trained, but rusty. If you've previously received CPR training, but you're not confident in your abilities, then just do chest compressions at a rate of about 100 a minute. (Details described below.)

The above advice applies only to adults needing CPR, not to children.

CPR can keep oxygenated blood flowing to the brain and other vital organs until more definitive medical treatment can restore a normal heart rhythm. When the heart stops, the absence of oxygenated blood can cause irreparable brain damage in only a few minutes. A person may die within eight to 10 minutes. To learn CPR properly, take an accredited first-aid training course, including CPR and how to use an automatic external defibrillator (AED).

Before you begin

Before starting CPR, check:

- Is the person conscious or unconscious?
- If the person appears unconscious, tap or shake his or her shoulder and ask loudly, "Are you OK?"
- If the person doesn't respond and two people are available, one should call 911 or the local emergency number and one should begin CPR. If you are alone and have immediate access to a telephone, call 911 before beginning CPR — unless you think the person has become unresponsive because of suffocation (such as from drowning). In this special case, begin CPR for one minute and then call 911.

- If an AED is immediately available, deliver one shock if instructed by the device, then begin CPR.

Remember the ABCs

- ✓ Airway,
- ✓ Breathing
- ✓ Circulation

Move quickly through airway and breathing to begin chest compressions.

Airway: Clear the airway

Put the person on his or her back on a firm surface.

Kneel next to the person's neck and shoulders.

Open the person's airway using the head-tilt, chin-lift maneuver. Put your palm on the person's forehead and gently tilt the head back. Then with the other hand, gently lift the chin forward to open the airway.

Check for normal breathing, taking no more than five or 10 seconds. Look for chest motion, listen for normal breath sounds, and feel for the person's breath on your cheek and ear. Gasping is not considered to be normal breathing. If the person isn't breathing normally and you are trained in CPR, begin mouth-to-mouth breathing. If you believe the person is unconscious from a heart attack and you haven't been trained in emergency procedures, skip mouth-to-mouth rescue breathing and proceed directly to chest compressions.

Breathing: Breathe for the person

Rescue breathing can be mouth-to-mouth breathing or mouth-to-nose breathing if the mouth is seriously injured or can't be opened.

With the airway open (using the head-tilt, chin-lift maneuver), pinch the nostrils shut for mouth to-mouth breathing and cover the person's mouth with yours, making a seal.

Prepare to give two rescue breaths. Give the first rescue breath — lasting one second — and watch to see if the chest rises. If it does rise, give the second breath. If the chest doesn't rise, repeat the head-tilt, chin-lift maneuver and then give the second breath.

Begin chest compressions to restore circulation.

Circulation: Restore blood circulation with chest compressions

Place the heel of one hand over the center of the person's chest, between the nipples. Place your other hand on top of the first hand. Keep your elbows straight and position your shoulders directly above your hands.

Use your upper body weight (not just your arms) as you push straight down on (compress) the chest 2 inches (approximately 5 centimeters). Push hard at a rate of 100 compressions a minute.

After 30 compressions, tilt the head back and lift the chin up to open the airway. Prepare to give two rescue breaths. Pinch the nose shut and breathe into the mouth for one second. If the chest rises, give a second rescue breath. If the chest doesn't rise, repeat the head-tilt, chin-lift maneuver and then give the second rescue breath.

That's one cycle. If someone else is available, ask that person to give two breaths after you do 30 compressions.

If you're not trained in CPR and feel comfortable performing only chest compressions, skip rescue breathing and continue chest compressions at a rate of 100 compressions a minute until medical personnel arrive.

If the person has not begun moving after five cycles (about two minutes) and an automatic external defibrillator (AED) is available, apply it and follow the prompts. Administer one shock, then resume CPR — starting with chest compressions — for two more minutes before administering a second shock. If you're not trained to use an AED, a 911 operator may be able to guide you in its use. Use pediatric pads, if available, for children ages 1 to 8. Do not use an AED for babies younger than age 1. If an AED isn't available, go to step 5 below. Continue CPR until there are signs of movement or until emergency medical personnel take over.

To perform CPR on a child

The procedure for giving CPR to a child age 1 through 8 is essentially the same as that for an adult. The differences are as follows:

- If you're alone, perform five cycles of compressions and breaths on the child — this should take about two minutes — before calling 911 or your local emergency number or using an AED.
- Breathe more gently.
- After five cycles (about two minutes) of CPR, if there is no response and an AED is available, apply it and follow the prompts. Use pediatric pads if available. If pediatric pads aren't available, use adult pads.

Continue until the child moves or help arrives.

To perform CPR on a baby

Most cardiac arrests in babies occur from lack of oxygen, such as from drowning or choking. If you know the baby has an airway obstruction, perform first aid for choking. If you don't know why the baby isn't breathing, perform CPR.

To begin, examine the situation. Stroke the baby and watch for a response, such as movement, but don't shake the baby.

If there's no response, follow the ABC procedures below and time the call for help as follows:

- If you're the only rescuer and CPR is needed, do CPR for two minutes — about five cycles — before calling 911 or your local emergency number.

- If another person is available, have that person call for help immediately while you attend to the baby.

Airway: Clear the airway

Place the baby on his or her back on a firm, flat surface, such as a table. The floor or ground also will do. Gently tip the head back by lifting the chin with one hand and pushing down on the forehead with the other hand. In no more than 10 seconds, put your ear near the baby's mouth and check for breathing: Look for chest motion, listen for breath sounds, and feel for breath on your cheek and ear. If the infant isn't breathing, begin mouth-to-mouth rescue breathing immediately. Compressions-only CPR doesn't work for infants.

Breathing: Breathe for the infant

Cover the baby's mouth and nose with your mouth.

Prepare to give two rescue breaths. Use the strength of your cheeks to deliver gentle puffs of air (instead of deep breaths from your lungs) to slowly breathe into the baby's mouth one time, taking one second for the breath. Watch to see if the baby's chest rises. If it does, give a second rescue breath. If the chest does not rise, repeat the head-tilt, chin-lift maneuver and then give the second breath.

If the baby's chest still doesn't rise, examine the mouth to make sure no foreign material is inside.

If the object is seen, sweep it out with your finger. If the airway seems blocked, perform first aid for a choking baby.

Begin chest compressions to restore blood circulation.

Circulation: Restore blood circulation

Imagine a horizontal line drawn between the baby's nipples. Place two fingers of one hand just below this line, in the center of the chest.

Gently compress the chest to about one-third to one-half the depth of the chest.

Count aloud as you pump in a fairly rapid rhythm. You should pump at a rate of 100 compressions a minute.

Give two breaths after every 30 chest compressions.

Perform CPR for about two minutes before calling for help unless someone else can make the call while you attend to the baby.

Continue CPR until you see signs of life or until medical personnel arrive.

3 minutes without breathing

Install and test smoke alarms in your home. Most victims of fire succumb to the smoke and toxic gases and not to burns. Fire produces poisonous gases that can spread rapidly and far from the fire itself to claim victims who are asleep and not even aware of the fire. Even if residents awaken, the effects of exposure to these gases can cloud their thinking and slow their reactions so that they cannot make their escape.

This is why it is so crucial for you and your family to have sufficient warning so that you can all escape before your ability to think and move is impaired. In addition, more than half of fatal fires in homes occur when people are asleep ' this represents only a third of a 24-hour day. Therefore, any fire protection system must be able to protect people who are asleep in their bedrooms when fire starts. If you have battery powered detectors make sure you replace batteries yearly as recommended by the U.S. Fire Administration.

Carbon monoxide (CO) is a deadly, colorless, odorless, poisonous gas. It is produced by the incomplete burning of various fuels, including coal, wood, charcoal, oil, kerosene, propane, and natural gas. Products and equipment powered by internal combustion engine-powered equipment such as portable generators, cars, lawn mowers, and power washers also produce CO. You will often read of people being sickened or dying of carbon monoxide poisoning during times of emergencies. Often these accidents are the results of use of portable fuel-burning camping equipment inside a home, garage, vehicle or tent that is not specifically designed for use in an enclosed space or failure to follow manufacturer's instructions for safe use in an enclosed area. The burning of charcoal inside a home, garage, vehicle, or tent can also led to CO poisoning.

Another common cause of carbon monoxide asphyxiation is from prolonged confinement in a running motor vehicle. It is important to remember that you can be overcome by carbon monoxide poisoning if you do not have enough ventilation in your vehicle. Whether you are running your vehicle at intermittent times or burning one of the coffee can heaters, you still need to crack at least one of your windows for fresh air. You should only run your vehicle for no more than ten minutes every hour. You also need to make sure the exhaust pipe of your vehicle is free of snow or mud.

Moving water is very dangerous. Just 6" of fast moving water can knock you off your feet. Cars, including heavy trucks, can get swept away in less than 2-feet of swift water. Never drive through moving water. Nationwide, 70% of all flood-related fatalities are in vehicles. With so many of today's vehicles coming with electrical controlled power windows and doors you should consider keeping an emergency auto-glass breaking tool in your vehicle. A vehicle's submergence in water will quickly short out the electric controls which unlock doors and power open windows, leaving you trapped inside. These tools are especially designed to quickly and easily break auto glass allowing you to escape.

There are any number of other emergencies which can occur which pose the threat of asphyxiation and/or drowning including flash floods, mud slides, tsunamis, gas leaks (residential, commercial), enclosed use of chemical solvents, misuses of common clean agents (the mixing of common chlorine bleach and household ammonia will cause a reaction that creates chlorine gas, chloramines and other noxious fumes. Accidental or deliberate mixing of bleach with fluids containing ammonia causes severe damage to the lungs). Always consider those which seem the most likely to occur in your area and try to create a plan accordingly.

XXII Survival Fire Safety

Our survival plans will rely heavily on fire for cooking, heating and lighting. What about Fire Safety? Do you have working fire extinguishers or another plan to deal with a fire if one erupts? If you are planning to use a generator it needs to be properly wired to prevent fire. And what about your fuel storage? Is it a hazard? After all, if services have deteriorated to this point, the local fire department isn't coming either.

Of all aspects of our daily life, Fire Safety is most commonly overlooked. The second step to mitigating any safety hazard, after removing the process entirely if possible, is to engineer out the hazard. Today, this is done for us in the form of model building codes, UL listings and other industry standards. Not surprisingly, it isn't forefront in our minds. But if an economic or societal collapse comes, we'll be trading our electric lights for kerosene lamps and candles, electric ranges for camp stoves and wood fires. Many things will be home-built or improvised from available resources. Not everything will have engineered-in safeguards?

The Science of Fire

To understand fire potential, and extinguishment, it is important to understand the dynamics of a fire. Some may recall learning about the "Fire Triangle" in school: combustion occurs when three components (oxygen, fuel and heat) are present. Removing one or more will extinguish the fire.

This first means that the fuel and oxygen components must attain proper chemical ratios or fuel to oxygen mixing to ignite. This usually requires the fuel, whether in liquid or solid form, to be heated until it vaporizes. This is where heat comes into play. "Flammable" means that it will vaporize at temperatures below 105 degrees F and generally includes liquids such as gasoline, alcohol, propane, etc. "Combustible" refers to fuels which vaporize at temperatures greater than 105 degrees F, thus requiring more heat input for the combustion process to occur. This is also why it is harder to start a campfire in the dead of a Canadian winter than summer in west Texas. As a fire burns, the combustion reaction produces large amounts of energy in the form of heat. This in turn becomes the heat necessary to sustain and/or grow the fire. The hotter the fire, the more fuel that becomes available and the more rapid the fire's growth.

The only limitation now is the available air. It is important to note, however, that not all fuels need to be in vapor form. Fine dust particles, when airborne in high enough quantity, can attain the proper mixing with oxygen to burn quite rapidly. This is important for anyone with bulk storage of grains, coal, sawdust and even dusty hay. The oxygen, or oxidizing agent, in this context comes from "standard" atmospheric air – roughly 20% oxygen, 79% nitrogen, etc.

As the fire burns, hot combustion gases expand and rise in a superheated plume. As these gases rise, fresh air is drawn into the fire at the base, heated, consumed in the fire and again released upward. This is what is referred to as convection currents and one reason why you aim a fire extinguisher at the base of the fire. Also note, however, that some materials, such as gunpowder, don't require outside oxygen combustion. Some chemicals, such as nitrates, contain sufficient quantities of oxygen within the molecules, and are easily released during the combustion process. These burn rapidly and are difficult to control.

If a fire breaks out, the first, we need to know what classification of fire it is (that is to say what materials are involved). This is important so we can determine the proper method of extinguishment.

Class A Fires involve "ordinary" combustibles such as wood, paper, cloth, etc. This is the most common fire you can expect and will most likely occur from a campfire that got out of control, a lantern getting knocked over, a lit candle or some similar incident. A little care can go a long way here. Water is going to be the best means to put out a Class A fire, but it may be a precious commodity. Snow is another excellent media since it is also very effective at blanketing the fire. If it is small, you can also try smothering it with a blanket or jacket, but make sure there is no flammable liquid involved or you'll set the blanket or jacket on fire. In the case of a small to medium fire outdoors, sand or soil shoveled onto the fire is also effective. However, sometimes it may be best to simply let the fire burn itself out while you prevent it from spreading.

Chimney Fires can creep up unwittingly. Unburned volatiles called creosote are given off primarily due to green/wet wood, low temperature fires and insufficient airflow. This creosote builds up until it either blocks the flue or is ignited by a hot fire. If a fire occurs, immediately close all inlet vents on the stove to smother the fire. If it is an open fireplace, extinguish the fire below then carefully try to close the damper if you can. Do not attempt to cover the chimney but do try to water down the roof if possible. There is otherwise very little that can be done for a chimney fire. Water sprayed into the flue will likely crack the flue liner. Moreover, the extreme temperatures generated are likely to damage to the chimney. Damaged flues and chimneys drastically increase the likelihood of a structure fire. It is best to take every precaution to avoid a chimney fire. Chimneys should be cleaned at least once per year!

Class B Fires generally involve flammable liquids such as gasoline, kerosene, paraffin, alcohol, etc. These pose a great risk because they ignite easily and spread quickly. Accumulated vapors can ignited with the smallest spark, even from static electricity. If you encounter a flammable liquid pool fire, do not use water. Remember, most flammable liquids we use are hydrocarbon based and float on water. Application of the water will cause ripples in the fuel, causing a flare up as well as spreading the fire. Flammable liquid fire must be extinguished by smothering. This is best accomplished by dry chemical or foam fire extinguishers, though small fires in containers may be carefully covered.

Say you are refueling a hot generator and it flashes over. You now have flames coming out of the fuel tank as well as the gas can. Get away! It is important to keep your distance as explosion or eruption is possible. This is a bad situation and there is little you're going to be able to do. A pressurized hose could be used to cool surfaces but at the risk of overflowing the tank or can, thus spreading the fire.

In the event of a leaking propane line that catches fire, shut off the gas at the source if it can be done safely. It is unlikely that anything else you try will be successful and even if it is, you'll be releasing raw fuel that is likely to re-ignite. Probably one of the most common and dangerous fires in this class is the grease fire. This generally occurs from superheating animal fats or vegetable oil and also applies to paraffin. Again, do not use water. Find something to cover it with, such as the lid to a pot if you are cooking. The next step is to do nothing. You see, as oil, grease or paraffin burns, its' auto-ignition temperature decreases. That means that if any air is introduced, it will flash over again unless it has cooled sufficiently.

Class C Fires involve energized electrical components such as wiring, motors, generators, etc. In this case, the ignition source is the electricity and the fuel is usually the wiring. The first step in this situation is to kill the electricity – trip the disconnect, turn off the ignition, shut down the generator, do what you have to. Now it is simply a Class A or Class B fire. DO NOT use water around live electricity.

Class D Fires involve metals, such as sodium, magnesium, aluminum, etc. These may be found in some fire starters and flares as well as around metal grinding and cutting. It is possible for two metals, along with a catalyst, to ignite. Such fires burn rapidly and extremely hot. However unlikely it is that you will encounter such a fire in a survival situation, this is one you can't affect without specialized firefighting equipment.

Fire Extinguishers are an indispensable safety item for every household. Each extinguisher will be labeled for the class of fire and fire size it is capable of being used on. There are several styles available so familiarize yourself with how yours operates before it is needed. There are also a number of different extinguishing agents so choose wisely. Water and water based foams will freeze and the powders used in dry chemical types wreak havoc with electronics. Do you homework. They also require some regular maintenance. For instance, dry chemical powders need to be "fluffed" every so often to keep them from caking. This can be accomplished by turning it upside down and hitting the bottom with a rubber mallet. And also check to make sure the bottle is free of rust or other mechanical damage

Doubtless, the most fearful fire of all is one that upon your person. In the event that your clothes become involved, don't run. STOP, DROP and ROLL to smother the fire. If you see someone else on fire, this is where your time on the high school football team comes in handy. Grab a blanket, preferably wool, and tackle them (albeit gently). The goal is to get them on the ground and covered with the blanket, smothering the fire. Depending on the circumstances and clothing involved, there will likely be some first aid required.

Combustion By-Products in Smoke

Aside from the inherent dangers of fire itself, combustion by-products may pose an even greater hazard. Incomplete combustion of organic materials, where adequate free air exists for the fire, carbon dioxide and water are produced. Carbon Dioxide (CO_2) is a colorless, odorless gas which, being heavier than air, collects in low areas. An increase of only 2-3% CO_2 in the air we breathe can result in impaired memory, loss of fine motor skills and weakness. Higher concentrations can cause unconsciousness and death. If you find someone a victim of CO_2 exposure, ventilate the area. Do not go rushing in and become a victim too (you won't do them or yourself any good like that).

Remove the victim to an area with fresh clean air. In some cases, the victim may require further medical treatment by trained personnel. If the fire is starved for oxygen, then carbon monoxide (CO) is produced. Again, CO is a colorless, odorless gas, but it is even more dangerous than CO_2. Generally, CO exposure causes a feeling of sleepiness in the victim, but also nausea, headaches and vertigo. Once the victim becomes unconscious, death soon follows. The complicating factor here is that CO molecules bond to hemoglobin, the oxygen carriers in the bloodstream, preventing oxygen from getting to the cells. Simply getting the victim to fresh air will not adequately purge CO from the system. Treatment for CO exposure usually requires 100% oxygen or hyperbaric treatment.

When inorganic materials such as plastic, paint, glue, particle board, wire insulation and other man-made materials burn, there is virtually no limit to the volatile and toxic chemicals that are released. These can result in serious illness and death very quickly and will almost certainly require medical treatment you cannot provide at your survival retreat.

Prevention

While we want to be prepared to deal with a fire if one starts, our best bet is to "engineer out" the hazard and prevent a fire altogether. Make sure that lanterns, lamps and candles are placed on a flat, stable surface. Candles should be in a proper holder or on a porcelain or tin plate with sides to catch melted wax. An empty tuna can works well for this. Ensure that all combustibles are kept away and be mindful of shirt sleeves and loose clothing when working with or around such items. Also, be careful around children and animals (remember Mrs. O'Leary's cow).

Chimney fires are best avoided by regular maintenance, starting with regular cleanings. If you burn strictly for heat in cold months, this means at least one cleaning before the burn season and possible more during the season. If you will be burning regularly for cooking, you'll probably be using a smaller fire, thus creating more creosote. Burning hot and staying away from "green" wood or wood heavy with resins such as pines will drastically help reduce buildup.

There are various products on the market which claim to help with creosote buildup. These products are simply burned periodically in the fire. However, while these would likely help, they are certainly no replacement for proper cleaning. Make sure you have a brush or two of the proper shape and size for each flue. In a pinch, a bundle of chain on a rope will work for small flues. If you experience a chimney fire, metal chimneys are expensive but easily replaced if you have spare parts. However, damage to masonry chimneys is much more difficult to repair.

Take extra care with flammable liquids. When stored, ensure that they are in approved containers with good seals. On his 1911-12 journey to the South Pole, Robert Scott left caches of food and fuel. On the return trip, he found that many of the fuel cans were empty, having leaked at the seals. The lack of fuel eventually led to their deaths. Flammable liquids should be stored out of sunlight and in a well ventilated area. Don't use anything with a flame around flammable liquids. Even a flashlight is a potential ignition source.

If you need to have something for light, get a small flashlight with a Class 1, Div.1 rating (ones from Pelican and UA are good choices). Also avoid using gasoline and the like for starting fires. The accumulation of fumes can have deadly results. A good alternative is to use gel starting fluid for pellet stoves. The gel is less volatile and won't flash or explode like gasoline will. Also be very mindful of the clothing you wear around or when starting a fire. Nylon, rayon and the multitudes of synthetic fibers used in clothing today are extremely dangerous. They ignite easily and melt even easier thus increasing the need for medical attention. Natural fibers such as cotton and wool are best. When possible, buy instead of building anything that uses a flame. This includes lanterns, stoves, burners, incubators, brooders and heaters. There are also several manufacturers of fire resistance coatings that can be applied to almost anything. Be careful with outdoor fires, especially when windy.

The last thing you want to do is start a fire that burns your house or shelter down with your supplies in it. Don't use stoves or flames inside of tents unless both the tent and the stove are intended for such a purpose. If you are planning to use a wood framed structure for your survival shelter, you may want to think about fire resistance. A number of manufacturers offer concrete fiberboard siding that is fire proof as well as water, weather and insect proof. There are also a number of options for roof coverings such as metal, clay and cement fiberboard.

Unless you are competent in electrical wiring, make sure to have everything checked out by a licensed electrician. If you plan to use an electric generator, use the proper connections and transfer switches. Don't try to jury rig this - the shock and fire potentials here are extremely high.

Smokey Bear always said "Only you can prevent forest fires". This is essentially true in a survival situation too. Many of us will be living in somewhat primitive conditions compared to what we are used to. We need to be vigilant at every moment. Think Safe, Be Safe.

XXIII Terrorist Attack

BEFORE

Learn about the nature of terrorism and how to protect yourself.

1. Terrorists often choose targets that offer little danger to themselves and areas with relatively easy public access.
2. Terrorists look for visible targets where they can avoid detection before or after an attack such as airports, large cities, major events, resorts, and high-profile landmarks.
3. Learn about the different types of terrorist weapons including explosives, kidnapping, highjackings, arson, shootings, and nuclear, biological and chemical weapons.
4. Prepare to deal with a terrorist incident by adapting many of the same techniques used to prepare for other crises.
5. Be alert and aware of the surrounding area. The very nature of terrorism suggests that there may be little or no warning.
6. Take precautions when traveling. Be aware of conspicuous or unusual behavior. Do not accept packages from strangers. Do not leave luggage unattended.
7. Learn where emergency exists are located. Think ahead about how to evacuate a building, subway or congested public area in a hurry. Learn where staircases are located.
8. Notice your immediate surroundings. Be aware of heavy or breakable objects that could move, fall or break in an explosion.

Preparing for a Building Explosion

The use of explosives by terrorists can result in collapsed buildings and fires. People who live or work in a multi-level building can do the following:

A. Review emergency evacuation procedures. Know where fire exits are located, in a dark and dusty atmosphere.

B. Keep fire extinguishers in working order. Know where they are located, and how to use them. Learn first aid and become CERT trained.

C. Keep the following items in a designated place on each floor of the building:

1. Portable, battery-operated am/fm radio and extra batteries.
2. Several flashlights and extra batteries and/or light sticks.
3. First aid kit and manual.
4. Several hard hats, work gloves, whistle, and dust masks.
5. Fluorescent tape to rope off dangerous areas.
6. Extra water.
7. A gas mask with extra filters.

Bomb Threats

If you receive a bomb threat, get as much information from the caller as possible. Keep the caller on the line and record everything that is said. Notify the police and the building management. After you've been notified of a bomb threat, do not touch any suspicious packages. Clear the area around the suspicious package and notify the police immediately. In evacuating a building, avoid standing in front of windows or other potentially hazardous areas. Do not restrict sidewalk or streets to be used by emergency officials. Move out of the way!

DURING

In a building explosion, get out of the building as quickly and calmly as possible.

If items are falling off of bookshelves or from the ceiling, get under a sturdy table or desk.

If there is a fire:

- Stay low to the floor and exit the building as quickly as possible.
- Cover nose and mouth with a damp cloth.
- When approaching a closed door, use the palm of your hand and forearm to feel the lower, middle and upper parts of the door. If it is not hot, brace yourself against the door and open it slowly. If it is hot to the touch, do not open the door - seek an alternate escape route.
- Heavy smoke and poisonous gases collect first along the ceiling. Stay below the smoke at all times.

AFTER

1 *Remain calm* and be patient. Think through the consequences of all your actions.
2 Follow the advice of local emergency officials.
3 Listen to your radio or television for news and instructions.
4 If the disaster occurs near you, check for injuries.
5 Give first aid and get help for seriously injured people.
6 Follow procedures for "General Post Emergency and Disaster Response"
7 Confine or secure your pets.

If you are trapped in debris:

1 Use a flashlight or a light stick. Try to avoid using matches - in case of a gas leak.
2 Stay in your area so that you don't kick up dust. Cover your mouth with a damp (if available) handkerchief or clothing.
3 Tap on a pipe or wall so that rescuers can hear where you are. Use a whistle if one is available. Shout only as a last resort—shouting can cause a person to inhale dangerous amounts of dust.

Note: Untrained persons should not attempt to rescue people who are inside a collapsed building. Wait for emergency personnel to arrive.

Chemical Agents

A. Chemical agents are poisonous gases, liquids or solids that have toxic effects on peoples, animals or plants. Most chemical agents cause serious injuries or death.

B. Severity of injuries depends on the type and amount of the chemical agent used, and the duration of exposure.

C. Were a chemical agent attack to occur, authorities would instruct citizens to either seek shelter where they are and seal the premises or evacuate immediately. Exposure to chemical agents can be fatal. Leaving the shelter to rescue or assist victims can be a deadly decision. There is no assistance that the untrained can offer that would likely be of any value to the victims of chemical agents.

Biological Agents

A. Biological agents are organisms or toxins that have illness-producing effects on people, livestock and crops.

B. Because biological agents cannot necessarily be detected and may take time to grow and cause a disease, it is almost impossible to know that a biological attack has occurred. If government officials become aware of a biological attack through an informant or warning by terrorists, they would most likely instruct citizens to either seek shelter where they are and seal the premises or evacuate immediately.

C. A person affected by a biological agent requires the immediate attention of professional medical personnel. Some agents are contagious, and victims may need to be quarantined. Also, some medical facilities may not receive victims for fear of contaminating the hospital population.

D. Quarantining yourself in your own home might be the best solution when professional help is unavailable.

Other preparedness considerations

A. Be prepared—keep a gas mask handy at home, at work (especially in high-rise office buildings where the mask can help you escape in smoky or dusty conditions), and in the trunk of your car. A gas mask by your bedside is a good option.

B. If you fear you have been exposed to biological agents (Anthrax, plague, Tularemia, Brucellosis, Q fever, smallpox, viral encephalitis, or hemorrhagic fever, etc.) do the following during the one to six day incubation period before symptoms arise.

NOTE: *Implement these suggestions at your own risk. Your success against these agents will vary according to exposure, the prior state of your immune system, and many other factors.*

Do NOT begin antibiotic treatment until symptoms appear. Early or excessive use of antibiotics will destroy the natural bacterial flora in your intestinal tract and render your immune system less effective.

A. Stop eating your normal, cooked food diet.

B. Begin a very light diet (almost light fasting) of raw fruits and vegetables and juices (no commercial products with artificial or natural sweeteners).

C. Drink a lot of water, but do not drink water from public water supplies; avoid chlorine or fluoride. It is recommended installing a water purifying system in your home before a major biological attack occurs. Once it does, there will be a run on equipment. Have several bottles of aerobic-type oxygen liquid on hand for water purification. Oxygen-based purifiers are far safer and better than chemicals or bleach.

1. If you begin to have symptoms, begin antibiotic treatment immediately, under the care of a physician, if available. Chances are high that despite government assurances, there may not be enough antibiotics to go around in a major biological attack, so it is important to live healthily and stockpile natural alternatives. Learn to live with alternative remedies before your life depends on them since it takes some skill and sensitivity to learn to recognize your own body's feedback signals giving you hints about what it needs. Remember, too, that natural solutions only work well when your body is NOT loaded down with food, especially junk food or cooked food, which have no live enzymes.

2. Leave any area where infection is growing. Find temporary housing in rural areas. It is best to make arrangements with friends and relatives beforehand. This is important to avoid continual exposure even to low levels of contaminants. Wear your gas mask in the car when leaving town. Don't worry about looking silly—it may save your life.

3. If you can't leave the area, follow the previous suggestions for "sheltering in place".

When in public wear a gas mask as long as you can do so without undue stress. You must remove it to eat and drink, unless it has a built in water straw. Remember most gas mask cartridges are good for no more than 24 hours, usually even less.

PREPARING FOR A PANDEMIC INFLUENZA OUTBREAK

The Self Imposed Reverse Isolation (SIRQ) Plan

1) Protecting the Family – Building a Safe Haven

a. Protecting the family from the influenza virus is central to the plan.

b. This requires that families sequester themselves from the outside world in order to avoid infection.

    i.   Children should not go to school or play with friends.

    ii.   Parents should work from home as much as possible.

    iii.   The family should not attend public events (sporting events, cultural events, religious services, etc.).

    iv.   If family members do have to leave sequestration, they must be educated and committed to maintaining protection.

c. Parents

    i.   Must establish their home as a protected cell.

ii. Must understand that as long as their family is sequestered they are safe, but safety is only good AS LONG AS EVERY FAMILY MEMBER REMAINS SAFE AND DOES NOT BRING THE INFECTION HOME.

iii. Must understand the importance of not allowing children to interact with others outside the family during the time the plan is in place.

iv. Must know how to remain safe when they leave the home:
    1 Protective equipment,
    2 Protective methods of interacting in an infectious environment.

v. Must have their homes prepared for a disruption in services.

d. Children. Are at high risk for transmission of disease because of less than ideal hygiene, close contact with others in closed environments, inadequate hand washing, etc.

i. Need to be sequestered in family groups.

ii. Need to be isolated from others who are potentially infected.

iii. Need to be trained in methods of protecting themselves from infection at their level.

2) Protecting the Individual

a. During an influenza pandemic, any individual that has to interact with the outside world must consider all they come in contact with as being infected.

b. Individuals must know how to interact in such an environment:

i. Need education and training about how to protect themselves.

ii. Need protective equipment to allow them to interact.

3) Protecting the Community

a. Community leadership must support the SIRQ plan and encourage its implementation:

i. Educating leaders, families and individuals about the plan.

ii. Implementation of reverse quarantine protection early (BEFORE THE INFECTION HITS THE COMMUNITY).

iii. Cancellation of schools, meetings, public venues, etc. (BEFORE THE INFECTION STARTS)

iv. Identify key services and individuals essential to these services:

v. Provide or strongly encourage personal protection use in all essential sectors early.

vi. Plan on contingencies

vii. Must provide venues for education of individuals and families.

viii. Should facilitate obtaining protective equipment for individuals or groups.

ix. Must lead by example.

This plan can be implemented without government or community support. A family or individual could use this plan and protect themselves as long as they are willing to keep themselves separate.

BIOLOGICAL AND CHEMICAL AGENT DISPERSION

Facts About Biological and Chemical Agents

1. Nerve gas and many other deadly gases cannot be sensed.

2. Some of the symptoms of nerve gas poisoning are as follows:

    a.   A feeling of tightness or constriction in the chest.
    b.   The onset of an unexplained runny nose.
    c.   Small, pin-point size pupils.
    d.   A drawing, slightly painful sensation in the eyes or unexplained dim vision.
    e.   Difficulty breathing.
    f.   Increased salivation and excessive sweating.
    g.   Nausea, vomiting, and abdominal cramps.
    h.   Generalized muscular twitching, jerking, and staggering.
    i.   Headaches, drowsiness, a sense of confusion, and a possible coma.
    j.   Death.

3. Biological agents are organisms or toxins that can kill or incapacitate people, livestock, and crops. They can be dispersed by aerosols, animal carriers, and food and water contamination.

4. Chemical agents are poisonous gases, liquids, or solids that have toxic effects on people, animals, or plants. They can be released by bombs, sprayed by aircraft and boats, and used to contaminate air, food, and water supplies.

5. In the event of a biological or chemical attack, you might be instructed to either take immediate shelter where you are and seal the premises or evacuate the area immediately. Follow the Instructions !!!

6. Become aware of the DOT warning placards used for in-transit hazardous materials

What to do *DURING* a Biological or Chemical Dispersion

1. What you should do is to evacuate the area for the amount of time that the authorities say. If an official evacuation is declared, **LEAVE IMMEDIATELY !**

2. In the event of an industrial accident or terrorist attack or other similar problem a broadcast might be made on the EAS (Emergency Alert System) following a general alert signal. It will be broadcasted on the radio, television, loudspeakers, and/or wide area broadcast systems. An example message would be as such: "Attention! Attention! A threat of (nerve gas contamination, radioactive contamination, or whatever the threat is) exists!" The direction of the cloud and the estimated time of arrival and path will be announced along with defensive action that each citizen should take.

3. If you have immediate access to a gas mask or scuba or scuba equipment, use it and then proceed to evacuate. If it is not immediately available do not go looking for it. It will be to late. If you can wear you PPE (Personal Protective Equipment) which includes: long-sleeved shirt, long pants, gloves, and a gas mask, so you can be as protected as much as possible.

4. Take your 72-hour kit (or preferably 96-hour kit). Lock your home or office.

5. Use travel routes specified by local authorities—don't use shortcuts because certain areas may be impassable or dangerous.

6. Listen to local authorities. Your local authorities will provide you with the most accurate information specific to an event in your area. Staying tuned to local radio and television, and following their instructions is your safest choice.

7. There should be **no** reason to stay behind when an official evacuation order is announced. But if the situation arises that you cannot evacuate, or you are asked to **"shelter in place"** the following are listed some precautions that can be made. If you are advised by local officials to **"shelter in place"**.

IN-PLACE SHELTERING

Authorities have long recognized that it would be extremely difficult to evacuate whole counties in the event of a disaster such as a bio-chemical hazard/incident or chemical spill. The population is too great with too few exit routes. Evacuation is preferable when possible, but if it isn't an option, people can do what is called "in-place sheltering" with some simple preparation. This means that a person sets up a shelter in their own home until the air-borne hazard passes, which could be in several hours or many days. "In place sheltering" involves two types of sheltering.

    a) Sealing yourself indoors
    b) Quarantining yourself indoors

Listen for OFFICIAL information to see what kind you need to do. To seal yourself indoors there are some special considerations to take other than just locking the doors. IN ADVANCE, select a room in your home where you would do the in-place sheltering. An upstairs and interior room is best, as some chemical hazards are heavier than air and travel along the ground and will enter basement shelters. Then make a list and keep it handy of what you will keep in that room or put there quickly if you have to shelter there. You will need to have:

Necessary:

    a) 200 sq. ft. (1 roll) plastic sheeting (4 mill is better than 3 mill but you can use down to 2 mil)
    b) 1 or 2 rolls of duct tape
    c) A battery powered radio or TV to check for OFFICIAL news
    d) Important personal medications for you and your family
    e) A flashlight or light stick - in case you lose power - do not use candles or lanterns that burn valuable oxygen

Optional:

    a) A port-a-potty, (5 gal. bucket lined with heavy duty lawn/leaf garbage bags and some RV/ holding tank toilet chemical or a pail of dirt and a lid or plastic snap-on toilet seat.
    b) Books, games, or other diversions (do not count on videos you will be covering your outlets)
    c) A FRS and/or ham radio to get information from local authorities - this does not displace official information sources - *REMEMBER* rumors are not official information.

d) A telephone or cell phone
e) Water or something to drink
f) Food to munch on but not salty foods

It's is better to have this planned in advance and readily accessible than to have to think it up and find it on the spot. Depending on the distance you are from the bio-chemical hazard/incident you could have as little a 5 minutes and as much time as an hour but not much more than that. Hazardous fumes, vapors and smoke follow the wind patterns. In most areas this is 2 - 3 miles per hour except around canyons and seashores where it can be anywhere from 2 to 40 miles per hour.

Most people can walk 2 - 3 miles per hour. SO, if you are not in the immediate path of danger you will have time to get to a place and shelter there. So run - don't walk. To calculate where a good place is, figure any where you can normally, walk to in 5 minutes, realizing that in the event of a incident panic and chaos set in. You will need to plan on being "sealed in" your place for a minimum ONE hour in the absence of official information or longer. Mother nature does a good job of cleaning up chemical hazards/incidents using normal wind patterns and sunlight. This means that most of the dangerous levels of toxic problems sealed against for about an hour.

NOTE: You may still need to stay quarantined indoors for a much longer time just not "sealed in". Our homes cannot provide us with sufficient oxygen to seal ourselves in for long periods of time. You WILL die of asphyxiation if you try this, so don't. Besides it is next to impossible to seal an entire house in a reasonable amount of time, so choose a single room large enough with oxygen for all the intended occupants.

Side note: Full size dogs use twice the amount of oxygen as a full grown adult so you determine if Fido is worth saving.

Quarantining yourself includes:

First:

Turn on a radio or TV for official information.

Second:

You will need to turn off all mechanical or electrical operated air intake or air exchange to your home, business, school, or church, etc., namely your furnace (and gas main shut off) or air conditioner, chimney flue dampers and any fans. Do not take the time to get on your roof to cover vents and/or chimney openings.

Third:

Close, lock and secure your home (windows, doors, animal entries, etc.).

Fourth:

1. Gather your family and any pets you want to save and the listed supplies into your selected room, and using the plastic sheeting and duct tape, make the room as air-tight as possible.

2. Wet some (soaking wet) towels and jam them in the cracks under the doors. Where possible select a room large enough to maximized the amount of oxygen you will have until it is safe to come out.

3. Cover over windows, heat vents, light switches, power sockets, fire places, baseboard gaps, light fixtures, and entire door frames with duct tape and/or plastic. It is best to have these pre-cut, well in advance to cover every opening. You can in advance, caulk some cracks and small air leaks into that room.

4. To determine oxygen needs and occupancy have everyone in the room in a standing position stretch their arms out fully. If they can do this without touching anyone else's outstretched arms/fingers there is enough oxygen for one hour. (i.e. a 8 foot by 6 foot typical bathroom holds enough oxygen for 2 adults and one child under 6 years of age.

5. Then limit activity and oxygen usage.

6. If the power goes out do not use lanterns or candles. This uses valuable oxygen. Light sticks or flashlights are a better source of light.

7. Stay inside you sealed shelter until you are told, *officially*, it is safe to leave. Realize you may still need to stay indoors, quarantined, for a longer amount of time. In the absence of official information you should leave your shelter after one hours time if you have only allotted yourself an hours worth of air.

Note: Quarantining yourself does not include or involve sealing yourself in with any kind of duct tape or plastic.

WHAT To Do *AFTER* a Biological or Chemical Dispersion

1. Follow the instructions of local and government authorities !

2. If you evacuated, do not return home until it is determined safe to do so.

3. If you feel or suspect you have been affected by the situation contact the local hospital to see if they are receiving patients, if so go get help. Some biological poisonings will require quarantine. If you are turned away by a hospital or treatment center quarantine yourself in your home for the time told to you by the authorities.

4. If you find that others have been affected you may still want to quarantine yourself for 2 weeks or longer depending on the extent of the problem.

Common other Biological / Chemical Agents

Name	Quarantine	Symptoms/Comments	Treatment
Aflatoxin	2 days	liver cancer	None
Anthrax	14 days spores	malaise, fatigue, cough, respiratory	antibiotics

		distress, fever, cyanosis, dyspnea, diaphoresis, stridor, toxemia	Ciprofloxacin tetracycline
Botulinum	0 days	weakness, dizziness, dry mouth nausea, vomiting, difficulty swallowing and talking, blurred vision, drooping eyelids, progressive paralysis, cyanosis, respiratory distress	oxygen, antitoxin
Brucellosis	2 days	joint and muscle dysfunction	Antibiotics like tetracyclines, rifampicin and the aminoglycosides streptomycin and gentamicin
Chlorine	2 days	eye and skin burns on contact, broncho-spasm, cyanosis	treat for burns, CPR, artificial ventilation
Cholera	6 -7 days	toxemia, vomiting, diarrhea, dehydration, shock	re-hydration, tetracycline erythromycin
Clostridium	2 days	Perfirgems - gaseous rotting of the flesh	Penicillin prophylaxis kills clostridia
Plague (bacterium)	90-100 days	bubonic, septicemia, pneumonic, high Fever , chills, toxemia, streptomycin headache, pneumonia, hemoptysis, malaise, meningitis, dyspnea, stridor, cyanosis, respiratory failure, death	antibiotic, streptomycin doxycycline Chloramphenicol Ciprofloxacin
Q-Fever	0 days	fever, chills, headache, severe sweats, malaise, fatigue, skin rash, respiratory problems	Tetracycline doxycycline
Ricin (toxin)	0 days	fever, nausea, vomiting, bloody diarrhea, abdominal cramps, difficulty breathing, kidney failure, paralysis circulatory collapse-paralysis	therapy for acute lung injury and pulmonary edema activated charcoal gastric lavage
Salmonella	2 days	diarrheal illness, headache, abdominal pain, nausea	re-hydration Ciprofloxacin
Small Pox (virus)	30 days	malaise, fever chills, vomiting, headache, 2-3 days later: flat red spots change to pus filled lesions on skin and mouth and throat	intravenous hydration, nutrition, pain control, antiviral drugs

Staphylococcal Enterotoxin B	l 2 days	SEB - fever, chills, shortness of breath, nausea, vomiting	artificial ventilation
Tularemia `	30 days	septicemia, pneumonic, high fever, chills, headache, hemoptysis, (bacterium) malaise, meningitis, dyspnea, stridor, cyanosis, respiratory failure, death	antibiotics

Common Nerve, Blood, Chocking and Blister Agents

Chemical	Comments	Treatment
GA	Tabun atropine, pralidoxime,	CPR. remove victim from area and wash entire body especially hair with soapy water
GB	Sarin - colorless liquid – evaporates quickly	pralidoxime, atropine, CPR, remove victim from area and wash entire body especially hair with soapy water
GD	Soman atropine,	pralidoxime. CPR, remove victim from area and wash entire body especially hair with soapy water
VX	thick oil like liquid	atropine, pralidoxime, CPR, remove victim form area and wash entire body especially hair with soapy water
H	distilled nitrogen mustard gas - blistering and burning of eyes and skin	irrigation of eyes and skin, CPR
HD, HS	mustard gas - blistering and burning of eyes and skin	irrigation of eyes and skin, CPR
HT	phosgene gas – Carbonyl Chloride	irrigation of eyes and skin, CPR
AC	Hydrogen Cyanide - lighter than air- asphyxiation	CPR, artificial ventilation
CK	Cyanogen Chloride – heavier than air - asphyxiation	CPR, artificial ventilation
MDI	Methyl Isocyanate – heavier than air- respiratory distress, skin rash, eye irritation	irrigation of eyes and skin induce vomiting

Nuclear - Chemical Decontamination Kit

- 1 5 or 6 gallon bucket with lid
- 1 - 2 Spray Bottle (s).
- 1 Bulb Syringe.
- 2 Large Bath Towels.
- - 8 Wash-Cloths
- 1 pkg. Baby Wipes
- 1 Small bottle of liquid soap.
- 1 Small bottle of shampoo.
- 1 - 4 39 gallon size (1 mil) yard bag(s)
- 1 - 4 Twist ties.

apart from "Decon Kit" but helpful and maybe necessary.

Before entering your shelter after a nuclear or chemical incident you need to decontaminate your entire body.

a. Carefully open and arrange your decon kit in such a way that you can reach everything and still keep all possible contamination in one localized area.

b. Step into the large basin or 39/55 gallon bag so it can catch all water and decontamination com ing off of your body.

c. Carefully strip off all of your clothes. Yes all of them. This is not a fashion show or a time to worry about modesty rather a time to worry about saving your life. Put ALL of your clothes in a 39/55 gallon bag. You may have to cut your clothes off. Speed is an issue. The faster the better. D. Remove ALL jewelry, eyeglasses, and plastic coated pictures, identification cards, etc. you may want to save and put them aside. These to will have to be decontaminated with water so realize you will not be able to save non-plastic coated papers or cloth items.

d. Shower completely with an *outside* shower or hose.

    1. **NOTE**: *If you do not have and outside shower or hose then do the following:*

    2. A Open a spray bottle and fill it with water and spray your entire body head to toe with emphasis on all the hair on your body, wherev er it is. Your hair must be cleaned well.

    3. B Take one washcloth and blot down (do not wipe the contamination into your pores) your entire body head to toe, not forgetting the genital areas and orifices, then the face then the rest of the body. Place the wash cloth in the 39/55 gallon bag.

    4. C Open the spray bottle again and fill it with 2 tablespoons of bleach - If it is a chemical incident. If it is nuclear incident straight water is okay. Spray your entire body again. Be careful around eyes, ears, nose, and mouth not to do this area if you are using the bleach solution. You do not need bleach in those parts.

    5. D Fill the small basin water and with the liquid soap, shampoo, the remaining water in the spray bottle, and a DIFFERENT wash cloth. Soap up and scrub your entire body, especially cracks and crevasses, your jewelry and id cards you want to save. You cannot save cloth or paper items.

6. E Fill up your spray bottle one or more times and rinse down your body completely.
7. F. Open the baby-wipes package and use one or more to clean around your eyes, nose, mouth and ears.
8. G. Dry off completely and step out of the large basin or bag. Place all towels, washcloths, and other cleaning instruments into the 39/55 gallon bag.
9. H. If it is a nuclear incident, with the Rad meter, take readings over your entire body AWAY from your decontamination basin and contaminated clothes and water. You need to bring the radiation level down to 1 R. or less. If the radiation level has not decreased continue washing until it does.
a. Repeat the process if necessary using clean towels and washcloths.
10. J. Seal up the 39/55 gallon plastic bag with the wire tie and place as far away from the shelter door as possible without risking further contamination.
11. K. Once you are "clean" you may enter your shelter and put on some clean clothes

XXIV Urban Survival

While we all want to do our best to prepare for a coming crisis, very few of us are really prepared to pack up the old Winnebago and head for the hills. Most Americans are going to stay in the cities. Most of us depend on the city for our livelihood. If we are going to live in cities, then we can be better prepared by at least earning a good income and collecting supplies while leaving options for exiting the city at the appropriate time.

Cities are artificial

Every city is an artificial construct. Modern cities formed as people came together to conduct business, participate in social interaction, and benefit from efficiencies in public services (such as schools, sewers, water, etc.) and a common defense. Yet cities cannot survive alone. They need resources from the country; most notably, food, water and electricity. While electricity and water can sometimes be created or found within city limits, the acreage requirements of food dictate that no city could possibly feed its own people.

Read that last phrase carefully: "No city can feed its own people." Not one. Cities are, by their very nature, dependent on the importation of food. The advent of just-in-time delivery systems to our grocery stores means that most cities would run out of food within a week if supplies were for some reason disrupted.

Since cities are not self-sufficient, they have for a long time been entirely dependent on the American farmer for their support – something almost all Americans take for granted (except the farmer, of course…)

Risks in the City

The city presents some serious risks during a crisis. The five most serious ones are

> 1 The collapse of social order (riots, loss of security),
> 2 The failure of the water treatment and delivery systems,
> 3 The depletion of food supplies
> 4 The failure of the power grid
> 5 The risk you may be quarantined.

While not every situation will appear in every city, every situation will most certainly appear in some cities. Will that include yours? We'll tackle these one at a time:

Solutions in the City Okay, so you're stuck in the city. You've made the decision to stay. You've read the problems above, you believe they make sense, and you're intelligently frightened.

What now? You really have two strategies. You can:

- Stay and defend your house
- Bug out (leave the city and head for the hills)

This is not an either/or situation. You can begin by staying in your house and assessing the situation. You'll want to have a "bug-out" vehicle stocked and ready, just in case, if you can afford one, but you may never actually choose to bug out. You'll have to be the ultimate judge of this. Just remember that when you bug out, you face major risks and disadvantages.

Among these:

1. You're severely limited in how much you can carry
2. You have limited range due to fuel
3. You expose yourself to social chaos, roadblocks, random violence, etc.
4. Your house will certainly be looted while you're gone
5. You run the risk of mechanical breakdowns of your vehicle
6. You must have a place to go that is in better shape than where you currently are.

In general, unless you have a specific, known safe place as your final destination, it probably isn't wise to bug out. Just "heading for the hills" is a very poor plan. You might not make it. But heading for Grandma's house or some known, safe place could be a very good plan indeed, depending on whether Grandma is ready, willing and able to accept you! For these reasons (and more), staying and defending your house is sometimes the only reasonable course of action, even if it seems dangerous.

For the most part, looters and people looking for food are going to have plenty of easy victims, so if you show a little willingness to use force to defend your property, you'll likely send people on to the next house. That is, until the next house is already empty and you appear to be the last house on the block with any food and water left. If you're in a bad enough area, your neighbors may "gang up" on you and demand your supplies or your life.

This is truly a worst-case scenario, and unless you literally have a house full of battle rifles and people trained to use them (and the willingness to shoot your neighbors), you're sunk. This is why the best situation by far is to keep your neighbors informed and help them get prepared. Then you (both your member and non-member neighbors) can act as a group, defending your neighborhood and sharing the supplies you have with anyone willing to help defend you. (And don't think for a second that your non-member neighbors won't remember all that food storage in your garage!) When you have this kind of situation, your neighbors realize you are their lifeline. You supply them with food and water, and they will help support you because they are, in effect, supporting their own lives. The best situation is when your neighbors have their own food and water supplies. That way, they aren't depleting yours, and they have a strong motivation for getting together with you defend your neighborhood.

Storing (and Hiding) Your Food

Storing food is just as important in the city as in the country, but hiding it is far more important. That's because in the worst areas, marauders will be going from house to house, demanding your food or your life. If you're dumb enough to put everything you own in the obvious places, you might as well not buy it in the first place. They will find it. To count on having any amount of food left over after the marauders break in, you'll need to hide your food.

One alternative is to plan on defending your home with force. If you have enough gun-wise people in the house, and enough firearms and ammo, you can probably pull this off. But most of us aren't nearly as experienced with firearms as the gang members.

The best way to hide your food may be to bury it. You'll need airtight containers, long-term food that won't rot and you'll need to plan ahead. Bury your food at night so nobody will notice, and make sure you don't leave the map on the refrigerator door! (Better to memorize it!) Try to get the ground to look normal after you're all finished. You'll want to bury your food as early as possible because it gives the grass time to regrow over the spot. If you're in an area that snows, you'll have a great concealment blanket! Most food marauders won't go to the trouble to dig up food, especially if you insist you don't have any. Best plan: Have some smaller amount of food stashed around the house, letting them find something. Better to give them something and send them on their way.

The art of hiding your food is an ancient one. You've got to get creative. Use the walls, the floors, and the structure of the house. If hiding your food is simply not an available alternative, then try not to advertise it. Keep it put away in your house or garage in as discreet a manner as possible. Don't make a point of telling people that you have a year's supply (or more). Word gets around fast that Bro. Jones has a ton of food in his garage. Boxes of food fit nicely under beds, behind furniture, in the attic, etc.. Be Creative!! To sum up the food storage, you really have three strategies here:

- Store it all in your house and plan on defending it by force.
- Bury it in your yard in case you get overrun by looters.
- Store part of it in your house, and hide the bulk of it.
- Relocate all of it as soon as you recognize a major disaster is in progress

An alternative to burying that would be faster and easier would be to simply build a false wall in your garage and seal up your food behind the false wall. Sure, you might lose 2-3 feet of useable space in your garage, but the tradeoff is knowing everything is safe and sound.

Storing Extra Water

Water can be stored in exactly the same way, although you might want to bury the barrel before you actually fill it with water. Make sure you treat your storage water, rotate it or have filters on hand when you get ready to use it.

If you don't have a yard, or it's not practical to bury your water, you'll have to store water inside your house. This can get very tricky because water takes up a lot of space and it's very difficult to conceal. It's best to get containers made for long-term storage, but in a pinch, use what you can find, just make sure it's clean and food grade material. But a lot of these containers will deteriorate quickly, and they may break easily. Also, consider what happens if your water may be subjected to freezing. Will your containers survive? Be sure to leave enough air space to handle the expansion.

In order to prepare yourself for the water shortage, assuming you're going to stay in the city, stock at least six months of water at a minimum two gallons a day per person. That's nearly 400 gallons of water if you have two people. Of course, even with the best in-house preparations, you may find yourself depleted of water supplies. In this situation, one of your best defenses is to have a really good water filter (like the Katadyn filter) that can remove parasites and bacteria from the water. You can also treat your water in other ways (iodine, distillation, silver solution, bleach, etc.). Armed with these items, you can safely use stream or river water (or even pond water) for drinking.

WATER WELLS

By far, the best solution for obtaining long-term water supplies is to drill a well. Buy the best quality handpump available (cast-iron pumps) and a good cylinder. They will last a lifetime if installed properly. With this setup, you'll have a near-unlimited supply of water. The total cost of doing this, depending on where you live, ranges from about $4000 - $6000. Is it worth it? If you've got the money, probably so. However, many cities simply don't allow the drilling of wells, so you may not be able to get one drilled even if you want to.

The deeper your well, the more expensive it gets. Most well drilling companies charge by the foot. When water is deeper, you also need a bigger pump and a more powerful cylinder, so the costs tend to really grow the deeper you go. If you can find water at 20', you're very lucky and it might not cost you even $2000. If you have to go down to 200', it might cost you $7500, and you're at the depth limit of hand-powered pumps anyway.

Defending Your Life and Property

Let's talk about force. No doubt, there are plenty of nice people in this country, and in small towns and rural areas, people will find ways to cooperate and get along. However, some cities will suffer complete social breakdown and violence will rule. If you happen to be stuck in one of these cities, you're going to need to use force to defend your house. Hopefully, you won't find yourself in these circumstances, but if you do, the information below may be valuable.

Important: Do not use your lights at night. If you are stocking propane-powered lanterns, solar powered flashlights, or other unusual supplies, using them at night will announce to everyone within line of sight that you have more than the "usual" supplies. Expect them to come knocking in your door. At most, let a fire burn in the fireplace, but in general, avoid drawing attention to your house.

Defending your house is a crucial element on your stay-in-the-city plan. Make your house your fortress, and hold drills to help other family members practice some of the more common activities such as hiding, defending, evacuating, etc.

Some useful items for home defense include:

- A guard dog
- Pepper spray
- Firearms
- Smoke bombs (military-grade)

- Trip wires

The guard dog is certainly a welcome addition to any family trying to defend their house. Although he probably eats a lot of food, the investment is worth it. Dogs also tend to sleep light, so let them sleep right next to the food storage areas, and make sure you sleep within earshot. If the dog barks, don't consider it an annoyance, consider it an INTRUSION.

Pepper spray is a great alternative to the firearm. It will incapacitate people and certainly give them a painful experience to remember. On the downside (potentially), it might just remind them that next time they come back for food, they better kill you first. So understand the limitations of pepper spray.

Firearms are useful for obvious reasons. In the worst-case scenario, when looting is rampant, you may have to actually shoot someone to protect yourself or your family. If you're squeamish about pulling the trigger under these circumstances, don't plan to stay in the city. Use the "bug out" plan instead.

Smoke bombs can be useful for covering a planned escape from your house. You can purchase high volume smoke bombs that will quickly fill up any house with an unbreatheable cloud of military-grade white smoke.

Trip wires are great perimeter defenses. You can buy them from Cheaper Than Dirt (they run a few hundred dollars). They will give you early warning if someone is approaching. You can connect the tripwires to flares, shotgun shells, lightsticks or other warning devices. This way, you can have an audible or visible alert, your choice.

In addition to these devices, you can make significant fortification-style improvements to your home. While none of these are very affordable, they certainly help defend your home:

- Replace glass windows with non-breakable Plexiglas
- Add steel bars to the windows
- Replace all outside door locks with heavy-duty deadbolts
- Replace all outside doors with steel doors, preferably without windows
- Remove bushes and other shrubs where people might hide
- Black out the windows entirely to avoid light escaping at night
- Build secret hiding places for food, coins, or even people
- Create escape hatches or passageways
- Rig pepper-spray booby traps

These aren't as absurd as they might at first sound. Many living in rough cities already have steel bars covering their windows, and removing extra bushes and shrubs is a well known tactic for making your home a safer place.

LIGHT

To light your home when there's no electricity, try the following:

- Use LED flashlights and rechargeable solar charged batteries.
- Use propane-powered lanterns. You can find these in the camping section of your local Wal-Mart. Be sure to purchase extra mantles and store lots of propane.

- Purchase quality oil lamps and stock up on oil. You can also purchase cheap kerosene lamps from the Sportman's Guide or Wal-Mart, then simply purchase and store extra kerosene.
- Buy extra candles.
- Purchase lots of olive oil. Not only can you cook with it (and besides, it's a lot healthier than corn or vegetable oil), olive oil also burns as a clean candle fuel. You can float a wick in a jar half-full of olive oil and light the wick. Viola, a home-made candle. Olive oil is a fantastic item for your storage anyway because even if you purchase all the grains in the world, you'll still need cooking oil, and you obviously can't buy powdered cooking oil. Well-stored olive oil can last for thousands of years.

STAYING WARM

Did you know that people won't steal giant logs? Although they may easily steal wood you've already chopped, most people won't have any way of stealing logs. They're too heavy, and the vehicles won't have any gas left. For this reason, your best bet in regards to stocking fuel for your house is to stock up on UNCUT wood logs.

It takes research to find out how to get them, but you can find a source if you look hard enough. Or you can usually get a permit to go out and cut your own. The effort is worth it, because this will give you a ready-to-go source of heat and fuel that cannot be easily stolen. The catch, of course, is that you'll need equipment to cut and chop the wood. A chainsaw is REALLY nice in this way, but it requires fuel. Fortunately, chain saws don't use much fuel, so if you have a way to store as little as 50 gallons or so, you've got enough to power your chainsaw for a few years.

You'll need fuel stabilizers, too, which you can buy at your local Wal-Mart. (Be sure to buy extra chains for your chainsaw, too.) You'll also need splitting hardware. You can buy log splitters or just buy an axe, a wedge, and a sledgehammer. Better yet, buy all four so you have a choice of what to use. And remember, wood splits much better when it's frozen, too, so you might just wait until the cold hits in Winter to start splitting your wood. Only split a little at a time, because you don't want to end up with a big pile of nicely-split wood sitting out in your yard. It will invite theft from people who don't have any.

If you already have trees on your property, you're all set. Cut down about 4-5 cords right now, so they can start drying out, then chop them as you need 'em. A "cord" of wood, by the way, is a volume measurement. It's 8' x 4' x 4', or 128 cubic feet of Wood (stacked). Some people that sell wood will try to rip you off, so make sure you know what you're buying. If you purchase logs, it's better to get a price per linear foot, based on the diameter of the log. For example, you might ask for logs that are an average of 10" in diameter, and you'll ask how much the charge per linear foot would be. Something in the range of $1 - $2 would be great.

Relations With Neighbors

We've already mentioned the importance of getting along with your neighbors. It really is crucial to your city-based survival plan. The best situation to be in, is to have neighbors who are aware of the issues and who are getting ready by stocking their own food, water, and other supplies. Every neighbor who becomes self-reliant is one less neighbor you'll have to support.

The range of neighbor situations, from best to worst, is as follows:

- Best case: your neighbor is aware of and prepared for an emergency with their own supplies and training.
- Good case: your neighbor is aware of a potential crisis, and even though they don't have their own supplies, they're willing to help defend yours as long as you share
- Bad case: your neighbor didn't prepare for it, figuring they would just steal from you if things got bad. They are aware of YOUR supplies but don't have their own.
- Worst case: your neighbor isn't aware of anything, he's a violent, angry neighbor just released from prison. He is going to be caught off guard by the ensuing events and will likely attempt to use violence to get what he needs or wants.

Your decision on whether to stay in the city may depend greatly on the quality and quantity of your neighbors. If you do live in a bad neighborhood, do what you can to relocate. If you live in a good neighborhood, do the best you can to educate and inform your neighbors.

One More Reason To Move Out

If you really feel you need a firearm to protect yourself and your family, your best bet may be to move to a city or state where people are a lot more accepting of firearms. You'd be surprised what a difference the locale makes. Check the gun laws in any state you're considering moving to. Obviously, "cowboy" states like Arizona, Texas and Wyoming will have fewer restrictions on firearms (and, interestingly, they have less of a problem with gun violence). States where the population is more dense (like Florida, California, New York) tend to have much greater restrictions on private ownership of firearms.

XXV Bugging Out

Suppose you've changed your mind about this city thing. You are right smack in the middle of one of the worst-hit cities in the country. The looting is getting worse, the power has been out for two weeks, and your water supplies are running low. You still have enough gas in your truck to make it out of town… if you can get past the gangs, that is.

You've decided to **BUG OUT !**

Some basic pointers:

- Don't try to bug out in a Chevy Geo. You will likely need a big heavy 4x4 truck in order to go off-road and around stalled vehicles
- Get something that can carry at least 1000 pounds of supplies. A big 4x4 pickup will do nicely! Yes, it requires more fuel, but you can carry the fuel as cargo.
- Don't bug out unless you can have someone ride shotgun, literally. You will need an armed passenger in case you run into not-so-nice people.

WHAT TO TAKE

Ahh, the bug-out supply list. All this will fit in your truck. Here's what you should take if you're preparing to bug out with two people:

- Your 96 hour kits for each person in the vehicle
- 20 gallons of water
- 40 gallons of extra fuel or more (and a full gas tank)

WHERE TO GO

If you have a designated place of refuge (Grandma's house, a cabin in the woods, etc.), head straight for it. If not, you're basically driving anywhere you can go, so try to head for an area that is forested and near a creek or river where you can get some water.

Choosing to remain in the city is a rational choice in many situations. However, the further away you can get from the population centers in general, the better your chances of surviving. Perhaps you have a difficult time actually accepting that a major disaster is going to be as bad as described. And after all, if you leave the city, sell out, quit your job, and move to the country – and then nothing bad happens – you will have disrupted your life, and you may find yourself broke, jobless, and homeless. You COULD assume it will be a mild event, which is also a credible possibility. In that case, surviving in the city will be quite feasible, especially if you have neighbors that can support your efforts and you don't live in a dangerous city with high racial tensions.

However, the very nature of a major disaster means that if only one or two major infrastructure components goes down, the ripple effect will quickly create a much worse scenario. It seems there is very little room for "mild" effects unless they are miniscule. The most likely scenario at this point clearly points to massive disruptions, severe shortages in food and water, loss of power in some areas, and a breakdown of social order in certain areas where the population density is high. But you can survive anything with good planning, an open mind, and plenty of practice. Why not start now?

WHAT STATES ARE BEST?

Today, millions of American families are considering a move to another part of the country because of the growing economic problems that the United States is experiencing. In the past, most Americans would normally just ride recessions out and would be able to safely assume that things would get back to "normal" sooner or later. But for many Americans, this time just feels different. Unemployment has never stayed this high for this long since the Great Depression. Thousands of our factories and millions of our jobs have been shipped overseas, and many of our formerly great cities (such as Detroit) have been turned into deindustrialized wastelands. The federal government and most state governments are essentially bankrupt and continue to get into more debt at an accelerating pace.

Meanwhile, Helicopter Ben Bernanke and his cohorts at the Federal Reserve have fired up the printing presses in a desperate attempt to revive the U.S. economy. Many believe that by flooding the financial system with paper money that they are setting in motion a series of events which will eventually lead to the death of the dollar. With so much wrong with our economy, is it any wonder why more Americans are deeply concerned about the state of the economy today than at any other time since World War II?

As the economy continues to crumble and as millions of Americans find it nearly impossible to find a good job, many of them have been wondering if things are any better in other parts of the country. And without a doubt, some areas of the U.S. are complete and total disaster zones at this point. For example, so many houses have been abandoned in Detroit that the mayor has proposed bulldozing one-fourth of the city. In Las Vegas, it was estimated that approximately 65 percent of all homes with a mortgage were "underwater" at the height of the housing crash. The number of people unemployed in the state of California is approximately equal to the populations of Nevada, New Hampshire and Vermont. Unfortunately, there is every indication that the U.S. economy is going to get even worse.

So if the economy does collapse, where should you go? What would be the best U.S. state to move to? Well, in choosing a place to live, the following are some of the factors that you will want to consider....

#1 You Need To Make Money

Unless you are independently wealthy or you work for yourself, you are going to have to find a way to make money. For most people, that means getting a job. Unfortunately, jobs are only going to become harder and harder to get in the years ahead. In fact, right now there are not a lot of areas in the U.S. where jobs are plentiful. It has been said that there is some work up in Montana and in the Dakotas because of all the oil that has been found there, but other than that there are not a whole lot of bright spots out there. Many Americans are trying to become independent and build their own businesses, but that is not always an easy thing to do either.

#2 Lower Housing Prices And A Lower Standard Of Living

Many Americans are packing up and moving from states that have a very high cost of living (such as New York or California) and are moving to areas where housing is cheaper and where it doesn't take as much money to live. After all, why pay half a million for a house when you can get the same house for $200,000 in another part of the country? Many people are discovering that a lifestyle with fewer bills and a smaller monthly budget can be extremely liberating.

#3 Food And Water Independence

More Americans than ever are becoming concerned about food and water independence. After all, if the U.S. economy does totally collapse someday, how will we all feed our families? 100 years ago, most Americans grew at least some of their own food. Today, very few Americans do that. Fortunately, a growing number of Americans have started to grow "survival gardens" and/or have started to store up emergency food supplies. If the inflationary policies of the Federal Reserve do end up totally trashing the U.S. dollar, the food that you and your family have stored up will end up being a **great** investment. In addition, in 2010 many Americans are looking for a place where it is possible to grow food and where water is plentiful when picking out a new area to move to. Owning a fertile piece of land is going to be a great asset to have in the years to come.

#4 Community And Crime

If the U.S. economy does collapse, rioting and gang violence will turn many American cities into war zones. Just remember what happened to New Orleans after Hurricane Katrina hit. That is a Sunday picnic compared to what could happen if the U.S. economy falls apart. Many Americans can see what is coming and they are moving out of the big cities. But wherever you move to, you will not be alone. So do your research ahead of time. Are you moving to an area where the people are friendly and helpful? Will you have family and close friends in the region? It is always good to have a support system around you - especially when times get hard.

#5 During Hard Times Weather Makes A Difference

During good times it is fairly easy to live just about anywhere, but if the economy falls apart the elements will become a bigger factor. For example, if you plan to totally rely on the power company, do you really want to live some place where it gets down to 20 or 30 below on a regular basis? What is your backup plan if basic services shut down for an extended period of time? How will you provide power and heat for your family? In addition, do you want to move some place incredibly hot if you can't always count on having air conditioning? The truth is that weather can make a huge difference in your lifestyle. The desert or the mountains may sound appealing now, but when you are trying to grow food they may not seem so great then.

These are just a few of the things to take into account when choosing a new place to live. There are certainly many others to think about as well. But all of us should be starting to think about these things. Now is the time to prepare - not later. If and When the U.S. economy does collapse, millions of American families will be scrambling to come up with a plan, but by then it will be too late. Unfortunately, we are already starting to see signs of inflation. The price of gas is rising again, and we've all seen the shocking price increases for agricultural commodities.

So what are some of the states that many Americans are choosing to move to?

Well, in no particular order, the following are some of the states that Americans have been moving to in an attempt to insulate themselves from the coming economic problems

1. Montana
2. Idaho
3. North Dakota
4. South Dakota
5. Wyoming
6. Colorado
7. Nebraska
8. Kansas
9. Alaska
10. Oklahoma
11. Arkansas
12. Missouri
13. Tennessee
14. Kentucky
15. West Virginia
16. Maine
17. Washington
18. Oregon
19. Vermont
20. New Hampshire
21. Virginia (the mountains)
22. North Carolina

XXVI Sarajevo War Experience

The 100 Items to Disappear First...

The 100 items to disappear first in Sarajevo at the start of the war...

1. Generators (Good ones cost dearly. Gas storage, risky. Noisy...target of thieves; maintenance etc.)
2. Water Filters/Purifiers
3. Portable Toilets
4. Seasoned Firewood. Wood takes about 6 - 12 months to become dried, for home uses.
5. Lamp Oil, Wicks, Lamps (First Choice: Buy CLEAR oil. If scarce, stockpile ANY!)
6. Coleman Fuel. Impossible to stockpile too much.
7. Guns, Ammunition, Pepper Spray, Knives, Clubs, Bats & Slingshots.
8. Hand-can openers, & hand egg beaters, whisks.
9. Honey/Syrups/white, brown sugar
10. Rice - Beans - Wheat
11. Vegetable Oil (for cooking) Without it food burns/must be boiled etc.,)
12. Charcoal
13. Lighter Fluid (Will become scarce suddenly)
14. Water Containers (Urgent Item to obtain.) Any size. Small: HARD CLEAR PLASTIC ONLY - note - food grade if for drinking.
15. Propane Cylinders (Urgent: Definite shortages will occur.
16. Survival Guide Book.
17. Mantles: Aladdin, Coleman, etc. (Without this item, longer-term lighting is difficult.)
18. Baby Supplies: Diapers/formula. ointments/aspirin, etc.
19. Washboards, Mop Bucket w/wringer (for Laundry)
20. Cookstoves (Propane, Coleman & Kerosene)
21. Vitamins
22. Propane Cylinder Handle-Holder (Urgent: Small canister use is dangerous without this item)
23. Feminine Hygiene/Haircare/Skin products.
24. Thermal underwear (Tops & Bottoms)
25. Bow saws, axes and hatchets, Wedges (also, honing oil)
26. Aluminum Foil Reg. & Heavy Duty (Great Cooking and Barter Item)
27. Gasoline Containers (Plastic & Metal)
28. Garbage Bags (Impossible To Have Too Many).
29. Toilet Paper, Kleenex, Paper Towels
30. Milk - Powdered & Condensed (Shake Liquid every 3 to 4 months)
31. Garden Seeds (Non-Hybrid) (A MUST)
32. Clothes pins/line/hangers (A MUST)
33. Coleman's Pump Repair Kit
34. Tuna Fish (in oil)

35. Fire Extinguishers (or..large box of Baking Soda in every room)
36. First aid kits
37. Batteries (all sizes...buy furthest-out for Expiration Dates)
38. Garlic, spices & vinegar, baking supplies
39. Big Dogs (and plenty of dog food)
40. Flour, yeast & salt
41. Matches. {"Strike Anywhere" preferred.) Boxed, wooden matches will go first
42. Writing paper/pads/pencils, solar calculators
43. Insulated ice chests (good for keeping items from freezing in Wintertime.)
44. Workboots, belts, Levis & durable shirts
45. Flashlights/Lightsticks & torches, "No. 76 Dietz" Lanterns
46. Journals, Diaries & Scrapbooks (jot down ideas, feelings, experience; Historic Times)
47. Garbage cans Plastic (great for storage, water, transporting - if with wheels)
48. Men's Hygiene: Shampoo, Toothbrush/paste, Mouthwash/floss, nail clippers, etc.
49. Cast iron cookware (sturdy, efficient)
50. Fishing supplies
51. Tools
52. Mosquito coils/repellent, sprays/creams
53. Duct Tape
54. Tarps/stakes/twine/nails/rope/spikes
55. Candles
56. Laundry Detergent (liquid)
57. Backpacks, Duffel Bags
58. Garden tools & supplies
59. Scissors, fabrics & sewing supplies
60. Canned Fruits, Veggies, Soups, stews, etc.
61. Bleach (plain, NOT scented: 4 to 6% sodium hypochlorite)
62. Canning supplies, (Jars/lids/wax)
63. Knives & Sharpening tools: files, stones, steel
64. Bicycles...Tires/tubes/pumps/chains, etc
65. Sleeping Bags & blankets/pillows/mats
66. Carbon Monoxide Alarm (battery powered)
67. Board Games, Cards, Dice
68. d-con Rat poison, MOUSE PRUFE II, Roach Killer
69. Mousetraps, Ant traps & cockroach magnets
70. Paper plates/cups/utensils (stock up, folks)
71. Baby wipes, oils, waterless & Antibacterial soap (saves a lot of water)
72. Rain gear, rubberized boots, etc.
73. Shaving supplies (razors & creams, talc, after shave)
74. Hand pumps & siphons (for water and for fuels)
75. Soy Sauce, vinegar, bullions/gravy/soup bases
76. Reading glasses
77. Chocolate/Cocoa/Tang/Punch (water enhancers)

78. "Survival-in-a-Can"
79. Woolen clothing, scarves/ear-muffs/mittens
80. Boy Scout Handbook, / also Leaders Catalog
81. Roll-on Window Insulation Kit (MANCO)
82. Graham crackers, saltines, pretzels, Trail mix/Jerky
83. Popcorn, Peanut Butter, Nuts
84. Socks, Underwear, T-shirts, etc. (extras)
85. Lumber (all types)
86. Wagons & carts (for transport to and from)
87. Cots & Inflatable mattress's
88. Gloves: Work/warming/gardening, etc.
89. Lantern Hangers
90. Screen Patches, glue, nails, screws,, nuts & bolts
91. Teas
92. Coffee
93. Cigarettes
94. Wine/Liquors (for bribes, medicinal, etc,)
95. Paraffin wax
96. Glue, nails, nuts, bolts, screws, etc.
97. Chewing gum/candies
98. Atomizers (for cooling/bathing)
99. Hats & cotton neckerchiefs
100.   Goats/chickens

From a Sarajevo War Survivor:

Experiencing horrible things that can happen in a war - death of parents and friends, hunger and malnutrition, endless freezing cold, fear, sniper attacks.

1. Stockpiling helps. but you never know how long trouble will last, so locate near renewable food sources.

2. Living near a well with a manual pump is like being in Eden.

3. After awhile, even gold can lose its luster. But there is no luxury in war quite like toilet paper. Its surplus value is greater than gold's.

4. If you had to go without one utility, lose electricity - it's the easiest to do without (unless you're in a very nice climate with no need for heat.)

5. Canned foods are awesome, especially if their contents are tasty without heating. One of the best things to stockpile is canned gravy - it makes a lot of the dry unappetizing things you find to eat in war somewhat edible. Only needs enough heat to "warm", not to cook. It's cheap too, especially if you buy it in bulk.

6. Bring some books - escapist ones like romance or mysteries become more valuable as the war continues. Sure, it's great to have a lot of survival guides, but you'll figure most of that out on your own anyway - trust me, you'll have a lot of time on your hands.

7. The feeling that you're human can fade pretty fast. I can't tell you how many people I knew who would have traded a much needed meal for just a little bit of toothpaste, rouge, soap or cologne. Not much point in fighting if you have to lose your humanity. These things are morale builders like nothing else.

8. Slow burning candles and matches, matches, matches

XXVIIPost Katrina Disaster Survival

The follow information was provided via someone heavily involved in the New Orleans disaster of hurricane Katrina:

I've had over 30 people staying with me since Sunday, evacuating from New Orleans and points south in anticipation of Hurricane Katrina. Only two families were my friends they told other friends of theirs that they knew a place where they could hole up, and so a whole bunch arrived here! I didn't mind, because there were six RV's and travel trailers, so we had enough accommodation. However, I've had the opportunity to see what worked - and what didn't - in their evacuation plans and bug-out kits, and I thought a few "lessons learned" might be appropriate to share here.

1. Have a bug-out kit ready at all times. Many of these folks packed at the last minute, grabbing whatever they thought they'd need. Needless to say, they forgot some important things (prescription medications, important documents, baby formula, diapers, etc.). Some of these things (e.g. prescriptions) obviously can't be stocked up against possible emergency need, but you can at least have a list in your bug-out kit of what to grab at the last minute before you leave!

2. Renew supplies in your bug-out kit on a regular basis. Batteries lose their charge. Foods have an expiration date. So do common medications. Clothes can get moldy or dirty unless properly stored. All of these problems were found with the folks who kept backup or bug-out supplies on hand, and caused difficulties for them.

3. Plan on needing a LOT more supplies than you think. I found myself with over 30 people on hand, many of whom were not well supplied and the stores were swamped with literally thousands of refugees, buying up everything in sight. I had enough supplies to keep myself going for 30 days. Guess what? Those supplies ended up keeping 30-odd people going for two days. I now know that I must plan on providing for not just myself, but others in need. I could have been selfish and said "No, these are mine" - but what good would that do in a real disaster? Someone would just try to take them, and then we'd have all the resulting unpleasantness. Far better to have extra supplies to share with others, whilst keeping your own core reserve intact (and, preferably, hidden from prying eyes!).

4. In a real emergency, forget about last-minute purchases. Stores will be swamped by thousands of refugees, as well as locals buying up last-minute supplies. If I hadn't had my emergency supplies already in store, I would never have been able to buy them at the last minute. If I'd had to hit the road, the situation would have been even worse, as I'd be part of a stream of thousands of refugees, most of whom would be buying (or stealing) what they needed before I got to the store.

5. Make sure your vehicle will carry your essential supplies. Some of the folks who arrived at my place had tried to load up their cars with a humongous amount of stuff, only to find that they didn't have space for themselves! Pets are a particular problem here, as they have to have air and light, and can't be crammed into odd corners. If you have to carry a lot of supplies and a number of people, invest in a small luggage trailer or something similar (or a small travel trailer with space for your goodies) - it'll pay dividends if the S really does HTF.

6. A big bug-out vehicle can be a handicap. Some of the folks arrived here with big pick-ups or SUV's, towing equally large travel trailers. Guess what? - on some evacuation routes, these huge combinations could not navigate corners very well, and/or were so difficult to turn that they ran into things (including other vehicles, which were NOT about to make way in the stress of an evacuation!). This led to hard feelings, harsh words, and at least one fist-fight. It's not a bad idea to have smaller, more maneuverable vehicles, and a smaller travel trailer, so that one can "squeeze through" in a tight traffic situation. Another point a big SUV or pickup burns a lot of fuel. This is bad news when there's no fuel available! (See point 10 below.)

7. Make sure you have a bug-out place handy. I was fortunate in having enough ground (about 1.8 acres) to provide parking for all these RV's and trailers, and to accommodate 11 small children in my living-room so that the adults could get some sleep on Sunday night, after many hours on the road in very heavy, slow-moving traffic. However, if I hadn't had space, I would have unhesitatingly told the extra families to find somewhere else - and there wasn't anywhere else here, that night. Even shops like Wal-Mart and K-Mart had trailers and RV's backed up in their parking lots (which annoyed the heck out of shoppers trying to make last-minute purchases). Even on my property, I had no trailer sewage connections, so I had to tell the occupants that if they used their onboard toilets and showers, they had to drive their RV's and trailers somewhere else to empty their waste tanks. If they hadn't left this morning, they would have joined long, long lines to do this at local trailer parks (some of which were so overloaded by visiting trailers and RV's that they refused to allow passers-by to use their dumping facilities).

8. Provide entertainment for younger children. Some of these families had young children (ranging from 3 months to 11 years). They had DVD's, video games, etc. - but no power available in their trailers to show them! They had no coloring books, toys, etc. to keep the kids occupied. This was a bad mistake.

9. Pack essentials first, then luxuries. Many of these folks had packed mattresses off beds, comforters, cushions, bathrobes, etc. As a result, their vehicles were grossly overloaded, but often lacked real essentials like candles, non-perishable foods, etc. One family (both parents are gourmet cooks) packed eighteen (yes, EIGHTEEN!!!) special pots and pans, which they were going to use on a two-burner camp stove... They were horrified by my suggestion that under the circumstances, a nested stainless-steel camping cookware set would be rather more practical.

10. Don't plan on fuel being available *en route*. A number of my visitors had real problems finding gas to fill up on the road. With thousands of vehicles jammed nose-to-tail on four lanes of interstate, an awful lot of vehicles needed gas. By the time you got to a gas station, you were highly likely to find it sold out - or charging exorbitant prices, because the owners knew you didn't have any choice but to pay what they asked. Much better to leave with a full tank of gas, and enough in spare containers to fill up on the road, if you have to, in order to reach your destination.

11. Have enough money with you for at least two weeks. Many of those who arrived here had very little in cash, relying on check-books and credit cards to fund their purchases. Guess what? Their small banks down in South Louisiana were all off-line, and their balances, credit authorizations, etc. could not be checked - so many shops refused to accept their checks, and insisted on electronic verification before accepting their credit cards. Local banks also refused (initially) to cash checks for them, since they couldn't check the status of their accounts on-line. Eventually (and very grudgingly) local banks began allowing them to cash checks for not more than $50-$100, depending on the bank. Fortunately, I have a reasonable amount of cash available at all times, so I was able to help some of them. I'm now going to increase my cash on hand, I think... Another thing - don't bring only large bills. Many gas stations, convenience stores, etc. won't accept anything larger than a $20 bill. Some of my guests had plenty of $100 bills, but couldn't buy anything.

12. Don't be sure that a disaster will be short-term. My friends have left now, heading south to Baton Rouge. They want to be closer to home for whenever they're allowed to return. Unfortunately for them, the Governor has just announced the mandatory, complete evacuation of New Orleans, and there's no word on when they will be allowed back. It will certainly be several weeks, and it might be several months. During that period, what they have with them - essential documents, clothing, etc. - is all they have. They'll have to find new doctors to renew prescriptions; find a place to live (a FEMA trailer if they're lucky - thousands of families will be lining up for these trailers); some way to earn a living (their jobs are gone with New Orleans, and I don't see their employers paying them for not working when the employers aren't making money either); and so on.

13. Don't rely on government-run shelters if at all possible. Your weapons WILL be confiscated (yes, including pocket-knives, kitchen knives, and Leatherman-type tools); you will be crowded into close proximity with anyone and everyone (including some nice folks, but also including drug addicts, released convicts, gang types, and so on); you will be under the authority of the people running the shelter, who WILL call on law enforcement and military personnel to keep order (including stopping you leaving if you want to); and so on. Much, much better to have a place to go to, a plan to get there, and the supplies you need to do so on your own.

14. Warn your friends not to bring others with them!!! I had told two friends to bring themselves and their families to my home. They, unknown to me, told half-a-dozen other families to come too - "He's a good guy, I'm sure he won't mind!" Well, I did mind... but since the circumstances weren't personally dangerous, I allowed them all to hang around. However, if things had been worse, I would have been very nasty indeed to their friends (and even nastier to them, for inviting others without clearing it with me first!). If you are a place of refuge for your friends, make sure they know that this applies to them ONLY, not their other friends. Similarly, if you have someone willing to offer you refuge, don't presume on his/her hospitality by arriving with others unforewarned.

15. Have account numbers, contact addresses and telephone numbers for all important persons and institutions. My friends will now have to get new postal addresses, and will have to notify others of this their doctors, insurance companies (medical, personal, vehicle and property), bank(s), credit card issuer(s), utility supplier(s), telephone supplier(s), etc. Basically, anyone who sends you bills, or to whom you owe money, or who might owe you money. None of my friends brought all this information with them. Now, when they need to change postal addresses for correspondence, insurance claims, etc., how can they do this when they don't know their account numbers, what number to call, who and where to write, etc.?

16. Have portable weapons and ammo ready to hand. Only two of my friends were armed, and one of them had only a handgun. The other had a handgun for himself, another for his wife, a shotgun, and an evil black rifle - MUCH better! I was asked by some of the other families, who'd seen TV reports of looting back in New Orleans, to lend them firearms. I refused, as they'd never handled guns before, and thus would have been more of a danger to themselves and other innocent persons than to looters. If they'd stayed a couple of days, so that I could teach them the basics, that would have been different but they wouldn't, so I didn't. Another thing - you don't have to take your entire arsenal along. Firearms for personal defense come first, then firearms for life support through hunting (and don't forget the skinning knife!). A fishing outfit might not be a bad idea either (you can shoot bait!). Other than that, leave the rest of your guns in the safe (you do have a gun safe, securely bolted to the floor, don't you?), and the bulk ammo supplies too. Bring enough ammo to keep you secure, but no more. If you really need bulk supplies of guns and ammo, they should be waiting for you at your bug-out location, not occupying space (and taking up a heck of a lot of weight!) in your vehicle. (For those bugging out in my direction, ammo supply will NOT be a problem...)

17. Route selection is very, very important. My friends (and their friends) basically looked at the map, found the shortest route to me (I-10 to Baton Rouge and Lafayette, then up I-49 to Alexandria), and followed it slavishly. This was a VERY bad idea, as something over half-million other folks had the same route in mind... Some of them took over twelve hours for what is usually a four-hour journey. If they'd used their heads, they would have seen (and heard, from radio reports) that going North up I-55 to Mississippi would have been much faster. There was less traffic on this route, and they could have turned left and hit Natchez, MS, and then cut across LA on Route 84. This would have taken them no more than five or six hours, even with the heavier evacuation traffic. Lesson think outside the box, and don't assume that the shortest route on the map in terms of distance will also be the shortest route in terms of time.

18. The social implications of a disaster situation. Feedback from my contacts in the LSP and other agencies is very worrying. They keep harping on the fact that the "underclass" that's doing all the looting is almost exclusively Black and inner-city in composition. The remarks they're reporting include such statements as "I'm ENTITLED to this stuff!", "This is payback time for all Whitey's done to us", and "This is reparations for slavery!". Also, they're blaming the present confused disaster-relief situation on racism "Fo sho, if Whitey wuz sittin' here in tha Dome waitin' for help, no way would he be waitin' like we is!" No, I'm not making up these comments... they are as reported by my buddies. This worries me very much. If we have such a divide in consciousness among our city residents, then when we hit a SHTF situation, we're likely to be accused of racism, paternalism, oppression, and all sorts of other crimes just because we want to preserve law and order. If we, as individuals and families, provide for our own needs in emergency, and won't share with others (whether they're of another race or not) because we don't have enough to go round, we're likely to be accused of me very much. If we have such racism rather than pragmatism, and taking things from us can (and probably will) be justified as "Whitey getting his just desserts". I'm absolutely not a racist, but the racial implications of the present situation are of great concern to me. The likes of Jesse Jackson, Al Sharpton, and the "reparations for slavery" brigade appear to have so polarized inner-city opinion that these folks are (IMHO) no longer capable of rational thought concerning such issues as looting, disaster relief, etc.

19. Implications for security. If one has successfully negotiated the danger zone, one will be in an environment filled, to a greater or lesser extent, with other evacuees. How many of them will have provided for their needs? How many of them will rely on obtaining from others the things they need? In the absence of immediate State or relief-agency assistance, how many of them will feel "entitled" to obtain these necessities any way they have to, up to and including looting, murder and mayhem? Large gathering-places for refugees suddenly look rather less desirable... and being on one's own, or in an isolated spot with one's family, also looks less secure. One has to sleep sometime, and while one sleeps, one is vulnerable. Even one's spouse and children might not be enough... there are always going to be vulnerabilities. One can hardly remain consciously in Condition Yellow while bathing children, or making love! A team approach might be a viable solution here.

20. Too many chiefs, not enough Indians" in New Orleans at the moment. The mayor has already blown his top about the levee breach: he claims that he had a plan in place to fix it by yesterday evening, but was overruled by Baton Rouge, who sent in others to do something different. This may or may not be true... My LSP buddies tell me that they're getting conflicting assignments and/or requests from different organizations and individuals. One will send out a group to check a particular area for survivors but when they get there, they find no-one, and later learn that another group has already checked and cleared the area. Unfortunately, in the absence of centralized command and control, the information is not being shared amongst all recovery teams. Also, there's alleged to be conflict between City officials and State functionaries, with both sides claiming to be "running things" and some individuals in the Red Cross, FEMA, and other groups appear to be refusing to take instructions from either side, instead (it's claimed) wanting to run their own shows. This is allegedly producing catastrophic confusion and duplication of effort, and may even be making the loss of life worse, in that some areas in need of rescuers aren't getting them. (I don't know if the same problems are occurring in Mississippi and/or Alabama, but I wouldn't be surprised if they were.) All of this is unofficial and off-the record, but it doesn't surprise me to hear it. Moral of the story if you want to survive, don't rely on the government or any government agency (or private relief organization, for that matter) to save you. Your survival is in your own hands - don't drop it!

21. Long-term vision. This appears to be sadly lacking at present. Everyone is focused on the immediate, short-term objective of rescuing survivors. However, there are monumental problems looming, that need immediate attention, but don't seem to be getting it right now. For example: the Port of Louisiana is the fifth-largest in the world, and vital to the economy, but the Coast Guard is saying (on TV) that they won't be able to get it up and running for three to six months, because their primary focus is on search and rescue, and thereafter, disaster relief. Why isn't the Coast Guard pulled off that job now, and put to work right away on something this critical? There are enough Navy, Marine and Air Force units available now to take over rescue missions. Another example there are over a million refugees from the Greater New Orleans area floating around. They need accommodation and food, sure but most of them are now unemployed, and won't have any income at all for the next six to twelve months. There aren't nearly enough jobs available in this area to absorb this workforce. What is being done to find work for them, even in states remote from the problem areas? The Government for sure won't provide enough for them in emergency aid to be able to pay their bills. What about mortgages on properties that are now underwater? The occupants both can't and won't pay; the mortgage holders will demand payment; and we could end up with massive foreclosures on property that is worthless, leaving a lot of folks neck-deep in debt and without homes (even damaged ones). What is being done to plan for this, and alleviate the problem as much as possible? I would have thought that the State government would have had at least the skeleton of an emergency plan for these sorts of things, and that FEMA would have the same, but this doesn't seem to be the case. Why weren't these things considered in the leisurely days pre-disaster, instead of erupting as immediate and unanswered needs post-disaster?

22. Personal emergency planning. This leads me to consider my own emergency planning. I've planned to cover an evacuation need, and could probably survive with relative ease for between two weeks and one month but what if I had been caught up in this mess? What would I do about earning a living, paying mortgages, etc.? If I can't rely on the State, I for darn sure had better be able to rely on myself! I certainly need to re-examine my insurance policies, to ensure that if disaster strikes, my mortgage, major loans, etc. will be paid off (or that I will receive enough money to do this myself). I also need to provide for my physical security, and must ensure that I have supplies, skills and knowledge that will be "marketable" in exchange for hard currency in a post-disaster situation. The idea of a "team" of friends with (or to) whom to bug out, survive, etc. is looking better and better. Some of the team could take on the task of keeping a home maintained (even a camp-type facility), looking after kids, providing base security, etc. Others could be foraging for supplies, trading, etc. Still others could be earning a living for the whole team with their skills. In this way, we'd all contribute to our mutual survival and security in the medium to long term. Life might be a lot less comfortable than prior to the disaster, but hey - we'd still have a life! This bears thinking about, and I might just have to start building "team relationships" with nearby [people of like mind]!

23. The "bank problem." This bears consideration. I was at my bank this morning, depositing checks I'd been given by my visitors in exchange for cash. The teller warned me bluntly that it might be weeks before these checks could be credited to my account, as there was no way to clear them with their issuing banks, which were now under water and/or without communications facilities. He also told me that there had been an endless stream of folks trying to cash checks on South Louisiana banks, without success. He warned me that some of these local banks will almost certainly fail, as they don't have a single branch above water, and the customers and businesses they served are also gone - so checks drawn on them will eventually prove worthless. Even some major regional banks had run their Louisiana "hub" out of New Orleans, and now couldn't access their records. I think it might be a good idea to have a "bug-out bank account" with a national bank, so that funds should be available anywhere they have a branch, rather than keeping all one's money in a single bank (particularly a local one) or credit union. This is, of course, over and above one's "bug-out stash" of ready cash.

24. Helping one's friends is likely to prove expensive. I estimate that I'm out over $1,000 at the moment, partly from having all my supplies consumed, and partly from making cash available to friends who couldn't cash their checks. I may or may not get some of this back in due course. I don't mind it - if I were in a similar fix, I hope I could lean on my friends for help in the same way, after all! - but I hadn't made allowance for it. I shall have to do so in future, as well as planning to contribute to costs incurred by those who offer me hospitality under similar circumstances.

25. People who were prepared were frequently mobbed/threatened by those who weren't. This was reported in at least seven incidents, five in Mississippi, two in Louisiana (I suspect that the relative lack of Louisiana incidents was because most of those with any sense got out of Dodge before the storm hit). In each case, the person/family concerned had made preparations for disaster, with supplies, shelter, etc. in good order and ready to go. Several had generators ready and waiting. However, their neighbors who had not prepared all came running after the disaster, wanting food, water and shelter from them. When the prepared families refused, on the grounds that they had very little, and that only enough for themselves, there were many incidents of aggression, attempted assault, and theft of their supplies. Some had to use weapons to deter attack, and in some cases, shots were fired. I understand that in two incidents, attackers/would-be thieves were shot. It's also reported that in all of these cases, the prepared families now face threats of retribution from their neighbors, who regarded their refusal to share as an act of selfishness and/or aggression, and are now threatening retaliation. It's reportedly so bad that most of the prepared families are considering moving to other neighborhoods so as to start afresh, with different neighbors. Similar incidents are reported by families who got out in time, prepared to spend several days on their own. When they stopped to eat a picnic meal at a rest stop, or an isolated spot along the highway, they report being approached rather aggressively by others wanting food, or fuel, or other essentials.

Sometimes they had to be rather aggressive in their turn to deter these insistent requests. Two families report attempts being made to steal their belongings (in one case, their vehicle) while over-nighting in camp stops on their way out of the area. They both instituted armed patrols, with one or more family members patrolling while the others slept, to prevent this. Seems to me to be a good argument to form a "bug-out team" with like-minded, security-conscious friends in your area, so that all concerned can provide mutual security and back-up. My take I can understand these families being unwilling to share the little they had, particularly in light of not knowing when supplies would once again be available. However, this reinforces the point I made in my "lessons learned" post last week plan on needing much more in the way of supplies than you initially thought! If these families had had some extra food and water in stock, and hidden their main reserve where it would not be seen, they could have given out some help to their neighbors and preserved good relations. Also, a generator, under such circumstances, is a noisy (and bright, if powering your interior lights) invitation saying "This house has supplies - come and get them". I suspect that kerosene lanterns, candles and flashlights might be a more "community-safe" option if one is surrounded by survivors.

26. When help gets there, you may get it whether you like it or not. There are numerous reports Of aggressive, overbearing behavior by those rescuers who first arrived at disaster scenes. It's perhaps best described as "I'm here to rescue you - I'm in charge - do as I say - if you don't I'll shoot you". It appears that mid-level State functionaries and Red Cross personnel (the latter without the "shoot you" aspect, of course) were complained about most often. In one incident, a family who had prepared and survived quite well were ordered, not invited, to get onto a truck, with only the clothes on their backs. When they objected, they were threatened. They had pets, and wanted to know what would happen to them and they report that a uniformed man (agency unknown) began pointing his rifle at the pets with the words "I'll fix that". The husband then trained his own shotgun

on the man and explained to him, in words of approximately one syllable, what was going to happen to him if he fired a shot. The whole "rescuer" group then left, threatening dire consequences for the family (including threats to come back once they'd evacuated and torch their home). The family were able to make contact with a State Police patrol and report the incident, and are now determined that no matter how much pressure is applied, they will not evacuate. They've set up a "shuttle run" so that every few days, two of them go upstate to collect supplies for the rest of the family, who defend the homestead in the meantime. Another aspect of this is that self-sufficient, responsible families were often regarded almost with suspicion by rescuers. The latter seemed to believe that if you'd come through the disaster better than your neighbors, it could only have been because you stole what you needed, or somehow gained some sort of unfair advantage over the "average victims" in your area. I'm at a loss to explain this, but it's probably worth keeping in mind.

27. There seems to be a cumulative psychological effect upon survivors. This is clear even - or perhaps particularly - in those who were prepared for a disaster. During and immediately after the disaster, these folks were at their best, dealing with damage, setting up alternative accommodation, light, food sources, etc. However, after a few days in the heat and debris (perhaps worst of all being the smell of dead bodies nearby), many found their ability to remain positive and "upbeat" being strained to the limit. There are numerous reports of individuals becoming depressed, morose and withdrawn. This seemed to happen to even the strongest personalities. The arrival of rescuers provided a temporary boost, but once evacuated, a sort of "after-action shell-shock" seems to be commonly experienced. I don't know enough about this to comment further, but I suspect that staying in place has a lot to do with it - there is no challenge to keep moving, find one's survival needs, and care for the group, and one is surrounded by vivid reminders of the devastation. By staying among the ruins of one's former life, one may be exposing oneself to a greater risk of psychological deterioration.

28. There is widespread frustration over the lack of communication and empathy by rescuers and local/State government. This is partly due to the absence of electricity, so that TV's were not available to follow events as they unfolded but it's also due to an almost deliberate policy of non-communication by rescuers. There are many accounts of evacuees wanting to know where the bus or plane was going that they were about to board, only to be told "We don't know", or "To a better place than this". Some have found themselves many States away from their homes. Other families were arbitrarily separated upon rescue and/or evacuation, and are still scattered across two or three States. Their efforts to locate each other are very difficult, and when they request to be reunited at a common location, all of those with whom I have contact report a blanket refusal by the Red Cross and State officials to even consider the matter at this time. They're being informed that it will be "looked into" at some future date, and that they may have to pay the costs involved if they want to join up again. This, to families who are now destitute! I'm very angry about this, but it's so widespread a problem that I don't know what can be done about it. I hope that in future, some means will be implemented to prevent it happening again. Lesson learned never, EVER allow yourselves to be separated as a family, even if it means waiting for later rescue and/or evacuation. Insist on this at all costs!

29. Expect rescuers (including law enforcement) to enforce a distinctly un-Constitutional authority in a disaster situation. This is very widely reported, and is very troubling. I hear repeated

reports from numerous States that as evacuees arrive at refugee centers, they and their belongings are searched without Constitutional authority, and any personal belongings seen as potentially suspicious (including firearms, prescription medication, etc.) are confiscated without recourse to the owner. I can understand the point of view of the receiving authorities, but they are acting illegally, and I suspect there will be lawsuits coming from this practice. Another common practice reported on the ground in the disaster areas is for people to be ordered to evacuate, irrespective of their needs and wishes - even those folks who were well-prepared and have survived in good shape. If they demur, they are often threatened and bullied in an attempt to make them abandon their homes, pets, etc. Lesson learned in a disaster, don't expect legal and Constitutional norms to be followed. If you can make it on your own, do so, without relying on an unsympathetic and occasionally overbearing rescue system to control you and your destiny.

30. Don't believe that rescuers are all knights in shining armor who will respect your property. There have been numerous reports of rescuers casually appropriating small items that took their fancy in houses they were searching. Sometimes this was blatant, right in front of onlookers, and when protests were made, the response was either threatening, or a casual "Who's going to miss it now?". Some of our field agents report that this happened right in front of their eyes. Another aspect of this is damage caused to buildings by rescuers. I've had reports of them kicking in the front door to a house, or a window, instead of trying to obtain access with as little damage as possible; climbing on clean, highly-polished tables with hobnailed boots in order to get at an attic hatch to check for survivors; etc. When they left the house, often the door or window was left open, almost a standing invitation to looters, instead of being closed and/or secured. When the families concerned get home, they won't know who caused this damage, but they will certainly be angered by it. I think that if one evacuates one's home, it might be a good idea to leave a clearly-visible notice that all residents have evacuated, so as to let would-be rescuers know that this house is empty. On the other hand, this might make it easier for looters, so what you gain on the swings, you lose on the round-abouts...

31. If you choose to help, you may be sucked into a bureaucratic and legal nightmare. Example: a local church in the beginning stages of the crisis offered its hall to house evacuees. Local and State officials promptly filled it up with over 100 people. Their "social skills" proved extremely difficult to live with... toilets were blocked, restrooms left filthy, graffiti were scrawled and/or carved on the walls, arguments and disputes were frequent (often escalating to screaming matches, sometimes to physical violence), evacuees roamed the neighborhood (leading to all sorts of reports of petty theft, vandalism, etc.), church workers were subject to aggressive begging and demands, etc. Requests to the authorities to provide better security, administrative assistance, etc. apparently fell on deaf ears - the crisis was so widespread and overwhelming that a small facility such as this seems to have been very low on the priority checklist. After two days of this, with complaints from the neighbors becoming more and more insistent, the church informed local officials that it wanted the evacuees removed at once, if not sooner. They were promptly subject to bureaucratic heavy-handedness (including threats to withhold previously promised reimbursement for their expenses); threats of lawsuits for daring to insinuate that the evacuees were somehow "lower-class" in their conduct, and for alleged racism, slander, and general political incorrectness; and threats of negative publicity, in that officials threatened to put out a press release denouncing the church for its "elitist" and "un-co-operative" attitude in a time of crisis. The church initially caved in to this pressure, and allowed the evacuees to stay but within a couple more days, the pressure from neighbors and from its own members became impossible to bear, and they insisted on the evacuees being removed to a Red Cross shelter. I'm informed that repairs to their hall will cost over $10,000. This is only one example among many I could cite, but it makes the point clear - if you offer your facilities to authorities, you place yourself (to a certain extent) under their control, and you're potentially liable to a great deal of heavy-handed, insensitive bureaucratic bullying. Those of you in the same position as this church (i.e. with facilities you could make available) might wish to take note.

32. Law enforcement problems will often be "glossed over" and/or ignored by authorities. In many cities housing evacuees, there have been private reports of a significant increase in crime caused by their presence but you'll find that virtually all law enforcement authorities publicly deny this and/or gloss over it as a "temporary problem". This is all very well for publicity, but it ignores the increased risk to local residents. I've been tracking crime reports in about a dozen cities, through my contacts with local law enforcement and the Louisiana State Police. All the LEO's I speak with, without exception, tell me of greatly increased crime, including rape, assault, robbery, shoplifting, vandalism, gang activity, etc. However, you won't see these reports in the news media, and will often see senior LE figures actively denying it. The officers with whom I speak are angry and bitter about this, but they daren't "go public", as their jobs would be on the line if they did so. They tell me that often they're instructed not to report certain categories of "incident" at all, so as not to "skew" or "inflate" the "official" crime figures. I've also heard reports from Texas, Alabama and Tennessee of brand-new high-end motor vehicles (e.g. Cadillacs, Lincolns, BMW's, etc.) with New Orleans dealer tags being driven through various towns, on their way North and West. The drivers were described as "gangbangers" (and sundry less complimentary terms). However, there have been no reports of stolen vehicles from New Orleans, because there are no workers to check out dealer lots, or report thefts, and no working computers to enter VIN's, etc. into the NICS database of stolen vehicles - so officers have had no choice but to let these vehicles proceed. Draw your own conclusions.

33. Your personal and/or corporate supplies and facilities may be commandeered without warning, receipt or compensation. I've had numerous reports from in and near the disaster zone of individuals (e.g. boat-owners, farmers with barns, tractors, etc.) and corporate groups (e.g. companies with heavy equipment, churches with halls, etc.) finding an official on their doorstep demanding the use of their facilities or equipment. If they demurred, they were told that this was an "emergency situation" and that their assistance was being required, not requested. Some of them have lost track of the heavy equipment "borrowed" in this way, and don't know where it is, whether or not it's still in good condition, and when (if ever) it will be returned - and in the meantime, they can't continue their normal operations without this equipment. Others have had their land and facilities effectively confiscated for use by rescue and relief workers, storage of supplies, etc. In some cases, in the absence of their owners, the property of the individuals and groups concerned (e.g. farm gasoline and diesel supplies, the inventory of motor vehicle dealers, suppliers of foodstuffs, tarpaulins, etc.) have been commandeered and used by law enforcement and relief workers, without permission, receipts, reimbursement, etc. Protests have been met with denials, threats of arrest, insinuations of being "uncaring" and "un-co-operative", etc. Lesson learned if you've got what officials need in a time of crisis, forget about Constitutional protections of your property! Sure, you can sue after the fact, but if you need your goods and facilities for your own survival, you're basically SOL. Those of us who stockpile necessities for potential crises like this might want to consider concealing our stockpiles to prevent confiscation and if you need certain equipment for your own day-to-day use (e.g. tractors for farmers, generators, etc.), you might have a hard time retaining possession of these things. This problem applies to relief workers also I've had several reports of private relief workers (e.g. those sent in by churches, etc.) having their vehicles and supplies commandeered by "official" relief workers, without compensation or receipt, and being kicked out of the disaster area with warnings not to return. The fact that the "private" workers were accomplishing rather more than the "official" workers was apparently of no importance.

34. If you look like you know what you're doing, you may be a target of those less prepared. There have been many, many reports of individuals who were more or less prepared for a disaster being preyed upon by those who were not prepared. Incidents range from theft of supplies, through attempts to bug out with these persons (uninvited), to actual violence. It's genuinely frightening to hear about these incidents, particularly the attitude of those trying to prey on the prepared they seemed to feel that because you'd taken steps to protect yourself and your loved ones, you had somehow done so at their expense, and they were therefore "entitled" to take from you what they needed. There's no logical explanation for this attitude, unless it's bred by the utter dependence of many such people on the State for welfare, Social Security, Medicare/Medicaid, etc. Since they've always been dependent on others, and regarded this as an "entitlement", in a disaster situation, they seem to automatically assume that they're "entitled" to what you've got! In one case, the family's pet dog was held hostage, with a knife at its throat, until the family handed over money and supplies. In two cases, families were threatened with the rape of their women unless they co-operated with the aggressors. In four cases that I know of, children were held hostage to ensure co-operation. There have also been reports of crimes during the bug-out process. Families sleeping in their cars at highway rest areas were a favorite target, including siphoning of gas from their tanks, assaults, etc. The lessons to be learned from this are obvious. One family can't secure itself against these threats without great difficulty. It's best to be "teamed up" with neighbors to secure your neighborhood as a whole, rather than be the one house with facilities in an area filled with those less prepared. If you're in the latter situation, staying put may not be a safe option, and a bug-out plan may be vital. When bugging out, you're still not safe from harm, and must maintain constant vigilance. 35. Those who thought themselves safe from the disaster were often not safe from refugees. There have been many reports of smaller towns, farms, etc. on the fringe of the disaster area being overrun with those seeking assistance. In many cases, assistance was demanded rather than requested, and theft, looting and vandalism have been reported. So, even if you think you're safe from the disaster, you may not be safe from its aftermath.

36. Self-reliance seems to draw suspicion upon you from the authorities. I've mentioned this in a previous e-mail, but I've had many more reports of it from those who survived or bugged out, and it bears re-emphasizing. For reasons unknown and unfathomable, rescue authorities seem to regard with suspicion those who've made provision for their safety and have survived (or bugged out) in good shape. It seems to be a combination of "How could you cope when so many others haven't?", "You must have taken advantage of others to be so well off", and "We've come all this way to help, so how dare you not need our assistance?" I have no idea why this should be the case... but there have been enough reports of it that it seems to be a widespread problem. Any ideas from readers?

37. Relief workers from other regions and States often don't know local laws. This is a particular problem when it comes to firearms. I've had many reports of law enforcement officers sent to assist in Louisiana from States such as New Jersey, California, etc. trying to confiscate firearms on the streets, etc., when in fact the armed citizens were legally armed, under local law. One can't reason with these officers in the heat of the moment, of course, and as a result, a number of people lost their firearms, and have still not recovered them (and in the chaos of the immediate post disaster situation, they may never do so, because I'm not sure that normal procedures such as logging these guns into a property office, etc. were followed). I understand that in due course, steps were taken to include at least one local law enforcement officer in patrols, so that he could advise officers from other areas as to what was legal, and what wasn't. Also, in Louisiana, law enforcement is conducted differently than in some other States, and officers from other States who came to assist were sometimes found to be domineering and aggressive in enforcing a law enforcement "authority" that doesn't normally apply here. So, if you're in a disaster area and help arrives from elsewhere, you may find that the help doesn't know (or care) about local laws, norms, etc. Use caution!

38. Relief organizations have their own bureaucratic requirements that may conflict with your needs. A good example is the Red Cross. In many cases, across three States, I've had reports that locals who needed assistance were told that they had to register at a particular Red Cross shelter or facility. The help would not come to them they had to go to it. If they wished to stay on their own property, they were sometimes denied assistance, and told that if they wanted help, they had to move into the shelter to get it. Also, assistance was often provided only to those who came in person. If you left your family at home and went to get food aid, you might be denied aid for your whole family because there was no evidence that they existed - only the number that could be physically counted by relief workers (who would not come to you, but insisted you come to them) would be provided with food. Needless to say, this caused much anger and resentment. I hope that these "lessons learned" are of use to you. I'm more and more convinced that in the event of a disaster, I must rely on myself, and a few friends, and never count on Government or relief organizations for the help I'll need. Also, I'm determined to bug out for a fairly long distance from a disaster in my home area, so as to be clear of the post-disaster complications that may arise. Once again (as it has countless times throughout history), we see that to rely on others (let alone Government) for your own safety and security is to invite complications at best, disaster at worst.

XXVIII   Defensive Weapons

In a massive social collapse, most people will be able to keep only that which they can defend. This includes their lives, their homes, their food, their money, and if they're male, even their wives and perhaps their children. This may disturb many people who are doing serious emergency planning; many do not have a "survivalist" background or mindset and they've never had any reason to physically defend that which is precious to them. A major disaster may change all that, just as it may change nearly everything else .

In an orderly, productive society with a stable division of labor, the harsh realities of life are not so obvious. You have laws that most people obey and you have professional police who enforce those laws. It's their job to defend the lives and property of the average citizen; if there's any violence to be done in that defense, the police handle that. The average person never has to consider defending what is his unless he is personally threatened by a criminal. The threat of force by the police keeps order in the society and tends to discourage aggressive criminal behavior. It also tends to hide a basic truth about the nature of human relations.

In a massive social collapse, law and public order break down and the truth about human rights is revealed: An individual has rights only as long as he can defend them. This is the subtle logic of violence. It has always been true but it's something to which most of us have never given a moment's thought. However, unless you understand and accept this basic fact of life, you may not survive the coming challenges. If a disaster crashes down hard upon us, it will destroy all the illusions and most of the rules we have lived by for the past hundred years or more. It will create harsh new rules. When the fundamental order of a society changes and new rules arise, those who fail to understand the new rules suffer the most.

It's not just having a weapon that's important, or even knowing how to use one; it's knowing full well why you need to use it and therefore not hesitating to use it when needed. *A gun in your hand is totally worthless against an assailant unless you're fully willing to use it to defend yourself.*

You must understand that the new rules brought on by a major disaster may require you to defend your life personally.

Who To Prepare For

Don't prepare for an idiot shooting at you from 200 yards away, prepare for the sneaky son of a gun that waits until you are distracted and gets to you when you less expect him. Obviously in war situations there are cases of people shooting enemies 1000 yards away. Killing someone that wants you dead before he gets close to you is perfectly logical. However it's impossible to name any cases of self defense where the person shot the bad guy 100 yards away.

If someone starts shooting at you 300 yards away, and you shoot back in self defense , that's ok, but that rarely, if ever, happens. There's no way can you know what a man's intentions are even at 100 yards away, unless he starts shooting at you like an idiot. And if he wants you dead that bad, he will get close enough and make sure that that one shot is the last thing you hear on this planet. Any bad guy who has survived puberty will be smart enough to get close, very close when you are distracted with some chore/fieldwork before he points a gun at you and asks you to calm down and walk into your house.

Criminals are not stupid, and they will spend days checking your home and YOUR ROUTINE. For example, if they see that you lock the gate at night, they will wait for you behind a tree until you are close - most of the time they sneak up on you. If they think that security is tight, they will just hide near the main gate, and wait for you to leave or return. When you stop and must get out of your vehicle to open/close the main gate or garage, they attack. The most frequent kind of attack is attacking by surprise when you enter/leave your home.

The most common times of attack - there is no "safe" hour of the day. Night is particularly dangerous. Maybe attacks during the day are faster, they want to get some money or jewelry and leave fast, while at night they might stay inside more time, maybe till the next day. But there are no fixed patterns. Eyes and ears wide open when you enter/leave your home. If possible, keep a gun on your hand when doing either one. If something looks, even "feels strange, then go around the block and check again, carefully. If you see them still there, either call the police (if still available) or get help. If you approach the house with a large number of people they will leave.

GUNS, AMMO AND OTHER GEAR

After a complete economic collapse, only the foolhardy believe the police will protect them from the crime wave that follows. A lot of people who are antigun before will run to the gun shops, seeking advice on how to defend themselves and their families. They'll buy a 38 revolver, a box of ammo, and leave it in the closet, probably believing that it would magically protect them from intruders. You will be smarter.

The likely worst case scenario is one in which there may be unrest and martial law in the urban areas and far less order than we're accustomed to (more akin to New Orleans) but nothing that resembles the Future War in The Terminator. Desperate people take desperate chances, the more base emotions become prominent in many people's behavior, and hunger, cold, lust, greed and fear take charge of people's actions. You probably won't have to worry about roving gangs; but your concern will be with one or two people breaking into your house for food or whatever may be available, stealing vegetables from your garden or firewood from your woodpile, etc. This is what you'll need to defend against and that is something you can handle.

BEST WEAPONS

The best weapon for home defense is a shotgun with a short barrel. There are three reasons why this is true. First, there is nothing scarier than looking at that big black hole at the end of the barrel of a shotgun when it's pointed at you. Second, when you fire a shotgun at close range it's impossible to miss; you're going to hit what you're aiming at. Third, when you hit someone with a shotgun, he doesn't get up and come at you. A short barrel gun is easier to handle than one with a long barrel.

There are several good basic shotguns on the market. One of the best is a 12 gauge Remington pump 870 Express Magnum with an 18" barrel. It's not fancy and it's not pretty but it will do the job.

Just hearing the unmistakable click of a pump shotgun being cocked will scare off most intruders. The Remington costs about $250 new. Mossberg also makes a good pump 12 gauge, along with several other manufacturers. If there is a good gun shop in your area, stop by and look at what's available. Ask questions; most gun shop employees are very knowledgeable and willing to share that knowledge with you.

The other useful weapon for home or personal defense is a handgun. Although an automatic shoots faster and loads quicker than a revolver, it is a more complex mechanism and may jam occasionally, whereas a revolver almost never jams. Also for a novice, a revolver is less intimidating to hold and shoot. Somehow a revolver just seems more familiar to someone who is not used to guns. The best revolver to have is a .357 magnum with a 4 inch barrel. It can fire both .38 and .357 shells (use the .38 ammo for practice because it's cheaper than the .357). A .357 is powerful enough to kill or seriously injure an assailant and its common enough to be affordable. Stick to a well-known brand such as a Smith & Wesson. Taurus makes a good handgun that is less expensive than the very top names. Again, ask at the gun shop. If the gun is for a small female, the .357 may be too heavy and awkward to use effectively. In that case a .38 or even a .32 may be a better choice. Remember that a smaller caliber weapon does not have the stopping power of a larger one, so if you have to shoot someone to defend yourself, keep shooting until you empty the gun. Once you've wounded someone, he's going to try to kill you if he possibly can, so you don't want to inflict a minor wound; you must stop him!

No matter which guns you get, be sure to get lots of ammunition. Any ammo you don't use or need could be a great trade item after a disaster. Wal-Mart generally has good prices on ammunition. Gun shows are always a good place to shop for ammo deals. If you know someone who has a good bit of knowledge and experience with guns, get him to teach you how to shoot safely. It is a terrible mistake to have a gun and not know anything about proper shooting and gun safety. If there is a gun course offered in your area, take it; ask about this at your local gun shop. Be sure to keep your guns away from your children! Put them where you can get to them quickly if needed but in a place to which they don't have access. There are lockable gun boxes on the market that are quick to get into if you know how, but impossible for a child to open; again, ask at the gun shop.

The cardinal rule about guns that should always be kept in mind:

Never point a gun at someone unless you are completely willing to shoot.

If your assailant senses hesitancy, he'll move quickly and take the gun away from you. Your life may depend upon this so it's essential to accept it completely. **In a disaster the rules have changed; understand that and you will survive; fail to understand that and you will perish.**

Selecting Survival Firearms

It is not especially surprising that a vast majority of folks are not well versed in firearms lore and the selection and use of weaponry. A rural background can help but by itself does not instill the knowledge to select a proper variety of firearms any more than living in Detroit makes you a car manufacturer.

You have to apply yourself to the study of weapon usage and capability, and to their use in the field to gain insight that keeps you from wasting your money on things that don't appreciably help your chances of surviving. Before you can make an intelligent choice, it would help if you knew what was out there? There are many hundreds of different firearms offered for sale today, and thousands of variations of barrel length, caliber, finish, sights, and other options, but hopefully we can condense that down into a more digestible group that are most pertinent to survivalists today.

The table below covers most of the types available:

Shoulder-Fired			Handguns		
Rifles	**Shotguns**	**Special**	**Revolvers**	**Pistols**	**Special**
Bolt Action	Pump	Single-Shot	S/A	S/A	Derringers
Semi-Auto	Semi-Auto	Interchangeable barrel	D/A	D/A	Single-shot
Lever Action	Over/Under	.50 Caliber	DAO	DAO	Bolt-Action
Pump	Side by Side	Other		Other	Other

- S/A Single Action Hammer must be cocked for each shot
- D/A Double Action Squeezing the trigger also cocks the hammer
- DAO Double Action Only Trigger-cocking for every shot

While every person has to decide just what role firearms will play in their own plans, disqualifying any type from your battery for semantic reasons (i.e., "handguns are evil", or "assault rifles kill babies") is both silly and dangerous. Without going into Second Amendment rights or discussion, if you need a pistol (for example), then you need it badly, and probably right now. Not having one because someone arbitrarily said you couldn't is just plain wrong. Every would-be survivalist should have the ability to protect themselves in a variety of situations, and have the ability to hunt small game and whatever else is in their area, or the area where they will be (expect to be) in case of emergency. Redundancy is recommended, great variety is not, unless you can afford to do it right.

Full Firearm requirements:

Three goals that stand out are to have the right firearm (tool) for the job, have enough firearms, and have spare parts and plenty of ammunition. It is not necessary to get carried away but to be fully prepared every adult contributing member would have (as a minimum):

- Rifle for defense/offense
- Rifle for hunting if a fighting rifle is not suitable
- Shotgun for defense/hunting

- .22 Rifle for small game & plinking (informal target practice)
- Handgun for defense
- Handgun for field work
- Handgun for concealment/defense

A couple of these, most notably the fieldwork handgun and the hunting rifle are of lower priority than the others. You can't carry all of these at the same time, so you may wonder why you need them. The answer is, you won't be fighting all the time, you won't be hunting all the time, you won't be carrying a rifle all the time and you won't need to conceal a handgun all the time. Also there are many other tasks that may need doing that are more important.

When considering what type of weapons to purchase, you also have to think about how many to get. While it seems prudent to get the defensive weapons first, if you accept the basic premise, you'll end up with the entire spectrum. At that point you should probably plan your back-up package. Consider the current Special Forces logistical doctrine, which holds with the PACE concept - Primary, Alternate, Contingency, Extra. While we as individuals do not have the budget of the Federal Government, we should keep this in mind as an excellent method of planning, and build redundancy into our plans.

- one fighting rifle, plus a spare for every two (people)
- a shotgun for every two
- a fighting handgun each, plus a spare for every two
- everyone should have one .22 and a working handgun
- a concealment handgun for every two

Calibers should be ones already in your inventory. It would be nice to have a complete battery both at home and at the retreat and have a weapon available in at locations where you might find yourself temporarily stranded.

The fighting rifle is where most controversy comes in. The entire family of semi-automatic, magazine fed rifles of suitable caliber (meaning 7.62 NATO, 7.62 x 39, or 5.56 NATO) is overpriced and over-restricted. In truth, however, pretty much all of the available choices are well constructed and serviceable, which makes selection mostly a matter of personal preference. The most commonly available weapons in this category are the AR-15, AK-47, SKS, M1A, FNFAL, HK's 91 & 93, and Ruger's Mini-14. The M1 Garand is part of this group, but you'll not find a great selection of the more esoteric rifles (such as the Galil, Valmet, Beretta, Sig, etc.) in this country, and spare parts & magazines could prove difficult to find if you didn't stock enough for a protracted emergency.

There are those who feel a magazine-fed semi-auto is not needed...that we are not likely to have to fight an infantry engagement. Regardless of who is right, they have some valuable insights in weaponry choices, and encourage the lever-action .30-30, .44 or .357 Magnum as a worthy alternative. Some of their arguments: Rapid fire repeater. Greater magazine capacity than most sporters. Much better trigger actions than most any battle rifle you'd care to name. Light weight. Cost is less than 20% of an assault rifle. These are some pretty significant considerations. You can buy two lever guns (at @ $200 each) and a thousand rounds of ammo (@ $500, if you shop around) for enough less than a state of the art auto ($1200 & up) to either get ANOTHER thousand rounds, or a handgun, shotgun, or a couple of .22's. Pretty convincing, especially when you consider the increased versatility over a .223, better shooting rifles than the .30 Russian Short (7.62x39), and much lighter weight than any .308 battle rifle available.

The hunting rifle is, for most of us, a fairly easy choice - if you live in the lower 48 and don't plan to hunt elk, moose, or grizzly, then anything from the .243 to the .300 Winchester Magnum is suitable, with something in the middle probably most appropriate. The .308 stands out mainly for its universal availability and the wide choice of bullets available, both loaded and separately as components. And of course, for its ammo interchangeability with a battle rifle.

The hunting rifle is probably a scope-sighted bolt-action job, with limited magazine capacity. It may be able to stand in for a "sniper" rifle, if it is accurate, your ammo and shooting skill are up to the task, and you don't have to drag it around on the ground, beat it against building walls, jump out of airplanes with it, or any of the myriad other tasks that military and law enforcement professionals routinely encounter.

Some of the most common & popular rifles today are the Remington 700 (choice of the U.S. Army & Marine Corps as the M24 & M40A1), Winchester's M70, and Ruger's M77. Savage sells their M110 & 112, which are super deals, both in price and accuracy, and recently introduced a short action which should be even stiffer & thus more accurate, while ending up lighter and shorter as well. There are lots of surplus Mausers on the market, of various model, manufacturer, and condition, as well as new production ones. There are many more types for sale than we can discuss here, so we are only listing some of the most. The main thing is to think about spare parts and ammo availability.

If you want to do some varmint hunting (coyote, groundhog, prairie dog, etc.) then you'll want a heavy-barreled .223 or .22-250, or something similar. If you think you can accurately shoot a deer or other large animal at long range, something more potent is called for. Starting at 7 millimeter (.28 caliber) magnums and working up through the .33 calibers, there are quite a few new cartridges that are very capable of taking out whatever you hit at ranges approaching 1000 meters. These cartridges send 160 to 250 grain bullets through the barrel at speeds up to 3600 FPS! Of course, to be able to hit anything at great distance requires immense amounts of practice and skill.

If you feel that life doesn't begin until 600 meters, there are several .50 caliber rifles on the market that have been proven in battle in the last dozen years or so. There are several accounts of **2 MILE** shots by Marine Corps snipers in Iraq during Desert Storm

The point about working rifles is that, given realistic evaluations of what you will expect them to do, there are countless rifles out there that will work, and most of them will do everything you want. Just stick with one of the most popular calibers (.270, .30-06, .308, etc.), and spending the money saved for more ammo to practice with and stockpile. There's nothing wrong with having a spare working rifle, along with your spare "fighting" pieces, but have a real good reason if it's not the same model and caliber.

The shotgun, often called the "front door gun, is the very picture of versatility. With slugs and a sighted, rifled barrel (is it still a shotgun if you put a rifled barrel on it?) it is deadly out to 125 yards or so. Everyone is familiar with its traditional bird-hunting role. With heavy loads of buckshot it is big medicine during building-clearing ops. With the near universal availability of replacement barrels, chokes, stocks, and other options, they can be customized to suit your requirements, and rapidly and easily changed to do something else. Remington's 870 is the popular choice in this category, but hard on its heels are Mossbergs 500 & 590 (choice of the Marine Corps in recent competition), and Winchester's 1200. These are all pump guns, but some autoloaders that make the cut are the HK/Benelli M1 Super 90, Beretta's 1201, and Remington's 11-87.

Probably the top shotgun accessories today are white light systems, the best of which is Laser Products Sure-Fire line. Available for most of the guns listed above, these units replace the factory forend with a completely self-contained flashlight/switch/forend combo that is extremely bright. It also allows single-hand control, something not possible before its introduction without dangling wires and taped-on switches. Additionally, the Side-Saddle spare ammo carrier that attaches to the side of the receiver and holds six extra rounds right at the balance point - accessible to either hand for tactical reloads while keeping the weapon on target - is virtually a standard addition to the tactical shotgun, and is well worth considering.

If you have ever lived or worked in the country, you'll immediately recognize the need for a .22 rifle. Whether you have rabbits in the garden, gophers in the yard, or starlings in the chicken feed, or simply want a way to spend an enjoyable afternoon, there is no other firearm that you will use as much or enjoy as much as a .22. Scopes are optional but useful. Marlin's line of bolt and semi-auto rifles have dominated the price wars for years, and are excellent buys, as is the Ruger 10/22 & bolt action 77/22, which is also available in .22 magnum, .22 Hornet, and now, .44 Magnum so strong is it's receiver. Ruger recently introduced its 96/22 lever-action rifle, and Winchester and Marlin also sell lever actions. Remington has a fine line (no surprises there) of bolt and semi-auto rifles as well. Don't overlook the variety of rifles that take-down for easier carry. These include Marlin's Papoose, the old Charter Arms AR-7 (now produced by Henry Arms), and Springfield Armoury's M6 combination .22/.410 shotgun. These are all lightweight rifles that are easily carried and offer a great improvement in accuracy for most shooters over trail handguns, while retaining the light weight that encourages their inclusion on your packing list for survival excursions or bug-out bags.

Nothing spells relief when things go bump in the night like a heavy handgun. The primary requirements are absolute reliability, adequate power and the accuracy to hit your target. The details are as numerous as the choices. The long-time favorite is the M1911A1-style .45. A large, heavy, and powerful handgun, its exploits are legendary. There are vastly more modern pistols, but very few approach the success of its long heritage, and none has the wide base of knowledge, spare parts, or accessories.

The Glock line is one that has been fantastically popular. There are those whom the lack of an external locking safety bothers, but the plastic Austrian gun's record doesn't reflect a problem. It's extreme reliability, light weight and accuracy have made converts of countless thousands of happy souls. Available in all the modern, effective calibers, in magazine capacities from 9 to 33 rounds, there is probably a Glock that is right for you.

The U.S. Military has purchased the Beretta M92 and the Sig/Sauer P228 for our standard military pistols as the M9 and M11, respectively, and many Federal and State agencies have followed their lead. Smith & Wesson, Heckler & Koch (HK), Walther, Browning, Ruger and Taurus round out the most popular autos with a variety of models to fill any need.

All this talk about semi-autos should not lead you to believe that revolvers somehow became ineffective the day everyone started switching to autos - far from it. A properly loaded revolver of quality design and manufacture is still potent medicine, and in the hands of a trained person can stand and deliver the goods. While autos will always have improved reload times and higher capacity, speedloaders and situational awareness, proper use of cover & concealment, and carrying the fastest reload of all - a spare weapon - will negate most of the arguments against them. No other handgun can compare with the .357's stopping record when using 125 grain hollow-points at a nominal 1400 FPS. And no other weapon is as versatile in as many conditions as a good four or six-inch barreled revolver.

The field handgun can double as the defense handgun, if you select carefully, and actually there is a lot to recommend such a course of action. This generally will be a revolver of suitable caliber, meaning either .357 Magnum, .44 Special or Magnum, .45 ACP or .45 Colt. The .38 Special is marginally acceptable, but since you can fire this cartridge in the .357, there is no need to limit yourself by choosing a .38 as your only chambering, at least in this larger revolver. In any case, if the field revolver is going to be your self-defense piece as well, it really must be a double action number with a swing-out cylinder for rapid reloading.

Some of the advantages of having a single weapon perform both missions are: You only have to store one caliber of ammo, You only need to practice with a single weapon to remain proficient, and initial procurement costs are cut in half or so - you'll still need a backup (ideally an identical duplicate), but generally a good revolver costs noticeably less than an equally good semi-auto, and it's ancillary items cost a lot less (speedloaders vs. magazines, anyway). If you opt for this course, stick with the .357, although you can get .44 Special (NOT magnum) guns built on medium frames these days, if you prefer big-bore bullet weights. You'll probably get tired of carrying the 50 oz. of a large frame .44 or .45 a lot quicker than a 32 oz. medium frame .357 or .44 Special. If you do not require it to do double duty – and if you can afford it - you can get away with a Single-Action revolver, preferably in a heavy caliber. An example is the stainless steel Ruger Super Blackhawk in .44 Magnum, with a 5-1/2 inch barrel.

Finally, the hideout piece. A smaller, lighter, and usually less-powerful firearm than your primary handgun, it is often the one you have with you when the unexpected happens. That being the case, don't neglect your training regimen with this weapon. It is probably more difficult to shoot well than your larger one, and, while marksmanship basics remain the same, they ARE more difficult to apply with grips and sights that are too small for most folks. Especially in dim or no light conditions, when your heart is racing, your hands are slippery and sweating, and you only went out for some milk for tomorrow's breakfast.

The hideout piece is a very important decision, but one that today is easier than ever before. For most folks this will be a small frame .38 Special, but with the proliferation of sub-compact autos in serious calibers, more people are choosing autos than ever before. Kahr Arms' 9mm, and their new MK-9, are both smaller than just about anything out there, Kel-Tec's P-11, S&W's Sigma 9 & .380, Colt's Pony & Mustang - the list just goes on and on. Also there are scads of .32, .25, and .22 miniature autos, and Freedom Arms' incredibly small .22 single-action revolver 5-shooters are wonders of micro-machining. For the traditionalist, or one who would rather depend on the proven .38, the S&W Centennial line are the ones to beat - concealed hammer, round grip frame, 2 inch barrel; at their best with an aluminum frame - they are also available in stainless and in .22, 9mm and .357 (stainless only) and with 3-inch barrels and adjustable sights. Colt has its new DS-II .38 6-shot revolver (the Smiths are 5-shooters) and lots of its old line such as the Agent and Detective Special are available used. Ruger's SP-101 is extremely robust for its size and is available in the same calibers as the Smith & Wesson offerings, and also in .32 H&R Magnum. Taurus's M85 revolvers are very popular in this role, as well.

There are those who live in states which allow civilian ownership of fully-automatic weapons who have or would like to have one. This is generally a mistake - at least, if you are including it in your defense planning. Owning one as a part of your shooting hobby is something else entirely. But, for those who can afford their prodigious ammunition appetite and don't mind the Federal paperwork and giving up their privacy rights (legally possessing - and don't think about having one illegally - an automatic weapon gives the BATF the right to unannounced inspections of your storage of it, and brings in an entire new spectrum of Big Brother). Anyway, if you feel you really need it for your defense planning a sub-machine gun (a compact, fully automatic weapon which shoots a pistol cartridge) is most effective up close (up to 75 meters or so), and a .30 caliber medium machinegun on a tripod is pretty good out to a thousand meters or so - if you can afford to practice enough to get good enough to hit at that distance.

A silencer, or more properly a sound suppressor, is a horse of an entirely different color. Being restricted by the same laws as full-automatics, a suppressor is something that is much more user friendly. It allows the shooter to hunt without giving away his position and to practice without earplugs. They ease the training of new shooters and help them avoid flinching, and in a more sinister context, allow such tasks as "sentry takedown" without alerting other guards. The military recognizes this and has a suppressor kit for the M9 Beretta, and the recent SOCOM (Special Operations COMmand) pistol contract specifies a sound suppressor as part of the package. EGW and Jonathan Arthur Ciener are two of the more widely known companies which sell suppressors in the States.

AMUNITION

Along with decisions about what firearms to own, come more choices concerning ammunition. The caliber of weapon you have obviously narrows down the choices considerably, but they can still be nearly overwhelming. If you have made the wise choice of purchasing military caliber weapons, take advantage of the availability of surplus ammo. Round for round you won't find a better deal, and you can't even reload .308 or .223 ammo as cheaply as you can pick up surplus stuff.

Be aware of the sometimes questionable quality or reliability of surplus ammo that may have been in very questionable conditions - widely varying temperature and humidity, perhaps contaminated with petroleum products - who knows? It may also be un-reloadable with Berdan primers, and could have corrosive primers as well. None of these are disqualifiers, but you need to know in advance and be prepared to compensate for these factors. It pays to check out a good sample of whatever lot you may purchase for reliability and accuracy, and make sure it's pressures don't exceed the strength of your rifle. There is an old axiom that will hold true as long as we have firearms - you can never have too much ammunition. In any case, keep at least 500 rounds per weapon, and if you have battle rifles, consider ten times that much.

Be sure your ammunition is stored properly. Don't ignore cleaning supplies or spare parts. Keep large quantities of cleaning solvent, patches, bore brushes, Q-tips, pipe cleaners, and lubricating oil & gun grease on hand so you can keep those valuable investments doing their job. At the same time, wouldn't you hate to have that rifle inoperative because your firing pin broke, or mainspring went soft, and you couldn't replace it? We're talking $5 or $10 parts, which could cost you a lot if neglected. In general, purchase firing pins, extractors, ejectors, and all internal and magazine springs, and any other parts with a history of breakage or early replacement. Manufacturer's manuals, disassembly and repair books, and any other reference on your specific type should be gathered as well, for the inevitable necessary repairs down the line. Please don't take the lack of mention of all the countless other manufacturers or models to mean they are somehow unsuited for use - the best gun in the world is the one you have when you need it. Take heart that despite the best efforts of the anti-gunners we still have some of the most liberal gun laws of anywhere in the world.

Whatever your feelings are toward the NRA, if you own firearms you should be a member - they are THE voice of law abiding citizens in Congress's ear. Despite its detractors, the NRA has been very effective in keeping our cause foremost in the American legislators mind. Join them and help support the right of all American citizens to keep and bear arms!

Gun Control in the Cities

No matter how you felt or thought about gun control in the past, it's time to face disaster-induced reality. The gun-control politicians (and the people who supported them) have placed Americans in a situation where not only can the police not protect us in a timely manner, but we cannot lawfully defend ourselves. Criminals unlawfully have firearms; citizens lawfully don't. Intentionally or otherwise, gun control supporters have created a situation where an unfortunate number of innocent men, women and children are going to be in danger during a crisis simply because they could not obtain the tools of self-defense.

It also happens that the cities where the rioting will likely be the worst are precisely the cities where firearms are most likely to be banned from lawful ownership and where criminals may wield near absolute power for a while. Perhaps when society recovers from it, we can review the fallacy in the cause / effect logic that keeps people voting for gun-control laws, but in the mean time, millions of people are going to have to resort to breaking the law in order to protect themselves. And yes, you too will have to resort to breaking the law if you are to acquire a firearm in an area where guns are entirely banned from private citizens (like New York, Los Angeles, etc.).

After the disaster hits, if the rioting gets really bad, you'll see local police begging law abiding citizens for help. Your firearm will be a welcome addition to the force of law and order, believe me. No local cop is going to mind you having a handgun if you're manning a roadblock protecting a neighborhood of families with children. Act responsibly, tell them what you're doing, and they'll probably give you a big thanks. But if you're carrying a gun while you smash a window of the Wal-Mart and walk off with a stereo; well that's a different story. Be prepared to get shot.

Cops don't mind private ownership nearly as much as we've all been led to believe. When the crisis hits, they'll be more than happy to have your cooperation. We're all going to need as many law abiding gun-toting citizens as possible in order to fend off the criminals and establish some degree of order.

XXIX Transportation & Mobile Shelter

CARS, PICKUPS, VANS, MOTORCYCLES

While zipping around town in a little Porsche is a whole lot of fun, you will wish you had something more practical when everything around you is falling apart. That means you need transportation which is:

- Inexpensive (there won't be much trade in value)
- Repairable by you
- Reliable
- Can carry a load
- Has good gas mileage

You aren't going to be able to meet all the above criteria in most modern vehicles. While they win on the gas mileage front, in general new cars are are expensive and not repairable by anyone who doesn't have a wide assortment of computer tools.

And forget the wonderful world of cars to come. It all sounded so easy: Impose higher average gas mileage standards on the auto industry and motorists would not only save money, but America would wean itself off oil. However, meeting the new regulations will cost thousands more than you will ever save on fuel costs. The American public should start getting used to paying more, because high-tech cars built for big increases in gas mileage and lower carbon emissions a decade from now are not going to be cheap. The cost of more ambitious goals that are being considered — 47 to 62 mpg by 2025 — would require more drastic changes in cars, such as massive weight reduction and plug-in electric motors, that could add $10,000 or more in today's dollars to sticker prices. New cars could be out of reach of many more potential buyers, and automakers could face lower sales as a "new normal".

You might consider a pre-90s truck or van, or even a collectable pickup from an earlier era, some are "cherried out" and are relatively inexpensive and can be repaired at the side of the road with a couple wrenches and a screwdriver. Classic cars also tend to increase in value, while new cars devalue as soon as they are driven off the lot.

Also consider buying a 4x4, even though you live in the city (it may need to be newer, get one while you can). A 4x4 allows you to drive over the sidewalk or through wasteland, away from roadblocks or riots. Those that have 4x4s simply go off road, climb over a boulevard and leave while the rest of the poor car owners have to stay. A 4x4 truck also has more mass and power in case that someone tries to cut you off or rams you with their car. It's less likely to stop running if you hit someone or several people (in a riot situation) since it's prepared for cross country use and the engine is much more protected.

FUEL STORAGE

You should also be stockpiling fuel, if you can. Five gallon metal jerry cans are probably what most people can obtain easily, but barrels with hand pumps would also help. Obviously, storage should be away from the home if possible. Chemical extenders can increase the shelf life of fuel, which does tend to degrade with time, losing the lighter molecules. Larger portable containers in the hundred gallon range are available for pickups for a few hundred dollars. Depending on their capacity, they can hold one or two barrels of gas and are seen at construction sites, and are not too expensive if bought used. Trailerable fuel tanks are pricier, running into the thousands of dollars.

DRIVING TIPS

If our country ever falls, remember some new rules will be in force whenever you see a traffic light. Windows and doors have to be closed at all times, a weapon must be within arm's reach. You never stop at a red lights or stop sign unless there is traffic, especially at night. At first, police will write you a ticket for not stopping at a red light if they see you (another way of saying that they will ask for a bribe if they see you pass a red light), but after a few months they will realize that nothing can be done, people would rather risk a ticket than risking their lives, so they decided to turn traffic lights to permanent yellow at night, after 8 or 9 PM. This is, of course, very dangerous. Night car accidents are both frequent and brutal since sometimes both cars hit each other at full speed.

Remember that a car is one heavy, powerful piece of machinery. especially a big truck with chrome-tube bumpers installed, especially for hitting those that are stupid enough to try and make you stop by standing in front of your car. If we devolve to the type of failed narco-state that Mexio has become, if someone tries to force you to stop your car by standing in front of it you will just aim at them and accelerate. At first, doing this will make you feel nervous, but it will become normal of necessity.

MOTORCYCLES BICYCLES & MOPEDS

Any two wheeled cycle can be nice to have in an emergency situation because they tend to be fuel misers. The question then becomes whether the model you get is practical, and whether your location is practical. Buying a Harley LowRider that is tricked out and expensive is unlikely to be a good option. If you live in a hilly area and you are out of shape could also make the most practical 15 speed mountain bike a waste of effort.

No matter what you choose, one consideration is to have carrying racks or bags that can attach to your cycle. While this may seem uber uncool now, think about how you are going to carry food for ten miles.

LIVING IN YOUR CAR

Living in a car isn't something that anyone would recommend. However, when you get laid off, your emergency fund runs out, your home is foreclosed (or you get an eviction notice) and there's nobody to help, living in your car might be the only choice, especially if you don't feel safe at a local shelter. Unfortunately, in many places, sleeping in your car is not only frowned upon, but also illegal. Here's how to get by until something better comes along.

Remember, you are not alone and you have a vehicle. Lots of people have survived and even thrived while sleeping in cars.

You can only live in your car successfully if your car works. You're going to need a new or "newish" car or be a good mechanic to live in an older car. If you have an old car keep in mind that you're liable to break down at an inopportune moment if you don't stay on top of maintenance.

Find a safe and inconspicuous place to park. First, check to see if there are any organizations or businesses in your area that designates parking lots specifically for people in situations like yours; If there are no such lots available, and you live in a city, look for streets with no sidewalks, no overlooking windows, and adjacent to woods; the area should be sparse enough to avoid nosy onlookers but populated enough that the car does not stand out. Parking lots of big-box retailers (especially those that are open 24 hours and have restrooms, such as Wal-Mart) are great to clean up in and have security, as long as you spend a couple of dollars there and don't park in one place too often. Parking lots however can be noisy, particularly in the morning as trucks arrive carrying food and goods.

Church car parks are often quiet during week days. If you check around, you may find a church that is less used than others. This could be a good place to park, and you may be able to ask for assistance at the church

Industrial estates and business parks are often noisy by day, but very quiet at night. Small ones close to residential areas are best. They have to be quiet at night. You may encounter security in some places like this, but if you are honest, saying you are just sleeping the night in your car, they usually won't bother you. Their main role is to protect the property.

University car parks. This is okay if you are a student, but not so good if you are not associated with the university. If required, get a parking permit

Camping grounds are another option, although they usually have time limits and some are almost as expensive as a hotel room. Some offer a shower for a nominal fee. National Forests have some free camping with time limits.

If there's no restroom, having a creek nearby helps for rinsing purposes. Know how to safely defecate outdoors and make a poop tube. A five gallon bucket with a lid and lye for odor can also work.

A free hospital parking lot is another option. If approached by a guard, you can say that you're waiting to visit a sick relative. If you can establish rapport with the manager of a retail store or restaurant, they may not give you problems about staying overnight, especially if they see your presence as a form of overnight security.

Once you find a spot, try to arrive late at night, and leave before 7am. This will draw as little attention as possible to yourself.

Due to noise, you might find that you will need ear plugs to sleep. Ear plugs will block a lot of background noise to like traffic, birds, animals, talking and background music. They will not block out very loud noise or close noise, such as someone tapping on your car.

Find a place to shower. The most logical place would appear to be a gym. This will help you keep your sanity and give you a purpose to your morning. Don't settle for the first gym you find, you may find nearly deserted gyms in which you can shower and fully clean yourself without embarrassment.

Gyms though can be an expensive option just for a shower. Many councils, churches and support organizations have free showers. It can be a false economy to use a gym just for showers, particularly as there are many free ways to keep in shape without a gym.

Try to remember the flip flops or water shoes as not to get a foot fungus and let the towel dry out in the car.

Community or Recreation centers that have gyms and showers are a cheaper option than the nationwide chains. Many Rec or Community centers yearly memberships cost about the same as the monthly memberships at a national gym. You may not be able to store your items as safely in these places though.

The next best choice is to check into an affordable trailer park one or two days a week. These usually range from about $18-$26 a night. You will have a spot to park your car, you can do laundry (usually an extra fee), fill up on water, have a shower and even pitch a tent if you have one. They usually have powered sites, so you can recharge your electrical devices or run a fan or heater.

Another option, though possibly more expensive, is to book into a cheap motel or hostel once or twice a week and clean up thoroughly there.

Public pools tend to have showers, depending on whether they have private stalls or are set up gang style, they may provide a discrete place to shower.

Another option to consider- when you can't shower, use unscented baby wipes to clean up, or take a "bum shower" in a public restroom where you feel comfortable doing so.

At a truck stop, you can ask around for a shower coupon, if you feel safe allowing people to know that you're without a place to stay. Truck stops are good to sleep at too. Truck Stops can be noisy at night though, so ear plugs are recommended. Some toll roads, especially state turnpikes, have large rest areas with free showers for truckers. Since these are usually open 24 hours, these plazas are also good places to sleep. Rest areas on National highways are good for a few hours and most have security.

Keep an eye out for community college athletic field houses-- they don't always check IDs, and can be a good free shower option. Check their fee schedule-- sometimes you can take a single class for a nominal price, thus becoming a legitimate member of the college community, with access to their gym, library, Wi-Fi, employment office and other resources (in addition to learning something).

Be discreet. Keeping your situation under wraps minimizes the embarrassment and helps avoid becoming a target for police officers and criminals alike. Rotate among several parking locations to avoid getting noticed.

When you move around in the parked car, move slowly to avoid rocking the car.

Consider using a car cover. Not only will it maintain privacy (especially since condensation on the windows will otherwise make it obvious that you're in there) but it will also keep the car warmer during winter. This is not a viable option, however, when it's hot outside.

When it's sunny in the daytime, use a sunshade for the windshield. You may find that you need and want more privacy than windows offer. Reflective window shades in your back and front window help. Similarly fold up shades on the side windows are good. You can also buy some cheap cloth and either stuff them in the windows, tape them in, or hold them in place by magnets.[11] Black cloth is best for privacy and blocking out light.

If you can afford it, local laws allow, and you don't mind driving with it. Get your windows tinted as dark as legally possible. This along with the front sunshade and dark cloth or towels can provide a lot of privacy. If you hang a towel or cloth on a untinted window it screams homeless person. You hang the same on a tinted window it'll be impossible to see inside and won't draw attention.

Keep the windows cracked open while you sleep, not wide enough for someone to reach in, but enough to allow fresh air and reduce condensation on the windows.

Get the things you'll need. The basic essentials for living in a car are a blanket, a pillow, and a mattress or some other padding. Due to the angles involved in the seating setup, you may develop dull back pain from the cramped quarters. Once you have your sleeping gear, you'll want a blanket to place over the back seat, and drape over the two front seats. This will block light and people's views.

A cheap cooler will help make life easier. The main thing the cooler needs is to be water proof. Cold food will cause condensation, while ice will melt. You don't want that water inside of your car. A cooler will help keep your perishable food cool. It will work most efficiently when full, so add bottles of cold water to it as you take out food. If you choose to buy an electric cooler, it will need good ventilation to work. For this reason, it will not work well in your car's boot. It is best placed within the car when running. Make sure it is only running when the engine runs, or use a low voltage cut out device. Make sure the cooling vent grille is not touching anything as it exhausts waste heat and may set some things on fire.

One essential item, if you can afford it is a porta potti, a chemical toilet. These devices can really make living in a car bearable. They can be purchased for under $100 new these days. If you can't afford a porta potti or don't have room for one, you can pee into wide necked bottles like Gatorade bottles, or make an improvised bucket style toilet.

Find alternate ways of generating electricity. A cigarette lighter converter is one option. These are useful for powering low consuming devices (100 watts), but if you plan on using your vehicle for cooking, then you'll need to draw power more directly from your battery or you'll blow the fuse. Running electric cooking appliances from your car is fairly impractical without an expensive dual battery and inverter system. There are small 12 volt water heaters and skillets, but these generally are not very efficient. You will also need a much more expensive inverter if you plan to run things that use mains voltage. You may need to idle the vehicle while drawing this power if you don't have a dual battery system; car alternators are not designed for such use and may not be able to produce the current you need.

A good buy for any car dweller is a low voltage cut out device. This device protects your car's battery by cutting off the electricity once the battery reaches a voltage where it can still start the car, but can't really run plug in devices much more. These usually retail for about $25-$40. Continual flattening of your battery will damage it, resulting in a costly replacement, and inconvenience of not being able to start the car.

An alternative to electric cooking devices is to use gas for cooking, but do not use this inside the vehicle for safety reasons. There are many dangers associated with cooking inside your car; unstable surfaces, fire hazards, burns from hot metal or spilled liquids, carbon monoxide build up, smells. Cooking is for outside of the car. If you live in a van with a stable set up for cooking, then cooking inside is okay, provided there is ventilation.

Have a place to store items that is portable. Get bags you can fill with your soaps, clothes, cell phone, etc. Keeping things in order will save you a lot of hassle. A vehicle may seem like a small space, but losing things can be extremely easy. Also, keeping things neat inside the car will draw less attention from people passing by who happen to look in the windows. Hiding your bedding might be a good idea (consider the trunk). If there is not room in the car for a week's worth of clothes and supplies, try to leave them at a friends for safe keeping and then you can have a reason to come over, and they may give you a shower and a place to hang out. When you do your laundry, be sure to get them bone dry, as you do not want damp clothes to mildew or smell bad in the car.

When you're not in the car, leave windows cracked and dryer sheets scattered about to keep the interior smelling decent. Wash your sheets once a month, or else you risk smelling like a homeless person, which will blow your cover and get you treated like a homeless person.

Keep dirty clothes separate in plastic bags so they do not smell up all your clothing.

Evaluate your food options. Peanut butter, tuna and crackers are great staples. Have a box for food so it does not get smashed. They will be limited by the lack of refrigeration. Gallons of water are a necessity for a lot of things. Fast food is expensive when you're living off of it. With old fashioned (large flake) rolled oats, powdered milk, bottled water, plastic cups, and chocolate protein powder, you can ensure that you always have a nutritious snack to fall back on.

Rent a P.O. Box or a Private Mail Box (PMB). Although PMBs tend to be more expensive, you can receive packages at them and some services will let you use a address format which makes it appear to be an apartment, which is useful for when someone requires a physical address.

Renew any paperwork that will require an address to process soon. Put valuables in a safe deposit box at a bank.

If you have friends or family who can't help you with your living situation at least ask them if you can use their address.

TRAILERS, CAMPERS, RVs & BOATS

This is a catchall for any mobile vehicle that you can sleep on, has a portable potty and where you can cook food. There are too many categories for us to cover adequately, other than just to give a few tips.

Don't buy a money pit – a lot of empty live aboard vehicles are empty for a reason. If you don't have experience with the particular mobile vehicle, have someone qualified give you both and estimate of its value, and what the repair costs will be.

Remember, this is not rent free living. There will generally be a storage/docking/hookup fee which might come to a sizeable amount.

If you aren't handy with tools, you probably shouldn't buy such a home. All repairs take three to ten times longer than estimated, so prepare for the amount of maintenance you will have to do.

If you buy a live aboard boat, the minimum length should be about 30 feet. If it isn't trailerable, you will have a regular sip fee. Also, boats tend to be very cold in the winter and noisy if there is water slapping at the sides. The following comments are addressed to RVs, but apply to boats as well.

RV's are designed to be fully self-contained, for at least a short period of time, and can easily get you through the first 72 hours of a disaster. Extending the time "off the hook" is not difficult if you learn how to **conserve** and make a few modifications.

Shelter is inherently taken care by an RV. The next thing to consider is an adequate water supply. Check the fresh water carrying capacity of your RV. Then at least double it with other containers providing you can safely carry the weight. Consider how many people you can accommodate and add enough more water storage to meet everybody's needs. Remember to include enough water for your pets' needs too, though if things are really bad te pet might need to fend for itself. Water is heavy, so, a balance of weight and carrying capacity needs to be thought through carefully. Water is plentiful if you have the means to be sure it is safe to use. You can acquire water along the way if your travel takes you that far where you would run out before you get to your planned destination.

Most RV's do not come with a water filtration or purification system. A simple sediment filter that attaches to the hose used to fill the fresh water tank is a good start. But, for drinking purposes a true high quality filtration system is essential. Equipping your RV with a passive filtration system such as a Berkey Light and with Berkey Black filters will solve all of your potable water problems. This will also eliminate the need for storing extra water, the space it would take up and the weight it would add.

Next consider a well stocked pantry. In addition to cupboards and drawers, every RV has numerous nooks and crannies where food can be stored. Search your RV for them. See if there are spaces under and behind drawers, voids around appliances, open areas in furniture, removable panels that access wall interiors.

Every time you do your grocery shopping pick up a few extra nonperishable items to stock in your RV. The more dried stock stored the better as it significantly decreases weight. Another thing to remember is that even with an RV you cannot carry enough foot to last a long time. Obviously pets or people with special needs must be planned for well in advance. Having a place to store food in advance at a remote destination that you can get to later is a real asset.

Cooking in a RV is usually done with propane fuel. So is heating and refrigeration. Keep your LP tanks full and ready. Availability of this resource will be limited or nonexistent in a mass emergency situation so conservation will be key. While in travel mode, using your onboard propane stove is the most practical. Once you arrive at a safe place where you can set up camp and collect fire wood, you can switch to cooking over an open fire outside. Having a few cast iron pots, pans, a griddle, and pot hangers would be very handy. If you don't know how to cook over an open fire, now is the time to learn, before the need to do it arises.

Electrical power isn't an absolute necessity but is certainly nice to have for lights at night and to power radios and small TV's so that you can keep abreast of what's happening in the world. Many folks that are medically dependant on electrical power must make plans for making their own power long term electrical power. Electrical power in most RV's manufactured in the United States are 12 volt and designed to run on battery power. The battery is charged by a converter when plugged into a 110 volt outlet. Fully charged batteries conservatively used can last for 72 hours until you get to a safe place. To continue having electrical power will require that the battery/batteries be charged. You can do this with a generator which will also supply power to run 110 volt items. But a generator requires fuel which you will have to carry with you in the likelihood it will not be available otherwise. Recharging the batteries and doing other electrically intensive things makes the best use of the gasoline.

Charging can also be done with a small trickle charging solar panel, an inexpensive option. The ultimate would be to install a full solar power system and have unlimited electrical power but it can be an expensive option. For true long term survivability, solar panels and other alternative power regenerative sources can make a key difference in comfort and livability. There are other less expensive methods of generating your own power than solar panels but they all have their respective limitations.

Your RV needs to have adequate sleeping space for everyone in your group. That doesn't necessarily mean a full bed for everybody but enough space for each person to lay down and get rest when needed. All of your crew needs to be well rested, especially in a stressful emergency situation, in order to function at their best. A well rested crew is a good crew, one that can be depended upon when in need. The recreational vehicle. A practical safe and secure way to evacuate with all the basic essentials needed for survival through an emergency. Shelter, water, food, safety, and comfort. A place that has power when the lights go out. Warm and dry from the storm and able to get out of harm's way. Your RV. A survival shelter on wheels.

XXX Clothing

Clothing is something that is not considered often enough in planning for a disaster. You'll find many chat room and discussion board references to food, water, housing, etc., but very few references to clothes. Yet finding suitable clothing will be a very real concern in a long term disaster. Clothes wear out or your kids grow out of them. In these normal times, you just drive to the mall or Wal-Mart or wherever and buy what you need. There's always plenty available.

This might not be true after a major disaster. It takes factories to make clothes; it takes international trade, a reliable banking system, dependable distribution systems, accurate billing systems, sophisticated telecommunications, the power grid, computers, computers, computers! Even in a less than worst case scenario, there will definitely be problems in some or all of these areas. If you want to have clothes for your family post crash, you will need to get them now.

No one will have the slightest interest in fashion after a disaster; we'll all be too concerned with getting enough food and keeping warm. We don't know how long the really nasty times will be, plan on at least 1 year of chaos followed by a couple years of rebuilding. This seems reasonable based on what we know about a large scale disasters. If you agree with this estimate, you'll need to have at least two full years of clothes for your family. Perhaps three years of clothes just to be sure. Since you already have clothes for everyone, you have part of this job done. You may have three years worth of clothes for your family in your house right now.

If you have children, this will take some thought. Will the clothes your oldest child wears become too small before they can be worn out, which means they can be handed down to younger siblings, or has your oldest essentially finished growing? Do you have boys or girls or both? Boys tend to wear out their clothes sooner than girls. Do you live in a cool northern area or a warmer southern one? The best way to figure out your family's clothing needs is to pretend they have nothing whatsoever to wear and you have been given the job of outfitting the entire family from underwear to topcoat. Actually you have been given this job, just not all at once. A disaster changes all that as it changes so many things. The bright side is that you can forget about getting them what's fashionable this year.

The only really tricky part is allowing for growth if you have children. Make a list with each family member on it and write down what each one needs, beginning with the oldest child. If the oldest still has some growing to do, figure that there will be hand-medowns available to younger siblings. Allow at least five long sleeve and five short sleeve shirts per child and five pairs of pants also. The oldest male can always hand down his outgrown shirts and pants to both younger brothers and sisters. Five pairs of underpants and undershirts, five pairs of socks, two sweaters, a jacket and a heavy coat per child should be the minimum. A few dresses and skirts for the girls would be nice.

You already have most of this, the only difference from your normal clothing concerns is the fact that you will need to buy clothes for growing children now instead of next year and the year after. There may not be much joy in your children's lives for a few years—things will be so terribly different from what they're used to—so have a few nice things tucked away for them, particularly for daughters. Kids are still kids and they love an attractive surprise. There may be some local social events in your area they'd like to look nice for so plan ahead for this, which means don't take those clothes shopping with you.

Shoes may be the worst clothing problem you have. Unless there is a cobbler in your area, which is very rare these days, there will be no way to repair shoes or resole them when they're worn out. The shoe purchase procedure is the same as with your other clothing concerns: figure out what each child will need for two or three years, allowing for growth, buy it now and put it away. Each child will need several pairs of everyday shoes to play in (or work in if things get really bad), plus a pair of nicer shoes for church or whatever social occasions may occur and some sturdy boots for winter snows.

Buy in a similar manner for you and your spouse or any other adults in the family. You don't have to buy everything new for adults or children; go to thrift shops or yard sales and stock up. If you find a good source of inexpensive clothes, buy lots of things in all the average sizes. Remember that most people will not be at all prepared for a crash so any clothes you don't need will be excellent barter items.

When choosing clothing for survival situations that suit that you wear to work may not be your best choice. Clothing needs to be durable. Another point to look at is the resources to wash your clothing, you need to pick survival clothes that will not fall apart when they get dirty or are used hard.

Levis or denim material: This material first became popular in the later 1800's with minors and cowboys, and it was for a reason it was because it was tough. A good pair of Levis and a sturdy work shirt will take you a long way and stand up to prolonged periods between washing. Denim material would be good clothing for around the home or in a situation where you had to spend some time in the forest. A good source for this type of clothing is Wal-Mart or any western store.

Military Surplus: There is a reason that the military uses the field clothes that they do. They are durable surplus pants and shirts are pretty easy to find, three great sources for military surplus survival clothing are, www.cheaperthandirt.com, www.sportsmansguide.com and your local military surplus store. Military surplus clothing is a good choice if you want to blend in or hide for some reason.

Shoes or Boots: Although shoes may seem like a small part of your apparel, if you have ever have had sore feet then you know that it can ruin your day. In the event of a long-term survival situation there may be a shortage of gasoline, if that is the case then you may be walking a lot. Saving money on clothing is one thing but I wouldn't recommend cutting corners on your shoes, however the question is what type of shoes do you get? Foot wear is largely a matter of preference although the preference would be a good pair of lace up hiking boots. Running shoes wear out too fast and they don't offer any support for your ankles. A good source for boots is www.cabelas.com.
Socks: You can have the best shoes in the world and if you still don't have quality socks your feet will still hurt. A good pack of gym socks will serve you well, they are not too thick and not to thin, many people try to by cheap socks however for survival use it would be a good idea to spend the extra money and put them away.

XXXI Fuels for Heating and Cooking

You will need fuel for three main purposes:

- Heating
- Cooking
- Transportation.

While there is some overlap, make sure you plan for the differences in safety and storage.

HEATING

Coal stores well if kept in a dark place and away from moving air. Air speeds deterioration and breakdown, causing it to burn more rapidly. Coal may be stored in a plastic-lined pit or in sheds, bags, boxes, or barrels and should be kept away from circulating air, light, and moisture. Cover it to lend protection from weather and sun.

Wood. Hardwoods such as apple, cherry, and other fruit woods are slow burning and sustain coals. Hardwoods are more difficult to burn than softer woods, thus requiring a supply of kindling. Soft woods such as pine and cedar are light in weight and burn very rapidly, leaving ash and few coals for cooking. If you have a fireplace or a wood/coal burning stove, you will want to store several cords of firewood. Firewood is usually sold by the cord which is a neat pile that totals 128 cubic feet. This pile is four feet wide, four feet high, and eight feet long. Some dealers sell wood by the ton. As a general rule of thumb, a standard cord of air dried dense hardwood weighs about two tons and provides as much heat as one ton of coal. Be suspicious of any alleged cord delivered in a ½ or 3/4 ton pickup truck. For best results, wood should be seasoned (dried) properly, usually at least a year. A plastic tarp, wood planks, or other plastic or metal sheeting over the woodpile is useful in keeping the wood dry. Other types of fuels are more practical to store and use than wood or coal.

Newspaper logs make a good and inexpensive source of fuel. You may prepare the logs in the following manner: Use about eight pages of newspaper and open flat. Spread the stack, alternating the cut sides and folded sides. Place a 1" wood dowel or metal rod across one end and roll the paper around the rod very tightly. Roll it until there are 6-8 inches left to roll, and then slip another 8 pages underneath the roll. Continue this procedure until you have a roll 4-6 inches in diameter. With a fine wire, tie the roll on both ends. Withdraw the rod. Your newspaper log is ready to use. Four of these logs will burn about 1 hour.

Propane is another excellent fuel for indoor use. Like kerosene, it produces carbon dioxide as it burns and is therefore not poisonous. It does consume oxygen so be sure to crack a window when burning propane. Propane stores indefinitely, having no known shelf life. Propane stoves and small portable heaters are very economical, simple to use, and come the closest to the type of convenience most of us are accustomed to using on a daily basis. The storage of propane is governed by strict local laws. As a rule you may store up to 1 gallon inside a building and up to 60 gallons outside. If you store more than these amounts, you will need a special permit from the fire marshal. The primary hazard in using propane is that it is heavier than air and if a leak occurs it may "pool" which can create an explosive atmosphere. Furthermore, basement natural gas heating units CANNOT be legally converted for propane use. Again, the vapors are heavier than air and form "pockets." Ignition sources such as water heaters and electrical sources can cause an explosion.

White gas (Coleman fuel). Many families have camp stoves which burn Coleman Fuel or white gasoline. These stoves are fairly easy to use and produce a great amount of heat. However, they, like charcoal, produce vast amounts of carbon monoxide. NEVER use a Coleman Fuel stove indoors. It could be a fatal mistake to your entire family. Never store fuels in the house or near a heater. Use a metal store cabinet which is vented on top and bottom and can be locked.

Kerosene (also known as Range Oil No. 1) is the cheapest of all the storage fuels and is also very forgiving if you make a mistake. Kerosene is not as explosive as gasoline and Coleman fuel. Kerosene stores well for long periods of time and by introducing some fuel additives it can be made to store even longer. However, do not store it in metal containers for extended time periods unless they are porcelain lined because the moisture in the kerosene will rust through the container causing the kerosene to leak out. Most hardware stores and home improvement centers sell kerosene in five gallon plastic containers which store for many years. A 55 gallon drum stores in the back yard, or ten 5 gallon plastic containers will provide fuel enough to last an entire winter if used sparingly.

Caution: To burn kerosene you will need a kerosene heater. There are many models and sizes to choose from but remember that you are not trying to heat your entire home. The larger the heater the more fuel you will have to store. Most families should be able to get by on a heater that produces about 9,600 BTUs of heat, though kerosene heaters are made that will produce up to 25,000 to 30,000 BTUs. If you have the storage space to store the fuel required by these larger heaters they are excellent investments, but for most families the smaller heaters are more than adequate. When selecting a kerosene heater be sure to get one that can double as a cooking surface and source of light. Then when you are forced to use it be sure to plan your meals so that they can be cooked when you are using the heater for heat rather than wasting fuel used for cooking only.

When kerosene burns it requires very little oxygen, compared to charcoal. You must crack a window about 1/4 inch to allow enough oxygen to enter the room to prevent asphyxiation. During combustion, kerosene is not poisonous and is safe to use indoors. To prevent possible fires you should always fill it outside. The momentary incomplete combustion during lighting and extinguishing of kerosene heaters can cause some unpleasant odors. To prevent these odors from lingering in your home always light and extinguish the heater out of doors. During normal operation a kerosene heater is practically odorless.

Charcoal. *Never* use a charcoal burning device indoors. When charcoal burns it is a voracious consumer of oxygen and will quickly deplete the supply in your little "home within a home." As it burns it produces vast amounts of carbon monoxide which is a deadly poison. Trying to heat your home by burning charcoal could prove fatal to your entire family.

COOKING To conserve your cooking fuel storage needs always do your emergency cooking in the most efficient manner possible. Don't boil more water than you need, extinguish the fire as soon as you finished, plan your meals ahead of time to consolidate as much cooking as possible, during the winter cook on top of your heating unit while heating your home, and cook in a pressure cooker or other fuel efficient container as much as possible. Keep enough fuel to provide outdoor cooking for at least 7-10 days.

It is even possible to cook without using fuel at all. For example, to cook dry beans you can place them inside a pressure cooker with the proper amount of water and other ingredients needed and place it on your heat source until it comes up to pressure. Then turn off the heat, remove the pressure cooker and place inside a large box filled with newspapers, blankets, or other insulating materials. Leave it for two and a half hours and then open it, your meal will be done, having cooked for two and a half hours with no heat. If you don't have a large box in which to place the pressure cooker, simply wrap it in several blankets and place it in the corner. Store matches in waterproof airtight tin with each piece of equipment that must be lit with a flame.

Sterno fuel, a jellied petroleum product, is an excellent source of fuel for inclusion in your back pack as part of your 72 hour kit. Sterno is very light weight and easily ignited with a match or a spark from flint and steel but is not explosive. It is also safe for use indoors. A Sterno stove can be purchased at any sporting goods store and will retail between $3 and $8, depending upon the model you choose. They fold up into a very small, compact unit ideal for carrying in a pack. The fuel is readily available at all sporting goods stores and many drug stores. One can of Sterno fuel, about the diameter of a can of tuna fish and twice as high, will allow you to cook six meals if used frugally. Chafing dishes and fondue pots can also be used with Sterno. Sterno is not without some problems. It will evaporate very easily, even when the lid is securely fastened. If you use Sterno in your 72 hour kit you should check it every six to eight months to insure that it has not evaporated beyond the point of usage. Because of this problem it is not a good fuel for long-term storage. It is a very expensive fuel to use compared to others fuel available, but is extremely convenient and portable.

Coleman fuel (white gas), when used with a Coleman stove is another excellent and convenient fuel for cooking. It is not as portable nor as lightweight as Sterno, but produces a much greater BTU value. Like Sterno, Coleman fuel has a tendency to evaporate even when the container is tightly sealed so it is not a good fuel for long-term storage. Unlike Sterno, however, it is highly volatile; it will explode under the right conditions and should therefore never be stored in the home. Because of its highly flammable nature great care should always be exercised when lighting stoves and lanterns that use Coleman fuel. Many serious burns have been caused by carelessness with this product. Always store Coleman fuel in the garage or shed, out of doors.

Charcoal is the least expensive fuel per BTU that the average family can store. Remember that it must always be used out of doors because of the vast amounts of poisonous carbon monoxide it produces. Charcoal will store for extended period of time if it is stored in air tight containers. It readily absorbs moisture from the surrounding air so do not store it in the paper bags it comes in for more than a few months or it may be difficult to light. Transfer it to airtight metal or plastic containers and it will keep almost forever. Fifty or sixty dollars worth of charcoal will provide all the cooking fuel a family will need for an entire year if used sparingly. The best time to buy briquettes inexpensively is at the end of the summer. Broken or torn bags of briquettes are usually sold at a big discount.

You will also want to store a small amount of charcoal lighter fluid (or kerosene). Newspapers provide an excellent ignition source for charcoal when used in a funnel type of lighting device. To light charcoal using newspapers use two or three sheets, crumpled up, and a #10 tin can. Cut both ends out of the can. Punch holes every two inches around the lower edge of the can with a punch-type can opener (for opening juice cans). Set the can down so the punches holes are on the bottom. Place the crumpled newspaper in the bottom of the can and place the charcoal briquettes on top of the newspaper. Lift the can slightly and light the newspaper. Prop a small rock under the bottom edge of the can to create a a good draft. The briquettes will be ready to use in about 20-30 minutes.

When the coals are ready remove the chimney and place them in your cooker. Never place burning charcoal directly on concrete or cement because the heat will crack it. A wheelbarrow or old metal garbage can lid makes an excellent container for this type of fire. One of the nice things about charcoal is that you can regulate the heat you will receive from them. Each briquette will produce about 40 degrees of heat. If you are baking bread, for example, and need 400 degrees of heat for your oven, simply use ten briquettes.

To conserve heat and thereby get the maximum heat value from your charcoal you must learn to funnel the heat where you want it rather than letting it dissipate into the air around you. One excellent way to do this is to cook inside a cardboard oven. Take a cardboard box, about the size of an orange crate, and cover it with aluminum foil inside and out. Be sure that the shiny side is visible so that maximum reflectivity is achieved. Turn the box on its side so that the opening is no longer on the top but is on the side. Place some small bricks or other noncombustible material inside upon which you can rest a cookie sheet about two or three inches above the bottom of the box. Place ten burning charcoal briquettes between the bricks (if you need 400 degrees), place the support for your cooking vessels, and then place your bread pans or whatever else you are using on top of the cookie sheet. Prop a foil-covered cardboard lid over the open side, leaving a large crack for air to get in (charcoal needs a lot of air to burn) and bake your bread, cake, cookies, etc. just like you would in your regular oven. Your results will amaze you. To make your own charcoal, select twigs, limbs, and branches of fruit, nut and other hardwood trees; black walnuts and peach or apricot pits may also be used. Cut wood into desired size, place in a large can which has a few holes punched in it, put a lid on the can and place the can in a hot fire. When the flames from the holes in the can turn yellow-red, remove the can from the fire and allow it to cool. Store the briquettes in a moisture-proof container. Burn charcoal only in a well ventilated area.

Wood and Coal. Many wood and coal burning stoves are made with cooking surface. These are excellent to use indoors during the winter because you may already be using it to heat the home. In the summer, however, they are unbearably hot and are simply not practical cooking appliances for indoor use. If you choose to build a campfire on the ground outside be sure to use caution and follow all the rules for safety. Little children, and even many adults, are not aware of the tremendous dangers that open fires may pose.

Kerosene. Many kerosene heaters will also double as a cooking unit. In fact, it is probably a good idea to not purchase a kerosene heater that cannot be used to cook on as well. Follow the same precautions for cooking over kerosene as was discussed under the section on heating your home with kerosene.

Propane. Many families have propane camp stoves. These are the most convenient and easy to use of all emergency cooking appliances available. They may be used indoors or out. As with other emergency fuel sources, cook with a pressure cooker whenever possible to conserve fuel.

Alcohol Stove Zen Basics The alcohol stove is really a great option for lightweight backpackers and has many advantages over other cook systems, but may not be suitable for every backpacker or situation. If you are interested in a stove that runs on odorless fuel, need to carry as little weight as possible, like to go cheap as possible, enjoy recycling, strive to use eco friendly renewable fuels whenever possible, and/or require the ability to find fuel while walking across North America then an alcohol stove is for you. If on the other hand you need to be able to melt tremendous amounts of snow to stay alive, demand the luxury of a gas range while camping, need bombproof durability, and/or like monster truck nitro injected power in your stove then the alcohol stove is not for you.

Here's a modified KISS (Komplete Individual Simple Stoves) synopsis on alcohol stoves:

Advantages

- Lightweight - few ounces versus a pound or more
- Simplicity - just add fuel and light a match - no pumping, priming or pre-lighting required
- Reliable - many designs are fail-proof
- Quiet - generally can't be heard
- Odorless - if you spill alcohol all over your gear, you won't smell like a gas pump for the rest of your trip
- Availability of Fuel - can be found at any hardware store or gas station (great for thru-hikers)
- No Maintenance - no time or repair kit need for adjustments and cleaning
- Safety - fuel not explosive and can be easily extinguished
- Easily Transportable Fuel - don't need a heavy metal container to transport fuel - a disposable plastic water bottle is more than ample
- Low Cost - the cheapest around or even free (use common recycled items)
- Eco Friendly - uses a clean renewable energy source
- DIY (Do It Yourself) - Tools, metal and fire! DIY stoving is so satisfying that is has become its own hobby

Disadvantages

- Reduced Output - about half the heat output per ounce compared to other liquid fuels (white gas, butane, etc) and not appropriate for groups, long treks (greater than a one to two weeks without refitting) or melting snow
- Invisible Flame - refilling with fuel or handling the stove can be dangerous to those that depend solely on the sense of sight for evaluating dangers
- Cold Sensitive - most setups depend on vaporization of fuel and may not work well in frozen environments
- Lacks Brand Name - North Face wearing, Mountain House eating, Starbucks drinking, Honda Element driving "outdoors people" will refer to you as "ghetto" and/or "trailer park"
- Durability - if you step on your stove made from pop cans, you might have to say goodbye to hot meals for the rest of your trip

- DIY (Do It Yourself) - Many of the stove designs out there require you to fabricate your own setup which can prove to be challenging or inconvenient for many

Alcohol Stove Types

There are several commercial alcohol stoves available on the market these days and a great many DIY versions. Each version has its own special characteristics, limitations and special little advantages over others, yet most share a few basic common features and can be categorized into six distinct designs:

- Open Flame
- Chimney/Updraft
- Low Pressure SideBurner
- Open Jet
- Hybrid SideBurner Jet
- Pressurized Jet

Open Flame Alcohol Stoves These are the simplest of all alcohol stove designs. Since enough alcohol vaporizes at room temperature to allow for easy ignition and generally not enough to be explosive under most conditions, you can simply burn alcohol in an open shallow metal tin. Simply open up a can of tuna or cat food, empty the contents, pour in some fuel and light. More refined versions incorporate a wick made of nonflammable fiberglass insulation, perlite (volcanic rock used in insulation and horticulture) or something comparable to help vaporize fuel and prevent spilling.

Chimney Alcohol Stoves - aka Open Vented and Updraft Stoves These stoves incorporate ventilation similar to a Bunsen burner to facilitate mixing of oxygen with fuel as air is "sucked" into the stove by the low pressure field created by an updraft from the burning fuel. This design allows for better air fuel mixing, more controlled burning when vents are sized properly (with or without a simmer accessory) and good heat feedback to the stove (needed to keep it running). Basically, they operate better than just a simple empty can, may be set up with adjustable heat output with the proper hardware and are more dependable than pressurized stoves.

- Mini Chimney Stove made from two 5.5oz V8 Cans
- Chimney Alcohol Stoves - Good heat output. Reliable.
- Cat Can Stove - Not too difficult to build. Burns hot.
- Brasslite - High quality. Durable brass. Heavy. Expensive. Built in pot stand. Adjustable heat output.

Low Pressure SideBurner Alcohol Stoves Most use a simple updraft concept to preheat the stove and fuel, but they also turn into pressurized sideburners when a pot is placed on top of them. Made with the right number, configuration of and sized holes/ventilation, and you'll have a very light weight and dependable stove that doesn't need a pot stand.

- Mini Chimney Stove made from two 5.5oz V8 Cans (Same stove as above)
- Low Pressure SideBurner Alcohol Stoves - Some are extremely simple to build. Don't need a pot stand. Can be very reliable.
- Super Cat Alcohol Stove - Very Simple to make.

- Jim Falk's 4 in 1 Cat Stove - Simple version of the Super Cat Stove.
- Jim Crandall's Mini Cat Can Stove - Simple stove.

Open Jet Alcohol Stoves These stoves work by vaporizing fuel and shooting them out little jets where the fuel is burned, creating a gas range-like effect. They are beautiful little gems, but may be more difficult to construct and more finicky than other stove types listed here. They are very simple to use – pour your fuel in the open center and light.

- TopBurner Stove - Good for small pots. Many simmer options.
- Trangia stoves - Durable brass. Stores fuel in stove. Inefficient. Heavy. Inexpensive.
- Pepsi Can Stove - Good for small pots. Many simmer options. Classic ultralight stove.

Hybrid SideBurner Jet Alcohol Stoves These are open jet stoves with jets on the side. Like the regular open jet stoves, alcohol is poured in an open center fuel port and lit. Once the jets ignite, you set your pot on top of the stove and seal off the center fuel port, creating a pressurized system. The advantage of these systems is that you don't need a separate pot stand to cook with.

- Zen Stove made from two 3oz Spam Spread cans
- Simplified Zen Sideburner Stove - Easy to build. Doesn't need a pot stand.
- Mini Zen Sideburner Stove - Fast fire up. Lightweight. Doesn't need a pot stand.
- SideBurner Stove - Doesn't need a pot stand.
- Tin Man's Pepsi Can Stove - Doesn't need a pot stand. Can purchase online.

Pressurized Jet Alcohol Stoves These stoves also have little jets like the open jet stoves, but lack the open center fuel port. Instead, the fuel port is generally closed off with a screw or are nonexistent (jets double as fuel ports). This allows for the stove to build up pressure as it heats up, forcing streams of fuel vapor through its jets. These stoves generally must be preheated by burning a small amount of fuel at the base or on top of the stove.

These can be very difficult to design and construct, but allow you the potential for very fast and hot cooking and possibly greater fuel efficiency.

- Pressurized Jet Stove - Burns hot. Possibly less wasted fuel. Difficult to build. Customizable heat output and distribution. Difficult to light (need primer pan). Can't simmer.
- Pressurized SideBurner - Doesn't need a pot stand.
- Photon Stove - Burns hot. Less wasted fuel. Difficult to build. Difficult to light (need primer
- pan). Very difficult to simmer.
- Mark Jurey's Penny Stove - An elegant setup and easy to build.

Fuels for Alcohol Stoves

Denatured Alcohol (ethanol with methanol (added as a denaturing agent), methyl ethyl ketone, acetone, water, and possibly other chemicals - aka methylated spirits, shellac thinner, marine stove fuel, liquid fondue fuel, chafing dish fuel)- and Found in marine shops and in the paint department of most hardware stores. Many brands of this solvent are specifically marketed for use as marine stove fuel and/or chafing fuel. This form of fuel has anywhere from 1% to 80% methanol and other poisonous chemicals in it. Because of the great variability of contents in denatured alcohol, some brands burn better than others. One trick to test the suitability of a particular brand of denatured is to burn a small amount in a dish and reject it if there is any residue left after it has burned.

Lab grade ethanol may have benzene or other chemicals mixed in with it.

Grain Alcohol (aka pure ethanol, pure grain alcohol, PGA, grain neutral spirits, GNS, rectified spirit, rectified alcohol, medical grade ethanol, ethyl anhydrous, moonshine) -

Everclear Grain Alcohol and Golden Grain alcohol from the David Sherman Corporation come in 95% (190 proof) bottles. This fuel works well but is an expensive option and may be illegal or difficult to purchase in many places. It is also non-toxic and can double for medicinal uses.

Grain alcohol can also be made at home in large quantities, though perhaps not legally in your area without special permits or permission (See TTB Forms).

Pure ethanol (aka absolute alcohol or dehydrated alcohol) can also be purchased from chemical supply distributors and as medical grade ethyl alcohol for a very high price. Since production of alcohol greater than 95.4% requires a special dehydration process that includes benzene or glycerine, these fuels can be very toxic.

Methyl Alcohol (aka methanol, wood alcohol, methyl hydrate, liquid fondue fuel, camp stove fuel, gas line antifreeze) -

Found in some hardware store paint departments as paint thinner or at gas stations and general stores as gas-line antifreeze such as HEET brand (Yellow is Methanol, Red is Isopropyl). You may also be able to purchase this for around US$3 per gallon at race shops that sell it as race fuel.

The vaporization pressures of methanol are much higher than ethanol throughout the applicable temperature ranges and the jets in your stove might light up faster when using this fuel. This is also a very poisonous fuel and you should consider the health concerns of this fuel if you decide to use it long term (thru-hikers beware and others may want to avoid storing contaminated stoves in their cook pots or bowls).

Isopropyl Alcohol (Isopropanol, 2-Propanol, rubbing alcohol) Not recommended –

Found in drug, food and general stores (HEET in red container). Rubbing alcohol is generally only 70% alcohol and won't work in many stoves. Alcohol with 91% or greater alcohol content will work, but will leave a sooty residue on your pot and brown water in your stove. The heat potential for this fuel is high, but it doesn't generally burn completely (yellow flame and unburned soot) and is generally mixed with water that isn't burned and hinders fuel efficiency. If you want to use rubbing alcohol (cheapest easily available fuel on this list) for fuel, you may want to use an open flame stove instead of a jetted stove. If you decided to use a jetted stove, you may need to use larger jets in your stove (#57 drill, pushpin size, ~1.4mm or larger) and try to empty as much left over liquid from your stove as you can after each use (as this will further hinder future fire ups) for it to operate.

Gelled Alcohol (Sterno, Canned Heat, jelled alcohol) –

This is either methanol or ethanol trapped in a network of solid calcium acetate forming a gel. This gel is a little safer to use than liquid alcohol since there is less of a spill hazard.

Unfortunately, most gelled alcohol stoves have small top openings and often don't get food hot enough to cook or bring water to a boil.

This fuel usually comes in a resealable can and may be the best choice for young and clumsy campers, since kicking it over is less likely to cause a significant fire hazard as would other liquid and gas stoves. Due to costs and limitations, it is not highly recommended for most long distance backpackers.

Diethylene Glycol (DEG, 3-oxa-1,5-pentanediol, diglycol, ethylene diglycol, or dihydroxy diethyl ether) Not recommended – Diethylene glycol is used in many brands of chafing fuels and must use a wick to burn. It is considered nonflammable by the US Department of Transportation, can be air transported and is therefore much more economical to transport and store. These transportation and storage classifications make it ideal for the retail market and it's safe to assume that any chafing fuel can with a wick uses diethylene glycol until proven otherwise.

This fuel is difficult to light and is extremely poisonous. It is in fact the deadly chemical implicated in the 1937 Elixir Sulfanilamide Incident that killed 107 and was the main motivation for hastening of the enactment of the 1938 Federal Food, Drug, and Cosmetic Act.

This fuel can be used but is not recommended for backpacking stove use due to its toxicity and nonflammable nature.

How to Make a Survival Stove (Car Heater) In colder climates, getting stranded in your car can become a dangerous possibility. As a result, everyone's emergency car kit should contain the ability to heat your car if you were stranded or holed up waiting the passage of a winter storm. Even if running your engine is an option, you may need to conserve fuel for the return trip. Also, carbon monoxide can build up inside a standing vehicle while the engine is running, even if the exhaust pipe is clear. Fortunately, you can make your own survival heater for your car that is cheap, safe to use, and easy to construct.

What You'll Need

- **A small empty metal can:** You want this to be slightly taller but thinner than a standard roll of toilet paper. Try an unused 1 quart aluminum paint can found in most hardware stores. You can also use an empty food can that fits this description.
- **A larger metal can that can easily accommodate the first one:** You can use a 1 gallon unused paint can (again found in most hardware stores). Another option is a coffee can, metal bucket and so on.
- **Some type of lid that can be placed over the larger can:** get a lid for the smaller can for as explain later.
- **Toilet paper (unscented)**
- **Six bottles of 70 to 91% isopropyl alcohol (rubbing alcohol)**
- **Matches or some other fire starter**

How to Put it All Together

Prepare the toilet paper: The first step is to take out the central cardboard tube from the toilet paper roll, leaving only the paper behind.

Squeeze the paper into the smaller can: Next you'll want to squeeze and roll the paper into the smaller can. If the can is so small that a full-size paper roll has no chance of fitting inside it, then you can remove some of the external sheets (just like you would if you were going to the bathroom) until it does squeeze into the can. It's important that it fills up the entire volume of the can.

Add the fuel: If you are now ready to use it, simply add the alcohol until the toilet roll inside the can is completely saturated. One of the benefits of using a 1 quart unused paint can is that you can store the stove with the fuel already added by placing the air-tight lid over the can. This saves space and allows you to have more fuel available. The lid can also be used to control the output of the flame.

Place the smaller can into the larger one and position it in your car: The larger can provides an insulating barrier and some protection for passengers and your car. You'll also want to position it in a place that's far enough from anything combustible. Use the palm check. Put the back of your hand against the surface you're worried about and if you can't keep your hand there without burning it then it's either to close or you'll need to adjust the flame.

Light the stove: First, open the window just a crack to provide some airflow and then carefully place a match (or throw some sparks using a firesteel) onto the saturated toilet paper and viola! you've got yourself a burning stove. Use caution in lighting as it will combust very quickly. It's best to partially cover the smaller can with a lid to decrease the size of combustion (you can always increase it later (see next section).

Controlling the Burn Rate You may notice if you follow the steps above, that a pretty sizable flame results from having the smaller can's opening completely exposed. While this is fine if you want to warm up faster, it does tend to go through the fuel fairly quickly and is not very efficient. A better way is to partially cover the smaller can with a lid. Or if you used a 1 quart paint can, you can make a small hole (about the size of a quarter) in the lid it comes with and place that on top of the can. Both of these methods control the burn rate and allow the stove to provide a constant heat. Another option is instead of completely saturating the toilet roll (as indicated in step 3 above) you can pour just a few ounces of alcohol on the paper and regularly add more as it burns out. This will also control the size of the flame and conserve fuel. The lid method is preferred since you don't have to regularly add alcohol (it's nice to sleep for a stretch of time and not have to regularly add fuel).

A Word on Carbon Monoxide "What about the dangers of carbon monoxide?" Carbon monoxide is produced from the partial oxidation of carbon-containing compounds. "Partial oxidation" is just a big word for what happens when combustion (fire) takes place in an area where there isn't much oxygen. This is most apparent when one operates a generator inside a home or if their wood stove is improperly vented. In the case of this alcohol stove, while there is risk of carbon monoxide emissions (rubbing alcohol contains carbon: C_3H_7OH) the risk is very minimal. Opening your window slightly should provide sufficient oxygen for a clean burn. If you still are concerned about it, you could purchase a battery-operated carbon monoxide alarm and turning it on (putting in the batteries) when running the stove. This will provide you ample warning should there be an issue.

Windshield Shade Solar Cooker

A simple way to make an instant portable solar oven. You can turn a reflective accordion-folded car windshield shade into a version of the solar funnel simply by attaching a little Velcro tabs along the long notched side.

Materials needed

- Reflective accordion-folding car sunshade
- Cake rack (or wire frame or grill)
- 12 cm. (4 ½ in.) of Velcro
- Black pot
- Bucket or plastic wastebasket
- Plastic baking bag

Instructions Making the funnel

Lay the sunshade out with the notched side toward you, as above. Cut the Velcro into three pieces, each about 4 cm. or 1 ½ inches long. Stick or sew one half of each piece, evenly spaced, onto the edge to the left of the notch. Attach the matching half of each piece onto the underneath size to the right of the notch, so that they fit together when the two sides are brought together to form a funnel. If using stick-on Velcro, you can align the two pieces easily like this: Stick down one side of the Velcro, then press the two pieces of Velcro together, fold the shade into the funnel shape and stick down the second side. Press the Velcro pieces together, and set the funnel on top of a bucket or a round or rectangular plastic wastebasket.

Place a black pot on top of a square cake rack, placed inside a plastic baking bag. A standard size rack in the U.S. is 25 cm. (10 in.). This is placed inside the funnel, so that the rack rests on the top edges of the bucket or wastebasket. Since the sunshade material is soft and flexible, the rack is necessary to support the pot. It also allows the sun's rays to shine down under the pot and reflect on all sides. If such a rack is not available, a wire frame could be made to work as well.

Note: The flexible material will squash down around the sides of the rack.

Tips

Cooker with stabilizing stick

- The funnel can be tilted in the direction of the sun.
- A stick placed across from one side of the funnel to the other helps to stabilize it in windy weather.
- After cooking, simply fold up your "oven" and slip the elastic bands in place for easy travel or storage.

This solar oven is extremely practical, lightweight and easy to carry along anywhere. It has reaches a higher temperature in a shorter time than most other models - a little above 350 degrees F hot enough to cook black beans in about the same amount of time as on a gas stove; You can use it to bake breads, granola, brownies, lasagna, all sorts of vegetables, and to purify water. Cost of the sunshade was about $3.00 USD; the Velcro about $.25.

XXXII Emergency Lighting

Should there be a temporary lapse in electrical power, alternative sources of lighting must be stored in advance. Before the event, this is relatively inexpensive and easy. After the event, it becomes very difficult, perhaps impossible as stores will be emptied quickly. In most emergencies with a several day time span (hurricanes, ice storms, etc.) battery operated lighting will often see us through. However, with a major emergency the duration can be much greater. There are many products on the market that will serve well for these longer emergencies.

There are now several solar products that can provide lighting, even after cloudy days. There are solar lanterns, solar flashlights, even solar battery chargers. The solar walkway lamps that line outdoor paths are available in home centers. These can be brought in at night to provide ambient lighting.

Solar photovoltaic panels or wind generators, hooked to batteries, can provide lighting and cost as little as $100 per light. With solar or wind, once the power is restored, you still have free, non-polluting lighting.

Kerosene lanterns and gas lanterns are common choices. With these be sure you have enough fuel stored safely away from the house. Gas lantern are very noisy but give off lots of heat. Kerosene lanterns can smell but scented fuel is available.

Candles should not be ruled out. However, common decorative candles have a short life. Emergency candles can have up to 100 hours of burn time and an indefinite shelf life.

Be sure to have a good quality fire extinguisher in each room where candles, kerosene and gas are being used. Most of the alternatives require a fire or flame, so use caution. More home fires are caused by improper usage of fires used for light than for any other purpose. Especially use extra caution with children and flame. Teach them the proper safety procedures to follow under emergency conditions. Allow them to practice these skills under proper adult supervision now, rather than waiting until an emergency strikes.

Cyalume sticks are the safest form of indoor lighting available but few people know what they are. Cyalume sticks can be purchased at most sporting goods stores for about $2 per stick. They are a plastic stick about four inches in length and a half inch in diameter. To activate them, simply bend them until the glass tube inside them breaks, then shake to mix the chemicals inside and it will glow a bright green light for up to eight hours. Cyalume is the only form of light that is safe to turn on inside a home after an earthquake. One of the great dangers after a earthquake is caused by ruptured natural gas lines. If you flip on a light switch or even turn on a flashlight you run the risk of causing an explosion. Cyalume will not ignite natural gas. Cyalume sticks are so safe that a baby can even use them for a teether.

Two-Mantle Gas Lantern

A gallon of Coleman-type fuel utilized with a two-mantle gas lantern has a burning time of approximately 40 hours. Light output is approximately the same as a 200W light bulb. Assuming an operating or burning time of 5 hours per day, the following approximate amounts of fuel would be consumed: White gas may be substituted in some camping equipment, but read and follow the specific instructions of the equipment manufacturer. A gas lantern gives a high intensity light and lots of heat, too—though the pressurized gas delivery system is quite noisy when operating.

Two-Mantle Gas Lantern Fuel Consumption

Period Fuel Consumed per 5 Hours of use.

- Day, 1 pint.
- Week, 1 gallon.
- Month, 4 gallons.
- Year, 50 gallons.

Kerosene Lanterns

Given today's technology, a kerosene lantern seems a bit old-fashioned and out of place! However, a kerosene lantern with a 1" wick will burn approximately 45 hours per quart of kerosene, saving lots of natural resources and utilizing approximately one-fourth as much fuel as a gas lantern. Kerosene lanterns are an effective and fairly safe lighting source. There are now scented lamp oils which replace kerosene. This lamp oil is generally available in retail stores. Make sure the oil is approved for use in your lamp. There is a difference in lighting quantity and quality, as the kerosene lantern is quite dim when compared to the two-mantle gas lantern. The light output of a kerosene lantern is comparable to a 40W-60W light bulb. As a rule of thumb, the typical kerosene lantern burns approximately 1 ounce of fuel per hour. Burning at the rate of 5 hours each day, the following approximate amounts of kerosene would be used:

Kerosene Lantern Fuel Consumption

Period Fuel Consumed per 5 Hr.

- Day, 1/4 pint.
- Week, 1 quart.
- Month, 1 gallon.
- Year, 12 gallons.

Kerosene lamps are excellent sources of light and will burn for approximately 45 hours on a quart of fuel. They burn bright and are inexpensive to operate. The main problem with using them is failure to properly trim the wicks and using the wrong size chimney. Wicks should be trimmed in an arch, a "V," an "A" or straight across the top. Failure to properly trim and maintain wicks will result in smoke and poor light.

Aladdin type lamps that use a circular wick and mantle do not need trimming and produce much more light (and heat) than conventional kerosene lamps. These lamps, however, produce a great amount of heat, getting up to 750 degrees F. If placed within 36 inches of any combustible object such as wooden cabinets, walls, etc. charring can occur. Great caution should therefore be exercised to prevent accidental fires.

The higher the elevation the taller the chimney should be. Most chimneys that come with kerosene lamps are made for use at sea level. At about 4500 feet above sea level the chimney should be about 18-20 inches high. If your chimney is not as tall as it should be you can improvise by wrapping aluminum foil around the top of it and extending it above the top. This will enable the light to still come out of the bottom portion and yet provide proper drawing of air for complete combustion. If the chimney is too short it will result in smoke and poor light. Be sure to store extra wicks, chimneys and mantles.

Tallow Candles Tallow candles burn brighter, longer, and are fairly smokefree when compared to wax candles. Tallow candles are generally available in specialty stores only, unless you make your own. Wax candles are available almost anywhere housewares are sold. Store tallow candles in a cool, dry location. Candles stored in the freezer will burn slower and without dripping.

Emergency Candles

Candles. Every family should have a large supply of candles. Three hundred sixty-five candles, or one per day is not too many. The larger the better. Fifty-hour candles are available in both solid and liquid form. White light colored candles burn brighter than dark candles. Tallow candles burn brighter, longer, and are fairly smoke free when compared to wax candles. Their lighting ability can be increased by placing an aluminum foil reflector behind them or by placing them in front of a mirror. However, candles are extremely dangerous indoors because of the high fire danger—especially around children. For this reason be sure to store several candle lanterns or broad-based candle holders.

Be sure to store a goodly supply of wooden matches. Save your candle ends for emergency use. Votive candles set in empty jars will burn for up to 15 hours. Non-candles (plastic dish and paper wicks) and a bottle of salad oil will provide hundreds of hours of candle light. The type made of hardened wax in a can has the capability of utilizing several wicks simultaneously. The other type is a liquid paraffin-filled bottle with a wick for easy lighting. The liquid paraffin burns without odor or smoke. This candle has a minimum 100-hour burning time and indefinite shelf life.

Tallow Candle Burning Rate

Height Diameter Approximate Burning Time in Hours

- 6" 1/2" 3
- 6" 1" 8
- 9" 2" 48

Trench candles can be used as fireplace fuel or as a candle for light. To make trench candles:

1. Place a narrow strip of cloth or twisted string (for a wick) on the edge of a stack of 6 to10 newspapers.

2. Roll the papers very tightly, leaving about 3/4" of wick extending at each end.

3. Tie the roll firmly with string or wire at 2-4" intervals.

4. With a small saw, cut about 1" above each tie and pull the cut sections into cone shapes. Pull the center string in each piece toward the top of the cone to serve as a wick.

5. Melt paraffin in a large saucepan set inside a larger pan of hot water. Soak the pieces of candle in the paraffin for about 2 minutes.

6. Remove the candles and place on a newspaper to dry.

Emergency Electric Lighting

Electric lighting has several advantages over other types, and some drawbacks. It's more portable and safer than fire based light. It can be extremely light weight and reliable. It's major drawback is the requirement of a power source. The most portable and available power source we currently have on the market is the traditional battery.

Emergency Lights

Light role Minimum Recommended

- EDC (Every Day Carry) 1 per kit 1 per person and kit with spares
- Low Level 2 per family 2 per family with spares
- Thrower 1 per family 1 per adult
- Headlamps 1 per family 1 per adult
- Small Lantern 1 per family 2-3 per family
- Large Lantern 1 per family 2-3 per family

Note, some lights can serve in more than one role. Especially multi level adjustable lights.

EDC

Short for Every Day Carry. These lights should be small enough that you won't mind carrying it around everywhere with you. You never know when you might need a light in an emergency. There will likely be no power and having a flashlight on you will give you additional flexibility in where you can go and when. You don't need to always always have it with you, but it's nice to have that option. Ideally it will run off a single cell, or two small cells. Having a bright mode is nice, but not essential, it can be just a low mode light, or just a high mode light. This light can also be multi role, act as a low level light and a thrower, maybe even a lantern when standing on its tail indoors. There are some nice lights out there but they can get expensive quick. If you use flashlights be sure to use krypton or halogen light bulbs in them because they last much longer and give off several times more light than regular flashlight bulbs on the same energy consumption. Store at least two or three extra bulbs in a place where they will not be crushed or broken.

Low Level This light is what you can get away with when traveling through known territory, around camp, through your house, a night trip to the out house/latrine, reading at home base. Conserves batteries, last a long time. Size is probably not important. This is probably the role that will see the most use, this is the easiest to find and is also the most important.

Thrower This is your big light. You may need it for search and rescue, a security patrol around a camp site, illuminating an area a long distance away (hence the name, it "throws" light far). It probably won't be in use every day, and it will eat batteries fast so you wouldn't want to run it all the time anyway. It's likely to be a larger light and only carried when a need is anticipated. Probably the least important, but when you need it, you need it .

Headlamp   This light will be used for night work or work in the dark where you need both hands free. If you've ever tried to do the dishes by hand, without power, or any other such similar task you will quickly appreciate what a headlamp can do for you. You may not have the ability to ask someone to hold a flashlight for you as you accomplish a task. It should be reasonably small and use small batteries. It is possible to rig up a flashlight to perform this role, for example, an EDC and a holder for it in a hat. A lantern can also perform this role to a degree, however, an actual headlamp still is a good idea.

Small Lantern   Sometimes you need to light up a room to socialize or you need a small light to read by. It mostly gives light to a small group of people. Other possibilities are using a flashlight in "candle mode", which is either with the bezel off the light exposing the lamp or just standing the flashlight on its tail and letting the light reflect off the ceiling.

Large Lantern   When more light is required than a small lantern provides, allows a group of people to have light in a small, usually stationary, place. Eating a meal at night, or socializing would be good examples.

Types of lamps for lights

Incandescent/Halogen/Krypton   These are not recommended for general flashlight use. They are not very durable, prone to break easily – especially when dropped. They are inefficient, consume batteries rapidly and generally get dim quite quickly with use. Really they are only suitable for use in a thrower type of light, and even then should probably be avoided due to their fragility.

LED   These are excellent for most all uses, more efficient than incandescent/halogen bulbs. Highly durable and only get more efficient as batteries deplete. You get what you pay for with these lights, really nice flashlights can be had. Do some research and get what fits inside your budget and meets your needs. They are getting better every year. Regulated lights are more efficient than the cheaper lights with resisters. High power production LEDs are now available that are just as efficient as Fluorescents. Unfortunately they can be expensive .

Fluorescent   Probably the best choice for large lanterns on a budget. Last a reasonably long time, they are not very expensive so you should own a few. The major drawback is they cannot be dimmed to save power, and don't work well in cold weather.

Self Powered Lights   Try a shake light. They appear quite durable, the mechanical part is only a loose magnet that goes back and forth inside a sealed container. Not prone to breakage, though the light level is low. Be aware that there have been reports of shake lights on the market that have coin cell batteries in them, they look nice and bright when you pick them up. Once the batteries dies (a few hours) they run on shake power which is nowhere near as bright as the batteries were. Solar lights are nice, but if you buy a solar battery charger you won't have to carry the bulk of a solar cell around when using the light. Internally a solar light is going to have a battery anyway. Self powered lights can probably only fill the role of a low level light.

A short course in Battery Chemistries

Primary Cells (single use, disposable cell)

The most common primary cells are Heavy-Duty and Alkaline, Lithium primary cells are also available but they can't always be used in devices that normally take Alkaline and Heavy-Duty batteries. Pure Lithium battery cells put out 3.0 volts rather than the normal 1.5. This requires either a different bulb or a "dummy" empty cell to be used to keep the overall voltage correct. But there are also new low voltage1.5v Lithium batteries as well.

Rechargeable Cells (multi use cells)

The most common today are probably NiMH cells. NiCd is an older technology. Lithium-ion is a newer technology, though it differs significantly from the more common cells.

Cell Type Shelf Life Capacity Sizes Available Cycles Cold Weather

- Heavy-Duty 8+ Years Low AAA, AA, C, D, 9V 1 Poor
- Alkaline 8+ Years Medium AAA, AA, C, D, 9V 1 Poor
- Lithium (Primary) 15+ Years High AAA, AA, C, D 1 *Excellant*
- NiCd 3 Months Med-Low AAA, AA, C, D, 9V 1-2K Good
- NiMH 2 Months Medium AAA, AA, C, D, 9V 500-800 Poor
- Lithium-ion 6 Months High R123A, other related sizes 300-500 Excellent

Shelf Life improves if you store the batteries in a cooler environment. After a rechargeable battery loses its charge due to shelf life, a simple recharge will put you back in business. Cold weather is defined as sub-freezing temperatures, and all cell types that have a "poor" rating can be warmed up in a pocket, put in an appliance and be expected to work again until they get too cold.

Battery cells should be treated like fuel. Take care of them, do not get them wet, do not throw them in fires, try not to drop them or get them banged up and they should be quite safe. Get water proof carry cases for your kits for them. You probably shouldn't store cells in devices if they are going to be packed away.

If you store quantities of Lithium batteries in a house they should be stored in a fire proof box with vent holes drilled into a side of the box as a safety precaution (do not place vent holes near flammable objects). Do not store them in a tent. Don't get paranoid about Lithiums, you probably use them every day in devices like a cell phone, but you've probably heard a story or two of "exploding" batteries. What they really do is "vent rapidly with flame" (quite rare), use caution and don't buy knock offs.

Primary cells should be in your emergency kits as well as a small reserve for extended on the go emergencies, rechargeable cells will be more useful in a longer term emergency when you can settle down a bit but power still doesn't exist. AA cells are the most available with the best prices, adapters can also be found to make them fit into devices that use C and D batteries. AA rechargeables also don't require nearly as long as D cells to recharge.

Heavy Duty (Single use, Disposable) Poor, not recommended. Cheap lights come with these batteries, it should also be taken as a sign that the light manufacture has cut every conceivable cost in the production and shipping of his light. Avoid them.

Alkaline (Single use, Disposable) Good value. Costs are very reasonable, just stay away from poor brands as they are likely to leak and damage your devices and the residue is usually toxic. Duracell, Energizer, Rayovac, and most storebrand names are fine (Costco, Rite-aid). Stay away from Western Family and unknown brands.

Lithium (Single use, Disposable) Expensive, but great cold weather performance for a primary cell, highest energy density. It would be good to have a few of these around for AA devices. Also in cases where weight, size, and capacity is more of an issue than cost.

NiCd (Rechargable) Most durable type of rechargeable cell. There is a reason that in an era of NiMH and Li-ion batteries power tools and other such items that see regular hard use still use NiCDs. You can expect these cells to give you 5 years of use from the date of manufacture, if you care for them. And they do require care, suck them dry once every month or two and they'll hold out the longest. For longer term storage, put them in a cool place at about half charge. Not a bad value, good cold weather performance without a high cost - have some of these if you plan on using a standard rechargeable. Toxic, please use care when disposing of these cells.

NiMH (Rechargable) Best value and convenience, an excellent value for what you receive with these batteries. They don't hold a charge long on the shelf but for regular battery use, they can't be beat. Some newer cells are available with a low self-discharge property at slightly reduced capacity (see Sanyo Eneloop or Titanium Enduro cells). They don't like the cold very much, so if it's cold outside you can put a flashlight in your pocket where it'll be warmer. Expect up to 3 years effective use from the date of manufacture, longer is possible but probably at reduced performance as the cell deteriorates.

Lithium-Ion (Rechargable) Rather exotic and requires special care and attention. Special chargers are required, only really an option when you have a larger power source available to charge off of, like a car or off grid electrical system, or if you know how to build your own solar system to run the charger. Good cold weather performance, good power density (superior to even NiMH). However they deteriorate rapidly with time. Even 1 year will see reduced performance. You've probably noticed this with your cell phone and laptop computer batteries. Not the best long term option.

Lead Acid Lowest self discharge of the rechargeable cells. Also the cheapest per unit of power. However they are also the least portable being the bulkiest. They can work well for area lighting and lanterns. Also for recharging smaller cells. Once you have a good idea what you want and have acquired a few items. Run a family home evening off your battery devices only. Spend 1, 2, or even 3 days without the grid electric lights, learn what your needs are and use this information to fill them.

XXXIII   Electrical Power

The real problem in a crisis starts when you spend more than just a few hours without light. In Argentina after the collapse in Buenos Aires in 2001 half the country went without power for 3 days. People got caught on elevators, food began to rot, hospitals that only had a few hours' worth of fuel for their generators ran out of power.

Without power, days get to be a lot shorter. Once the sun sets there is not much you can do. If you are reading under candle light and flashlight your head starts to hurt after a while. You can work around the house a little, but only as long as you don't need power tools. Crime also increases once the lights go out, so whenever you have to go somewhere in a black out, carry the flashlight on one hand and a handgun on the other.

Being in a city without light is depressing. Spending your nights alone, listening to the radio, eating canned food and cleaning your guns under the light of your LED head lamp isn't a Carnival cruise. To pass the short term crises, you will need batteries.

BATTERIES

Rechargeable batteries are a must. Get a solar powered battery charger if you can or else you'll end up broke if lights go out often. Have a healthy amount of spare quality batteries and try to standardize as much as you can.

Keep about 2 or 3 packs of regular, Duracell batteries just in case, they have a long shelf life.. Rechargeable NM batteries have the disadvantage of losing power after a period of time, so keep regular batteries as well and check the rechargeable ones every once in a while.

You need a battery charger that has both solar panel and a small crank, they are relatively inexpensive. Get a couple of these. Even if they don't charge as well as a regular rechargeable from an outlet, it will put out enough power to charge batteries for LED lamps at least.

A note on flashlights. Have two or three LED head lights. They are not expensive and are worth their weight in gold. A powerful flashlight is necessary, something like a big Maglite or a SureFire, especially when you have to check your property for intruders. But for more mundane stuff like preparing food, going to the toilet or doing stuff around the house, the LED headlamp is priceless. Try washing the dishes on the dark while holding a 60 lumen flashlight on one hand. LEDs also have the advantage of lasting for almost an entire week of continuous use and the light bulb lasts forever.

EMERGENCY GENERATORS

Generator Basics

Generators are shaft-driven machines that produce electric power. Broadly speaking, they range in size and capacity from the tiny devices used as sensors to the extremely large machines used at commercial power plants. The term "alternator" is also used and means essentially the same thing.

The term "generator set" or "genset" is sometimes used to describe a generator along with a gasoline or diesel engine or other power source. Generators are rated in terms of the amount of power they can produce. This is measured in Watts (W) or Kilowatts (kW). A Kilowatt is equal to 1,000 Watts. Some household items list their power requirement in Watts, such as light bulbs and small appliances. Others only list Amperes (abbreviated A or Amps). Most household electrical loads (including all cord connected appliances that plug into a standard outlet) run on 120 Volts, and since Watts = Amps X Volts, you can determine Watts by multiplying the amp requirement by 120. Large heating and cooling appliances, and well pumps, sometimes use 240 Volts. This can be determined from the nameplate. For these loads, wattage is determined by multiplying amps by 240.

Generator Types

Commercially available generators useful for small-scale standby power fall into these categories:

Type Wattage Price Range

- Small portable units marketed primarily Generally less than 2 kW $400-$600 for camping
- Midsize portable units 3-5 kW. $400-$2,000
- Large trailer-mount units without engines, 15-60 kW $2,000-$5,000
- PTO driven by a tractor
- Large trailer-mount units designed for 10 kW or more.. construction or industrial use
- Large standby units designed. 5-40 kW or more $4,000-$12,000 for permanent installation

Costs vary depending on ruggedness, reliability, and features.

The more expensive units typically include features like:

- Better quality engines, with pressure lubrication, cast iron cylinder blocks (or cast iron sleeves), oil filters, and electronic ignition. The primary benefit of these is longevity, although the better engines may be somewhat more reliable.
- Larger fuel tank for long, unattended runs.
- Low oil shutdown to prevent engine damage
- Electric start
- Built in battery charger for 12V car batteries
- Quieter design, achieved through better mufflers, soundproofing, and lower operating RPM
- Ground fault circuit interrupters (GFCI) for safety
- Wheels. Even the smaller generators are heavy.

There are a wide variety of brands available. All of them work, and most are adequate for occasional standby use. The generators that are driven by a farm tractor are a good buy if you already own one or more farm tractors. Unlike car and truck mount generators, tractor-driven ones produce ample power. Tractors are better suited to continuous, stationary operation than cars and trucks.

Generator Uses

Generators can be useful in a long-duration power outage by providing power to run essential equipment, such as refrigerators, freezers, lighting, water pumps, sump pumps, and furnaces. They are also useful for providing power w here it is inconvenient, costly, or impossible to bring commercially produced power.

Sizing

Determining the exact size generator required for a household involves adding up the wattage required by each load, including the starting power required by the largest motor and any others that will be started at the same time. It is difficult to get accurate results since starting current requirements often vary and because nameplate ratings sometimes overstate the power required. If a generator is too small for its load, the voltage will drop. This can cause damage to the generator, the load, or both. Circuit breakers and thermal protectors may trip and prevent damage, but cannot be relied upon. Do not connect loads to the generator that are too large for its capacity.

If you only want to run a few critical items, you can use this chart as a guide:

Generator size Loads typically supported

- 1000W or less Lights, radio, battery chargers, clocks, fax, or computer
- 1500W Above items, also small manual defrost freezer or refrigerator
- 3500W 240V Same as 1500W, plus ½ H.P. well pump (if 240V)
- 3500W 120V Most refrigerators and freezers, clothes washer, gas clothes dryer,
- sump pump, ½ H.P. furnace blower, ½ H.P. well pump (if 120V),
- nearly any plug-connected appliance with a standard 120V plug
- 5000W 240V Same as 3500W, plus most well pumps up to 2 H.P.
- 15,000W 240V Will run all the loads in most households including electric water heaters, dryers, well pumps, and ranges; will run many central air conditioning units.

Electric heat systems need to be considered case by case as many larger systems use more power than even a big generator like this produces.

Measuring the Load

Sometimes it helps to measure the amount of power a particular piece of equipment (or an entire household) uses. This may be the only way to determine power requirements accurately if there is no nameplate listing the power required. Clamp-on ammeters are available at most building supply stores for about $50-$100 that will measure the number of amps flowing through a wire. They usually include an attachment that you can use for cord-and-plug connected devices. More sophisticated ammeters that measure starting current are available but are costly ($400) and require some expertise to use.

Electrical Hookup

There are three ways to hook up generators:

- Plug in loads directly, using extension cords if necessary.
- Transfer switch
- Suicide wiring

Plugging in loads to the generator's outlets directly is the simplest and works OK when only a few small loads are used. This method is used in remote areas and for construction, where no electric wiring is present. It also works in standby situations for running a handful of things, say, a freezer, refrigerator, sump pump, and a couple lights. Generators must be operated outdoors unless specifically designed for indoor operation. Those designed for indoor use have an exhaust system that vents outside. Since the generator is usually outside and the load is inside, extension cords are needed. Be sure they're big enough. Most of the orange extension cords sold use 16 gauge wire and are rated for 13 amps. These are fine for a couple of small appliances but create a fire hazard when used for heavier loads.

Transfer switches

Transfer switches allow you to connect a load to either the generator or the commercial power source simply by flipping a switch. They are the only reasonable and safe alternative for running an entire house from a generator . They are also the only way to run equipment that can't be unplugged, such as furnace blowers, well pumps, and the like. Different configurations are available that allow switching of all or part of a household's electrical circuits. They are expensive and must be installed by an electrician or other qualified person. Some examples: Transfer switches that have 4-6 different handles, each of which switches a single circuit, are available for around $200 from many retailers that sell generators. They wire into the house's breaker or fuse panel. You only hook up the circuits that you will need in an emergency, which reduces the cost, and you can switch them one at a time so all the motors don't start at once. Some designs include an ammeter so you can see how much power you're using. Some designs, including one from Square D, use circuit breakers to perform the switching and have an interlock so you can only turn on one circuit breaker – either the generator breaker or the commercial power breaker. These can go for as little as $60 plus the cost of the circuit breakers.

Again you only hook up the circuits that you think you will need in an emergency. These panels hook up to your main breaker panel as a sub-panel. Large transfer switches switch the power to a house or group of buildings and are wired between the meter socket and breaker (or fuse) panel. These cost $300-$600 depending on capacity. They are costly to install as well. Automatic transfer switches will start the generator and switch the load to it without intervention. Some standby systems have these built in. One catalog lists a 200A model as costing almost $2,000. Telephone companies, hospitals, radio and TV stations, and the like use larger versions of these. Transfer switches are wired with a large, flexible cord and plug for use with portable generators. The cord and plug are not normally included with the transfer switch and must be purchased separately. Welding supply companies are a good, inexpensive source for the heavy gauge wire required. If you plan to connect the generator to building wiring, consider the transfer switch part of the cost of the generator.

Suicide wiring

Any method of connecting a generator to a building's electrical system, other than by using a transfer switch, falls under the category of suicide wiring. You can be killed. And you can kill an electric lineman if you fail to isolate your generator from the power company's lines, by causing electricity to back-feed into the commercial power system. You can also burn up your generator or your house. It is also against the law in many jurisdictions.

Plan ahead. Buy a transfer switch. Get it installed. Don't use suicide wiring.

Generator Safety

Here's some basic advice on generator safety. Read the instructions for your generator or check with a dealer or licensed electrician for authoritative safety rules.

1   Follow the safety instructions that come with the generator.
2   Keep the generator outside so you don't breathe carbon monoxide and die. Protected locations, such as a garage with the garage door open, are helpful if the weather is bad.
3   Follow whatever grounding instructions come with the generator. Generators should be grounded but the recommendations for how this is done vary depending on manufacturer.
4   You can get a bad shock by touching a wet power cord or plug while the generator is running. Shut off the engine before fiddling with the power connections if it is wet out.
5   Don't refuel a hot engine. If you refuel at night, use a source of light that won't ignite the gas. The cyalume sticks work well for this.
6   Don't overload extension cords.
7   Use a transfer switch.
8   Store gasoline outside, in a safe container.

More accidents happen during power outages than occur when power is available, particularly fires. Here are some general tips for safety during power outages:

1   Don't leave candles or oil or gasoline lanterns burning unattended.
2   Realize that smoke and carbon monoxide detectors will not work without power.
3   Have fire extinguishers at hand.
4   Have some water drawn up in buckets or pans to use in case the water supply fails.

Fuels and Fuel Storage

Most portable generators run on gasoline. But gasoline is a poor choice for standby use, because it is unsafe to store in residential areas and is prone to deterioration when stored for any length of time.

Gasoline is extremely flammable and should not be stored in any quantity in a house or garage. There is no safe way to store gasoline in a building. Building and zoning codes, and insurance requirements, vary; some municipalities prohibit permanently installed gasoline tanks and limit the size of portable ones.. Gasoline suppliers usually recommend that bulk storage tanks be at least 10' away from garages and other buildings. If you are serious, some may want to store gasoline in 5 gallon cans in its own little building a long way from all the other buildings.

Gasoline can be stored in full, sealed containers for 1-2 years or more without deterioration, provided that high temperatures are avoided. Air, water, and heat all contribute to deterioration. You can use a commercial fuel preserving additive in the gas tank for your generator, but there is no consensus on misc.survivalism that such additives materially improve the storage life of gasoline. Larger, generators are sometimes available with diesel engines. These engines are, as a rule, noisier gasoline engines and are more difficult to start in cold weather. For standby use, they may be worth having because of fuel storage considerations. Diesel fuel and kerosene are much safer to store than gasoline.

It is still common to store fuel oil, which has similar properties, indoors in houses in quantities up to 250 gallons. Building and zoning codes and insurance rules may limit the amount or method of storage. These products should not be stored in red cans because of the potential for confusion with gasoline. These fuels can be stored 2-3 years before they deteriorate. Midsize and larger generators designed for permanent installation and standby use are available for use with LP gas or natural gas. The engines are like gasoline engines in most respects but replace the carburetor with a mixing system designed for LP o r natural gas. LP gas standby generators are widely used in industrial/ commercial settings. The chief benefit is that LP gas can be stored indefinitely without deterioration. LP gas conversion kits are available for many small generators.

Readiness

Anecdotal evidence suggests generators frequently fail to start when they are needed, even in industrial settings where regular maintenance and testing is performed. Electric start generators sometimes fail to start because the battery is dead. Batteries that are continuously trickle-charged may start the engine while being charged but fail when the charger is turned off, as in an actual emergency. Battery terminal s also have a way of getting corroded. Stale gasoline can contribute to starting problems, especially in cold weather. Using starting fluid will sometimes make up for this. Spare parts and supplies should be kept on hand. At a minimum, some extra motor oil, suitable starting aids, air and oil filters (if used), and a spark plug should be available. You should periodically operate your generator, and hook up whatever loads you plan to use, to make sure that everything is ready if needed. Once a month is probably often enough to catch most problems.

How Practical Is a Generator?

Severe weather can be extremely disruptive to power systems and the unlucky individuals whose own lines are knocked down in a storm end up at the end of the power company's list for repairs. Power losses can be costly if you stand to lose the contents of your freezer, or if cold weather and no heat threatens to freeze pipes. Unless you can afford a fully automatic, permanently installed system, you had better be able-bodied. It's work to pull out the generator and start it and hook it up even if you have a good setup. Big generators are noisy. Everyone in the neighborhood will know that you're running one. You may wish to consider running the generator during only part of a 24-

hour period. Most refrigerators and freezers will maintain temperature if operated 50% of the time, depending on ambient temperature, condition of the door seal, and how often the door is opened. Fuel availability is a thorny issue. Gas stations require electricity to be able to pump gas. If you are fortunate, you may live in a setting where it is possible to store ample quantities of fuel to run the generator for a week or more. Even the worst power outages are ordinarily corrected after a week, two at the most. Those concerned about The End Of The World scenarios should consider alternatives that do not rely on fuel availability.

Other Ways to Produce Electricity

Several companies sell inverters that produce 120V electricity using the power from a car or truck's battery and alternator. These are not suitable for most standby uses because the output power is too low. The largest car and truck alternators produce no more than 2000 watts, and this only at high engine speeds. The really big inverters – 2000W and over, capable of running a refrigerator – are expensive, big, heavy, and require heavy cabling to the battery. The logistics of operating a vehicle while stationary must also be considered: how do you secure the vehicle, potential for damage due to low oil or high temperature while unattended, potential for transmission bearing damage due to extended idling, poor fuel economy.

There are some belt-driven and PTO-driven generators for cars and trucks that have similar problems. In addition, most of these units must be operated at a specific speed. Unless the vehicle is equipped with an engine governor, this is difficult.

Uninterruptable power supplies (UPS) are designed primarily for use with computers and communications equipment. They generally are designed for short duration outages, 15 minutes or less.

Solar, hydroelectric, and wind generators are a topic in their own right and are beyond the scope of this book. Many products marketed for use with alternative power systems are also useful for standby use. It might make sense in some cases to have low- voltage DC wiring for lights that can be operated from batteries in an emergency.

Non-electric Alternatives

There are a number of low-tech techniques that can reduce your dependence on electricity. Some are effective by themselves, and others will reduce the size generator you need or the hours you need to run it. Use something besides electricity for the primary source of heat. Although any modern central heating system requires some electricity to operate, you can run a natural gas, LP gas, or oil-fired furnace from a generator of modest size. Electric heat systems can't be operated except by very large generators. Replace electric appliances with gas. Houses that are served by a natural gas supplier rarely have gas outages and electric outages at the same time (except possibly in earthquake-prone areas). LP gas is stored in tanks and is independent of electrical and other utilities. A gas stove can be used without electricity if the burners are lit with a match. Most gas water heaters don't require electricity at all (except for horizontal exhaust and other power-vented units).

Have a wood stove or fireplace insert that is capable of heating your house. Have enough wood on hand to be able to use it in a power outage. A wide variety of non-electric lighting is available.

Aladdin lamps, which burn kerosene and produce a bright light, are practical and safer to use inside than gasoline lanterns. Lamps that operate on LP gas supplied through pipes are available. They mount permanently to a wall or ceiling, and are bright, safe, and cheap to operate. Inexpensive kerosene wick lamps are widely available and produce more light than candles. LP gas and kerosene operated refrigerators and freezers are available. Some will also operate on electricity. Full-size units are expensive but no more so than a good generator installation. Smaller refrigerators, such as those used in RVs, are available too – though some require a 12V DC power source to operate the controls and ignition system even when running on LP gas.

SOLAR POWER

This is a beginner's course in solar electricity. Specific guidance on how to install your own solar electric systems can be had from manufacturers. This process can be like trying to build an automobile by purchasing parts from a NAPA dealer. You can buy a brake drum, wheel bearing, and oil filter, but since your car does not yet exist, how do you know what parts you need, what parts will fit with other parts, and how should these parts be wired together.

System types

Some solar power systems are 12-volt DC due to the many low voltage RV and boating lighting and appliances available, and do not have a utility line connection. These DC only systems can be used to power several DC lights in a remote cabin, or a DC well pump in a field for watering cattle. Some solar power systems have an inverter to convert a 12, 24, or 48-volt DC battery voltage into 120-volt AC power to operate standard household appliances. Some grid connected solar power systems are designed for direct connection to your utility line and do not use any batteries at all.

Hybrid solar power systems can include a battery bank, a solar array, a generator, and even a wind turbine to provide power at all times with the utility grid serving only as backup. Inverters and solar arrays are available in many different styles, voltages, and wiring configurations. Some solar arrays are mounted on the roof, some on the top of a pole, and some are ground mounted, with each having different wiring rules. If you visit a solar home that has a well designed and properly installed solar power system, you will find the concept is actually fairly simple. The hard part is knowing what wiring layout was best for this specific home, what size and quantity of each system component was required, and what wire size and fuses were needed to keep from burning down the house.

Batteries

One of the most misunderstood parts of a solar power system is the battery or battery bank, and that is where our class begins. Some solar battery banks use wet cells, like golf cart batteries, while others use sealed or gel cell batteries, and each have different temperature, mounting, and ventilation requirements. Every battery is designed for a specific type of charge and discharge cycle. Car batteries have thin plates to keep their weight down and are designed for a heavy discharge lasting a few seconds, followed by a long period of slow re-charge. A 6-volt golf cart battery (size T-

105) is the minimum battery for a residential solar application. You will need to buy these in "pairs" to make 12 volts.

Golf cart batteries have very thick plates and are designed for hours of heavy discharge each day, followed by a fast recharge in only a few hours each night. This is similar to the duty cycle of a residential solar application, only in reverse. A solar battery must be able to provide long periods of deep discharge each evening and night, followed by a full recharge in only a few hours of sunlight each afternoon. Very few batteries can take a deep discharge-recharge cycle every day, and the 6-volt golf cart battery is the least expensive and easiest to find locally.

For some reason, everyone wants to use a sealed marine battery for their homegrown solar system. But sealed marine battery can "explode" after being connected to a small solar charger for several months. Even a small 12-volt DC 5-amp solar charge controller powered from a single 50-watt solar photovoltaic module can provide enough energy to gradually overcharge the battery and evaporate all of the electrolyte even though it is a "sealed" battery. A low electrolyte level can expose the plates which will gradually warp or "grow" in thickness as they oxidize. This can cause an internal short circuit and ignition of the hydrogen gas. Plate damage can also occur when there is a large buildup of sediment after the upper plate areas become exposed from reduced water levels and begin to "flake" off. Most liquid acid batteries do not vent gasses while discharging. However, near the end of a typical charging cycle, when the battery is almost "full," the sulfuric acid and water electrolyte will begin to break down into hydrogen and oxygen—a very explosive combination.

When ignited by a nearby spark or flame, an "explosion" can result, though this flash lasts only a fraction of a second, which is usually too fast to ignite nearby walls. However, this is still a very explosive reaction, with plastic battery parts becoming acid-covered shrapnel. Always wear eye protection and acid proof gloves when working around batteries, and have lots of water and baking soda nearby. This will neutralize any acid spills from battery refilling and prevent further corrosive damage. A typical 6-volt golf cart battery will store about 1 kilowatt-hour of useful energy (6 volt X 220 amp-hr X 80% discharge = 1056 watt-hours). Since this would only power two 50-watt incandescent lamps for 10 hours (2 X 50 X 10 = 1000 watt-hours), your alternative energy system will most likely require wiring several batteries together to create a battery bank.

Since each golf cart battery weighs almost 65 pounds, there are weight considerations as well as battery gas venting issues to think about. An area of a garage or storage building having a concrete floor is the most common location for a battery bank, although some large systems have their own specially designed battery room. You are probable installing a much smaller system and will only require four to eight batteries.

If you need more than the 220 amp-hr capacity contained in each golf cart battery, you can switch to the larger "L-16" size traction battery, having a 350 amp-hour rating, which may allow using fewer batteries. This battery is the same length and width as a golf cart battery, but is much taller and twice as heavy. This is an excellent battery for solar applications and can take very heavy charge-discharge cycling. This industrial rated battery may be more difficult to find, as it is only available from battery wholesale distributors. Batteries can lose over half of their charge when exposed to extreme temperature swings, so be sure your proposed battery location stays in a 50° to 80° F range, or you will need to insulate the battery box.

Since liquid electrolyte batteries require refilling and battery terminal cleaning to remove corrosion several times each year, the floor area selected should be able to take an occasional acid spill and water wash down. Battery venting is very important, and if you build an enclosure around your batteries, it should be designed to direct all vented gasses to the outside. A 2-inch PVC pipe makes a good vent, but be sure it is located at the highest point in your battery enclosure where the lighter hydrogen gas will accumulate. Be sure it also includes a screened vent cap to keep out rain and insects.

Do not locate your battery bank near a gas water heater or other open flame appliance that could ignite any accidental hydrogen accumulation. A battery box can be built using standard 2 x 4 framing construction, with pressure treated plywood lining the interior surfaces. A hinged top door is needed for periodic battery maintenance, and should include a gasket to prevent gases from entering the room. The top of the site-built battery box should slope up to a high rear area where PVC vent pipes are located. The interior plywood surfaces of this wood frame construction were painted with several coats of fire and acid resistant paint. Since batteries lose capacity with lower temperatures, your batteries should not rest directly on a cold uninsulated concrete floor.

Pressure treated 2 x 4s on edge, spaced every 6 inches and covered by a fiberglass laminated concrete board, makes an excellent base for your battery box. This heavy sheet material is sold in most building supply outlets as a backing behind ceramic tile work in wet shower stalls, and is usually available in smaller 2-foot by 4-foot sizes. By careful planning, you may be able to use the entire sheet without cutting or splicing.

If you can afford to invest in the more expensive gel or absorbed glass matte (AGM) batteries, you will have more flexibility in locating your battery bank, since these batteries do not need to be refilled and do not normally generate explosive gasses. Large battery banks with the batteries mounted close together in a vertical steel rack are possible. You do not need a vapor proof enclosure or vent pipe when using these batteries, however they cost almost 30 percent more without providing any additional life or storage capacity.

Most solar or generator based backup and off-grid power systems will require a battery bank to store energy for use later when the sun is not shinning or the generator is not running. A battery bank is like the gas tank in your car. The larger the tank, the longer you can go between fill ups. However, a larger tank also means it will take longer to fill up when you do stop. Also, the larger the car's engine (electrical load) the faster you will drain the gas tank (battery), which means you will need to stop more often for gas (recharge).

A battery bank storage system should be sized to get you through several days of stormy weather, but if the battery bank is too large for the size of your solar array or generator powered charger, you may not have time to recharge back to 100% before needing to power the loads again. If the battery load each day is greater than the solar or generator charging each day, the battery bank voltage will drop lower and lower each day until it will no longer be able to supply the loads. Once a solar charged battery bank has been depleted, you will need to turn off all loads until the next sunny day, or utilize a backup generator or wind turbine to help you through the extended period of cloudy days. A dual source charging system allows using a smaller battery bank than a solar only system.

Battery life

Assuming we can put back what we take out each day, there are advantages to having a storage battery larger than needed to meet the daily appliance and lighting loads. A good quality lead acid battery designed for daily charge/discharge cycling may be advertised to have a 2,000-cycle life, when discharged 20% each time (80% charge remaining). However, this same battery may only have a 400-cycle life if each cycle took the battery down to 90% discharged (10% charge remaining).

Since we don't want to replace the batteries every year (400 cycles/365 days), in order to increase battery life we must reduce the depth of discharge (DOD) the battery reaches during each charge/discharge cycle. This is accomplished by using more batteries, larger batteries, or reducing the system load. 6-volt 350-amp-hour batteries with "Flag" terminals allow bolt-on type cable interconnects. Although an occasional period of stormy weather may require your battery bank to be heavily discharged, your normal average daily discharge should not go below 50%, with 40% a better goal (60% charge remaining).

Battery ratings When selecting a battery it is the amp-hour (A-Hr) rating that defines its energy storage capacity, and a battery's advertised amp-hour rating can be listed for different discharge time periods, so be sure you are not comparing apples and oranges. For example, an "L16" size deep discharge battery typically used in solar powered homes has a 350 amp-hour capacity when slowly discharged over a 20-hour period (C20). However, this same battery has a 460 amp-hour rating when discharged over a 100-hour period (C100), but only a 259 amp-hour rating when discharged over a 6-hour period (C6). The 400 amp-hour battery you find on sale could actually have a smaller capacity than a 350 amp-hr battery if you are comparing amp-hour ratings for different discharge periods. Since a typical four-hour solar charging period per day or four hours of generator run time per day leaves 20 hours per day for slow discharge before the next charging cycle, the advertised C20 rating will be the closest published discharge rating to the typical daily cycling of most residential off-grid systems.

Battery Sizing

Say you want to power a 12-volt DC lighting system for an off-grid cabin that has no other source of power. You have four fluorescent fixtures and they each are 36-watts and draw 3 amps (36 watt/12 volt = 3 amp). If all lights are operating at the same time, this means the total lighting load will be 12 amps (4 lights x 3 amps). Now let's say you will operate these lights from 5:00 pm until 11:00 pm each night, or six hours per day. Your battery system must supply 72 amp-hours (12 amps x 6 hours) of energy each day to meet your daily power needs, if we ignore all efficiency losses.

Two 6-volt batteries in series provide 350 amp-hour capacity at 12-volts. If we select a battery having a 350 amp-hour rating, this battery will deliver 175 amp hours (350 x 0.50) before needing recharging if discharged to 50%. NOTE: discharging a battery below 50% will greatly reduce battery life. With 175 amp-hours of battery capacity to work with, this means our lighting system can be powered for two days (175 amp-hr/72 amp-hr) before needing recharging. This also means your solar array will need to put into the battery bank a minimum each day of what you are taking out, plus at least 20% more to account for system and charging losses.

Now comes the confusing part. The 350 amp hour battery used in this example was a 6-volt battery, and our lighting system requires double that voltage or 12-volts to operate, so we will need two batteries wired in series to provide the 12-volts. Unfortunately this does not also double the amp-hour capacity of this battery bank which will stay the same. Multiple batteries wired in series have the same amp-hour capacity as each individual battery. Only when we wire batteries in parallel do we obtain multiples of the amp-hour capacity, but wiring batteries in parallel does not increase battery voltage.

Although theoretically you could wire batteries together in as many series and parallel configurations as needed to provide any voltage and amp-hour capacity, having a large number of batteries in parallel is not desirable. If a battery or battery cell fails in an individual series wired string, the battery bank voltage for that series string drops or the voltage output stops completely. If a battery or battery cell fails in a group of batteries wired in parallel, the adjacent string of good batteries will try to flow current into the string having the bad battery or battery cell, which becomes another system load.

Since most battery interconnect wiring uses fairly large size cables, a cell failure can result in very large currents discharging from one parallel string into another, causing melted battery cables or a boiled dry cell giving off lots of smoke and explosive gasses. It is a good idea to limit your battery bank to no more than four battery strings wired in parallel, with two parallel strings that much safer. You can also reduce the risk associated with batteries wired in parallel by installing a "catastrophic" fuse in each individual series string of a parallel-wired battery bank.

The easiest way to increase battery bank capacity is to switch to a higher voltage system. Since most of today's 12-volt DC appliances, DC lighting, and DC to AC inverters are now available in 24-volt and 48-volt versions, a 24-volt system will need four 6-volt batteries in series and a 48-volt system will need eight 6-volt batteries in series to achieve the higher voltage. For example, a 48-volt battery bank having sixteen 6-volt batteries would only require two parallel strings of eight batteries each (8 batteries x 6-volts).

NOTE: In all of these wiring examples, the positive (+) and negative (-) connections are located at opposite ends of each battery bank. This causes the electrical path to be equal in length and resistance regardless of which way the electricity flows, resulting in an equally balanced charge and discharge for each individual battery.

If you have ever dropped a wrench across the terminals of a car battery you know how easy it is to melt metal, even at this low voltage. Every wire connected to the positive (+) terminal of any battery or group of batteries should pass through a fuse to prevent serious damage if there is a system short. You should also understand that an AC fuse or AC circuit breaker would not safely protect a DC wiring circuit. DC electricity does not cycle to zero volts like AC electricity, and a constant DC electrical flow will try to "weld" the switch contacts together when the arc forms as the fuse or circuit breaker starts to open.

Safety devices rated for DC use need to be of much heavier construction than the same amp capacity device intended for AC circuits. When using multiple batteries to increase the voltage and capacity of your battery bank, be sure to use the proper size and type cables for these interconnects and keep them as short as possible. Do not use automotive or marine type cables or welding cables, as these are not UL listed for residential wiring. UL listed red and black battery interconnects 9 and

12 inches long, made from #2/0 multi-strand flexible copper cable, with machine crimped all copper terminals on each end, are fairly inexpensive and available from any solar supplier.

Using improper safety devices or undersized low cost non-copper cables and connectors is no place to save money. Be sure your backup power system uses the correct wire sizes for the loads and batteries used, and be sure each circuit is protected by the proper size and type safety device.

Inverters

Since all solar photovoltaic modules generate DC electricity, unless all of the lights and appliances being powered are DC, an alternative energy power system will need to include an inverter. This device is used to convert the DC electricity from the solar modules and batteries into AC electricity.

Inverter basics Early inverters for the consumer market were used mainly for mobile applications like boats and recreation vehicles, and most were designed for 12-volt DC battery ignition systems. Due to an upper capacity limit of approximately 200 amps for the internal power components and heavy welding cables that were being used for connecting these mobile 12-volt systems, 2,400 watts was about the largest capacity inverter that could be made for these applications (12V x 200A = 2,400 W).

To keep inverter costs low and the designs simple, these early inverters generated a "modified" sine wave output to simulate the 60-cycle 120-volt AC line voltage. The more "steps" in the modified waveform, the closer the output voltage will be to a normal AC sine wave. Until the explosive increase in personal computers and microprocessor controlled appliances and audio/video equipment, most electrical loads that included older technology would work fairly well on a modified sine wave inverter. Incandescent lights and power tools also worked well, although some fluorescent fixtures and light dimmers had problems. An AM radio may produce an objectionable hum in the background, and a microwave oven will take much longer than normal to cook the same food, but most of these devices would still operate on a modified sine wave inverter.

In the early 1990s, quality modified sine wave inverters were being sold by Trace Engineering and Heart Interface. Although still limited to about 2500-watt output using a 12- volt DC input, these became the standard for residential off-grid and back-up power systems. Many of these early models are still in operation and have an excellent reputation for robust design and reliability. By the mid-90s, lower costs for solar photovoltaic modules and the need to power more sophisticated appliances, computers, and digital audio/video systems created a demand for larger inverter capacities and a smoother 60-cycle voltage waveform. Manufacturers responded with inverter outputs up to 5,500-watts by using higher voltage 24 to 48-volt DC inputs and more sophisticated internal electronics to increase the number of "steps" simulating the 60-cycle sine wave.

Some newer inverter models include a communications "link," which allows interconnecting multiple inverters to provide synchronized higher wattage and voltage outputs. Since these changes resulted in much higher inverter prices, most manufacturers still offer lower cost modified sine wave models when lower capacity and power quality are not a concern.

The Trace (now Xantrex) SW series 3,600, 4,000 and 5,500-watt inverters and the Outback FX 2000 and 2,500-watt inverters are popular residential inverters for back-up and off-grid power systems, although there are several other excellent brands now on the market. As long as it includes a battery powered inverter, any alternative energy system can continue to power the lights and appliances directly from the batteries after the sun goes down, the wind stops blowing, or the generator is turned off.

Grid-tie systems As the price of solar photovoltaic modules continues to fall and the price of peak afternoon electricity continues to increase, it is becoming cost-effective in some states to install solar modules just to reduce daytime metered electricity usage and sell any excess power generated back to the utility. Since these systems are not intended to provide emergency power, a grid-tie inverter can be less expensive since there are no battery chargers, battery bank, or costly high amperage components to buy. Obviously, if these special application inverters require the utility grid to serve as their "battery," a grid-tie solar system without a battery bank cannot serve as a source for emergency or back-up power.

Increasing the voltage for a given wattage allows reducing the current (watts = volts x amps). Since these inverters are designed for much higher DC solar array voltages than low voltage battery based systems, this can substantially reduce solar array wire size and wiring costs. However, with grid-tie solar array wiring in the 300 to 400-volt DC range, the potential for shock or fire causing arcing is substantially increased over a 12 to 48-volt DC battery based system.

All roof mounted solar photovoltaic arrays must be protected by DC ground fault circuit breakers. In recent years there have been several American made grid-tie inverters that did not meet promised efficiency performance, and several grid-tie inverter manufacturers have gone out of business which created a shortage in the American grid-tie inverter market. As a result, several European manufacturers moved in and filled this market niche with inverters that had excellent product quality and provided high operating efficiencies. The "Sunny Boy" line from Germany and the more recent Fronius line from Austria are becoming major contenders for this domestic grid-tie inverter market. Inverter features

Not all inverters are created equal, and there are more differences and options to pick from than just having to decide between a modified sine wave and a pure sine wave unit. Since this 1500-watt StatPower (now Xantrex) modified sine wave inverter mounted on a battery pack may be the most expensive component in your alternative energy system, there is a tendency to under-size the inverter just to save a few dollars. Don't fall into this trap, as you can always install fewer solar modules now and add more later, to save some up-front costs.

Many models of inverters are available with a built-in load transfer relay. This transfer relay is useful for back-up emergency power applications. Unlike a straight DC to AC inverter, an "AC input" connection is provided to connect the inverter to a spare circuit breaker in the main house panel. The AC output connections on the inverter are then connected to a new subpanel that will supply all critical loads in the house. This usually includes some of the lighting circuits, kitchen appliance outlets, refrigerator, and audio/video center.

Although a well pump would be considered a critical load, most inverters have a 120-volt AC output and most well pumps are 220-volt. This will require either buying two matching inverters or using a step-up transformer. As long as utility power reaches the inverter's AC input side, the transfer relay will continue to pass this AC grid power directly through the inverter to the sub-panel's critical loads. Any interruption in utility grid power results in the transfer relay automatically switching to the battery powered inverter output so the subpanel's loads will now be supplied from the battery bank. Although these inverters are not advertised as suitable as a computer UPS power supply, the relay transfer time is fast enough to not affect most computers.

Inverters that include the AC input terminals and transfer relay may also include a built-in battery charger. This circuit monitors the battery state of charge and will keep the battery fully charged when utility grid power is available and the transfer relay is switched to grid power. A word of caution is in order however. Most inverter battery chargers are very heavyduty and charging outputs over 100 amps are not uncommon. Special care must be taken to insure all of the battery charging setpoints are correct on the inverter for the size and type of batteries being used, or this high capacity charger could easily damage a very expensive battery bank.

Some inverters are available with a separate generator start relay. This is a real necessity for back-up and off-grid applications. These inverters may also include a second AC input specifically for generator power. This generator-start option allows programming the generator to either start as soon as the utility grid fails, or start when a low battery charge level has been reached. Since the inverter is only operating the generator to recharge the batteries, the generator will operate fewer hours than a straight generator-only power system.

When using these more sophisticated battery-charging inverters with a solar array, you must take care to properly balance the battery charging setpoints on the inverter with the setpoints on the solar charge controllers. If not set correctly, the inverter will easily "over-power" the output from the solar array and provide all of the battery charging from the utility grid regardless of the available sunlight. Some of the more expensive sine wave inverters are very versatile and provide many different system and battery charging setpoints for system finetuning. However, this versatility also requires more knowledge to properly set up a system to maximize its performance. Although these inverters may work right "out of the box," this does not mean the default settings are right for your specific application. If this appears to be too much of a challenge, you may want to consider a less sophisticated inverter model or hire a professional solar installer.

Almost all inverter manufacturers offer a remote display panel option. From a basic on/off switch to a more sophisticated data display screen, these are really useful if your inverter and battery bank are located in a hard to access crawl space or garage. You might want to locate these remote displays in the kitchen where you pass several times each day for a quick check on system status. Some inverters include a separate unused control relay that can be programmed by the installer to switch almost anything. For example, a battery room exhaust fan could be turned on by this relay when the battery voltage reaches a high limit during heavy charging and out-gassing begins. An alarm bell or light could be activated by this relay when a low battery charge is reached to tell the occupants to reduce their electrical usage or to start a manually operated generator. Not all inverters have these features, so if they are important to your application, be sure to shop carefully. Something to consider when shopping for an inverter is the balance of system (BOS) components you will also need, as these are not normally included in the advertised inverter base price.

In addition, the inverter list price for any battery powered inverter almost never include the required battery hook-up cables, which can run as high as $200 for a 10-foot pair. A grid-tie inverter purchase is usually more straightforward, since you will not need heavy battery cables, batteries, or large DC disconnects. A 2500-watt SMA Sunny Boy grid-tie inverter has a list price of $2,845. Since this includes a cover with digital display and built-in ground fault circuit breakers for multiple solar array inputs, the only other electrical component you will need is a $5 circuit breaker to feed the new inverter AC output to your existing main house circuit breaker panel.

Inverter shopping tips

1. If you are on a tight budget or are building a remote cabin system that will only need RV or boat-type 12-volt DC lights and appliances, you still may need to power a limited number of small AC appliances. Consider the 1500-watt StatPower (now Xantrex) low cost modified sine wave inverter designed for mobile applications. This is about the smallest size inverter that can still power a power saw, refrigerator, or microwave oven. Although these are normally 12-volt input inverters, they are available in many different outputs. For a slightly higher price, the Heart Interface (also now Xantrex) 2500-watt RV and marine line of modified sine wave inverters have higher capacities and more features. Most lower cost inverters are fairly reliable, but they do not have the same robust overload and control features that are found on more expensive models. An accidental system overload when starting a well pump or clothes washer may result in inverter or battery damage when using lower priced and lower wattage models.

2. If you just want to reduce your utility bill and do not need to power lights and appliances after the sun goes down or during a power outage, then your solar power system may not need a battery bank. This will allow using the lower cost "gridtie" inverter models such as Sunny Boy, Sharp, StarInverter, or Fronius. This will also allow using a much higher voltage solar array, which can reduce solar array wire size and associated installation costs.

3. If you plan to install a system that will have a battery bank, and your loads will include more power sensitive computer and digital audio/video equipment, you will probably want to consider one or more Trace (Xantrex) or Outback sine wave inverters powered from a 24 or 48-volt DC battery bank.

4. Wind turbines can quickly recharge a battery bank during unusually high wind conditions. Shutting off a wind driven generator as soon as the batteries are charged can cause over-speed of the now free turning blades. To avoid blade damage, many wind power systems include a "diversion load" control. This allows automatically switching the power output from battery charging to a second load such as electric heating elements in a hot water tank. This provides Sunny Boy grid-tie inverter, optional disconnects, and check meter Fronius grid-tie inverter and optional AC & DC disconnect free water heating while keeping the wind generator under a constant load. There are several new grid-tie inverters just entering the market specifically designed for wind generator type power output.

5. Using a small-scale (under 25-kW) grid-tie inverter to sell power back to the utility is a fairly new concept, and many states and electric utilities require an exterior safety disconnect and a utility inspection process before you can do this legally. Many utilities may also want you to install a special electric meter that totals electric flow in both directions. Be sure to check with your local

utility before installing any solar system that will be used to sell electricity back to the utility, as some state regulations are very strict.

Solar Arrays

Many people want to power their all-electric four-bedroom home with three or four solar modules., but we need to dispel some of these solar array misconceptions. Forget powering a conventional all-electric home with solar modules unless you want to spend what your house cost in the first place. Today's solar modules can convert 14% to 18% of the solar energy they receive into electricity under ideal conditions. This means the more square-feet of solar array you have, the more power you will generate. However, outdoor temperatures, cloud-cover, site elevation, and shadows reduce this electrical power output substantially.

Reviewing many popular sizes of modules available from several different manufacturers, one finds the average nameplate rating of about 11 to 12-watts per square foot. Remember, this performance was measured at perfect "solar-noon" conditions using a sun simulator, not the real sun. Since there will be some efficiency losses for less than perfect "real world" conditions, 10-watts per square-foot of roof area is a good "rule-of-thumb" for most areas in North America. Those in sunny southern latitudes can expect better performance than those of you in cloudy northern latitudes, but this will be a good starting point for our discussions.

Basic array sizing Using the above average peak output of 10-watts per square-foot, this means it will take 100 square feet of solar array for each kilowatt (kW) of solar output we want. Individual solar modules are now being manufactured with a much higher wattage per- module to reduce wiring and installation expense. You will want to arrange your array layout using standard size modules, and the actual roof required may be larger than your initial square foot estimate based on wattage. You will want to leave some space between modules to allow for expansion, and between rows for wiring .

Residential-size solar systems typically have a 24 or 48-volt battery-bank, unless they are grid-tied systems without batteries. Therefore, you should use a module count that is a multiple of two, since most modules have a nominal voltage of 12 or 24-volt. For example, if you wanted to install a solar array in the 2 kW size range, you could install 24 modules at 80- watts each (1,920 watts total), but should not use 25 modules just to make it match a nominal output goal. This will allow equally dividing the voltage and current among other system components, such as array circuit fuses, charge controllers, and wire runs.

Expected system performance While the sun shines all day, at the lower sun angles before 9:00 am and after 3:00 pm, the solar array will have a much lower power output. During shorter winter months this "solar day" is even shorter. There are weather tables available giving total sun-hours for most cities in the United States, but if you are looking for a ballpark sun-hour per day value, use 4-hours for winter months, and 6-hours for summer months. Those of you in more southern latitudes may exceed these averages, while those of you in more northern latitudes may have fewer peak sun-hours per day, especially during winter months.

From our earlier example of a 1,920-watt array, this results in 7.68 kWh/day in the winter (4 hr. x 1,920 watts) and 11.5 kWh/day in the summer (6 hr. x 1,920 watts). Remember, these are manufacture nameplate performance values using sun simulators. Your installation will have a lower output due to the system losses we have already discussed. For most systems and site locations, your actual system useful AC wattage output will be 20 to 30 percent below the module nameplate DC wattage values, even with ideal weather conditions.

Solar module types

We've discussed battery-based inverters and grid-tied inverters that do not use batteries. You can use the same solar modules for both system types, but how the modules are wired together will be different. Some solar module manufacturers start with a round, single-crystal of silicon that is sliced into very thin wafers. These have electrical conductors plated to each side, and are then sandwiched between a tempered glass front panel and a vacuum sealed plastic or vinyl material backing. This assembly is then mounted in an aluminum frame, which allows easy attachment to mounting racks or a building structure.

Other solar module manufacturers start with a "block" of multi-crystalline silicon, which is also sliced into very thin wafers, and follows the same type assembly as the single-crystal module. Since a multicrystalline material can be cast into larger square blocks than a round single-crystal can be "grown," a square-shaped solar cell is easier to place close to each adjoining cell, allowing less material waste and more cell surface area per module frame size. To achieve the same cell density, most round single-crystal cells have each side cut off to create a square shape with rounded corners. This allows the same cell density per module frame-size, but at a higher material waste and cost.

A third cell technology that offers significant manufacturing cost savings is a solar cell that is "plated" onto the back of the glass front, then this silicon material is "cut" into individual cells using a laser. Unfortunately, the wattage-per-square-foot output for this amorphous cell technology is substantially lower than the more conventional modules, so you need significantly more roof area for the same output. However, since amorphous modules sells for a much lower price-per-module, your actual array cost per watt will be almost the same. Single-crystal cells with squared sides do allow closer cell placement

There are some solar manufacturers mounting solar cells directly onto a metal or vinyl backing without any glass front plate. These modules are for applications subject to physical damage, like the deck of a sailboat or vehicle roof. Some modules are flexible and can be rolled up or tied down to irregular mounting surfaces. These are excellent for portable applications, but are not normally available in higher wattage sizes.

Most of the solar module brands you will see in the marketplace today are from large brand name manufacturers and carry excellent product warranties. Some may have a heavier frame than others, and some may have a different size or exterior finish, but they are all very similar. However, their cost-per-watt and watt-per-square foot values will be different.

Stay with name brands and solid warranties. If you do encounter a technical problem or need warranty replacement, that low cost, high volume Internet solar distributor may be long gone when you have a technical problem.

XXXIV   Master Preparedness List

This list is based on a family of two/three adults and two/three children that want to take their preparedness beyond the simple 96 hour kits and become more fully prepared for whatever may come. The items within each category are listed by "Purchase Priority". The quantities listed are for a 30 day to one-year crisis. Because some items are impossible to store indefinitely or it would not be cost-effective to store the quantities necessary to maintain our current lifestyle, it is assumed that alternate sources or substitutes will be found or changes in lifestyle will occur if the crisis lasts over one year. Quantities could be adjusted for other estimated lengths of crisis. There are 3 major groupings that are based on the duration of the "Crisis", 30 Days, 90 Days and 1 Year.

Within each of these three durations, items are prioritized. It should be your goal to Obtain all of the "30 Day" items in sequence from Priority 1 to 3, by April 1st. Then move onto your "90 Day" items in the same manner obtaining them by July 1st, and finally onto your "1 Year" items by October 1st. This will allow you to build up your preparedness in stages, 30 Days first (as these items would be needed in EVERY scenario) 90 Days second (as they build on the 30 day list), and finally your 1 Year equipment that rounds out your preparations.

The purchase priority is not how important the item is. everything on this list is important. The purchase priority is how soon the item should be purchased *to avoid shortages should other people decide to start "stocking up" on the same items.* A priority "1" item should be purchased ASAP. A priority "2" item should be purchased before most people figure out what is going on. Priority "3" items should be available until later. These are common household items which should be manufactured and shipped right up until the last minute. The purchase date is a guideline of when to make purchases. Items with a "Last minute" listing are perishable and you want as long a shelf life as possible. Signs of shortages or panic should be watched closely to avoid missing out on these items. The final three columns indicate whether the item would be necessary for a 1 month, three month, one year to indefinite crisis.

Clothing

Keep in mind that a crises will as like as not be during the winter and adjust this list for your climate. Warm, Waterproof, Windproof clothing. Think Wool, Gore-Tex, Polarfleece, Polypro, Thinsulate. Avoid Cotton!

Item	Qty.	Priority	Plan Date	Duration
Bandanas	24 each	3		
(*inexpensive shield face, head cover, wash cloth, bandage, sanitary pad*)				
Balaclava	1/person	3	April 1	30 Day
Boots	2/person	2	April 1	30 Day
Boots, (insulated)	1/person	2	April 1	30 Day

Bra athletic	2/female	3	April 1	30 Day
Clothes line	100 ft	3	April 1	30 Day
Clothes pins	250	3	April 1	30 Day
Clothes Wringer (hand crank)	1	2	July 1	90 Day
Coats	1/person	2	April 1	30 Day
Hats	1/person	3	July 1	90 Day
Iron-on patches.	2 pkgs.	3	April 1	30 Day
Laundry detergent	5 (5gal)	3	April 1	30 Day
Long sleeve shirt/high collar	5/person	3	April 1	30 Day
Long underwear	3/person	2	April 1	30 Day
Needles	Assortment	3	July 1	90 Day
Non-electric washing machine	1	1	April 1	30 Day
Jean Pants	6/person	3	April 1	30 Day
Rain Parka/Rain Pants	2/person	2	April 1	30 Day
Safety pins	Assortment	3	July 1	90 Day
Sewing patterns	Assortment	3		1 Year
Sewing supplies	Assortment	2	April 1	30 Day
Shirts	6/person	3	April 1	30 Day
Shoelaces	20	3	July 1	90 Day
Snow Jacket	1/person	3	April 1	30 Day
Socks heavy	12/person	3	April 1	30 Day
Stove iron	1	1	July 1	90 Day
Sweats/nightclothes	2/person	3	April 1	30 Day
Tennis Shoes	2pair/person	3	April 1	30 Day
Thread	Assortment	3	July 1	90 Day
Underwear	12/person	3	April 1	30 Day
Wash board	2	1	July 1	90 Day
Wash tub	2	1	July 1	90 Day
Winter gloves	1/person	2	April 1	30 Day
Work Gloves	3	2	July 1	90 Day
Zippers and buttons	Assortment	3	April 1 30	30 Day

Communications

The phone/address books are of friends and family so that you can look them up after the worst has passed. If phones are not working you may have to travel to their home to check on them. Keep these items in waterproof containers. Many survival and camping stores sell flat, water tight pouches. If you have a food vacuum sealer, this is another great use for it!

Item	Qty.	Priority	Plan Date	Duration
Addresses of friends	1 set /family	3		
CB Radio/ Cell phone	1	2	April 1	30 Day
Frequency lists/books	1	2	July 1	90 Day
Map of your local area	2	2	April 1	30 Day
Phone numbers of friends/family	1 set			
Pre-addressed, stamped postcards	1 set			
Radio (hand cranked)	1	1	April 1	30 Day
Road Flares	8	3	July 1	90 Day
Short-wave Radio	1	1	July 1	90 Day
Signal Flares	12	2	July 1	90 Day
Signal Mirror	1/person	3	July 1	90 Day
Signal Whistle	2/person	3	July 1	90 Day

Documents

Item	Qty.	Priority	Plan Date	Duration
Bank account numbers			Now	30/90/Year
Birth, death, marriage certificates and divorce decrees			Now	30/90/Year
Charge card account numbers, "lost or stolen" notification numbers			Now	30/90/Year
Deeds and contracts			Now	30/90/Year
House and life insurance policies			Now	30/90/Year
Inventory valuable household items			Now	30/90/Year
Medical records including immunizations			Now	30/90/Year
Passports, where pertinent for each family member			Now	30/90/Year

Social security numbers			Now	30/90/Year
Stocks and bonds			Now	30/90/Year
Vaccination records			Now	30/90/Year
Wills			Now	30/90/Year

Entertainment & Education

Item	Qty.	Priority	Plan Date	Duration
Bible & scriptures	1/person	3	April 1	30 Day
Board Games	1 set	3	April 1	30 Day
Books for pleasure reading	Many	3	April 1	30 Day
Book on Edible plants	1	3	October 1	1 Year
Card game book	1	3	April 1	30 Day
Cards	4 sets	3	April 1	30 Day
Crayons	2	3	April 1	30 Day
Domino game book	1	3	April 1	30 Day
Dominoes	1	3	April 1	30 Day
Erasers	10	3	April 1	30 Day
Home School Curriculum	1/child	2	October 1	1 Year
How To Books	Many	1	July 1	90 Day
Hoyle game rule book	1	3	April 1	30 Day
Magnifying Glass	1 each	3	April 1	30 Day
Non-electric pencil sharpener	2	3	April 1	30 Day
Paper	100 pads	3	April 1	30 Day
Paper Clips, assorted sizes	1 box	3	April 1	30 Day
Pencils	100	3	April 1	30 Day
Pens	50	3	April 1	30 Day
Reference books	1	3	July 1	90 Day
Safety Pins, assorted sizes	1 box	3	April 1	30 Day
Toys		3	April 1	30 Day

First Aid Supplies

Item	Qty.	Priority	Plan Date	Duration
Ace bandage	5	3	April 1	30 Day

Band aids	6 large assort	3	April 1	30 Day
Band aids Finger tip	1 large box	3	April 1	30 Day
Band aids Knuckle	1 large box	3	April 1	30 Day
Bandages (Ace) elastic, 4"	2	3	April 1	30 Day
Bandages, gauze, 2", 3", 4"	4 boxes	3	April 1	30 Day
Bandages, gauze, 18" x 36"	1	3	April 1	30 Day
Bandages, burns (Second Skin)	1 box	2	April 1	30 Day
Bandages Triangular	3	3	April 1	30 Day
Birth supply kit	1	3	July 1	90 Day
Burn Dressings Assorted (*Burn Free*)	2		April 1	30 Day
Butterfly closures/Leukostrips	1 large box	3	April 1	30 Day
Cold/heat Pack, instant	5 each	3	April 1	30 Day
Cold/heat Pack, reusable	1	3	April 1	30 Day
Cotton Balls	1 box	3	April 1	30 Day
Cotton Swabs	1 large box	3	April 1	30 Day
Eyedropper	1	3	April 1	30 Day
Eye pads	1 large box	3	April 1	30 Day
First aid manual	1	3	October 1	1 Year
Gauze 2"	5 rolls	3	April 1	30 Day
Gauze 3"	5 rolls	3	April 1	30 Day
Latex gloves	1 box	3	April 1	30 Day
SAM splint	1	3	October 1	1 Year
Scalpel	1 box	3	April 1	30 Day
Scissors, Surgical pointed	1	3	October 1	1 Year
Shears	2	3	October 1	1 Year
Snake bite kit	1	3	July 1	90 Day
Space Blankets	4	3	April 1	30 Day

Sterile pads 4" x 4"	1 large box	3	April 1	30 Day
Sterile pads 5" x 9"	1 large box	3	April 1	30 Day
Surgical tape	10 rolls	3	April 1	30 Day
Thermometer	4	3	April 1	30 Day
Tongue Depressors	6	3	April 1	30 Day
Tweezers	4	3	April 1	30 Day

First Aid, Perishables

Item	Qty.	Priority	Plan Date	Duration
Alcohol	6	3	July 1	90 Day
Alcohol Moist Towelettes	100	3	Last minute	30 Day
Analgesic Cream (*Camphophenique*)	1 tube	2	Last minute	30 Day
Antacid(*Mylanta, Tums, Pepto-Bismal*)	1 box	2	Last minute	30 Day
Antibiotic (*Amoxicillin Erythromycin Tetracycline for general infections*)	1 set	2	Last minute	30 Day
Anti-Diarrheal (*Imodium, Diasorb, Lomotil*)	1 box	2	Last minute	30 Day
Anti-fungal (*Desenex, Micatin, Tinactin, Lotrimin*)	1 box	2	Last minute	30 Day
Antihistamine (*Benadryl, Claratyne*)	1 box	2	Last minute	30 Day
Antiseptic Ointment (*Neosporin*)	3 tube	2	Last minute	30 Day
Aspirin	6 (100)	3	Last minute	90 Day
Bee sting ointment	6 tubes	3	Last minute	30 Day
Bicarbonate of Soda	1 box	2	July 1	90 Day
Bronco Dialator (*Primatine Mist*)	1	2	Last minute	30 Day
Burn Ointment (*Hydrocortisone, Derm-Aid*)	1 tube	2	Last minute	30 Day
Cold/Flu Tablets (*Nyquil*)	1 box	2	Last minute	30 Day
Constipation (*Ex-Lax, Dulcolax, Durolax*)	1 box	2	Last minute	30 Day
Cough Syrup (*Robitussen, Dimetap*)	1 bottle	2	Last minute	30 Day
Epsom Salts	1 box	2	July 1	90 Day
Eye Drops (*Visine*)	1 bottle	2	Last minute	30 Day

Eye Wash	1 bottle	2	Last minute	30 Day
Hemorrhoid Relief (*Preparation H, Anusol*)	1 tube	2	Last minute	30 Day
Hydrogen peroxide	6 bottles	3	July 1	90 Day
Ibuprofen (*Advil, Motrin*)	1 box	2	Last minute	30 Day
Itching, Insect/Rash (Caladril, Calamine)	1 bottle	2	Last minute	30 Day
Itching (*Dibucaine, Lanacane*)	1 tube	2	Last minute	30 Day
Lice (*Nix or RID Lice Shampoo*)	1 tube	2	Last minute	30 Day
Lip Balm (*ChapStick, Blistex*)	1 tube	2	Last minute	30 Day
Lubricant, Water Soluble (*K-Y Jelly*)	1 tube	2	Last minute	90 Day
Meat Tenderizer bites & stings	1 bottle	2	July 1	90 Day
Nasal Decongestant (*Actifed, Sudafed Sinex*)	1 bottle	2	Last minute	30 Day
Nausea, Motion (*Kwells, Dramamine, Meclizine*)	1 box	2	Last minute	30 Day
Non-Aspirin Pain Reliever (*Tylenol*)	1 box	2	Last minute	30 Day
Pain, Fever Reducer (*Panadeine, Mobigesic*)	1 box	2	Last minute	30 Day
Pain Reliever with Codeine (*Tylenol 3*)	1 box	2	Last minute	30 Day
Prescriptions	(as needed)	1	Last minute	30 Day
Petroleum Jelly (*Vaseline*)	1 jar	2	Last minute	30 Day
Poison Ivy/Oak (*Neoxyn*)	6 bottle	2	Last minute	30 Day
Poison Absorber (*Activated Charcoal*)	1 bottle	2	Last minute	90 Day
Soap, liquid, antibacterial	1 bottle	3	Last minute	30 Day
Sunburn Relief (*Solarcaine*)	1 can	2	Last minute	30 Day
Sunscreen (SPF 15 at least)	1 bottle	2	Last minute	30 Day
Vomit Inducer (*Ipecac*)	1 bottle	2	Last minute	30 Day
Yeast Infection Treatment(Gyne-Lotrimin, Monistat)	1 tube	2	Last minute	30 Day

Food Preparation

The fire place insert would ideally be designed to cook on. The fire grate is for cooking outside over an open fire. Crisco shortening is listed because it can be stored for a long time.

Item	Qty.	Priority	Plan Date	Duration
Plastic Wrap	1 roll			
Aluminum foil, Heavy	6 large rolls	3	April 1	30 Day
BBQ grill (charcoal/propane)	1	3	July 1	90 Day
Boning Knife	2	3	April 1	30 Day
Bread Loaf Pan	4	3	April 1	30 Day
Butcher Knife	1	3	April 1	30 Day
Butter churn	1	2	October 1	1 year
Camp Stove	1	2	April 1	30 Day
Can opener (hand cranked)	2	3	April 1	30 Day
Can Opener, heavy duty	1	3	April 1	30 Day
Canning books	1 set	2	July 1	90 Day
Cast iron cook set (*Complete!*)	1 set	2	April 1	30 Day
Cheesecloth	1 roll	3	April 1	30 Day
Cheese press	1	2	October 1	1 Year
Coffee filters	100	3	April 1	30 Day
Coffe maker, metal	1	3	April 1	30 Day
Coleman metal dinner plates	1 set	2	April 1	30 Day
Coleman Cooler	2	3	April 1	30 Day
Corkscrew	1	3	April 1	30 Day
Crock pot, Large	1	1	October 1	1 Year
Cultures	1 set	3	Last Minute	90 Day
Dish Cloths	6	3	April 1	30 Day
Dishwashing liquid	5 gal	3	April 1	30 Day
Dutch Oven, small with lid	1	2	April 1	30 Day
Dutch Oven, large with lid	1	2	July 1	90 Day
Fire grate	1	1	July 1	90 Day
Fireplace insert	1	1	April 1	30 Day
Grain mill (hand cranked)	1	1	April 1	30 Day
Grater	1	3	April 1	30 Day
Hot Pad	1 set	3	April 1	30 Day
Kettle, huge, for boiling water	1	2	July 1	90 Day

Latex disposable gloves	1 box	2	July 1	90 Day
Mixing Bowl, Large	1 each	3	April 1	30 Day
Mixing Bowl, Small	1 each	3	April 1	30 Day
Molds	1 set	3	April 1	30 Day
Napkins	10	3	April 1	30 Day
Pancake Turners, metal	2	3	April 1	30 Day
Paper cups	100	3	April 1	30 Day
Paring Knife	1	3	April 1	30 Day
Plastic knives, forks, spoons	200	3	April 1	30 Day
Pressure cooker	1	2	July 1	90 Day
Rennet	1	3	October 1	1 Year
Rubber dish gloves	4 Sets	3	April 1	30 Day
Sauce Pan, large with lid	1	3	April 1	30 Day
Sauce Pan, small with lid	1	3	April 1	30 Day
Scrub pads	50	3	April 1	30 Day
Skillet, large with lid	1	3	April 1	30 Day
Spoons, large metal	2	3	April 1	30 Day
Spoons, Wooden	2	3	April 1	30 Day
Strainer	1	3	April 1	30 Day
Thermos	1/person	2	April 1	30 Day
Yeast	1 box	3	Last minute	30 Day
Yogurt culture	1 box	3	Last Minute	90 Day
Ziploc Bags - Sandwich	100	3	April 1	30 Day
Ziploc Bags - Storage	50	3	July 1	90 Day
Ziploc Freezer Bags, gallon	2 boxes	3	July 1	90 Day
Ziploc Freezer Bags, quart	2 boxes	3	April 1	30 Day

Food Storage

Item	Qty.	Priority	Plan Date	Duration
1 gal. plastic bags	300	3	July 1	90 Day
Baskets/crates	24	1	October 1	1 year
Boiling canner	1	1	October 1	1 year

Bucket opener	2	1	October 1	1 year
Canning book	1	1	October 1	1 year
Canning jars	100	1	October 1	1 year
Canning lids	500	1	October 1	1 year
Canning salt	20lb	1	October 1	1 year
Canning supplies (Misc)	Assortiment	1	October 1	1 year
Canning Utensils	Assortiment	1	October 1	1 year
Colander	1	1	October 1	1 year
Desiccants	60 (66gm)	1	April 1	30 Day
Food storage buckets	30 (5 gal)	1	July 1	90 Day
Jar lifter	1	1	October 1	1 year
Jars Assortment	1	1	October 1	1 year
Lids	Assortment	1	October 1	1 year
Mesh bags	24	1	October 1	1 year
Oxygen absorbers	50 (500ml)	1	July 1	90 Day
Parafin Wax	5lb	1	October 1	1 year
Pressure canner	1	1	October 1	1 year
Saucepan	2	1	October 1	1 year
Saucepot	3	1	October 1	1 year
Scale	1	1	October 1	1 year
Storage/garden books	Assortment	2	October 1	1 year
Timer	1	1	October 1	1 year
Tongs to remove jars	2	2	April 1	30 Day
Water storage	10 (5 gal)	1	April 1	30 Day
Water storage	2 (55 gal)	1	April 1	30 Day
Wax for canning				

Fuel & Power

The amount of firewood will depend on your climate and the efficiency of your stove or fireplace. The kerosene is for the lamps under "General Household". Sta-bil is an additive which allows gasoline to be stored longer than normal. The barrel is to transport gasoline in if it can be purchased.

Item	Qty.	Priority	Plan Date	Duration
Barrel	(55 gal)	1	July 1	90 Day

Item	Qty.	Priority	Plan Date	Duration
Charcoal	500 lb.	1	April 1	30 Day
Fire starters	2	1	July 1	90 Day

(jelly, ribbon, tablets, impregnated peat bricks, wax-coated pine cones, magnesium block, flint)

Item	Qty.	Priority	Plan Date	Duration
Fire wood	10 cords	2	April 1	90 Day
Fuel filter for generator	1	2	April 1	30 Day
Fuel pump	1	1	April 1	30 Day
Gasoline	500 gal	2	October 1	1 Year
Gas cans	(5 gal) 6	2	April 1	30 Day
Kerosene	50 gal	2	July 1	90 Day
Kerosene storage barrel	1 (55gal)	2	July 1	90 Day
Lighter Fluid	5 cans	2	April 1	30 Day
Matches	20 (250)	1	April 1	30 Day
Propane	500 gal	2	July 1	90 Day
Spark plug for generator	1	2	April 1	30 Day
Sta-bil	8 qt	1	April 1	30 Day
Starter fluid	5 gal	1	April 1	30 Day
White Gas Coleman(for campstove)	10 (1 gal)	2	April 1	30 Day

Gardening

Non-hybrid seeds will reproduce true to the parent plant. Hybrid seeds may reproduce with a recessive gene. The polyethylene is for covering young plants to maintain warmth and moisture. The styrofoam cups are for coverings seedlings during late winter frosts.

Bug spray. Malathion, Sevin, Dursban and Diazanon. Dursban and Diazanon. Dursban and Diazanon can have severe side effects in humans, for use outside of house, not necessarily on the garden. Fine for flower gardens. Sevin is safer to use on the vegetables.

Item	Qty.	Priority	Plan Date	Duration
Black polyethylene	1	2	October 1	1 year
Bleach	5 gal	2	October 1	1 year
Clear polyethylene	1	2	October 1	1 year
Garden hoses	2	3	April 1	30 Day
Herb Seeds	Assortment	2	October 1	1 year
Hoe	2	3	July 1	90 Day
Misters for seedlings	2	2	October 1	1 year
Miracle Gro	2	2	October 1	1 year

Non-hybrid seeds	Assortment	1	October 1	1 year
Organic fertilizers	Assortment	2	October 1	1 year
Perennial flowerseeds	Assortment	3	October 1	1 year
Pull wagon	1	3	July 1	90 Day
Rototiller	1	2	October 1	1 year
Seed starting containers	Assortment	2	October 1	1 year
Seed starting medium	Assortment	2	October 1	1 year
Thermometers	2	2	October 1	1 year
Soil testing equipment	1	1	October 1	1 year
Sprayer/Pumper-2 gallon size	1	3	July 1	90 Day
Styrofoam cups	1000	2	October 1	1 year
Watering can	1	2	October 1	1 year
Wheel barrel	2	2	October 1	1 year

Hardware & Building Supplies

Item	Qty.	Priority	Plan Date	Duration
A few cases of silicone caulk.				
Bolts	Assortment	3	July 1	90 Day
Bricks, rocks	Assortment	3	October 1	1 Year
Cable	100 ft	3	July 1	90 Day
Cable clamps	8	3	July 1	90 Day
Cement	10 bags	3	October 1	1 Year
Chains and padlocks	Several	3	July 1	90 Day
Chicken wire, barbed wire, etc.	2 rolls	3	October 1	1 Year
Duct tape	10 rolls	3	April 1	30 Day
Extra axe handles	2	3	October 1	1 year
Long polls	10	3	October 1	1 Year
Fencing material	Assortment	3	October 1	1 Year
Lumber	Assorted	3	October 1	1 Year
Mouse traps	5	3	April 1	30 Day
Nails	100 lbs.	3	October 1	1 Year
Nuts and bolts	Assorted	3	April 1	30 Day

Item	Qty.	Priority	Plan Date	Duration
Pipe	Assorted	3	April 1	30 Day
Plumbing repair supplies	Assorted	3	April 1	30 Day
Polyethylene Black	2	3	July 1	90 Day
Polyethylene Clear	2	3	July 1	90 Day
Pulleys	4	3	July 1	90 Day
Rigging book	1	3	July 1	90 Day
Rope	Assorted	3	April 1	30 Day
Screws	Assorted	3	July 1	90 Day
Spare keys to all locks (set to same key)	1 set	2	April 1	30 Day
Spare parts for wheelbarrow	1 set	3	July 1	90 Day
Spare toilet parts	1 set	3	July 1	90 Day
Tarps	4	3	April 1	30 Day
WD-40	1 gal	3	July 1	90 Day
Wire	Assorted	3	April 1	30 Day

Household Items

The water filter is assuming you have a stream or other reliable source of water. The ni-cad batteries are rechargeable for the radio. Other batteries should be sized according to your needs.

Item	Qty.	Priority	Plan Date	Duration
Backpack with Frame (for Hauling)	1/person	2	April 1	30 Day
Batteries AA	100	1	Last minute	30 Day
Batteries AA, Ni-Cad	8	1	April 1	30 Day
Batteries C	20	1	Last minute	30 Day
Batteries C, Ni-Cad	8	1	April 1	30 Day
Batteries D	100	1	Last minute	30 Day
Batteries D, Ni-Cad	8	1	April 1	30 Day
Battery Charger, SOLAR	2	1	April 1	30 Day
Blankets	10	1	April 1	30 Day
Camera	1	3	July 1	90 Day
Camera batteries	1 set	3	Last minute	90 Day
Camera film/mem cards	3 rolls	3	Last minute	90 Day
Candles 10 hour	50	1	April 1	30 Day

Candles 36 hour	25	1	April 1	30 Day
Candles (liquid parafin) 100 hour	25	1	April 1	30 Day
Candle holders	1 set	2	April 1	30 Day
Candle wax/wick	10lbs	2	July 1	90 Day
Carpet sweeper hand operated	1	3	April 1	30 Day
Clocks wind up	3	3	April 1	30 Day
Fanny pack for short excursions	1/person	2	April 1	30 Day
Fire extinguishers	4	3	April 1	30 Day
Flashlights	5	2	April 1	30 Day
Flashlight bulbs	2/light	3	April 1	30 Day
Handwarmer, lighter fueled	1	3	April 1	30 Day
Kerosene Heater	2	1	April 1	30 Day
Kerosene lamps	4	1	April 1	30 Day
Kerosene lamp wicks	10	1	April 1	30 Day
Lighters (disposable)	50	2	April 1	30 Day
Light sticks (12 hour)	18	3	April 1	30 Day
Matches stick(boxes of 250)	20	2	April 1	30 Day
Matches, water/windproof	5 boxes of 20	2	July 1	90 Day
Mosquito Netting	1 roll	3	July 1	90 Day
Paper towels	100	3	April 1	30 Day
Pet Food	as needed	3	April 1	30 Day
Permanent Ink Maker	2	3	April 1	0 Day
Propane Heater	2	2	April 1	30 Day
Sleeping bags	1/person	1	April 1	30 Day
Sleeping Bag Mattress Pads	1/person	1	April 1	30 Day
Tents (2 person)	2	2	April 1	30 Day
Trash bags	10 Boxes	3	April 1	30 Day
Treadle Sowing Machine	1	2	July 1	90 Day
Walkie talkies	1 pair	1	April 1	30 Day
Watches	5	3	April 1	30 Day
Wool Blankets, heavy	2/person	2	April 1	30 Day

Infant Supplies

Item	Qty.	Priority	Plan Date	Duration
Baby Food	???	2	Last Minute	30 Day
Baby Clothes	3 sets	1	April 1	30 Day
Baby Powder	2 bottles	1	April 1	30 Day
Baby Wash	2 bottles	1	April 1	30 Day
Blankets	2 each	1	April 1	30 Day
Bottles	3 each	1	April 1	30 Day
Diaper Cover		1	April 1	30 Day
Diapers, disposable (24 count)	26 boxes	1	April 1	30 Day
Diaper Rash Ointment	1 bottle	1	April 1	30 Day
Formula	? cans	1	Last Minute	30 Day
Lotion 2 bottles	1	1	April 1	30 Day
nursing bras	1 each	1	April 1	30 Day
Nursing pads 1 April 1 30 Day	4 each	1	April 1	30 Day
Teething Ring	1 each	1	April 1	30 Day
Towelettes, Pre-moistened	2 boxes	1	April 1	30 Day
Toys	As needed	1	April 1	30 Day

Miscellaneous

Guns are like tools, it's difficult to have too many. The quantity and types of guns required will vary tremendously from one person to another. Self defense is an important consideration and, if wild game is in the area, hunting can provide fresh meat. The maps should be very detailing showing back roads in case major highways are closed or clogged. The safe is for storing records, documents, cash, and gold or silver. A burn barrel is for disposing of household garbage and a spark arrestor is a grated top to prevent accidental fires.

Item	Qty.	Priority	Plan Date	Duration
5 gallon emergency toilet	1	2	April 1	30 Day
Ant spray concentrate	1	3	April 1	30 Day
Binoculars	2	3	April 1	30 Day
Book on using compass	1	1	April 1	30 Day
Burn barrel	2	3	July 1	90 Day
Compass	2	1	April 1	30 Day
Fishing tackle	Assortment	3	October 1	1 year

Metal bucket for charcoals/ashes	1	3	April 1	30 Day
Night vision scope	1	1	April 1	30 Day
O.D. parachute cord	200ft	3	July 1	90 Day
Safe	1	1	April 1	30 Day
Spark arrestor	2	3	April 1	30 Day
Sponges	10	3	April 1	30 Day
Toilet seat	1	3	July 1	90 Day
Trash bags - 13 gallon size	1 box	3	April 1	30 Day
Trash bags - 33 gallon size	1 box	3	April 1	30 Day
Water buckets 5 gal	2	3	April 1	30 Day
Glue various types (*wood glue, super glue, weather stripping adhesive, etc.*)	several	3	July 1	90 Day
Paint	10 gal	3	October 1	1 year
Rolls of 10 mil"Visqueen"	3	3	April 1	30 Day
Tape (*duct, masking, packing tape, etc.*)	Assortment	3	April 1	30 Day
Window screen	2 Rolls	3	October 1	90 Day

Money

$1000. in cash and change (during times of disaster charge cards and checks will not be honored* *Money is always hard to tuck away and pretend it isn't there, but in this instance, it is a necessity. One can't assume expenditures on credit cards during a crisis. Whenever you make a purchase, it is always verified by a telephoned authorization number. If phone lines are down and these numbers are not obtainable, chances are your purchase won't be allowed.

Item	Qty.	Priority	Plan Date	Duration
Cash	$1000/person	1	April 1	30 Day
Gold	10oz/person	1	October 1	1 Year
Silver	100oz/person	1	July 1	90 Day

Personal Toiletries

Solar showers use the sun to heat water for bathing. Lime is used to keep down odors from human waste. Quantities are not given for feminine or baby needs because of lack of familiarity with them.

Item	Qty.	Priority	Plan Date	Duration
Baby wipes	1 box	3	April 1	30 Day
Bar soap	100	3	April 1	30 Day

Barber scissors	2 pair	3	April 1	30 Day
Birth Control	3 boxes	3	July 1	90 Day
Brushes	3/person	3	April 1	30 Day
Camping Potty	1	2	April 1	30 Day
Chapstick	24	3	April 1	30 Day
Combs	3/person	3	April 1	30 Day
Contact cleaning supplies	1 set	3	last minute	30 Day
Cotton swabs	4 (500)	3	April 1	30 Day
Dental floss	12	3	April 1	30 Day
Deodorant (men's)	12	3	April 1	30 Day
Deodorant (women's)	12	3	April 1	30 Day
Fingernail clippers	1/person	3	April 1	30 Day
Fingernail file metal	1/person	3	April 1	30 Day
Fluoride Rinse	2 bottles	3	July 1	90 Day
Glasses	2 pair	2	July 1	90 Day
Insect Repellent	4 cans	3	July 1	90 Day
Kleenex	50 boxes	3	April 1	30 Day
Lime	100 lbs.	3	April 1	30 Day
Liquid Hair Shampoo (Adult	2 bottles	3	April 1	30 Day
Liquid Hair Shampoo (Child)	2 bottles	3	April 1	30 Day
Liquid Hand Soap (antibacterial)	5 bottles	3	April 1	30 Day
Lotion	12	3	April 1	30 Day
Mouthwash	2 bottles	3	July 1	90 Day
Panty Liners	1 box	3	April 1	30 Day
Razor blades (men's)	30	3	April 1	30 Day
Razor blades (women's)	30	3	April 1	30 Day
Sanitary Pads	1 box	3	April 1	30 Day
Shampoo	24	3	April 1	30 Day
Sunglasses	2/person	3	April 1	30 Day
Tampons	1 box	3	April 1	30 Day
Toenail clippers	3	3	April 1	30 Day
Toilet paper	100 rolls	3	April 1	30 Day

Shaving Cream 3 April 1 30 Day	2 cans	3	April 1	30 Day
Solar Shower	2	1	July 1	90 Day
Toothbrushes	2	3	April 1	30 Day
Toothpaste	5 tubes	3	April 1	30 Day
Towelettes, Pre-moistened	2 boxes	3	April 1	30 Day
Towels	15	3	April 1	30 Day
Tweezers, pointed	2	3	April 1	30 Day
Wash Cloths & Towel	4/person	3	April 1	30 Day

Security Supplies

Common Caliber Ammunition is the best all-around barter item. Top choices are: .22 long rifle, .223 Remington (5.56 mm NATO), .308 Winchester (7.62 mm NATO), .30-06, 12 gauge (2-3/4 inch #4 Buckshot), .45 ACP, and 9mm Parabellum

Item	Qty.	Priority	Plan Date	Duration
.22 shells	1000	2	July 1	90 Day
Gun safe	1	1	April 1	30 Day
Guns/Ammo	Assortment	1	April 1	30 Day
Military rifle bore cleaner 1 oz. bottles	10	2	July 1	90 Day
Ammo reloader	1	2	October 1	1 Year
Ammo Cans	5	2	April 1	30 Day
Gun accessories	1 set/weapon	2	April 1	30 Day
Gun cleaning equipment	1 set/weapon	2	April 1	30 day
Military web gear *pistol belts, magazine pouches, etc.*	2/person	2	April 1	30 Day
Perimeter alarm	1 set	2	April 1	30 Day
Solar powered perimeter Lights	5	3	April 1	30 Day
Waterproof dufflebags *(dry bags)*	1/person	2	April 1	30 Day

Tools

The generator is for emergencies and occasional use like pumping water from a well. It is not feasible to store enough fuel to run a generator full time to maintain our current lifestyle. A cant hook is a tool for rolling logs so that you can move them in to position to cut them for firewood. A list of hand tools could be as long as the rest of the list. At a minimum it should include pliers, wrenches, screwdrivers, and a hammer. The funnels are for transferring fuel and other liquids from bulk storage containers to daily use containers. A come-a-long is a portable cable winch. It could be used for moving heavy objects like dead cars or fallen trees.

Item	Qty.	Priority	Plan Date	Duration
1 gal. gas can for mixed gas	1	3	April 1	30 Day
10" Wire Cutters	1	3	April 1	30 Day
2 cycle oil	6	3	July 1	90 Day
24" or 30" Bolt Cutters	1	2	July 1	90 Day
Axe	1	3	April 1	30 Day
Bar oil	1	3	July 1	90 Day
Blades	Assortment	3	April 1	30 Day
Bow saw	2	3	April 1	30 Day
Bow saw blades	2	3	April 1	30 Day
Bungee Straps (variety of lengths)	6	3	April 1	30 Day
Bush or Tree Saw	1	3	July 1	90 Day
Caulking gun	1	3	April 1	30 Day
Chain	1	3	April 1	30 Day
Chainsaw	1	3	July 1	90 Day
Chainsaw extra	2	3	July 1	90 Day
Chimney cleaning brush	1	3	October 1	1 year
Chisel/Wedge	1	3	April 1	30 Day
CO Detector, battery powered	2	3	April 1	30 Day
Come-a-long	1	3	April 1	30 Day
Crowbar	1	3	April 1	30 Day
Drill, Hand-operated	1	3	April 1	30 Day
Dust Mask	1box	3	April 1	30 Day
Duct/100 MPH Tape	1box	3	July 1	90 Day
Extra air filter	2	3	July 1	90 Day
Extra spark plug	2	3	July 1	90 Day
Funnels	Assortment	3	April 1	30 Day
Garden fork	2	3	July 1	90 Day
Generator	1	1	April 1	30 Day
Hacksaw	1	3	April 1	30 Day

Hammer	1	3	April 1	30 Day
Hand tools	Assortment	3	April 1	30 Day
Hatchet	1	3	April 1	30 Day
Ladder	1	3	April 1	30 Day
Maul	1	3	April 1	30 Day
Oil for generator	12 qt	3	April 1	30 Day
Paint brushes	2	3	October 1	1 year
Pick	1	3	April 1	30 Day
Pins	1 box	3	April 1	30 Day
Pliers, needle nose	1	3	April 1	30 Day
Pliers, regular	1	3	April 1	30 Day
Post Hole Digger, auger type	1	3	April 1	30 Day
Rope, Nylon	100 feet	3	April 1	30 Day
Saw horses	2	3	April 1	30 Day
Scissors 2 3 April 1 30 day	2	3	April 1	30 Day
Screwdriver, Flat Head	2	3	April 1	30 Day
Screwdriver, Phillips	2	3	April 1	30 Day
Sharpening files	1	3	April 1	30 Day
Sharpening instruments	1 set	3	July 1	90 Day
Sharpening stone	Assortment	3	April 1	30 Day
Shovel, round	2	3	April 1	30 Day
Shovel, sharpshooter	2	3	April 1	30 Day
Shovel, Snow	1	3	April 1	30 Day
Shovel, square	2	3	April 1	30 Day
Sledgehammer	1	3	April 1	30 Day
Smoke Detector battery powered	2	3	April 1	30 Day
Staple Gun and Staples	1	3	April 1	30 Day
Swiss Army Knife	1/person	3	April 1	30 Day
Tin snips	1	3	April 1	30 Day
Tow Chain/Straps	1	3	April 1	30 Day
Twine or Heavy String	100 feet	3	April 1	30 Day
Two man tree saw	1	3	October 1	1 year

Vice Grips	1	3	April 1	30 Day
Wedge	1	3	April 1	30 Day
welding outfit	1	3	July 1	90 Day
Wench and Cable (come along)	1	3	July 1	90 Day
Wire Cutters	1	3	April 1	30 Day
Wood Saw	Assorted	3	April 1	30 Day
Wood Screws		3	April 1	30 Day
Wrenches	Assorted	3	April 1	30 Day

Transportation

Vehicle maintenance shouldn't be a problem in the short run or the long run if fuel supplies dry up. A "midlength"crisis could call for some basic maintenance though. Bicycles should come in hand for short trips and to avoid drawing attention to yourself when most people are walking. Buy an old rebuilt car. No electronic ignition.

Item	Qty.	Priority	Plan Date	Duration
12 volt air compressor	1	3	April 1	30 Day
Antifreeze	2 gals	3	April 1	30 Day
Bicycle	1/person	3	April 1	30 Day
Bicyle chain repair kit	1/bike	3	April 1	30 Day
bicycle tire repair kit	1/bike	3	April 1	30 Day
Bicycle tube hand air pump	1/bike	3	April 1	30 day
Fan belts	1set/auto	3	July 1	90 Day
Fuses	1 set	3	April 1	30 Day
Handlebar Basket	1/bike	3	April 1	30 Day
Hi-Lift Jack	1	3	April 1	30 Day
Hoses	1set/auto	3	July 1	90 Day
Jacks and stands	1 set	3	April 1	30 day
Jumper Cables	1	3	April 1	30 Day
Manuals	1set/auto	3	July 1	90 day
Oil filter	4	3	July 1	90 Day
Oil	24 quarts	3	July 1	90 Day
Ramps	1 set	3	July 1	90 day
Snow Chains	1set/auto	3	April 1	30 day

Spare bicycle tires	2/bike	3	April 1	30 Day
Spare bicycle tubes	2/bike	3	April 1	30 Day
Spare replacement car parts	1 set	3	April 1	30 day
Tire pressure gauge	1	3	April 1	30 day
Tires and blocks	1/auto	3	April 1	30 day
Tire sealer/inflator (can)	2/auto	3	April 1	30 Day
Tire wrench	1/auto	3	April 1	30 Day
Car specific Tools	1 set	2	April 1	30 day
Torx screwdrivers	1 set	3	April 1	30 Day
Tow chain	1	3	April 1	30 Day
Tow strap	1	3	April 1	30 Day
Tube repair kits	1/bike	3	April 1	30 Day

Water

Item	Qty.	Priority	Plan Date	Duration
55 gallon water drums	2/person	2	April 1	30 day
Bleach (5.25%)	1 gallon	3	April 1	30 day
Bung Wrench Hand pumps for drum	2	2	April 1	30 day
Pool tarp- 11 x 16 ft.	1	3	April 1	30 day
Pool water testing kit	1	3	April 1	30 day
Water bag (collapsible) 5 gallon	1	3	April 1	30 day
Water can - 5 gallon	2	3	April 1	30 day
Water chlorinating granules (pool)	1 box	3	July 1	90 day
Water Distiller	1	3	October 1	1 Year
Water filter	1	1	April 1	30 Day
Water filter replacement cartridge	1	1	April 1	30 Day
Water funnels	2	3	April 1	30 day
Water jug bottles, 2qt	2/person	2	April 1	30 Day
Water pump	1	1	July 1	90 Day

Made in the USA
Charleston, SC
15 June 2011